ASP 3.0:
A Beginner's Guide

Dave Mercer

Osborne/**McGraw-Hill**

Berkeley   New York   St. Louis   San Francisco
Auckland   Bogotá   Hamburg   London   Madrid
Mexico City   Milan   Montreal   New Delhi   Panama City
Paris   São Paulo   Singapore   Sydney   Tokyo   Toronto

Osborne/**McGraw-Hill**
2600 Tenth Street
Berkeley, California 94710
U.S.A.

For information on translations or book distributors outside the U.S.A., or to arrange bulk purchase discounts for sales promotions, premiums, or fund-raisers, please contact Osborne/**McGraw-Hill** at the above address.

ASP 3.0: A Beginner's Guide

1234567890 VFM VFM 01987654321

ISBN 0-07-212741-4

Publisher   Brandon A. Nordin
Vice President & Associate Publisher   Scott Rogers
Acquisitions Editor   Ann Sellers
Project Editor   Elizabeth Seymour
Acquisitions Coordinator   Timothy Madrid
Technical Editors   Robert Sutherland, Michael Davis, Jeffrey Davis
Copy Editors   Lunaea Weatherstone, Marcia Baker
Proofreader   Linda Medoff
Indexer   Robert J. Richardson
Computer Designers   Gary Corrigan & Tara Davis
Illustrators   Lyssa Sieben-Wald & Michael Mueller
Series Design   Gary Corrigan
Cover Design   Kevin Curry

This book was composed with Corel VENTURA™ Publisher.

To Tina, Lucy, Trish, and Bob.

*What a blessing it is to have sisters
and a brother to share my life with.*

*As the songwriter said,
"What a long strange trip it's been."*

About the Author

Dave Mercer has been building databases professionally since 1993, and built his first Web site in 1995. He holds a degree in Business from San Diego State University, and has a diverse background, including 15 years in industrial engineering. Dave has worked on Web sites for businesses such as flower shops and car dealerships to real estate appraiser directories. He's taught Web site design and development classes since 1996, and has been writing books for the computer market since 1998.

Dave is currently CTO of a Web site design and database development company, helping to establish the new Internet economy in which he feels all of us are gradually coming to live and work. He lives in Spring Valley, California, with his wife, JoAnn, and their cat, Taffy (who actually does much of the programming late at night after Dave and JoAnn have gone to bed. Hey, he's a smart cat and knows his stuff).

Contents

Introduction

I've always been fascinated by computers. My first home computer was a Commodore 64, although at work I made heavy use of an Apple they had sitting around. Eventually I bought a cloned 286 (with a yellow monochrome display) and I can remember asking my relatives and friends why they hadn't bought a computer. The standard answer was "I don't know what I'd do with it." Most people were getting along fine without them, and didn't see the (to me) obvious advantages.

I was happy using my computer (an early version of DOS was the operating system) to run Enable, a suite containing a spreadsheet (on which I kept my checkbook), a word processor, and a database. One day I decided to investigate connecting to an online bulletin board service, so I installed a 1200 baud modem. I ended up getting an account with Compuserve. (I was no pioneer; BBSs had been around for quite a while, and the Internet was quietly growing towards critical mass.) However, I didn't use my Compuserve account much. It was still text based (this was just before they introduced the graphical interface) and it seemed rather boring to me to wade through the menus to get a bit of text flowing back to the screen on some subject or another. Plus, I didn't want to rack up extra charges for special services.

The only event that really stands out in my mind was when we had a large earthquake (we're in Southern California, so earthquakes are not uncommon, but this was a big one). My son Mike demanded that we go online and check the wire service. Sure enough, the wire service, through Compuserve, immediately started reporting details about the earthquake, such as location, strength, damage reports, and so on. What impressed me was that we received this information *about five minutes before a news anchor on the TV started quoting the exact same information to the general public.*

Because I felt I wasn't getting much out of my Compuserve account I closed it a few months later, and didn't sign up for any other online services until 1994. In 1994 my boss asked me to investigate the Internet for our agency, to see what benefits, if any, might accrue if we adopted the technology. I opened an account with CTS, a local ISP, bought a 14.4 modem, and connected it to my upgraded 386 (the same 286 with a new motherboard, CPU, and RAM). I wrote a detailed report about the Internet, and it was easy for me to see the potential. What impressed me most was the graphical interface and hypertext links (rectangular images on a gray background, with nice blue links). I could connect to anywhere in the world, and even by that time there were easily hundreds or thousands of Web sites.

Later in 1994 I was teaching myself HTML from monthly articles in Boardwatch magazine, and I found the code for making forms. This was awesome, because it meant two-way communication between user and Web master. The commercial possibilities were now officially endless. The average person could put up a site for $50 a month, perhaps a few scanned photos, and a little easy-to-learn HTML, and compete with the largest businesses in the world. Interactivity opened up whole new worlds.

At the time, I was designing databases using Paradox for Windows (with the Programming Applications Language, or PAL) and I realized how powerful interactivity could become with a database and some programming logic behind the scenes. I wrote a little database application that could generate, based on the data in the database records, text files that were actually customized Web pages, each containing a few records from the database. It was going to be a classified ad service, but unfortunately I couldn't conjure up enough paying customers to make it profitable. The potential was impressive, though.

The point of this story is that we now have a tool whose capabilities are almost limitless. Everyone and everything is or soon will be connected, not just people and their desktop computers, but literally everything. Any kind of sensor or input device can communicate with any programming logic contained in any device with communications and computation capability, many of which will soon become too small to even see. We're very close to living in a smart, connected world. And the basic technology many of the new applications will depend on is Active Server Pages.

Active Server Pages is not a programming language, or database, or markup language, or application. Instead, it is more a "glue" technology, a means of harnessing the awesome power of logical instructions (programming), connectivity (the Internet), data sources much more than just databases), and communications between devices (the user interface or IO functions). In one fell swoop it creates an environment in which you can put all these things to work, for whatever purpose you desire. And it's only getting better. This is definitely a technology you need to know and understand.

Who Should Read This Book

So welcome to Osborne's *ASP 3.0: A Beginner's Guide*. As the name suggests, this book is for everyone from raw programming trainees to programming professionals breaking into ASP for the first time. If you intend to program interactive Web sites this book is for you. If you intend to manage those who program interactive Web sites, this book is for you. If you own a business and wish to understand one of the primary technologies by which developers will program interactive Web sites for you, this book is for you.

We hope you'll find the material interesting, well-rounded, clear and concise, and just plain fun. For my money, Active Server Pages is one of the easiest, most immediately accessible, and most fun technologies for working with the Web, and at the same time, one of the most powerful.

What This Book Covers

This book is broken into 13 modules and several appendixes. The modules contain pretty much all you need to know to immediately begin programming interactive Web sites, from simple responses and server components all the way to complete database manipulation and e-mail applications. Because modern Web sites are built from many different languages, technologies and components, this book touches on HTML and Web site design, XML, Javascript, VBScript, SQL, ASP objects and components, and database construction with Microsoft Access and SQL Server. You'll be exposed to working code fashioned in a plain, easy-to-understand format, demonstrating clearly all the basic functions you'll need to grasp and work with daily.

At the back of the book there are several appendixes (the first being an answers guide) containing valuable reference material for quick review when you need a specific value or constant. On the Web site all the code is available for easy download and insertion into your own site. If you follow along with the examples written in the book and produce code and databases to match, you can use the samples to immediately add powerful functionality to any Web site you already have.

Module 1, "Active Server Pages—Getting Set Up"—In this module we discuss how ASP is related to Web sites, operating systems, and how it affects Web site design. The installation of IIS 5.0 is covered, as well as hosting issues. Manual and automated development environments are reviewed, and an overview of all the objects and components of ASP is included.

Module 2, "ASP and the Web—Programming Basics"—HTML and ASP are intimately related, as are several other common programming languages. We discuss how HTML, JavaScript, and VBScript fit into the scheme of things, and the role of SQL. Good Web site design practices are outlined, and we begin to discuss fundamental programming syntax and structures. Finally, error handling and debugging are reviewed.

Module 3, "The Request and Response Objects"—The Request and Response objects are the workhorses of ASP, and we discuss using them for basic interactions with your users in detail. Reading and writing data, cookies, buffering and flushing, and other methods and properties are explored in the module's project.

Module 4, "The Server Object"—This module reviews typical Web Server operations, and covers Server-side includes as well as new (in ASP 3.0) methods such as Transfer and Execute. The correct syntax and implications of creating object instances is explained, and the methods and properties of the server object are used in the module's project.

Module 5, "The Application and Session Objects"—Applications written with ASP use the Global.asa file to manage state and scope in many instances. This module reviews state and scope and how they can be managed using the Application and Session objects. The correct syntax is shown, and the properties and methods of each are outlined in examples and in the module's project.

Module 6, "The Scripting Object Model and SOM Objects"—Any application programming technology eventually needs access to the file system, and the SOM provides this functionality for ASP on the Server. The Dictionary object is covered in this module, as well as objects that allow access to drives, folders, files, and individual text streams.

Module 7, "Major Active Server Components"—ASP Components include the Ad Rotator, the Browser Capabilities, and several others, all of which are reviewed in this module. Their relation to well-designed Web sites is discussed, and typical usage of each component is demonstrated in the module's project.

Module 8, "More Active Server Components"—Other installed components such as the Page Counter and the Permission Checker are reviewed, and third-party component issues are covered. Properties and methods of each are outlined, and the module's project includes code for running them all.

Module 9, "ActiveX Data Objects and SQL Overview"—ActiveX Data Objects (ADO) is a set of components used with ASP to access databases, and the design and construction of an Access database is covered in this module. The SQL database query language is presented in basic format, so the syntax becomes clear, and common SQL queries are shown. Finally, ADO objects (Connection, Command, and Recordset) are discussed.

Module 10, "ADO Connection-Related Objects"—Making connections to databases via connection strings is the subject of this module. Correct usage of the Connection object is shown, and several types of connections are made. Stored procedures are discussed, and a stored procedure is created and run in the module's project.

Module 11, "The ADO Recordset-Related Objects"—Manipulating data in a database gets going nicely using recordsets. The Record and Stream objects are reviewed, and an application allowing basic record navigation and edits, updates, and deletes is constructed in the module's project.

Module 12, "ASP Transactions"—Part of working with data sources is forming changes into transactions, and the fundamentals of transactions are covered in this chapter. A working SQL Server database is created, so that a transaction-based ASP application can be demonstrated in the module project.

Module 13, "ASP Collaboration and Security"—E-mail is easy to send from an ASP application, using CDONTS. The basic workings of CDONTS and the structure of ASP e-mail applications is covered, and an easy-to-use application is built as the module's project.

Appendix A, "Answers to Mastery Checks"—Each chapter contains questions at the end (called Mastery Checks) that check to make sure you've absorbed the basics, and Appendix A provides the answers to these questions.

Appendix B, "HTML 4.0"—This is the most recent recommendation of the W3C for HTML.

Appendix C, "JScript"—This is a list of operators, commands, and other JScript components.

Appendix D, "VBScript"—This is the most recent version of Microsoft's VBScript.

How To Read This Book

This book can be read from beginning to end, starting with the first module, but you can also open any module for an easy-to-follow introduction to the specific ASP objects and capabilities you are interested in. Each module explains in detail the objects it covers, and includes many working examples demonstrating the capabilities of the object or components in question. In addition, at the end of most of the modules is a project that illustrates, step-by-step, the creation of a working application using the most important parts of the material discussed in the module.

Special Features

Throughout each chapter are **Hints, Tips,** and **Notes,** as well as ***detailed code listings.*** The code all works fine and the source code can be downloaded in full from zip files on the Web site, at **www.e4free.com/ASPBeginnersGuide/ ProjectFiles/Module01/** and then the name of the project file (in the Module01 folder you'll find the zip files for Module 1 projects). All of the project files for this book are also available at **www.osborne.com.** There are ***1-Minute Drills*** that check to make sure you're retaining what you've read (and help focus your attention on the more important points). There are ***Ask The Expert*** question-and-answer sections that give in-depth explanations about the current subject. Included with the book and on the Web site are ***Projects*** that take what you've learned and put it into working applications. At the end of each module are ***Mastery Checks*** to give you another opportunity for review, and the answers are contained in ***Appendix A.*** The Properties and Methods of each ASP object are listed and explained, and coding techniques are discussed and illustrated. Overall, our objective is to get you up to speed quickly, without a lot of obtuse, abstract, and dry reference to formal coding practices.

There is quite a bit of additional information at the Web site mentioned in the chapters, from the Microsoft Web site to the W3C Web site to third-party ASP coding Web sites. And I've built some Web pages containing links to Zip files that have all the code and examples found in the book, so you can visit and download what you need, rather than copying from the book. You can find the URL to each chapter project listed next to the module's project heading.

So let's get started. You won't believe how easy and fun it is to program Active Server Pages to create a smart Web site. Good luck!

Part 1

The Basics of ASP Programming

Module 1

Active Server Pages—
Getting Set Up

The Goals of This Module

- Understand ASP as an interactive Web technology
- Explore operating systems (OSs) and their relationship to ASP
- Install and configure Internet Information Server (IIS) 5.0
- Review manual and automated (Visual InterDev) development environments
- Examine ASP objects, components, and ADO
- Cover issues and concerns of Web site and application hosting

Welcome to *Active Server Pages 3.0: A Beginner's Guide*. You're on the road to knowledge that will most likely change your life and will certainly change the world. If you've been around the computer scene for long and remember early Web pages, you know that the information they contained was static—that is, it was fixed and didn't change. As exciting as it was to view text and images from around the world at the click of a button, the interactivity ASP makes possible is far more powerful and valuable. So let's get started! Chapter 1 lays the ground rules for the work you'll do throughout this book.

Why Active Server Pages (ASP)?

The impact ASP has on a Web site is determined by its ability to produce a high degree of *interactivity*. This means that things are happening in real time (while the user is using the site), and with each exchange of information or data between the user and the Web site, responses are modified based on the exchange.

There is simply no real limit to the amount of processing or customization the site can perform in response to user input when ASP and ASP-compatible technologies are used. Today's best Web sites know their customers and greet them by name when they return to the site; the best commercial Web sites often perform individually targeted marketing based on stored user profiles and past purchases.

Currently, two primary platforms host the majority of Web sites—either some flavor of UNIX or Windows NT. On the UNIX side, you'll hear things like Common Gateway Interface (CGI) and Practical Extraction Reporting Language (Perl) in interactivity discussions. On the Windows NT side, it's ASP and VBScript. We'll discuss the merits and drawbacks of each in depth later on, but for now just remember that both technologies perform many of the same functions. ASP, for a variety of reasons, seems to be the easier, cheaper, and better performing of the two.

Note

You can buy a version of ASP that will run on UNIX machines. Check **http://www.chilisoft.com** or use your favorite search engine to find companies offering non-Windows NT versions of ASP.

ASP is now in version 3.0, and the platform this book focuses on is Windows 2000. Internet Information Server 5.0 comes with Windows 2000 (Advanced Server version) and ASP 3.0 is built in. To run Windows 2000 Advanced Server edition, you need at least 128MB of RAM and a Pentium 166, but the recommended hardware is significantly more powerful than that. However, all the material for this book was created with the minimal hardware (Pentium 166 and 128MB of RAM), so you can feel comfortable at that level.

In addition, it is really best to run your examples from a separate machine running Internet Explorer 5.0. While you can run your examples directly on the server, or from another browser, some examples take advantage of IE 5.0's special features (these will be pointed out, of course). Running examples from a separate client machine also means you'll detect problems with permissions that may not be evident when you're logged directly into the server as an administrator.

Windows 2000 Advanced Server Edition

Windows 2000 has been on the market since February 2000 and, as of this writing, there are a number of patches, service packs, or other fixes available (although I'm sure we'll see more by the time you read this). You can find them listed at the Web site **http://www.microsoft.com/windows2000/downloads**. Download and install at least the latest security patches and upgrades.

During installation of Windows 2000, you'll need to answer quite a few questions about how you want Windows 2000 configured. The most important questions affecting your use of Active Server Pages concern the installation of Internet Information Server and how your hard disk drive partitions are formatted.

Microsoft recommends installing Windows 2000 as an application server if you intend to run the machine primarily as a Web server. Doing this will make it use memory more efficiently. Since Windows 2000 installs as a file server by default, you need to follow this procedure to switch to an application server:

1. On the desktop, right-click the My Computer icon and select Properties from the shortcut menu.

2. Select Local Area Connection and right-click to open its properties.

3. Select File and Printer Sharing for Microsoft Networks and right-click to open its properties.

4. On the Server Optimization tab, select Maximize Data Throughput For Network Applications.

For non-production servers, you should install Windows 2000 to a file allocation table (FAT) partition, and set aside another partition entirely for the installation of IIS. The IIS partition should be formatted as an NT file system (NTFS). This will make your Windows 2000 installation viewable by other FAT formatted operating systems, while allowing IIS to maintain the highest levels of security with NTFS.

Installing Internet Information Server

IIS 5.0 is the latest incarnation of Microsoft's industrial-strength Web server. Microsoft also produces the Personal Web Server for distribution with FrontPage 2000, but it will not be installed if another Web server has been installed when you install FrontPage. Since you're working in Windows 2000, you'll most likely be working with IIS.

IIS 5.0 is installed by default during installation of Windows 2000 Advanced Server, unless you already have another Web server installed. While you are installing the operating system, you will have the opportunity to specify configuration options for IIS. However, after the operating system (OS) installation, you'll immediately see a Configure Your Server screen (shown in Figure 1-1) that lets you start a variety of service installation and configuration wizards. We'll use this screen to walk through and discuss the options available for IIS 5.0.

When you choose Web/Media Server (from the choices on the toolbar along the left side of the Configure Your Server screen), a drop-down menu will appear (shown in Figure 1-2) and you'll be able to choose between Web Server and Streaming Media Server. Choose Web Server, and you'll see the screen shown in Figure 1-3.

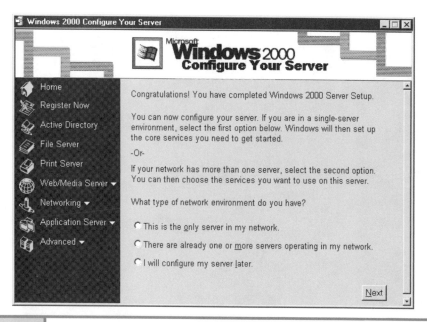

Figure 1-1   The Configure Your Server Screen

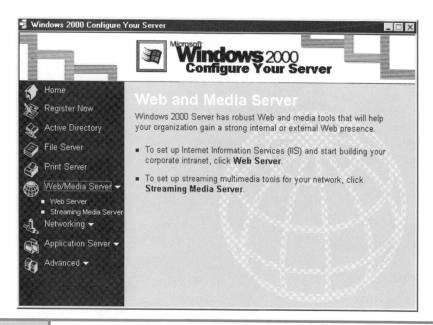

Figure 1-2   Web/Media server choices

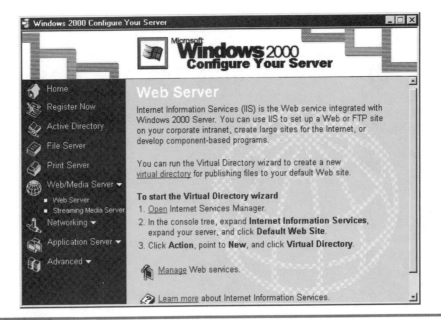

| **Figure 1-3** | The Web Server screen |

The Web Server screen offers three choices. You can

- Create a new virtual directory.
- Manage Web services.
- Learn more about Web services.

If you choose the option to learn more about IIS 5.0, a Help window will appear offering six new options, discussed next:

- Installing IIS
- Software Checklist
- Troubleshooting
- Electronic Mail
- Newsgroups
- FrontPage Server Extensions

1

Installing IIS   The information about installing IIS simply gives you the procedure for installation in the most basic terms, rather than explaining any of the configuration options or, more importantly, why you would want to configure IIS a particular way and the consequences of your decisions. The basic procedure to start installation is explained in Project 1-1, later in the chapter; here we'll give you more information about the issues you face when configuring IIS.

Software Checklist   Prior to beginning installation, you must have TCP/IP installed. The Windows TCP/IP Protocol and Connectivity Utilities is the name Microsoft uses to denote this set of utilities. It should be installed by default when you run the Setup program. Microsoft also recommends installing Domain Name Service (DNS) on one of the computers on the network so that users can enter "friendly" names (such as **http://www.bertandernie.com**) to access other computers, rather than IP addresses (such as **http://209.38.476.19**). That one is up to you. As mentioned earlier, IIS should be installed on an NTFS partition (there's more information about partitions and formatting schemes in the "Ask the Expert" section, later in this chapter).

Troubleshooting   The information about troubleshooting gives you a method for determining whether your Web server is working. Essentially, you must ensure that there are browser-readable (HTML—Hypertext Markup Language) files in your wwwroot folder, open your browser, and enter the proper URL to find one of the HTML files. The URL should be the name of your computer preceded by http:// and followed by a slash and then the name of the file to display, like so: **http://cx847962-a/myfile.htm**. You can find the name of your computer in the Control Panel under Network settings.

Electronic Mail and Newsgroups   If you want to send e-mail or read newsgroups, you should install Simple Mail Transport Protocol (SMTP) and Network News Transport Protocol (NNTP) during the OS installation, or later from the Configure Your Server screen (shown previously in Figure 1-1). The next two choices under Learn More About Internet Information Services (Electronic Mail and Newsgroups) each give you a URL you can use to review documentation for these services. The paths are file:\\%systemroot%\help\mail.chm for e-mail and file:\\%systemroot%\help\news.chm for newsgroups.

FrontPage Server Extensions   If you plan to use Microsoft FrontPage for Web site or page creation, installing FrontPage Server Extensions is a must. Although you can create great Web pages that will run on any server with FrontPage, the advanced features of FrontPage are dependent upon the server extensions. For example, if you want to add the simple, built-in search engine function to your site, server extensions must be installed. Same with the built-in hit counter component, the e-mail form handler, and the registration form handler.

Ask the Expert

Question: What are FAT and NTFS?

Answer: Information about the files on your hard drive, such as location, size, and so forth, is stored in a file allocation table, or FAT. A single physical hard drive can be logically divided up into multiple hard-drive partitions, each with its own drive letter. Partitions can be formatted differently from one another, although, depending on the formatting structure, they may or may not be able to "see" each other.

Several formats are in common use, such as FAT16, FAT32, NTFS, and others for UNIX and proprietary operating systems. Networked operating systems, unlike desktop operating systems, usually have a means to store permission information for each file/folder along with the data just mentioned. Windows 2000 can be installed on a FAT16 partition, but IIS should be installed on NTFS, because NTFS stores permissions information for each file and folder.

Question: What permissions information can be stored?

Answer: Permissions information dictates what user or group can see, read, write, move, execute, author, delete, and edit files. Various levels of permissions can be assigned, and the operating system reviews stored permissions information to decide if the user making the request has sufficient permission to perform the request.

Question: How can I tell if my drive is FAT or NTFS?

Answer: Open Windows Explorer and select the drive (partition) on which the operating system or IIS is installed. Right-click it to display the shortcut menu, and select Properties. On the General tab, the file system type is shown.

Question: **How can I change the format of a partition on my hard drive to NTFS?**

Answer: Partitions can be formatted to NTFS from Windows Explorer. Just find the partition you want to change in Windows Explorer, right-click it, and choose Format from the shortcut menu. Note that once you change a partition to NTFS it cannot be changed back to FAT (at least, not according to Microsoft's documentation).

project1-1.zip

Project 1-1: Install and Configure IIS 5.0

This project will install IIS 5.0 on a machine running Windows 2000. The installation process will ordinarily be performed during the initial installation of Windows 2000, but the steps required for either procedure are very similar, and the configuration parameters used are the same.

Step-by-Step

1. Click the Start button from the desktop, choose Control Panel, and double-click the Add/Remove Programs icon.

2. Choose Configure Windows, click the Components button, and then begin installing, removing, or adding components to IIS. Start by clicking Internet Information Server, and then click the Details button.

3. Inside the Details screen are several choices for IIS components, such as Common Files, Documentation, NNTP service, and so forth. Choose the components you want and then click OK. (For this project you can install all items except NNTP, because you're not going to be running newsgroup services.)

The next screen will show Windows installing and configuring IIS according to the choices you've made.

Ask the Expert

Question: What are load balancing and performance throttling, and when should I use them?

Answer: Load balancing is part of a general set of topics that refer to your ability, as a designer, to scale up the hardware and software components of your Web site for an increased number of visitors and/or more activity per visitor. Performance throttling/tuning is related as a means of controlling CPU performance, bandwidth consumption, and application performance.

The discussion really starts with *clustering*. Clustering lets you use clustering software to connect multiple servers, so that they provide services to clients such as Internet Explorer as though they were one computer/server. In addition, clustering allows servers to offer robust features not available with stand-alone server nodes, such as load balancing. Clustered servers can share clustered hard-disk drives, further improving performance and reliability of critical database-contained information.

Often you'll hear of *Web farms* or *CPU farms*, terms that are sometimes used interchangeably with clustering. Increased performance and reliability are the chief reasons for adding multiple servers in a cluster arrangement. For example, if one server dies within a cluster, other servers can immediately pick up the slack. This is called *failover*. When the dead server is reanimated and it resumes carrying its load, the term is *failback*.

Performance throttling is also part of a larger discussion about controlling and tuning resource usage among the various services at work on your server, so you can offer maximum performance for each service while not unnecessarily restricting or limiting usage of any service. The problem is rather complex and involves several issues.

First, any online services compete to use the CPU, the applications you've created, and the bandwidth available. Available bandwidth is determined by the data transfer speed of your Internet connection, so that a 28.8K modem is capable of transmitting 28,800 bits each second, while a T-3 line can transmit 45,000,000 bits each second. File size and protocol *overhead* (a percentage of the file size dedicated to non-file data, such as packet source and destination addresses) added together equal the amount of data that must be transmitted to accomplish a given purpose, such as sending e-mail or fulfilling an HTTP request for a Web page. Data transfer speed (bandwidth) determines the maximum amount of data that can be transmitted and, therefore, the total number of files or communication requests that can be transmitted. Each online application will compete for bandwidth; if some applications are transmitting larger files or more communications requests, other applications may slow down or stop altogether for a while, disrupting those services.

You can throttle bandwidth usage at the Web-site level, and these settings will override settings made at the level of the entire computer. If you are running multiple Web sites on IIS, you can throttle each individually—an important consideration for Web hosting companies and Internet Service Providers (ISPs). System monitoring tools can tell you how well your settings are performing. A good rule of thumb is that if you are exceeding 50 percent of your available bandwidth during peak usage times, you should consider getting a better (higher data-transfer speed) connection.

The Development Environment

The environment in which a Web site is constructed and maintained is called the development environment. The term *development environment* refers specifically to the platform, process, and tools used to design, build, manage versions, and maintain all the files/objects/data that go into a modern Web site. Web sites can be as simple as a few HTML pages or as complex as complete application-driven sites with a multitude of file types, objects, and components interacting harmoniously. In general, development environments can be broken into two broad categories: manual and automated.

Manual Development

Some programmers prefer to write all the code themselves, and a complex site can be developed manually with tools as basic as Notepad or WordPad. Typically, however, Notepad and WordPad are used for quick editing of existing files rather than construction from scratch.

Using Notepad

Notepad is a simple and lightweight text-editing tool that is supplied with all normal installations of Windows as part of the accessories group. It is capable of creating and saving text files, searching for text strings, and producing ASCII text plus carriage-return and line-feed characters. It is ideal for creating small HTML files or for editing HTML files, including scripting such as ASP, VBScript, and JScript. It is a popular tool because it is free, small, and leaves no formatting characters in the file. However, there are almost no automated functions, so it pales in comparison to the more sophisticated page and scripting creation and debugging tools.

Using WordPad

WordPad also comes with standard installations of Windows, under the accessories group, and it is a somewhat more advanced text or word-processing tool. It allows you to save files in formats other than plain ASCII text, but this is actually a drawback for most page creation and editing. It's useful because it can display large files. However, it is necessary to ensure you do not save files in the wrong format (such as a Rich Text Format Document, with an rtf extension to the filename), because the excess formatting characters can completely mess up your pages. Use it with caution.

1-Minute Drill

- **What service do you need to install if you want to send e-mail from your server?**
- **Web pages have a file extension of .htm or .html, but what is the file format for Web pages?**
- **What does the File Allocation Table do?**

Automated Development

In contrast with plain-vanilla text editors, automated development environments provide a rich set of tools that make the common chores of HTML and ASP development easier, faster, less error-prone, and often

---

- **SMTP**
- **ASCII text**
- **Maintains file location, sequencing, and size information**

more intuitive. Even in FrontPage, which primarily performs HTML editing, the code view is color-coded for clarity. Some tools offer a higher degree of automation than others, but the trade-off is less understanding of what is going on behind the scenes. Too much automation can put you at the mercy of a program when things don't seem to function as you want and you'd like to get in and make changes by hand.

Text Editors with Automated Features

There are text editors on the market that offer a variety of features specific to Active Server Pages development. For example, you can find an evaluation version of ASP Express by clicking the word Tools in the Reference section at the 15 seconds Web site (**http://www.15seconds.com**). ASP Express functions as an HTML text editor, but also includes a SQL statement generator, debugging tools, and other automated utilities.

Microsoft FrontPage 2000

Microsoft FrontPage started with FrontPage 97, progressed to FrontPage 98, and now exists as FrontPage 2000. Each new version built upon the strength and eliminated some of the flaws of the previous version. FrontPage 2000 contains many powerful WYSIWYG tools for creating Web pages, as well as scores of pre-built templates for pages, graphics, and even whole site layouts. The advanced features of FrontPage require FrontPage Server Extensions to run, so FrontPage comes with the Personal Web Server (PWS) to run them on during development. FrontPage also contains publishing tools, online development capability, wizards to automate site creation and maintenance, and some rudimentary reporting and project management tools. The primary drawback of FrontPage is that it uses some proprietary, or Microsoft-only, non-HTML-compatible tags and functions, limiting your choice of browser or server in some circumstances. For example, anyone looking at your site with Netscape Navigator will not be able to view the MARQUEE tag, but FrontPage allows you to use the MARQUEE tag without any warning.

FrontPage also comes with some ASP scripting tools, notably the Database Results Wizard. This feature generates canned ASP scripting that connects to a database (making a new connection for you, if necessary) and retrieves result sets for display in groups on the page in which you inset the display region. It is useful for this function, but often you'll find that it limits what you can do, so you'll end up remaking the scripting in standard ASP. In addition, FrontPage will remove any custom scripting you add to the page. Unless you are sure you're not going to need more advanced retrieval or processing capabilities, it's hard to recommend using this FrontPage 2000 feature.

Using Visual InterDev

Visual InterDev, Microsoft's high-end Web site development tool, uses a component-driven model for automating application production. It provides a rich development environment for coding and debugging, and even a visual scripting model that provides a graphical user interface (GUI) for setting up functions.

Visual InterDev contains a site designer for overall site construction, an integrated page editor for page construction, database tools such as the Data View and the Query Designer for working with databases and data sources, and debugging and collaborative development tools. Osborne's *Visual InterDev 6 from the Ground Up* by Joseph O'Neil (ISBN: 0-07-882509-1) is an excellent resource for learning more about Visual InterDev.

Ask the Expert

Question: How is a Web site created on the server?

Answer: When IIS is installed, a default Web site is created. You can add other Web sites, but you'll want to make sure that each has its own unique identification (IP address). Your system administrator or Web hosting company can provide you with additional IP addresses.

Question: How are Web pages published to the server?

Answer: The easiest way is to create your pages and then copy them to the default Web site folder on the server. If you are publishing remotely, you can FTP your pages (use File Transfer Protocol) or use an HTML editor such as FrontPage to create and save your content directly to the server in real time. If you use a stand-alone FTP program to copy your files to the server, FTP must be running on IIS and you must know your *hostname* (the IP address of the FTP server), your username, and your password.

Question: What is the difference between a *normal* Web site and an *application-driven* Web site?

Answer: Normal (or static) Web sites deliver their content by request without having any idea whether the requestor has just been there or is visiting for the first time. There is no continuity between requests, nor is there any continuing information between requests. In technical terms, normal Web requests and responses are *stateless*. In addition, normal Web pages are built and then displayed as is. Little or no information in them is updated automatically, and they certainly aren't constructed on the fly or in direct response to user input or conditions.

Application-driven (or dynamic) Web sites, on the other hand, can keep track of each user and store information across page requests (or even across the entire Web site for all users) about the state of interactions with the user(s). Dynamic Web sites can also build pages automatically, on the fly and in response to conditions on the server, at the client, or unique to the user.

Active Server Pages: An Overview

Active Server Pages (ASP) is built into IIS and Windows 2000 and is automatically installed when the operating system and Web server are installed. ASP is, quite simply, a technology for interacting with the user by intercepting incoming requests and processing outgoing responses. Ordinary HTTP requests and responses follow an inflexible pattern during normal use and are not suitable for dynamic interactions.

Web hosting with a version of the UNIX operating system was, until recently, the default method of publishing your Web content. Common Gateway Interface (CGI) is the method used to interact with the Web server on the UNIX side.

When you have a Web site hosted on IIS and you run ASP scripts, the server checks each file to see whether it contains ASP (and server-side includes, discussed later in this book). If it does, the server routes those files to ASP for processing prior to sending them out to the client. ASP then processes the scripting and generates the appropriate content for transmission back to the browser/client. Because ASP has a chance to process output before it gets back to the user, all manner of functionality can be built in, such as database access, component usage, and the ordinary programmatic functionality available with VBScript, JScript, or any other scripting language you'd care to use. VBScript is the default language ASP uses, but both VBScript and JScript scripting engines are included with Windows 2000.

ASP Objects

Active Server Pages is not a programming language per se. It is more like the glue that holds together scripting, objects, components, and interactions with the Web server. Technically, ASP is made up of objects, which are called from VBScript or JScript to perform certain highly useful functions, such as capturing data submitted by users, responding to user inputs, managing applications and sessions, and manipulating the server.

Included ASP Objects

Objects included with ASP are as follows:

- **The Request and Response objects**   These objects capture incoming data from the user and respond with processed text, HTML, and other data.

- **The Application and Session objects**   These objects allow the designer to set the functionality of the Web site as an application whose variables have scope over the entire set of pages in use, and as a session whose variables have scope over the pages in use by an individual user.

- **The Server object**   This object allows the developer to manipulate the server, encode HTML and URLs, set timeouts for scripts, and create instances of other objects and components within the application.

ADO Objects

ActiveX Data Object (ADO) is the term used for one of the most valuable components ASP can call. ADO objects allow direct and convenient access to databases and other data sources, and this functionality serves many common purposes on application-driven Web sites.

Included ADO Objects

ADO includes the following objects:

- **The Connection object** This object creates a connection between your ASP scripts and a database or data source.

- **The Command object** This object allows you to run specific commands against a data source.

- **The Recordset object** This object gives you control over a set of records and fields from a data source, so you can perform all the common record functions available when working with a database table, such as finding, editing, adding, deleting, and so forth.

ASP Components

As mentioned previously, ADO is an ASP component. ASP also includes other components, and you can buy third-party components online. Components are valuable because they offer pre-programmed functionality that would take many hours of effort to duplicate yourself, even assuming you had excellent programming skills. Built-in components are essentially free, and the cost for most third-party components is relatively low. Third-party components are usually tested and debugged for reliability, and they expose methods and properties you can easily call and use, just like built-in objects.

The scripting engines provide access to their own set of objects, most notably the Dictionary object, FileSystemObject object, Drive object, Folder object, and File object. Collectively, these are called the *Scripting Runtime Library* objects. Another class of objects that comes with ASP, called installable components, is discussed in the next section.

Included (Installable) ASP Components

Installable components included with ASP 3.0 are

- The Ad Rotator component
- The Browser Capabilities component
- The Content Linking component
- The Content Rotator component
- The Counters component
- The Logging Utility component
- The MyInfo component
- The Page Counter component
- The Permission Checker component
- The Tools component

These components will be discussed in much more detail later on in this book.

Relational Databases and Other Data Sources

Relational databases, such as Microsoft Access, SQL Server, and many others, contain data structured as tables, records, and fields. You can connect to these databases with the Connection object, as mentioned previously, but you can also connect to and manipulate many other data sources with the tools developed for ASP 3.0. For example, you can connect to spreadsheets and word-processing documents as well.

Just the same, you'll be primarily using databases with ASP for the immediate future; and while Microsoft Access isn't very scalable for production Web sites, it is a good tool for rapidly prototyping databases and the functionality required for a particular project. There are conversion and migration tools available that make it easy to go from a prototype in Access to a full-fledged, industrial-strength, database-management system when you've stabilized the functionality required.

1

Developing Online Applications

Online applications are Web sites that offer much more functionality than static Web pages or normal Web sites. On a normal Web site, you can fill out a form, and when you press the submit button, the contents of the form are sent to a CGI script and processed into an e-mail, or perhaps turned into a text file on the server. Everything else is simply the display of text and graphics in your browser, with a little hypertext linking around the Web for fun.

Online applications take their name from the familiar application programs you use, such as TurboTax, except that they don't run on your desktop—they run online. To build an application that will do your taxes on a Web site, for example, you will do software development much like the programmers of TurboTax did.

The default Web site created for you when IIS is installed is the place where applications start. Assuming you know what functions you want to build in, you can code them with ASP and VBScript (or another scripting language that appeals to you). For speed and scalability, you may want to program particular functions of your program as executable components (ActiveX) using C++ or Visual Basic, or perhaps you'll buy some components off the shelf.

Most likely you'll also create some databases to store subscriber or customer data behind the scenes, as well as tables of information that may not change much, such as tax tables and forms.

Finally, you'll tie the functions, components, databases, and user sessions together using Active Server Pages objects and the scripting language you've chosen. ASP functions will manage user interactions and call the other components of your application, within the scope of the application and session parameters you set.

Client/Server or Tiered Applications

It's easy to think of servers as computers, rather than software services running on them, because the hardware is often called a *server*, while the server software running on them is called *services* these days. In any case, a server or software service is so called because it serves up files or performs services for other computers, such as delivering Web content. A *client* requests services from a server. Typical clients are Web browsers and e-mail programs. Just for fun, the distinction between servers and clients is beginning to blur, and servers and clients can also be clients and servers.

The term *client/server* aptly describes the interaction between a Web browser and a Web server. The client makes a request for a Web page or other Web site resource, and the server provides copies of the Web page (and associated files) to the client. Obviously, the server (like most servers) is built to handle multiple client requests at once.

Related to client/server is another type of client/server interaction called *multi-tiered applications*. Multi-tiered applications involve several levels of interactions. For example, suppose you use your client to request data from a server, and the server must in turn request processing functions and data from a data source or an intermediate data interpreter or conversion program. These intermediaries are often referred to as the *middle tier* in a multi-tiered application, and there may be a number of layers of processing going on between you and the data or functionality you are using. Ideally, these layers should be transparent, so the functions of the application perform in a uniform way, using the interface you understand (your client).

Multi-tiered applications can consist of components spread out anywhere online or on a network, so that applications can be more easily scaled, more reliable, and more powerful and data-rich. After all, think what you could do if you could combine multitudes of the resources available on the Internet into a monolithic application, even in just one industry or area of interest.

Virtual Directories

A *virtual directory* is a folder that is not in your home or root Web site folder, but appears that way to browsers. It is actually an *alias* to another directory elsewhere on the server. Among the advantages of using virtual directories is the fact that users don't know the real location of critical files on your server (so they can't mess with the files). It's also easier to change directories later if you decide to move content (just change the alias mapping, not every URL reference in the Web site).

You can use the Virtual Directory Creation Wizard to create a virtual directory. Just follow these steps:

1. Open the Internet Services Manager from the Desktop by choosing Start | Programs | Applications | Internet Services Manager.

2. Find the Default Web site and right-click it to see the shortcut menu. Choose New | Virtual Directory. The Virtual Directory Creation Wizard will open, as in the following illustration.

3. On the first screen requiring an entry, enter the alias or name for your virtual directory, as in the illustration.

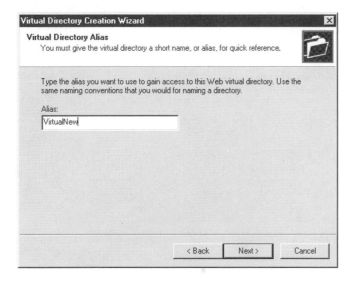

4. On the next screen, enter (or browse to) the physical folder represented by the name you entered on the previous screen, and then click Next, as in this illustration.

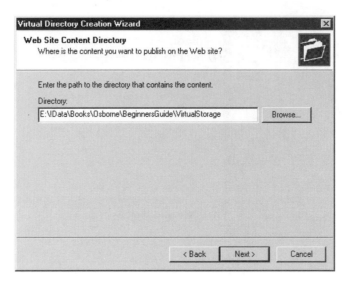

5. On the next screen, choose which actions will be allowed within the directory, such as Read, Run Scripts, and so forth. Make your choices, click Next to go to the final screen, and then click Finish when you've finished. Your Virtual Directory will appear in the Default Web site with the alias you chose, as in the following illustration.

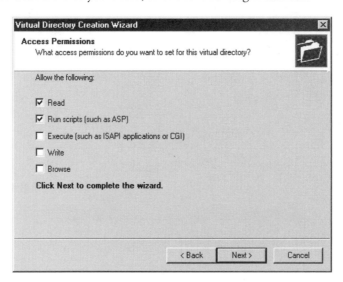

1

The Web Site as Communications Channel

Physically, the Internet is simply a network of networks, using mainly TCP/IP as the communications protocol among nodes. A systems engineer can tell you about the various network layers (or protocols) involved in network communications, how data is broken into packets that follow a variety of routes from one computer to the next across the local network or the Internet, and so forth. It's easy to begin to think of the Web as simply a subset of the Internet (which it is, in fact) and Web site communications as simply another method of advertising, like TV or radio.

However, building a successful Web site (and especially an online application-driven Web site) involves many more factors than simply getting the mechanical functions right. Not only must you build in plenty of useful interactivity, you must structure it in such a way that the user feels right at home. Perhaps you remember the days when the term *user friendly* was the buzzword. Your Web site must be so user friendly that the rankest novice can immediately grasp how to make it function, while at the same time not turning off advanced users. This is no easy task, but some insightful tips are offered in the next section. And in Chapter 2, you'll learn more about how to make a site interesting without resorting to useless flashiness.

Development Issues

Even though you may be certain that you'll be hosting your site on Windows 2000 (most Windows-hosted sites are currently on Windows NT 3.51 or 4.0, but this is beginning to change to Windows 2000 as hosting companies migrate to the new platform), there are other issues you'll encounter as you make decisions about your hosting and design requirements. This section covers most of them and provides some tools for making those decisions.

Establishing Objectives

You've made the decision that the Web is the way to communicate a particular set of information or provide a particular process with real-time interactivity. Now you are faced with a multitude of other decisions regarding how to set up the site so it can perform the functions required to support your objectives. However, if those objectives are vague or undefined, you will end up backing your way into them. It's better to establish specific objectives in the beginning so they can lead you to the right answers for development and deployment of your site.

For example, if a major objective of the site is to allow users to make online purchases, you'll need to take the following into consideration:

- Target market and demographics

- Projected sales, unique visitors, and hits

- Integration of online and offline inventory systems

- The purchasing process

- Security, privacy, and customer/technical support

Target Market and Demographics   Understanding your target market is not only important for business purposes, it also plays a big role in the structure of your Web site. If no one in your target market owns a computer or has an Internet connection, you won't get many sales. At this writing, probably only 10 percent of the world's population is connected on a regular basis (although that's still a huge number—around 600 million). If your target market is high-end corporate or academic types with high-speed access at all times, you can use heavier file types to communicate with them. By the same token, if most of your users connect to your site with mobile phones or personal digital assistants (PDAs), you need to consider using a conversion service so your site will be compatible.

Projected Visitors and Hits   The number of visitors and hits is important because it has a direct impact on the availability of your site. If you need millions of visitors per day to fulfill the sales objectives of your site, you'll probably need multiple servers and a ton of bandwidth to remain rapidly available for most users (not to mention excellent DBMS software and well-tuned OSs, Web servers, and applications running in the background).

Whatever bandwidth is available needs to be large enough to accommodate your highest expected levels of visitors and hits. Another consideration regarding bandwidth is the amount you use. Most hosting companies impose some kind of limit on bandwidth usage, even when they claim usage is unlimited (read the fine print of your contract). Exceeding this limit usually means paying extra charges or at least renegotiating the contract.

Integration of Online and Offline Inventory Systems

You've probably seen that commercial making fun of companies that don't have tight integration between their online and offline inventory systems. Naturally, consumers expect that if they buy something online they will be able to get it; but if no coordination exists between online and offline inventory databases, what seemed to be in stock may actually not be. Brick-and-mortar stores going online must ensure a constant connection between inventory displayed online and purchases made offline. Some stores are connecting everything to the online system to reconcile inventory problems.

The Purchasing Process   Purchasing should be fast, easy, and fun, rather than confusing, tedious, and boring. Consumers should be able to find and add to their shopping cart every product they are looking for, with instant updates to totals, taxes, and shipping charges, and an easy and intuitive method for deleting products when they change their minds. The act of making a purchase and charging with a credit card should be clearly defined, and links to customer service, privacy statements, terms and conditions, and security information should be provided.

Security, Privacy, and Customer Support   While you may not want to advertise to the world the security measures you employ, a general reference should be offered to alleviate consumer concerns. The effort you put into establishing security during the installation of Windows 2000 and IIS is, at least generally, part of your marketing and a valuable selling point. Privacy concerns are growing daily, so your privacy statement is probably just as important. And if your customers are concerned before the sale or after, they should have a customer support number to call for reassurance. If you like, you can even set up a call through their computers, although this can be rather expensive and require some heavy investment in software and hardware for your call center.

Hosting the Web Site

Although the best situation when creating a Web application is to have complete control over your servers, this is frequently not the case, and freelance developers in particular may have little choice in the matter. Sometimes you'll be forced to use a company's existing Web hosting service, and other times the company may not be in a position to buy or lease its own servers. Understanding the variation in Web hosting services and how to get the most out of them (and when to recommend changing hosting companies) is a key skill for ASP programmers. The hosting company and their hardware/software setup will have a major impact on your applications.

There are many Web hosting companies to choose from (go to the Web site **http://www.boardwatch.com** to review an extensive list of hosting companies in the United States), and two of the best are **http://www.e4free.com** and **http://www.dynamic-e.com**. E4free is hosting the site upon which the application developed for this book is running. Both of these companies offer all the amenities, including plenty of space, plenty of bandwidth, multiple high-speed Internet connections, secure servers, e-mail features, domain name registration, and so forth. The best idea is to choose a company that specializes in Web hosting rather than an ISP that also hosts Web sites. ISPs that provide hosting as a sideline feature may not offer the same degree of service as a hosting-only company.

Hosting Issues

It's very important to establish a rapport with the technical support folks at your hosting company early on. Hopefully, they are competent; if not, you should complain or switch. In addition, get full details on what hardware/software combinations they are running and in what configuration. Depending upon the configuration, what works for one client on one platform may not work for another client on the same platform.

Choosing Connection Types   The primary considerations when choosing a connection type or evaluating the Web hosting company's connections are how many ways are they connected, and at what speed?

Each Web hosting company or ISP purchases their Internet connections from larger companies upstream on the Internet (their upstream provider) until you get to the largest Internet connection providers. If your Web hosting company claims to be *multi-homed*, it is saying it has connections to several upstream Internet connection providers. This is important because even the biggest Internet connection providers have been known to fall out of service for days and weeks at a time, although this is relatively unusual. Having connections to between three and seven upstream providers is not uncommon at the better hosting companies.

The amount of bandwidth available depends on the type of connection the company has to the Internet. The amount of bandwidth available to you depends on how many other sites are vying for the same bandwidth (either on your machine, or on all the machines in your cluster). To estimate the amount of bandwidth required to support a given number of users, you can use a procedure similar to the following:

1. Find the size of the files to be transmitted. For HTML pages, multiply the number of characters per line (approximately 80) by the number of bits per character (8), times the number of lines per page (around 66), times the number of pages in the document, times an overhead factor of 1.5. So, for a 10-page HTML document filled with code, there would be 10 pages times 66 lines per page (= 660), times 80 characters per line (= 52,800), times 8 bits per character (= 422,400), times 1.5 for overhead. The total bits to be transmitted would be 633,600, or about two-thirds of a million bits.

2. Divide the number of bits to be transmitted by the bandwidth available to find out how long it will take to transmit the page. If your page is really two-thirds of a million bits, it would take around 04 of a second to transmit if you're running a T–1 line (1.54 million bits per second). Conversely, dividing transmission speed by file size gives the number of pages that can be transmitted per second (about 2.36 for this example).

Note

This calculation is not representative of typical HTML pages, because most do not contain characters in every column of every line. However, pages do usually contain graphics files that must be transmitted separately. All the files making up a page should be included in your calculations of bandwidth requirements. In addition, it's important to note that most people can't receive at T-1 speeds; if they are using a 28.8K modem, you'd better make sure your pages are about one-tenth the size discussed above, including graphics and related files.

3. Figure out how many users your available bandwidth can support. The number of users is commonly measured as the amount of pages (meaning all the files associated with a page) per day times the typical file size downloaded, in kilobytes or megabytes. If you have 1.54 million bits per second available (a T-1 line dedicated to your Web server only), you can transmit (after the overhead factor) 11,088,000,000 bytes per day, or a little over 10Gb. If each page hit averages 30K, you can support approximately 333,000 page hits per day.

4. If each page hit is spread apart from the others, no user will suffer performance degradation. However, it is much more common to see users congregate at your site during peak times. Therefore, you should also calculate the number of simultaneous users your site can support and still maintain acceptable download times. This is done by calculating the number of page hits that can be processed and transmitted within an arbitrarily chosen time frame. For example, if you want all your users to receive their page requests within three seconds of clicking, you would calculate the maximum transmission speed of your connection for the average page hit. If each page hit is 3.75KB, and you're running a T-1 line, you can fit approximately 100 users into a three-second time frame.

1

☑ Mastery Check

2. What is the primary functionality ASP brings to a Web site, and why is it so important?

_____

_____

_____

3. What is a partition, and why does it matter how it is formatted when installing IIS?

_____

_____

_____

4. What process is advisable to use when designing a Web site?

A. Start developing pages and functions first, and ask questions later.

B. Do exactly as the client says.

C. Use reverse-engineering and usability testing to figure out how to arrive at the desired functionality, and then conform to the client's wishes as closely as possible.

D. None of the above.

5. What is bandwidth and why is it an important consideration in modern Web site design?

_____

_____

_____

Module 2

ASP and the Web— Programming Basics

The Goals of This Module

- Learn and practice HTML and use HTTP
- Define how ASP works with HTML, VBScript, JavaScript, and SQL
- Review the basics of Web site layout and design
- Explore the fundamental interactivity methods in ASP
- Learn basic ASP scripting structure and syntax
- Practice error-handling techniques
- Examine good and bad debugging procedures

More and more, Web sites are becoming complete online applications. Whereas early Web sites used static pages to display text and graphics, today's Web sites perform very complex functions, much like traditional applications programs. Therefore, the development effort that goes into modern Web sites is similar to traditional software development efforts. Programming is a fundamental part of those efforts, and the same kinds of tools and procedures used to develop software are being transformed and used in Web site development.

This module covers programming basics, such as using HTML, VBScript, JavaScript, ASP, and SQL, and also touches on error handling and debugging. In addition, we'll offer some advice about site layout, as well as construction and process flow.

Web Site Coding Languages

Web sites are a mixture of HTML and graphics files; scripting (both on and off the server); databases; and other file types, programs, and components. Working together, they make beautiful music, but for the user it means being multilingual. Because ASP applications will ordinarily be used with Web pages, and because Web pages are mostly made up of HTML, we will spend some time defining how Web pages are typically constructed with HTML. Although there are plenty of high-quality HTML editors out there, you're going to be working closely with the code as you build functions with ASP. It pays to understand the HTML code, and practice will help you feel comfortable with it.

Source code commands in HTML are called tags. They are recognizable by their enclosing angle brackets (greater-than and less-than signs) at each end. For example, the <BODY> tag is appropriate to begin the body of your page. This simple device is all that separates HTML commands from the ordinary text that makes up most of the content of Web pages. Browsers read through the tags and construct the Web page onscreen according to those tags. The tags are simple enough to write manually, and you can use simple text-editing tools (such as Notepad, WordPad, or Simple Text) to create and modify your HTML code. Be sure to save your files as plain text when using WordPad, however. Embedded characters such as carriage returns and line feeds shouldn't bother the browser, but other embedded characters might cause problems.

Static Web Pages

Static Web pages are so called because they are not generated on the fly. The content in them doesn't change, except when the Webmaster uploads revisions. At this writing, Web pages usually contain

- A header that, except for the title, contains information invisible to the viewer

- The body, into which the bulk of the content goes

- JavaScript or VBScript for limited programmatic functionality

- Graphics or multimedia to lend a pleasing appearance

HTML 4.0 is the latest version of the HTML specification (you can find more information about the spec, or recommendation, at **http://www.w3.org/MarkUp/**). Basic HTML tags usually have a beginning and ending tag, differentiated by the slash, as in the beginning and ending bold tags (<B> and </B>). Think of them as bookends, alerting the browser to begin boldfaced font with the beginning tag, and end boldfaced font with the ending tag. Like most rules, there are exceptions. The image tag (<IMG SRC="image.gif">) is an example of an HTML tag that has no ending tag. Some HTML tags have ending tags that are required, some have ending tags that are not required, and some have no ending tags at all (and it is forbidden to use them). Appendix A lists all HTML tags, as well as details about proper usage.

Some HTML tags, in normal use, offer users the opportunity to communicate with the server. For example, if you build a link into your page, the viewer will be able to click that link and request another page from your server (or any Web server in the world, for that matter). Graphics files are accessed using a similar mechanism in the image tag. Form tags have the ability to specify the path and filename of a program or script to run when the Submit button is clicked. ASP takes advantage of these mechanisms as a means to run scripts.

Coding HTML

There are many fine HTML primers and tutorials, both in print and on the Web, so we won't spend an inordinate amount of time on the HTML tags here (but we will cover essential tags as we encounter them in our scripting exercises). However, because you will be mixing HTML and ASP code frequently, there are some things you should know about HTML conventions in general:

- HTML is not case sensitive, but URLs, paths, and filenames may be.

- HTML tags consist of the tag itself and any attributes or properties they may possess.

- HTML tags can be separated from ASP scripting within an HTML document by means of the ASP separation characters (<% and %>) and can also be generated in server output using the HTMLEncode function in ASP.

- JavaScript and VBScript can also be generated by or embedded in ASP scripts.

Far from their humble beginnings as a way to access and display text and graphics data, HTML and compatible languages and technologies now form a set of tools capable of creating full-featured applications. Think of HTML and its peculiarities as a text-based GUI tool, and ASP, VBScript, JavaScript, and SQL as programming languages for the HTML tool.

Browser Wars

No discussion of HTML would be complete without mention of the differences in Web browsers. Not only do browsers run the gamut from text-only to fully 3-D capable, they also vary widely in their ability to handle conforming HTML tags, HTML extensions (the most popular of which are created by Microsoft and Netscape), and various file types. HTML extensions, by the way, are nonconforming HTML tags that can be properly interpreted (out of the box) only by the maker's browser, unless another browser maker builds acceptance of these tags into their product. In the war for market dominance, the big players seldom adopt each other's extensions.

To add to the confusion, various browser versions also differ in their ability to interpret tags, and sometimes tags fall out of favor or are replaced by more effective tags (they may become *deprecated*, meaning they are scheduled to be phased out).

Bottom line is, you'll have to be aware of the workable tags and how they are interpreted by your users' most common browsers, or you could alienate large portions of your target audience. Fortunately, ASP comes with built-in functions that can detect browser types, and you can compensate by using lowest common denominator tags or by creating multiple versions of your pages and displaying them selectively.

Hypertext Transport Protocol (HTTP)

The World Wide Web Consortium (the same organization that develops HTML specifications) also builds the Hypertext Transfer Protocol, currently in version 1.1. Like most Internet-related specifications, it is tracked as a Request For Comment (RFC), and the most recent RFC for HTTP 1.1 is RFC 2616 (you can find it at **http://www.w3.org/ Protocols/rfc2616/rfc2616.html**).

The HTTP protocol is, according to the abstract, "an application-level protocol for distributed, collaborative, hypermedia information systems. It is a generic, stateless protocol that can be used for many tasks beyond its use for hypertext, such as name servers and distributed object management systems, through extension of its request methods, error codes, and headers." In practical terms, it is the mechanism by which client and server communicate when using the Web.

In the introduction to HTTP 1.1, the authors note that HTTP is a request/response protocol, and describe some of the aspects of typical communications between client and server. In particular, they note that there may be several programs acting as servers and several acting as clients when Web pages (or resources) are being requested and supplied.

They refer to the roles of Web servers, gateways, proxies, caching, and browser (or other user agents) as clients, servers, and sometimes both client and server at the same time. For instance, a proxy may be a client when it is requesting a page from a Web server. At the same time, it may be a server for the browsers it is making requests for as it serves them the pages it receives from the Web server. Also noted is HTTP 1.1's capability to support caching, the holding of recent copies of a page at a closer, more accessible location for faster retrieval. We discuss caching and how ASP helps you manage it in greater detail in Module 3.

Section 4 of the specification mentions HTTP headers, which form an important part of any communication between client and server, or vice versa. HTTP headers "include general-header (section 4.5), request-header (section 5.3), response-header (section 6.2), and entity-header (section 7.1) fields," and "follow the same generic format as that given in Section 3.1 of RFC 822 [9]. Each header field consists of a name followed by a colon (":") and the field value. Field names are case-insensitive. The field value MAY be preceded by any amount of LWS [(linear white space)], though a single SP [(space)] is preferred."

Module 3 covers how to use ASP objects to show the value of request and response headers. HTTP headers can be read, modified, and created using ASP objects, and may affect application behavior. Headers' capabilities will be discussed in detail as they are encountered and used within applications.

Note

All HTTP 1.1 listings include both the object or message and the section of the specification where further information may be found, in this and other modules.

General Header Fields   In Section 4.5 of the HTTP specification, there are a few general header fields that apply to both request and response messages. They are listed next.

Cache-Control	Pragma	Upgrade
Connection	Trailer	Via
Date	Transfer-Encoding	Warning

Request Headers   In Section 5 of the HTTP specification are the request headers. One of the most important parts of a request message is the header containing the method by which data is conveyed to the server. Current allowable methods are listed here (note that the most common are GET and POST):

OPTIONS	POST	TRACE
GET	PUT	CONNECT
HEAD	DELETE	

Section 5.3 of the HTTP specification also lists allowable request header fields. The fields include data about the character set and language employed, the browser type, expiration, and other important message data. The following list contains these request header fields:

Accept	Accept-Charset	Accept-Encoding
Accept-Language	Authorization	Expect
From	Host	If-Match
If-Modified-Since	If-None-Match	If-Range
If-Unmodified-Since	Max-Forwards	Proxy-Authorization
Range	Referer	TE
User-Agent		

Response Headers   After a server has been contacted by a client, and has read and interpreted the request, it builds a response message consisting of a status line, headers, and a message body. The message body includes the HTML that makes up the returning page, while the status line indicates the status of the request.

Status-line components (including the status code and status message) are built in the following way. The status code is a three-digit code meant to be interpreted by machines (although some are well-known to humans, such as the "*HTTP 404*–Not Found" code/message combination). It is followed by the status message (or Reason-Phrase, to be technically correct). The status message is the Not Found portion of the status line mentioned previously. There are several categories of allowable status codes based on the first digit of the code, as follows:

● **1*xx*: Informational**   The request was received, continuing process.

● **2*xx*: Success**   The action was successfully received, understood, and accepted.

● **3*xx*: Redirection**   Further action must be taken in order to complete the request.

● **4*xx*: Client Error**   The request contains bad syntax or cannot be fulfilled.

● **5*xx*: Server Error**   The server failed to fulfill an apparently valid request.

Note

According to the specification, the status messages are recommendations, and may be changed without affecting the protocol's operation. This means you can modify these messages using ASP without affecting the server's standard use of them.

Response Status Codes and Messages   The HTTP 1.1 specification defines the following response status codes and messages. First, here's the 100 and 200 Series HTTP response header status codes/messages:

100	Continue
101	Switching Protocols
200	OK
201	Created
202	Accepted
203	Non-Authoritative Information
204	No Content
205	Reset Content
206	Partial Content

And here's the 300, 400, and 500 Series HTTP response header status codes/messages:

300	Multiple Choices
301	Moved Permanently
302	Found
303	See Other
304	Not Modified
305	Use Proxy
307	Temporary Redirect
400	Bad Request
401	Unauthorized
402	Payment Required
403	Forbidden
404	Not Found

405	Method Not Allowed
406	Not Acceptable
407	Proxy Authentication Required
408	Request Time-out
409	Conflict
410	Gone
411	Length Required
412	Precondition Failed
413	Request Entity Too Large
414	Request-URI Too Large
415	Unsupported Media Type
416	Requested Range Not Satisfiable
417	Expectation Failed
500	Internal Server Error
501	Not Implemented
502	Bad Gateway
503	Service Unavailable
504	Gateway Time-out
505	HTTP Version Not Supported

Response Header Fields   Response header fields give information to the client (or requester), outlining the server type, whether authentication is required, the age of the response, what methods to allow, and more. Allowable response header fields are

Accept-Ranges	Age	ETag
Location	Proxy-Authenticate	Retry-After
Server	Vary	WWW-Authenticate

The lists displayed previously constitute some of the most important aspects of the HTTP 1.1 specification that you will encounter using ASP, but should not be considered a comprehensive review of the specification. Visit the World Wide Web Consortium and review the specification and the descriptions associated with the various codes, messages, and headers mentioned in this module to gain a better understanding of how they work. They will be covered in greater depth as we go along, but this book does not attempt to make you an HTTP master.

Ask the Expert

Question: Where do Web site languages and protocols come from?

Answer: Hypertext Markup Language (HTML) is a language defined by Standard Generalized Markup Language (SGML). The HTML 4.0 specification (technically just a recommendation) is a formally defined SGML Document Type Definition (DTD). The DTD defines the allowable HTML tags and attributes that produce Web pages according to the current version of the HTML specification.

VBScript is a subset of the Visual Basic programming language, created by Microsoft. It acts as an interpreter for scripting code within Web pages and on the server.

Active Server Pages is also a Microsoft-created technology. ASP is, according to Microsoft, "an open, compile-free application environment in which you can combine HTML, scripts, and reusable ActiveX server components to create dynamic and powerful Web-based business solutions. Active Server Pages enables server-side scripting for Internet Information Server (IIS) with native support for both VBScript and JScript."

JScript is Microsoft's version of Sun's JavaScript; Microsoft calls it "a powerful scripting language targeted specifically at the Internet, [and] the first scripting language to fully conform to ECMAScript, the Web's only standard scripting language."

SQL stands for Structured Query Language. Specifically developed for interacting with relational databases, it has a specification independent of the versions customized to work with individual vendors' RDBMS products. Versions of the language can be traced as far back as 1974; in 1986, an ANSI standard for SQL was adopted. SQL is the universal language for accessing databases, and is used in all popular DBMS products.

Question: What role does each language play?

Answer: HTML is the basic construction tool for Web pages today. Scripting languages such as VBScript, JScript, and JavaScript, add programmatic functionality to Web pages, both on and off the server. ASP is a technology rather than a programming language, and provides built-in objects that enhance the developer's ability to work easily with HTML, as well as script languages, programs, components, and data sources. SQL is the language used to query and work with relational databases and other data sources.

Question: Do I really have to understand how to program them all? Aren't there automated tools that will do the programming for me?

Answer: You don't have to be an expert in programming each of these languages, and there are many tools available to make working with them easier. For example, few people still code all their HMTL by hand. Instead, they use FrontPage or Dreamweaver to do the bulk of the work. However, you should be familiar with each of them, and understand their strong and weak points, as well as how they interact. Making them work together is your job.

Question: Is there any way to change HTTP headers? How does this affect the browser?

Answer: You have access to HTTP headers via the Request and Response objects, so you can view their contents. However, some of them cannot be changed directly. Instead, you might have to store their value (a cookie, for example) in a variable and then change it on the return trip (when you send a new cookie back, for example). Changing headers, such as status messages, can directly affect the browser. For example, if you change the status message to **307–Temporary Redirect**, you can send the browser to a location different than the one requested.

Dynamic Applications

Unlike static Web pages, ASP scripts make your Web site come alive with interactivity. The built-in ASP objects make it easy to communicate with the server; to start, control, and manage the site as a persistent application; and to work with individual users during separate sessions. The highly integrated nature of ASP and HTML, VBScript/JavaScript, and databases/SQL means you must be on good terms with all of them; but if you have any programming background, you'll find the commands and syntax very easy to understand and use. If not, learning the basic structures of these languages will assist you with any other programming languages you choose to learn.

ASP and HTML

If you have a working knowledge of HTML, or are proficient with a good HTML editing program such as FrontPage or Dreamweaver, you can create ASP pages the same way you would an ordinary HTML Web page. In fact, for ASP 3.0 and IIS 5.0, Microsoft recommends that you create all your pages (even static HTML pages) with an .asp filename extension, because the ASP processing engine can process ordinary HTML pages nearly as fast as the Web server itself.

Looking at ASP Code   The reason you can start ASP pages as Web pages is that there is a lot of HTML-based content in the output ASP scripts generate. For example, suppose you want to return to the user the value of a form field that was submitted. You would use something like the following:

```
<HTML>
<HEAD>
<TITLE>The Title of this Page</TITLE>
</HEAD>
<BODY>
<% Response.Write(Request.Form("fieldname")) %>
</BODY>
</HTML>
```

Notice the ASP code delimiters are slightly different from the HTML delimiters, in that they contain the % sign. This tells the ASP processing engine that there are ASP-related commands in the code, and that they need special attention.

If no delimiters are found in the code, the engine streams the code straight to the Web server, so processing takes place almost as quickly as if the server processed it firsthand. Code containing ASP commands is processed line by line in the normal fashion.

Scripting with ASP

You can also use the HTML script tags (<SCRIPT>) to identify scripting elements within your pages, and these tags can be placed anywhere you want. They would look something like this pseudocode:

```
<HTML>
<HEAD><TITLE>The title goes here</TITLE></HEAD>
<BODY>
<SCRIPT>
VBSCript and ASP code go here
</SCRIPT>
</BODY>
</HTML>
```

Client-Side Scripting   Client-side scripting, as its name implies, is executed on the client. For routine calculations that don't require any special security measures, or for which users reading the code is not a concern, client-side scripting has the advantage of utilizing the user's processing cycles. Client-side scripting is the default when ASP scripts are embedded in Web pages, but they can also be explicitly set using the RUNAT attribute, as follows:

```
<SCRIPT RUNAT="client">
```

Server-Side Scripting   Server-side scripting must be explicitly set with the RUNAT attribute when using the <SCRIPT> tags. Script that is run at the server will not be seen in the finished page; rather, the user will see the results of processing. If you use the source attribute within a <SCRIPT> tag, you can include any script file you choose within the Web page for processing at the server:

```
<SCRIPT RUNAT="server" SRC="mypath/myscript.asp"></SCRIPT>)
```

To make the separate script file, you can use a plain text editor such as Notepad. The script file should contain only script code, not HTML commands, and the <SCRIPT> tag itself must contain no other code.

The advantage here is that you can reuse the same script many times throughout your Web site; changing the script once changes the function of each page. It is sometimes more useful to use the server-side include instruction. The only limitation on server-side includes is that each block of code must be delimited, meaning you must end a block of code in the current page before you call a block of code from an external script file. This instruction will be used extensively in ASP code examples in later modules.

Built-In ASP Functions

ASP version 3.0, as installed with Windows 2000 and IIS 5.0, comes with a variety of built-in objects, properties, and methods. These provide the foundation that makes ASP work so well with HTML, VBScript/JavaScript, SQL, and Active Data Objects (ADOs). They also allow access to HTTP and the HTTP headers, to make your life easy when creating dynamic Web applications. Let's take a look at capturing and sending data to users first.

Capturing Data   The Request object exposes collections that capture data as it travels in a stream from the browser via a hypertext link or a form submittal. Data that can be captured includes HTTP variables, cookies, query strings, and the contents of form fields (including the field names). For example, capturing data submitted by a form can be accomplished using the Request.Form(*fieldname*) object/method combination in ASP.

Sending Data   The Response object allows you to insert data in the response stream heading back to a particular user, such as strings, the values of variables, cookies, and custom HTTP headers. For example, sending a message back to the user for display in a Web page can be accomplished using the Response.Write(*string*) object/method combination in ASP.

Creating Applications   The Application object, created when the first page is requested by the client, stores variables and object references that any page in the application can access. Using the OnStart event, statements can be processed whenever the application is first opened.

Creating Sessions   The Session object is created whenever a user connects to your application, and is unique for each user (the user must accept cookies for the Session object to work). It can hold variables and object references for the entire session. The session ends when the timeout period expires.

The Server Object   The Server object is used for instantiating Component Object Model (COM) objects, as well as translating characters into the proper format for URLs and within HMTL.

ASP and VBScript/JScript

By default, ASP supports both the VBScript and JScript scripting engines. You can install other scripting engines to interpret PerlScript and TCL. Microsoft also introduced Microsoft Windows Script Interfaces, a new way for scripting engine vendors to add scripting and OLE automation capabilities. According to Microsoft, any language or runtime environment—including VBA, VBScript, Perl, and Lisp—can run as a scripting engine on a Windows script host (such as Internet Explorer). ASP uses the default scripting engine, which is set in the Application Configuration dialog box shown in Figure 2-1. Since VBScript is so widely used with ASP, the remainder of this section is devoted to the VBScript language.

VBScript is a subset of the Visual Basic programming language. Rather than being compiled, it is *interpreted*, meaning it is converted into machine language on the fly as the browser or server reads it. This makes it run more slowly than a precompiled program (like any interpreted language). However, the programs are generally much shorter and tend to run quickly, so you usually won't notice the difference.

A big advantage to using VBScript is that it is similar in usage and syntax to Visual Basic. It is possible to use VBScript and JScript in the same document, although for heavy use this may not be the most efficient use of the server. Keep in mind that for each scripting engine used, ASP has to load that engine and send code to it. It's best to avoid switching in and out of ASP script in a single page. Keep your code inside one set of ASP delimiters (<% *code* %>) and you'll only have one processing job to execute. For small jobs or scripts, this may not be a problem; but for larger or more complex scripts, switching can slow things down considerably.

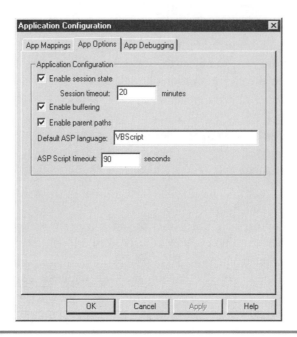

Figure 2-1 The Application Configuration dialog box

VBScript Basics

The 5.0 versions of Internet Explorer and Internet Information Server both support VBScript 5.0. There are several interesting new language elements in VBScript 5.0, including the Class object and Class statement, the Eval function, the Ignore Case property, the Length property, the Timer function, and the With statement. We've assembled a VBScript 5.0 appendix (Appendix D), and we'll cover commonly used and essential VBScript commands, reserved words, and structures here. For an up-to-the-minute reference, the Microsoft VBScript documentation can be downloaded at **http://msdn.microsoft.com/scripting/vbscript/ download/vbsdoc.exe**.

Variables in VBScript   Variants are the only data type available in the VBScript scripting engine. Because they can store many types of data, they take more room and require more processing cycles, and so are not as efficient at storing or processing data—but they have some excellent advantages. For instance, inside a variant, values are stored as individual subtypes, and they automatically convert data types appropriately in most situations. You must exercise caution when ordering VBScript statements to make sure you'll get the correct result (this will be discussed in greater detail later in this module, when we discuss the VarType method).

Variables can be declared anywhere within code, simply by using the Dim statement. However, it is wise to use the Option Explicit statement (<% Option Explicit Dim var1, var2 %>) at the beginning of your code, because it forbids the use of variable names that have not been explicitly dimensioned. This means that if you accidentally include a variable that doesn't exist, an explicit error will emerge, making debugging your code a much easier job.

VBScript Features   Microsoft organizes VBScript (by features included) in one section of the documentation, and we'll follow that convention. Please note, comments can be included using the REM (for "remarks") keyword or simply an apostrophe ('). Programming features include, for example, Array Handling (the first feature mentioned in the online documentation), which contains

- **Array function**   Array (*arglist*)
  Returns an array of Variant type, where *arglist* is a comma-delimited list of values.

- **Dim statement**   Dim *varname*[([*subscripts*])][, *varname*[([*subscripts*])]] . . .
  Declares variables, including arrays.

The Set statement is used frequently as the Assignment feature, such as when you are setting a recordset equal to a particular set of records from a database table. The syntax is

- **Set statement**   Set *objectvar* = {*objectexpression*}
  Makes the object equal to the object expression, where the expression results in the selection of records from a table via a database connection. Can also be used to associate a procedure reference with an event or create a new instance of a class.

VBScripts include the following *constants* and *literals* (constants are always the same value; literals describe, literally, conditions of variables):

- **Empty**   Used to indicate an uninitialized value (but not Null)

- **Nothing**   Used to remove an association from an object variable, as in *vRecordset* = Nothing (where vRecordset is a recordset that was associated with records from a database table)

- **Null**   Used to indicate that a variable contains no valid data

- **True**   Contains a value of −1 (not 1)

- **False**   Contains a value of 0 (zero)

Control Flow Structures   Some of the most important and frequently used VBScript structures are the *control flow* structures, such as If...Then and Do...While. You'll most likely use all of them repeatedly in your scripts.

- **Do...Loop**   Do [{While | Until} *condition*] [*statements*] [Exit Do] [*statements*] Loop
  This structure repeats a block of statements until a condition is true or while a condition is true, depending on how it is set up.

- **For...Next**   For *counter* = *start* To *end* [Step *step*] *statements*] [Exit For] [*statements*] Next
  This structure simply repeats a block of statements until the counter runs out. You can set the value the counter must reach, as well as the step size for each iteration. The step can be either positive or negative.

- **For Each...Next**   For Each *element* In *group* [*statements*] [Exit For] [*statements*] Next [*element*]
  This structure repeats a block of statements for each element in an array or collection. You'll use this with every collection you encounter in ASP objects.

- **If...Then...Else**   If *condition* Then [*statements*] [ElseIf *condition-n* Then [*elseifstatements*]] . . . [Else [*elsestatements*]] End If

2

This structure is also used often, and specifies conditional execution of VBScript statements. You can nest them to check multiple conditions, but you should examine the Select Case structure for complex conditional checking.

● **Select Case**   Select Case *testexpression* [Case *expressionlist-n* [*statements-n*]] . . . [Case Else *expressionlist-n* [*elsestatements-n*]] End Select This structure is useful for checking many conditions and selecting statements to perform based on the valid condition.

● **While...Wend**   While *condition* Version [*statements*] Wend This structure can iterate through statements based on a condition, but it is more practical to use the Do...Loop structure to do this.

● **With**   With *object statements* End With This structure is new to VBScript (although it has a history in VBA and Visual Basic) and is a welcome addition to the language. It allows you to reference an object once and execute multiple statements against that object, without re-referencing the object for each statement.

Data Type Conversions   VBScript can perform the normal data type conversions from variant subtypes, such as

● **CStr function**   Returns a variant of subtype String

● **CInt function**   Returns a variant of subtype Integer

● **Cdate function**   Returns a variant of subtype Date

● **Abs function**   Returns the absolute value of a number

● **Asc and Chr functions**   Asc returns the ANSI character code of the first letter in a string, and Chr returns the letter associated with an ANSI code

● **Hex, Oct, Fix, and Int**   Return the hexadecimal, octal, and integer portions of numbers, respectively, with Fix rounding down for negative numbers and Int rounding up

Common date/time functions in VBScript include

- **Date**   Returns the current system date

- **Time**   Returns the current system time

- **Day**   Returns a whole number representing the day of the month

- **Month**   Returns a whole number representing the month of the year

- **Year**   Returns a whole number representing the year

- **Now**   Returns both the current system date and time

Error Handling   Not surprisingly, errors sometimes occur in VBScript code, and there are statements you can use to handle them (On Error Resume Next and On Error GoTo 0). On Error Resume Next enables inline error handling, and you should include one of these statements in each procedure to handle any errors that crop up. On Error GoTo 0 disables error handling.

Hint

The behavior that occurs when errors are encountered at runtime depends on the host running the code. Sometimes hosts notify users of errors and stop code execution, and sometimes they don't. Make sure to take this behavior into account when building ASP applications.

Eval, String, IO, Math, and Variant Functions   The Eval function is new to VBScript among the expressions, and it removes confusion in statements such as (x=y) as to whether to perform an assignment or a comparison. In JScript the assignment operator (=) is different from the comparison operator (==), so no confusion exists. For example, you can use the Eval function as part of an If…Then structure, to test whether one value is equivalent to another, whatever the subtype.

Formatting strings can be performed using several functions, among them the FormatCurrency function. This function returns a currency value that uses the currency symbol defined in the system Control Panel.

There are also several input/ouput functions, such as the MsgBox function. This function displays a message box with text you specify (literally or using a variable) and then waits for input from the user. It can display 16 different button combinations, and will return values (from 1 to 7) indicating OK, Cancel, Abort, Retry, Ignore, Yes, or No, depending on the button types you set it to display.

Math functions included with VBScript are limited compared to other languages. One statement often employed is the Randomize statement. This function initializes the random number generator, and can be used in conjunction with the Rnd function to produce random numbers. Other math functions include Tan, Cos, and Sin (tangent, cosine, and sine); and Exp, Log, and Sqr (exponent, logarithm, and square root).

VBScript has a fairly complete complement of operators, including addition (+), subtraction (−), multiplication (*), division (/), exponentiation (^), less than (<), greater than (>), string concatenation (&), and Boolean operators such as And and Or. These operate in the normal fashion.

Besides the string functions mentioned earlier (Asc and Chr), there are a few more you can use with VBScript. Find the number of characters in a string with the Len function, or reverse the order of characters in a string with StrReverse. Join strings in an array with the Join function, and convert case in a string with the LCase and UCase functions.

Finally, there are the variant functions, which help determine the subtype of variants. These include IsArray, IsDate, IsEmpty, IsNull, IsNumeric, each of which returns a Boolean value as an indicator, and the VarType function, which returns a specific value indicating the subtype.

The VBScript functions listed here are only a subset of all the ones available; refer to Appendix D in this book and Microsoft's online documentation for more information. In later modules, the many examples of VBScript coding with ASP will demonstrate the correct syntax and usage of the VBScript language.

ASP and Databases

Database access is one of the most important and most frequently used capabilities of ASP. Technically, the objects used to access databases aren't ASP. They are Active Data Objects (ADOs), and they make it easy to connect to, retrieve, and manipulate records from a database table. As defined by Microsoft, ADO consists of a COM type library with a program

ID (ProgID) of ADODB (this will crop up again in Module 9). There are six objects in the ADO object model:

- **Command** Maintains information about a command, such as a query string or parameter definitions. Use it to execute a SQL query string on a Connection object.

- **Connection** Maintains connection information on the data provider (the database you are accessing, for example).

- **Error** Contains extended error information (as distinct Error objects in the Errors collection if two or more errors result from the same incident).

- **Field** Contains information from a single column of data in a recordset. Each Field object exists as part of the Fields collection in a recordset.

- **Property** Defined by the data provider, this is a characteristic of an ADO.

- **Recordset** A set of records from a database table or a cursor pointing to those records. You can set the properties of recordsets so that they are read-only or updateable to various degrees. If you open a recordset using the Connection object, you can open multiple recordsets on the same data provider.

In typical ASP scripts, you'll first make a connection to the data provider using a DSN or an on-the-fly connection (more on these in Module 9), and then you'll execute a SQL query string against the database table or tables from which you want to retrieve records. Of course, if you are inserting records (rather than retrieving records) you may use an INSERT statement instead of a SELECT statement. Once the recordset is populated, you can begin manipulating the field values—editing, adding, or deleting records, or simply navigating records as you see fit.

ADO includes many methods specifically designed for working with records, such as

- **AddNew** Creates a new record

2

- **Delete**   Deletes the current record or group of records

- **Move and MoveFirst/Last/Next/Previous**   Moves to the specified record

- **Open**   Opens a cursor and also allows you to specify the cursor type and lock type

- **Update**   Saves changes made to the current record

- **Requery**   Refreshes data in the recordset

There are also a number of properties useful for working with records in ADO, especially BOF (beginning of file) and EOF (end of file). Among the most valuable are

- **RecordCount**   Returns the current number of records in a recordset

- **PageCount**   Indicates how many pages of data are in a Recordset object

- **MaxRecords**   Indicates the maximum number of records to return to a Recordset object

- **BOF and EOF**   Indicate that the current record position is either before or after the first or last record in a recordset. This comes in handy when you want to know if there were any records returned following a query string execution (recordset.EOF equals true indicates no records were returned).

1-Minute Drill

- **What is the difference between HTML and HTTP?**
- **What is the difference between ASP and VBScript?**

- HTML is a markup language for writing Web pages that can be understood by any browser. HTTP is a protocol for sending Web pages across the Internet and relaying messages from the browser to the server and vice versa.
- VBScript is one of several scripting languages that can be used to write programs either on the server or on the browser. ASP is a technology for using those scripting languages plus a built-in set of special functions to create highly interactive Web pages.

Ask the Expert

Question: Can you describe, step by step, what happens when a user enters my Web site's URL in their browser? I'm curious about exactly what gets sent where, and how the server, the scripting engines, the database, and ASP interact.

Answer: The request goes initially to the Web server. Depending on the file extension (.htm, .html, .asp, .shtml, and so on), the contents of the file are returned to the user or processed by ASP or a scripting engine. If processed by ASP, any connections to data sources are opened, and input or output is accomplished and then returned to ASP. ASP returns the processed output to the server for relay back to the user. Think of it like this:

- HTML-only file (including client-side scripting)—Retrieved by Web Server and returned to client, finish processing performed at client.

- ASP file (including HTML, ASP, and perhaps ADO and SQL)—Retrieved by Web Server, sent to ASP and other scripting engines for processing, perform ADO/SQL database functions, finish processing by ASP and other scripting engines, and returned to client.

Question: Which scripting language should I use, VBScript or JScript?

Answer: That depends on your familiarity with these languages. VBScript and JScript scripting engines each possess a standard installation of ASP, so the deciding factor will be your comfort level with either language. Their capabilities are nearly identical, so there's not much to base a decision on there.

Question: I've heard it can be tough to use SQL, especially when you have to insert variable values in a SQL statement. Any tips to make the going easier?

Answer: Fortunately, SQL is similar across vendors. Unfortunately, the differences seem to be in the way they handle variable insertion. My recommendation is to use the built-in SQL generators most of the popular Relational Database Management System (RDBMS) programs have, and read everything you can on the specific syntax required for each program (or version).

Question: **What are the pros and cons of database programs on the market? Do I need to use SQL Server or Oracle, or can I put Microsoft Access to productive use?**

Answer: Microsoft Access 97 and 2000 are very good desktop-level RDBMS programs, useful for quickly prototyping desktop and small-scale Web applications. Beyond a certain size and number of concurrent users, however, Access won't perform well; so you'll need to make sure SQL Server, Oracle, and other major RDBMS programs are in your plans. These programs are industrial-strength databases, and although they are more expensive than Access, they supply the tools, capabilities, robustness, and performance required by higher-level Web sites and enterprise applications.

Laying Out the Web Site

Before you begin building pages or creating content, you should go through a process of imagining the structure and layout of the site, based on your objectives. This step is overlooked at many sites in the rush to get something (anything) up before the idea is stolen. The fact is, ideas for most Web sites have already been implemented, so there's nothing to steal; and what counts is not the idea so much as good execution. For the next few years, just about any reasonable (and quite a few not so reasonable) ideas will be viable. At the end of the day, users will find and return to a site if it has any or all of the following qualities.

Convenience

To determine whether your idea is convenient, look at existing processes people use to accomplish the same thing, and see if doing it online is truly more convenient. For example, if you're already connected to the Web with high-speed access and a clear understanding of what you're doing, going online to shop may seem like the most convenient thing in the world. For someone with low-speed access or with limited experience online, Web shopping may be a pain, and just cruising down to the local store could seem a lot more convenient. Making your Web site as convenient to use as possible can bring in even these reluctant visitors.

Affordability

The Internet and the Web definitely have an effect on pricing, thankfully often in favor of consumers. As an example, my wife and I were shopping for a used car recently. I wanted to trade in my old Mazda truck. To determine what it was worth, I went online and found a site that provides Blue Book values in real time (an excellent example of an online application, by the way). I entered the make, model, year, mileage, and condition of the truck and was instantly presented with two values, one representing what a dealer should be prepared to pay and the other the price I should get if I sold it to the general public. Armed with this knowledge (and with the price we could expect to pay for the Bonneville we wanted), I was able to find the car at a local dealer and felt confident that I was getting good prices on both counts.

To top it off, during the purchase we were offered Lojak (the popular security system that helps recover your car if it is stolen). While we were deciding, the salesperson mentioned that the price was $595, rather than $995, because "everybody knows you can get it for that price on the Internet, so we don't even try to sell it for the recommended retail price." Well, I didn't know that, but the fact that it was on the Internet dissuaded them from selling it at a higher price.

This explains the popularity of auction sites, both for buyers and sellers. The Web provides a valid mechanism for finding appropriate pricing for goods and services; and if your site gives the perception of reducing costs, it will be popular.

Coolness

Coolness is in the eye of the beholder, to borrow a phrase, and tends to light upon sites that have new features or gimmicks and are controversial. Coolness can linger for a time, but more often it fades rapidly. It's good to be cool, but it's better in the long run to emphasize the other qualities listed here. Your site can still be popular and productive (in a business sense) long after its 15 minutes of fame have faded!

Originality

There are millions of Web sites, and it's easy to assume that all the really good ideas have been executed. In reality, there will always be room for innovative designers and entrepreneurs to develop original sites. Each new technology and each shift in attitudes presents opportunities for creative sites.

Stability and Reliability

When coolness is gone, when a hundred imitators copy your formula, when everyone lowers their prices by a penny under yours, what will you have left in your favor? If you got out there first with advertising, you may have the market share. But how do you increase it or even hang on to it against the competition? Assuming you do an adequate job of advertising, product development, and cover all the business basics, your key to continued success is rock-solid stability and reliability. Make sure your site is always up, mirrored, backed up, and secure. Make sure your hosting company doesn't overload their servers and bandwidth or fail to notify you of planned outages. The same goes more so if you are hosting the site yourself. Take some extra time in these areas, even if it means getting off to a slower start in the market. Good marketing can compensate for a slow start, to a degree, but keep in mind that positioning yourself first or near first is still important.

You should now have an idea of what you want to achieve with your site. Take the time to write out a simple, focused report outlining how the Web site you're building will attain these objectives in terms of the company's overall goals. Later, as you plan the budget, give consideration to the expected return on investment. Remember that there could come a time when you'll have to justify (or provide support for someone else's justification) why thousands of dollars were spent on those neat features written in ASP.

Structuring Your Web Site

The structure of Web sites is currently most easily depicted graphically as a site map showing what pages link to other pages. Using the storyboard method, you can turn out a rudimentary site map in 15 minutes with pen and paper. However, this method is not as useful as it used to be, especially for Web sites that are really applications. Use the storyboard method for pages that are static (and it will be more common to have no static pages in the future); use the traditional software development flowchart method for application-based pages. After all, there may be twists and turns to your application that are rarely seen, but required; and it's more useful to know under what circumstances they will appear rather than to place a box with several hundred lines going to it on a two-dimensional drawing.

Navigation   Site navigation is crucial to any Web site. If folks can't find what they're looking for, they can simply click to one of the myriad other sites available. That doesn't mean you're forced to use the same layout as everyone else on the Web, just that you should spend some time making sure it is intuitive and perhaps test it on a few friends first. If a person unfamiliar with the site cannot find their way around, it is obviously not laid out in an intuitive manner.

Remember, traffic planners, department stores, and many other businesses spend big money on consultants to determine the best traffic pattern or store layout to accomplish their purposes. Consider using similar usability techniques for your Web site. If you're not sure how, consider hiring a consultant who specializes in testing Web sites for usability and making them more user friendly.

From an ASP standpoint, setting cookies can give you a glimpse into users' traffic patterns (click-stream) as they traverse your site. Combined with hit statistics, the data can be a valuable tool for determining flaws in your site's design, as well as for discovering or inventing ways to encourage sales and make life easier for users. And take user feedback seriously. For every user who provides feedback to you, there are probably many others with a similar complaint but less inclination to tell you about it.

Graphics   A well-dressed person gets attention and commands respect, and the same goes for excellent Web site graphics. Graphics take on different meanings depending on the content of the site, but overall they should be easy to download, and eye catching (though not necessarily pleasing), and should not detract from the message the site is communicating.

2

Do take into consideration that the touch of a professional graphic artist is required in most cases. While anybody can create a Web page, well-trained, experienced, and talented graphic artists have the ability to properly build graphics and page layouts (if they are suitably trained for Web work, a much different medium than print).

Ask the Expert

Question: There are millions of Web sites out there focusing on every subject from basket weaving to fly fishing. Is there a strategy to help me decide what mine should look like and what it should contain, without going crazy looking at hundreds of sites? How can I tell the good from the bad?

Answer: Use your favorite search engine to produce a list of all the Web sites in a given category, and narrow the list as much as possible before browsing the sites. Chances are, there will be only a few (10 or 20) sites that are in direct competition with yours. Separating the good ones from the bad is obvious. Poor-quality graphics, lack of relevant content, slow loading times, confusing navigation, and incomplete or nonexistent features (such as a lack of security on the order forms) are the marks of a badly executed site. Other than that, just about anything interesting goes.

Question: I'm a Web site developer. How closely should I work with my clients? What should we expect of each other?

Answer: Although time consuming and sometimes frustrating, working closely with a client produces the best results. Keep in mind that it is your job to bring in the site's customers and users. Without their acceptance, the Web site won't fulfill its objectives. Knowing that's your goal, your client should expect you to learn as much as possible about his or her business, and you should expect full access to any information you need, such as input from employees who will use the application.

Question: How long does it take to create a Web page, on average, and how much does it cost?

Answer: You'll get this question often from people who want a simple formula to quantify the cost and time required to build a site. It's likely that any answer you give will change later. The dilemma is, one page may be graphically complex yet easy to compose, while another page may have a simple appearance but requires complicated programming. The best way to handle it is to pull out your handy dandy estimation tool and go through the process of defining roughly what's required. I like to use project management software to define all the tasks required to complete the Web site, including costs and times for each. Later, when requirements change, you can go back to the same rough estimate and modify it, and then produce another estimate. This gives the quantifier what they want (the estimate), while making sure that they understand that changes will incur extra costs.

project2-1.zip

Project 2-1: Design the Structure for a Web Site Application

This project will take you through the process of designing the layout for a new Web site from scratch. Consider this project to be a subset (with more detail) of step 5, Project 1-2, in Module 1. For graphics and layout, a graphic artist or professional layout designer may be needed, particularly if you don't possess those skills yourself. It's up to you to apply the information supplied here as you and your colleagues make design and layout decisions along the way.

Step-by-Step

1. Build a basic flowchart of the user and management pages on the site. Typical pages for a commercial site include About, Contact, Order, Terms, Privacy, and Catalog. On the flowchart, draw a box representing each page (or the response to each page), and draw lines between the pages showing how they link together.

2. Be sure to include spaces or controls for all the data captured or information displayed. Make sure your clients agree that the pages outlined give them enough data to perform their business processes, and that the data is sufficient to support the calculations and processing required by your scripting or components.

3. If the project warrants it, conduct usability testing of several graphical formats, as well as layouts. Make sure users can find what they are looking for and are able to navigate the site intuitively. For this project, usability testing can be simple; you might just present the format ideas to a person unfamiliar with the project and with the Web site creation process. Ask him to tell you if there are things he doesn't understand while trying to navigate the site.

4. List the number of Web pages that will be created; and for each page, list the languages involved. For behind-the-scenes processing, list the scripts that will be required, giving each one a descriptive name. This list will grow as you gain a greater understanding of how ASP works; but for now, building a conceptual list is fine.

5. Copy the flowchart, page formats, displayed and captured information, number and language requirements for each page, and scripting requirements for the application into a folder and review each design with the client. For this project, simply collecting the materials you've generated into a folder is enough. These materials become the basis for decision making and construction of the Web site.

Proper Coding Techniques

There are many ways to code an ASP script, but some of them are more practical, readable, and easier to troubleshoot than others. This section reviews common coding practices that can enhance the value of your code, and typical problems you might encounter that require debugging. The remainder of this module will provide techniques for creating high-quality code that is reusable and maintainable. Some of the examples refer to ASP and ADO scripting that have not been covered yet, but they will be in later modules—so be patient and focus on the techniques presented.

What's Wrong with My Code?

The first step in solving a problem is recognizing that a problem exists. You may say that your code has always worked fine and you don't see a reason to change. You may stick to some standards and not others because you've done what works for you. While coding style is one of those things that has a lot of personal bias associated with it, there must be a balance between personal style and using techniques that work. This section will demonstrate examples of problematic code, explain why the code is problematic, and show how to correct the problems. The reasons for using most of these techniques have to do with performance and maintainability issues.

Problem 1: The Straight-Through Approach

The straight-through approach is basically taking a plain HTML page and adding a little ASP code to it, as in this example:

```
<html><head><title>My Web Site</title></head>
<body>
<h1>Welcome to my web site</h1>
<h3>Today is <% = FormatDateTime(Date, vbLongDate) %> </h3>
</body>
</html>
```

This is a simple example, where the page makes a single call to a built-in function to generate the date. The straight-through approach knows no size limitations, however. You could easily create a 100-line ASP file using this approach to display a database table.

In some cases, this approach appears to be valid. A simple page that needs just a little ASP code to perform some function not available in HTML might be one case. You might also decide that the page is temporary and will be replaced with an improved version later. These justifications ignore the fact that most applications and pages grow in complexity and required functions before you're done with them. The page that simply dumps a database table may evolve to show a list of all the available tables. It may also let the user type in a query to be executed. A simple page that uses one function may quickly turn into a much more complex page with many functions. Using the straight-through approach, you are probably postponing the inevitable rewrite of the code to support more functions. If you're going to write the code once, add a few extra lines to allow the page to support more functions in the future.

Problem 2: Mix-and-Match

This approach is typically used on pages made up of half ASP and half HTML. The signs and symptoms are chunks of code that look like this:

```
<html><head><title>My Web Site</title></head>
<body>
<h1>Welcome to my web site</h1>
<h3>Today is <% = FormatDateTime(Date, vbLongDate) %> </h3>
<% If Day(Date) = 5 Then %>
<h3>Today is Thursday!</h3>
<% ElseIf Day(Date) = 1 Then %>
<h3>Today is Sunday!</h3>
<% End If %>
</body>
</html>
```

The mixing and matching come with the ASP wrapping around HTML that is only read if the If…Then condition allows it. Like the previous approach, this is not limited to a few lines of code. In early applications, the HTML was too complicated to try to convert into the equivalent Response.Write statements. Also, it is easier to change the HTML later, if necessary.

The major problem with this approach is how the server handles HTML versus ASP. In order for the ASP to be processed, the file extension must be .asp. IIS reads the extension and loads the ASP engine to process it. As it's reading the ASP code, however, it encounters plain HTML. IIS then has to load the HTML processing engine to handle it. This continues through the whole page. Even with the new versions of ASP and IIS used for the examples in this book, processing can be slowed down.

The preferred approach is to use ASP to generate all output using Response.Write. This method allows the ASP engine to handle all processing and finish processing faster.

Tip

Double-quote characters in your HTML must be converted to two double-quote characters, or ASP/VBScript gets confused. This is a minor annoyance when you consider the performance gains.

Problem 3: Form Processing Separation

If you've built ASP forms, you've handled the back end of form processing. The user types some data into the form, and you provide ASP code to handle the response. The most common way to do this is to have two separate ASP pages: one to generate the form, and one to handle the validation and any necessary action. Control then passes to the next ASP page, which is usually set up as a split personality, too.

In this case, the data capture process is separated into two different places. This means both pages have to know about the form, how the data is laid out, and how the database is used. It also means you can't share code between them (except via server-side includes). Any changes to one file must be made in the other or you'll have problems down the road. The solution is to keep the form and its validation in the same ASP page. The trick is that if you're using the straight-through method, you can't handle this type of page. By employing a combination of flags and some simple routing code, you can handle a virtually unlimited number of functions in a single ASP page. You gain the ability to share code in the same ASP page, as well as decrease the number of files, especially welcome in a large application. Instead of having a form.asp and form_process.asp for each of 100 entities, you have a single file per entity.

Problem 4: Declaring Variables

One of the holdovers from the original versions of Basic was the ability to start using a variable without first declaring it. In VB and VBScript, variables can be declared using the Dim statement, as shown here:

```
Dim intVariable
```

Visual Basic adds a data type designation to this declaration; VBScript does not. Why would you want to declare your variables when you don't have to? Take a look at this example:

```
<html><head><title>My Web Site</title></head>
<body>
<h1>Welcome to my web site</h1>
<h3>Today is <% = FormatDateTime(Date, vbLongDate) %> </h3>
<% strInput = Request.ServerVariables("SCRIPT_NAME") %>
<% If Day(Date) = 5 Then %>
```

```
<h3>Today is Thursday!</h3>
<% ElseIf Day(Date) = 1 Then %>
<h3>Today is Sunday!</h3>
<% End If %>
<% Response.Write stInput %>
</body>
</html>
```

For some reason, the name of the script (stored in the SCRIPT_NAME variable) isn't being printed out. Is the Request.ServerVariables collection working? Are you losing memory somewhere? No, you've got a typo in the name when you are printing it out at the bottom of the script. VBScript sees that you have a new variable, allocates space for it, and goes on its way. The variable, of course, starts out with no content, so strInput never gets printed. The solution to this is twofold. First, always use the Option Explicit statement as the first line in every ASP page. This forces you to declare your variables by disabling VBScript's auto-declaration feature. It works best as the first line in a common include file. The second part, which comes immediately after doing the first part, is to declare all your variables. It's also good to list the type in a comment following the variable, like so:

```
Dim dcnDB    ' As ADODB.Connection
```

It doesn't do anything different, but it does provide documentation for what the variable does. The three-letter prefix also helps. While VBScript will let you put any type of data into a variable, using the prefixes on your variables provides a visual indication of the type of data that is supposed to be in the variable.

Problem 5: Hard-Coding Values

One of the annoyances with code is fixing hard-coded values. This means that everywhere a value is needed, such as a database connection string, the exact value is copied over and over. As an example, say every page in a company's intranet had an entire connection string copied everywhere it was necessary. The minute the database connection changes, each page has to be changed individually. This happens in both numerical and textual data, as in one site that had a form with drop-down list boxes where one of the items was "Not Selected" and had a −1 for its value. This is a good idea, since you can trap the −1 in your error handling and validation code. However, the −1 was hard-coded everywhere it was needed.

Another less obvious example comes when pages are generating links to other pages. How many times have you had code that looked something like this?

```
Response.Write "<a href=test.asp?action=validate&id=" & intID & ">click
here</a>"
```

This code is using the variable to supply the ID parameter to the URL, but what about all the hard-coded values in the URL? What hard-coded values?, you might ask. Here's a list of all the hard-coded values in this particular link:

- Page name

- Action parameter

- Action parameter value

- ID parameter in URL

If you have to move your site to a different location, or if you rename your files, you'll have to find all the references to test.asp in your ASP code in order to make the application work again. If you are building your URLs and misspell the word "action" in either the generating code or in the code that checks the parameter value, you'll get errors that are tough to trace. The same thing goes for the value for the action parameter, as well as the name of the ID parameter. The solution is to use constants for everything: the page names, the parameter names, and so on.

Problem 6: Access and Security Control

How many times have you gone to a store and attempted to open the door, only to discover the store was closed? The owners of the store forgot to put out a sign saying they were closed, so you had to try the door first. Many computer programs use this method for security. They let you modify a record; and then when you're ready to save the record, the program displays an error message saying you don't have the security rights to do it. All that work down the drain without more than a rude warning. The point is, don't let your users think they can do something when they can't. If they can't add a record, don't give them the opportunity to try to add a record. Hide the link or issue a warning on the page that tells users what's going on before they attempt a procedure and fail.

Problem 7: Poor Documentation

Early computer science classes emphasized that documentation was important. If you write the program, are the only one using it, and know what you're doing in the code, why is documentation necessary? Well, years pass and the old memory isn't quite what it used to be. In addition, you've got at least ten different applications' codes running around in your head, and it's confusing. If you write an application that works well, you might not revisit it until you need to add some enhancements. Depending on how busy you are, it may be several months before you put in those changes. Inevitably, you will open up a piece of code and stare at it for hours, trying to figure out what you were thinking at the time you wrote it. The solution to this problem is simple: document everything in your code. If there is a complex bit of logic, add a line of comment to explain what's going on. If you made an assumption about input or output data, add a comment to remind yourself about it. File header documentation blocks are useful for tracking changes and additions to the file in a central location.

The point is not whether the code works, but whether the code is going to be useful in a different application or as part of an expanded application. If the code breaks these rules, the end result is code that will have to be reworked or entirely rebuilt.

How Can I Fix My Code?

With potential problems identified, let's work on some easy solutions for writing reliable and reusable ASP code. While the techniques will be presented individually, the best approach is to combine all these techniques. A complete example will be shown at the end of this section, using all of these examples.

Declaring Variables

In order to prevent unknown variables from popping up, declare your variables. Even though it's easier not to declare them, things will run smoother if you do. The easiest way to force yourself to declare them is to add Option Explicit as the first line of code in every ASP file. If the statement is not on the first line, you'll get an error when you load your ASP file. Once you have Option Explicit in your file, you have to declare your variables. The minimum requirement for variable declaration looks like this:

```
Dim test
```

This declares test as a variable in the program. However, just using the name "test" doesn't tell you anything about the variable. You can't tell if the variable holds numbers or text, or how the variable is used in the program. The first thing you can do to solve this problem is to show the type of variable. While VBScript does not allow you to specify a data type with the As clause (which is available in Visual Basic), you can specify the type in a comment after the variable. Here's an example, using the same variable as before:

```
Dim test      ' As String
```

This tells you that the variable is designed to hold string variable data. This is a good start on defining your variables, but the second step is even more useful. While this will tell you at the top of a subroutine or a page what data type the variable is, you don't want to scroll to the top of the file every time you need to know the data type of a variable. The solution is to prefix each variable with the data type you intend to store in the variable. While this doesn't change the fact that you can put any data type into a variable, it does help you keep things straight when you have 20 variables, all of different data types. Here is a revised declaration for our variable:

```
Dim strTest      ' As String
```

The As String is redundant, but for users who don't know the prefixes, it's helpful. It is also helpful when you start declaring objects, such as the following:

```
Dim objCustomer      ' As ESObjects.Customer
```

The prefix "obj" is used to identify an object variable, but the declaration specifies that this object will hold a Customer object from the ESObjects library. For the basic data types, Table 2-1 shows prefixes for each data type.

Arrays are a bit different, because they use two data types: array and one other type. For these variables, prefix the prefix with **a_**, so an array of integers might be declared as follows:

```
Dim a_intData(5)    ' As Integer
```

This helps distinguish an array from a single variable. If a variable is declared outside of a subroutine in the page, add **g_** to the variable, as shown here:

```
Dim ga_intData(5)     ' As Integer
```

This particular array is a global array of integers. While there is an "obj" prefix for objects, try a different set of prefixes for objects dealing with Active Data Objects. Using these prefixes makes it easier to read code, considering how often it is necessary to use ADO in an ASP page. Table 2-2 shows prefixes for the various data objects.

The final use for naming conventions is in HTML forms. There are a number of input tags you can use in your forms, and when the data is submitted, all of the data comes in through the Request object. Using the prefixes shown in Table 2-3 will help you identify what type of data to expect when you retrieve values from the Request.Form collection.

Prefix	Data Type
Int	Integer
Lng	Long integer
Sng	Single-precision, floating-point number
Dbl	Double-precision, floating-point number
Cur	Currency
Dat	Date/time data
Str	String
Obj	Object
Bln	Boolean
Var	Variant
Byt	Byte

Table 2-1   Prefixes for Variable Data Types

Prefix	Object
Dcn	ADODB.Connection
Rs	ADODB.Recordset
Cmd	ADODB.Command
Fld	ADODB.Field
Par	ADODB.Parameter

Table 2-2　Prefixes for ADO Variables

With these naming conventions and all others, the key is to be consistent. If you prefer to use all three-letter prefixes, that's fine. If you want to use five-letter prefixes, that's fine, too. Just be sure to document what you choose and stick to it.

Prefix	Input Type
Txt	Text box or TEXTAREA tag
Cbo	List box or drop-down list box
Opt	Radio button
Chk	Check box
Cmd	Input buttons

Table 2-3　Prefixes for HTML Form Field Names

1-Minute Drill

● **Why is it important to document your code and use consistent names for your variables?**

● **What happens when you switch from HTML to ASP code?**

● Without documentation, you may forget the purpose of the functions you wrote; and without consistent variable names, it may be confusing to understand which variable holds which type of data.

● Each time you go from one type of code to another, the server must redirect processing, which consumes additional time.

Project 2-2: Create a Simple ASP Application

Now it's time to tie together the loose threads of HTML, ASP, and VBScript by writing a simple application. Throughout this book, you'll use these projects to build ASP applications that work properly and illustrate usage of the concepts, conventions, and syntax covered in this module. Start with an application that displays text in a variety of ways, using some simple ASP and VBScript.

Step-by-Step

1. Display text in an HTML document. In this step, build an HTML page that can connect to an ASP script. Use the hyperlink tag to make the connection. This is easy to code, so use Notepad to code the HTML page. Open Notepad, create a new file, and enter the following code (see Figure 2-2 for a look at what the browser produces):

```
<HTML>
<HEAD>
<TITLE>My First ASP-Connected Web page</TITLE>
</HEAD>
<BODY>
<center>
This is the first Web page I've created that connects to an
ASP script.<P>
I can access the script using the following link:<P>
<A HREF="asp1.asp">Click Here</A>
</center>
</BODY>
</HTML>
```

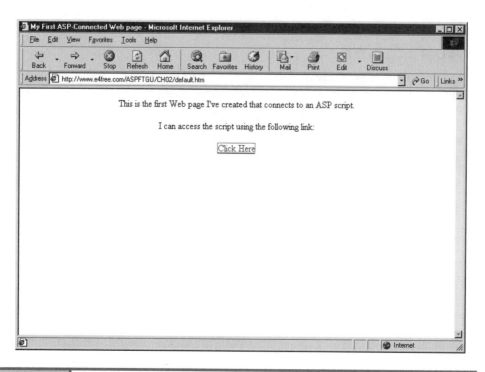

Figure 2-2 The HTML Web page in the browser

2. Now create an ASP script that demonstrates what ASP can do. Run through a series of VBScript commands that respond to the request (using a For...Next loop), even though no data is sent, and return the processed results, like so (see Figure 2-3 for the results in the browser):

```
<HTML>
<HEAD>
<TITLE> The Results of the ASP Processing</TITLE>
</HEAD>
<BODY>
Here are the results from the processed ASP script!<P>
<center>
<%
intI = 1
For intI = 1 to 6
%>
```

```
<H<% Response.Write(intI) %>>These are different heading
sizes</H<%
Response.Write(intI) %>>
<% Next %>
</center>
</BODY>
</HTML>
```

The way this script works is simple. Notice that all the code in both files is embedded within HTML. This feature alone makes ASP very powerful, because scripts can be written quickly and simply right inside ordinary Web pages. It's like writing HTML and then throwing in some VBScript for good measure. If you're familiar with writing both HMTL and VBScript (or at least JavaScript), this shouldn't present much of a challenge.

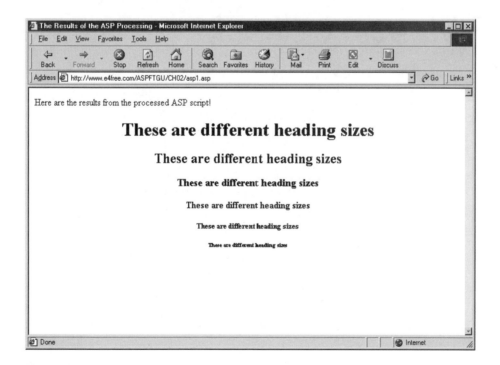

Figure 2-3   The ASP-processed results

Notice that the results in the browser are the processed results from the script, not the script code itself. This occurs even though the server is not explicitly set to run the script. The ASP will automatically process script contained inside the delimiters (<% and %>), so your source code is protected.

Notice also that you don't have to explicitly declare the variable intI to use it as a counter in the For…Next loop. It comes into existence as soon as you use it. It is easy to embed HTML code in between the ASP code (although to do so means you're switching in and out of ASP processing, which may slow things down for more complex scripts). Even though you're switching in and out of processing, the loop still works and carries the HTML code through the loop with it into the final output.

☑ *Mastery Check*

1. What languages are commonly used to construct Web pages and online applications?

A. Hypertext Markup Language

B. Visual Basic Scripting

C. Active Server Pages

D. Practical Extraction and Reporting Language

E. All of the above

2. Hypertext Transport Protocol defines communications between Web server and Web browser. What kinds of messages are included in these communications?

A. Time and date

B. Browser and server type and version

C. Cookies

D. Status and error messages

E. Web pages

F. All of the above

2

☑ *Mastery Check*

3. Delimiters are characters used to define commands in programming languages. The delimiters for HTML are ___ and ___. The delimiters for ASP code within HTML are ___ and ___.

4. Describe three common coding practices that make your code more readable, more debuggable, and less error prone.

_____

_____

_____

5. Who decides on the layout and look of a Web site? Who should have input?

A. The client or manager paying for the job

B. The users

C. The designer/programmer

D. The graphic artist

E. All of the above

Module 3

The Request and Response Objects

The Goals of This Module

- Practice using the Request and Response objects

- Capture data using the QueryString, Form, and ServerVariables collections

- Learn about and understand how cookies and ClientCertificate collections work

- Insert data and text into Web pages

- Redirect the browser from one page to another

- Buffer and flush processed content

With static HTML, you can construct Web pages that display text and graphics, and you can construct forms that allow the user to send data back to the server. Traditional Common Gateway Interface (CGI) scripting allows you to capture data returned to the server and process it. That processing can include data and HTML tags being returned to the user, in effect "talking to" the user.

However, as discussed in Module 2, these "conversations" can be difficult to construct and maintain with static HTML and CGI. Active Server Pages provides a couple of built-in objects that make Web conversations much easier. This module discusses these objects in detail and provides many examples of using VBScript to conduct Web conversations.

Creating Web Site Interactivity

One of the most important and enabling features of Web-based communication is the ability to provide interactivity, or real-time, two-way communication. Browsers communicate with Web servers using the HTTP protocol (discussed in Module 2), and user communications are accomplished via the same protocol. As anyone who has ever used Perl (Practical Extraction and Reporting Language) will tell you, it can be a complex undertaking to establish and maintain communications with HTTP. ASP, fortunately, eases the burden with two built-in objects called the Request and Response objects.

The job of the Request object is to capture and make available data coming from the user, while the Response object provides a means of responding to the user with plain text or HTML-encoded data. The way these objects do their job, and the simple syntax used to access or create data streams, makes using them both easy and common. Most of your applications/scripts will make heavy use of these two objects.

Web-Based Communications

Using a browser is pretty easy: just point and click to get to a link, or fill out a form and press the Submit button to send information. Beneath the ease and simplicity, though, is a fairly complex transaction—a two-way communication between the Web server and the client (the browser, or in more precise terms, the *user agent*). Understanding what's going on behind the scenes is important to your ASP programming efforts, and it's also important to remember that browsers aren't the only clients that might access your Web site.

Let's use the example of a browser to illustrate in detail how things are done. Suppose a user opens his browser and enters your domain name in the address field. When he presses ENTER, his browser makes a connection with the Web server across the Internet and then requests the default page (assuming he's entered no filename after the domain name). As he traverses the Web site, his browser requests each page he clicks by its full path and filename. Using the full path and filename is required because the Web is *stateless*, which means that the Web server doesn't maintain a continuous connection to each client and, therefore, doesn't know one page request from the next.

The actual content of the request may contain much more information than just the path and the filename. For instance, the request may include the time, date, accepted application file types, cookies, host IP address, browser type, connection type, and so forth.

If the requested page is available *anonymously* (meaning no username and password is required to access the page), the server will respond with similar information plus the HTML content of the page. The returned information may include date, time, server type, connection type, cookies, and so on. This response is also the source of those annoying messages such as "HTTP1.1 404 Not Found." If the request is valid, the page will be displayed; if not, the user will see the HTTP version and the appropriate error message.

The Request Object

When a link is clicked or a form is submitted, the request object captures all the data within the request, including the HTTP variables, cookies, query strings, security certificates, and certain properties of the request that can be used to manage communications. All this data is then immediately available to the activated ASP script.

Request Object Collections

The Request object includes five built-in collections, each of which captures specific kinds of data:

- **Query string**   The name/value pairs attached to the end of a requested URL, or the name/value pairs resulting from the submission of a form where the method equals GET (like this: <FORM ACTION="someaction.asp" METHOD="GET">)

- **Form**   The name/value pairs resulting from the submission of a form where the method equals POST (like this: <FORM ACTION="someaction.asp" METHOD="POST">)

- **Server variables**   The names and values of the HTTP header plus the names and values of several environment variables from the Web server

- **Cookies**   The values of all cookies sent with the user's request (by default, the only cookies sent are those that are valid for the domain of the Web server)

- **Client certificate**   The values of the fields/entries in the client certificate offered to the server

The Request object captures all this data in these collections and then makes it easily accessible by your scripts for further processing.

Request Object Properties and Methods

The only property of the Request object is TotalBytes, which represents the total number of bytes in the body of the request. You probably won't be using this very frequently (unless you have an unusual application); more likely, you'll be interested in the contents of each name/value pair.

The only method of the Request object is BinaryRead. BinaryRead retrieves a specified number of bytes from a request sent using METHOD="POST" and is somewhat complementary to the Form collection. Both are ways to get data from the request when the POST method is used, and use of either one prevents use of the other. This

3

means that if you use the BinaryRead method, it will return the data it finds as a Variant array and, at the same time, prevent successful use of the Form collection. As its name implies, BinaryRead reads data in binary form; it is not currently used much. We'll discuss it in more depth in the Response object section (see "The Response Object"), later in this module.

Note

The Form collection, if used first, will prevent subsequent use of the BinaryRead method (for a single request, not all future requests).

Accessing Values from Forms or URLs

The QueryString and Form collections capture values from forms and appended to URLs. Accessing these values is a matter of coordinating your scripts to the fields received, and there are a number of ways to accomplish this. If you are familiar with Visual Basic, you are used to using collections and the syntax will be easy to follow. You can use both the name of a field or an integer value representing its order in the fields collected. Project 3-1 demonstrates these things with a simple HTML form and HTML response.

Project3-1.zip

Project 3-1: Create a Quick HTML Form Page and Response

You'll use HTML forms frequently in your applications, so the first project for this module covers the creation of such forms from scratch.

Step-by-Step

1. Make a typical HTML form page with the following tags (although the following tags will create a complete form, you will make forms that look better than this does onscreen):

```
<HTML><HEAD><TITLE>My Form</TITLE></HEAD>
<BODY BGCOLOR="lightblue" TEXT="black">
<FORM ACTION="someaction.asp" METHOD="POST">
Name:<INPUT TYPE="text" SIZE=40 NAME="fullname"><BR>
Address:<INPUT TYPE="text" SIZE=60 NAME="address"><BR>
```

> **Note the reference to the ASP file.**

```
Phone:<INPUT TYPE="text" SIZE=20 NAME="phonenumber"><BR>
<INPUT TYPE="submit" VALUE="Send Info"><INPUT TYPE="reset"
VALUE="Clear">
</FORM>
</BODY></HTML>
```

You can find this form on the Web site (see the following illustration for a look at it as it appears in the browser). Notice that each field (generated by the INPUT TYPE tags) has a unique but descriptive field name included in the tag. If you write some variables into your ASP script and set their values equal to the appropriate request object collection items (and notice that the field names are called out in your ASP script), you can then manipulate those values within your script.

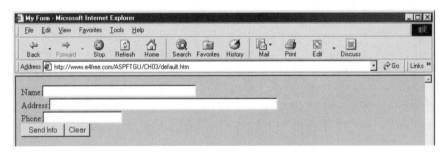

2. To demonstrate that you've retrieved these variables, use the Response.Write object to write their values back to the user (although the Response object won't be covered in depth until a little later in the module). For example, you could write a response page using code such as this:

```
<HTML><HEAD><TITLE>My Form Results</TITLE></HEAD>
<BODY BGCOLOR="lightblue" TEXT="black">
<% vName = Request.Form("fullname")    ◄────── Note use of the
vAddress = Request.Form("address")             ASP delimiters <%.
vPhone = Request.Form("phonenumber")
Response.Write(vName) %><BR><%
Response.Write(vAddress) %><BR><%
Response.Write(vPhone) %><BR>
</BODY>
</HTML>
```

Thereafter, in this script, the variables vName, vAddress, and vPhone contain the values retrieved from the submitted form contents, and you can use them in any of your subsequent VBScript code. You can get the results shown in the following illustration by filling out the default.htm form on the Web site and clicking the Submit button. You could also just access them directly in your code by calling out the full Request.Form and field name combination.

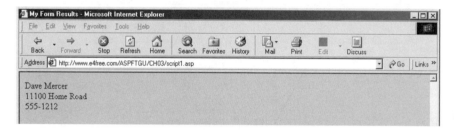

Another way to access these values is to specify the integer index of each field, as shown in the following code:

```
vName = Request.Form(1)
vAddress = Request.Form(2)
vPhone = Request.Form(3)
```

Although you can use the integer index to access values, it's much better practice to use the given names of the fields, because if their order on the page changes, the wrong values will be picked up. In addition, the index is more difficult to read through and debug.

3. Finally, if you'd like to retrieve the whole set of name/value pairs at once, you can do so by simply using Request.Form without a field name or index. Using your example, you could write

```
vFormContents = Request.Form
```

The contents submitted from the form would take the form of one string of name/value pairs (first the field name, then the equal sign, and then the value, starting with the first field on the form) separated by the ampersand (&). This result can be obtained using the default2.htm form on the Web site. Of course, this format is rather unpleasant to deal with, because it comes out looking like this:

```
fullname=thenameentered&address=theaddressentered&phone=thephoneentered
```

Even worse, from a readability standpoint, all white spaces between words entered as values in fields will be replaced with plus signs (see the example results shown in the following illustration). If you happen to be feeding this string of data directly to another application that is designed to interpret this kind of formatting, great; but for most uses, it is inappropriate.

Referencing Each Item in a Collection

The Request.Form collection provides a *Count* property, meaning you have access to the value representing the number of items in the collection. Using this value, you can set up a looping structure to iterate through each item in the collection. You could use the integer index method by incrementing a variable each time the loop is traversed, as shown here:

```
For intIncr = 1 To Request.Form.Count
     Response.Write Request.Form(intIncr) & "<BR>"
Next
```

The HTML form and output results look the same as our first example (shown in the illustrations in steps 1 and 2), but the ASP script uses the For . . . Next loop to do the work. Notice that instead of using the ASP delimiters (%) to separate the ASP code from the HTML, only the actual <BR> tag is located inside quotes. This works just as well as the previous technique, and relieves you of switching in and out of ASP code. (Also, you would typically want to do something more useful than simply writing back the values in the collection, such as entering them into a database—but more on that subject in later modules.)

If you'd like to gather the names as well as the values of each item in the collection, you can use the For Each looping structure, in the following fashion.

```
For Each collItem In Request.Form
    Response.Write collItem & " = " & Request.Form(collItem) & "<BR>"
Next
```

This will display both the names of each collItem (and you can create whatever name you want for collection items, such as objItem, myItem, and so forth) and then the value associated with it (with an equal sign in between), as shown here:

```
fullname = theirname
address = theiraddress
phonenumber = theirphonenumber
```

Use the default4.htm form to produce the results shown in the following iillustration.

So far, we've been using text box form elements, each with a unique name, to capture and retrieve data from the contents of a form submission. HTML does not force designers to give each text box element a unique name; and although it is not common, there are some instances in which the names of text boxes may be identical. In addition, names of other form elements, such as radio buttons and check boxes, are identical for elements of the same group. Include some of these elements in your simple HTML form, and then examine some handling techniques. Here is the simple

HTML form with some added formatting for looks (consisting of table tags and headings) and a few new elements to play with:

```
<HTML><HEAD><TITLE>My New Form</TITLE></HEAD>
<BODY BGCOLOR="lightblue" TEXT="black">
<CENTER>
<FORM ACTION="script5.asp" METHOD="POST">
<TABLE BORDER=1>
<TR>
<TD>Name:</TD><TD><INPUT TYPE="text" SIZE=40 NAME="fullname"></TD>
</TR><TR>
<TD>Address:</TD><TD><INPUT TYPE="text" SIZE=60 NAME="address"></TD>
</TR><TR>
<TD>Phone:</TD><TD><INPUT TYPE="text" SIZE=20 NAME="phonenumber"></TD>
</TR><TR>
<TD>Product Choices</TD>
<TD><SELECT NAME="Product" SIZE="3" MULTIPLE>
    <OPTION VALUE="Product1">Coat
    <OPTION VALUE="Product2">Shirt
    <OPTION VALUE="Product3">Pants
    <OPTION VALUE="Product4">Tie
    <OPTION VALUE="Product5">Shoes
    <OPTION VALUE="Product6">Socks
  </SELECT>
</TD>
</TR><TR>
<TD>Credit Card Type</TD>
<TD>MC<INPUT TYPE="radio" NAME="CCType" VALUE="MC">
 Visa<INPUT TYPE="radio" NAME="CCType" VALUE="Visa">
 Discover<INPUT TYPE="radio" NAME="CCType" VALUE="Disc">
</TD>
</TR><TR>
<TD COLSPAN=2><INPUT TYPE="submit" VALUE="Send Info"><INPUT TYPE="reset"
VALUE="Clear"></TD>
</TR>
</TABLE>
</FORM>
</BODY></HTML>
```

> **Notice the table is inside the form, and is used to format the form elements.**

This form is listed as default5.htm on the Web site (see Figure 3-1 for a screen shot) and produces a more structured form page, although it still has quite a way to go before it becomes the professional-looking form you'll be using later. Notice that each radio button carries exactly the same name and that only one name (Product) appears for the SELECT element as well.

Radio buttons are *mutually exclusive,* meaning only one can be selected. When a radio button item is selected, the browser returns the value for that button and only one instance of the name for that button in the Request.Form collection. If you leave the VALUE attribute out of a particular radio button element and that element is selected, the browser

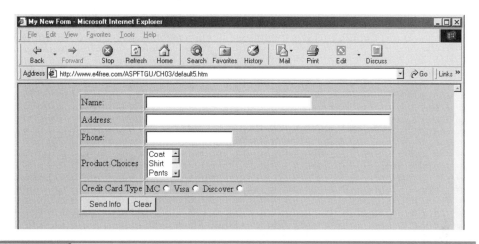

Figure 3-1 The formatted HTML form with added form elements

returns the word "on" to describe the value of that element. Needless to say, knowing that the value is "on" might be enough to accomplish the processing required, but it is just as easy and frequently more useful to have a specific value associated with each radio button.

An example of a group of check boxes is not included in your form, but their behavior is similar to the behavior of the SELECT form element. Both elements have a single name for all their choices, and one or more of the choices may be selected when the form is submitted. The browser will return the name of the element plus all the values selected, separated by commas. For example, if you used your form to select the options Coat, Shirt, and Socks, and then clicked the submit button, the result would look like the following illustration.

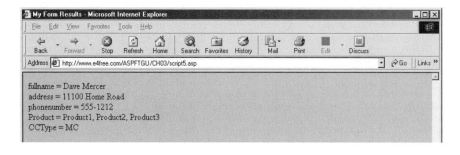

An interesting aspect of the behavior of the SELECT element is that if you leave the VALUE portion out of the tag, the browser will return the plain-text label next to it, as shown here:

```
Product = Coat, Shirt, Socks
```

Other Controls Providing Values

The form elements of INPUT TYPE="submit" and INPUT TYPE="image" can also send values to the server (but not INPUT TYPE="reset" or INPUT TYPE="button"). The value of the submit button (which is also the caption for the button) will be returned with the contents of the form, while the X and Y coordinates upon which the user clicked (on your image) will be returned when INPUT TYPE="image" is used.

Because it is possible to put several INPUT TYPE="submit" buttons on a form, these buttons can be used to provide several different results depending on which value your script receives. For example, you could make a menu bar that's composed of submit buttons that navigate your entire site, using the redirect method of the Response object. It wouldn't be pretty, but it would be functional.

Perhaps a better and more appealing way to achieve the same effect would be to use an image as a menu bar and insert it in your form using INPUT TYPE="image" SRC="menubar.gif". The form named default6.htm on the Web site shows an example of including an image as a menu bar.

When an image is used as a submit button in this manner, the X and Y coordinates are returned, named X and Y and followed by their value in pixels. Although the order in which these values are returned may be unknown, they can still be accessed by name, and their values can be used to determine the location on the image that was clicked and, therefore, to redirect the user to a specific page.

To demonstrate this, check out the following very simple menu bar image that uses Microsoft Image Composer. The image is inserted as a submit button into default6.htm, using the code shown here:

```
<TD COLSPAN=2><INPUT TYPE="image" SRC="menubar.gif"><INPUT
TYPE="submit" VALUE="Send Info"><INPUT TYPE="reset"
VALUE="Clear"></TD>
```

The existing submit and reset buttons have been retained, which doesn't hurt anything (but does look a little awkward). The X and Y coordinates on the image while in Image Composer were used to map the various areas of the image to specific pages, and the following code was used to build the conditions in VBScript:

```
<% If Request.Form("X") < 100 Then
     Response.Redirect "about.htm"
Else
   If Request.Form("X") >200 Then
       Response.Redirect "contact.htm"
   Else
       Response.Redirect "default.htm"
   End If
End If
 %>
```

Notice the lack of any ordinary HTML formatting in this script. No values will be transmitted back to the user, so no HTML tags are required. Also notice that you've been obliged to produce about and contact pages; otherwise, the browser would not find anything when attempting to redirect the user to these pages. If you intended to process these results in any way, of course, you'd retrieve those values and possibly send a thank-you note back to the user, constructed from normal HTML tags. And, by the way, the Response.Redirect method is used here. Browser redirection is covered in greater depth later on in the Response object section in this module (see "The Response Object").

The QueryString Collection

A query string carries names and values after a URL it is pointed at. It can be created with the hypertext link tag and looks like this:

```
<A HREF="www.mydomainname.com/myscript.asp?fullname=Dave">
Click Here
</A>
```

The filename shows the intended script target, and the data following the question mark consists of names and values separated by the equal sign. As mentioned earlier, the contents of the QueryString collection can be retrieved from a hypertext link, or from the values submitted from a form using the GET method in the form tag. If you happen to know the names of the value pairs, you can retrieve them individually by name (or you can iterate through them using the same techniques used with the Request.Form collection). You can also simply retrieve the entire string by omitting the field or pair name (like this: Response.Write Request.QueryString). Either way, the values will be available for further processing, as shown in the following illustration, which can be activated using the Click Me link at the top of the form named default7.htm on the Web site.

Ask the Expert

Question: I know I can get data from a form submitted by a user. Do I have to create a form for everything?

Answer: No, you can sometimes use the QueryString method to get data more effectively, by attaching the necessary values to the URL within the HTML anchor tag. And often you can simply display a button to click without field elements by using the hidden HTML form elements.

Question: What if the user modifies the form by hand? Doesn't this present a security risk?

Answer: Yes, and in the more advanced applications you'll always find extensive, server-side validation of form field values precisely because of this problem.

3

Question: There seems to be several ways to write the syntax for the Response object. Which is best?

Answer: It depends on what you are doing; but as a general rule, you should try to avoid inserting lots of HTML and ASP blocks within each other. If you have some HTML tags that have to go back to the user with your other output, use the Write method of the Response object to output the HTML tags as text strings.

The ServerVariables Collection

When a request is sent from the browser, certain HTTP headers are sent. When they arrive at the server, the server also generates a set of variables. Both of these sets of values are accessible through the ServerVariables collection. To view these variables, you need to modify your responding script slightly, as follows:

```
<HTML>
<HEAD>
<TITLE>My Form Results</TITLE>
</HEAD>
<BODY BGCOLOR="lightblue" TEXT="black">
<CENTER>
<TABLE
BORDER=1><TR><TD><B>Name</B></TD><TD><B>Value</B></TD></TR>
<% For Each collItem In Request.ServerVariables %>
<TR><TD><% Response.Write collItem %></TD><TD> <%
Request.ServerVariables(collItem) %></TD></TR>
<% Next %>
</TABLE>
</CENTER>
</BODY>
</HTML>
```

This script produces raw ServerVariables output in tabular format, and at the top lumps together multiple-value variables. For easier reading, the table is broken into smaller table sections in Tables 3-1 through 3-7, with a more reasonable number of variables.

Name	Value
ALL_HTTP =	HTTP_ACCEPT:image/gif, image/x-xbitmap, image/jpeg, image/pjpeg, */*
HTTP_ACCEPT_LANGUAGE	en-us
HTTP_CONNECTION	Keep-Alive
HTTP_HOST	cx847962-a
HTTP_REFERER	http://cx847962-a/ASPBEG/CH03/default8.htm
HTTP_USER_AGENT	Mozilla/4.0 (compatible; MSIE 5.01; Windows NT 5.0)
HTTP_COOKIE	ASPSESSIONIDGQGQGLZQ = 00DPIFCBBDGJKPJ0PMBPHLPA
HTTP_ACCEPT_ENCODING	gzip, deflate

Table 3-1 The HTTP Variables, Including Cookie, User Agent, and Host

Name	Value
ALL_RAW	User-Agent: Mozilla/4.0 (compatible; MSIE 5.01; Windows NT 5.0) Cookie: ASPSESSIONIDGQGQGLZQ=00DPIFCBBDGJKPJ0PMBPHLPA Accept-Encoding: gzip, deflate Accept: image/gif, image/x-xbitmap, image/jpeg, image/pjpeg, *.* ACCEPT_LANGUAGE: en-us Host: cx847962-a Referer:http://cx847962-a/ASPBEG/CH03/default8.htm

Table 3-2 The ALL_RAW Variable

3

Name	Value
APPL_MD_PATH	/LM/W3SVC/1/Root
APPL_PHYSICAL_PATH	e:\inetpub\wwwroot\
AUTH_PASSWORD	
AUTH_TYPE	
AUTH_USER	
CERT_COOKIE	
CERT_FLAGS	
CERT_ISSUER	
CERT_KEYSIZE	
CERT_SECRETKEYSIZE	
CERT_SERIALNUMBER	
CERT_SERVER_ISSUER	
CERT_SERVER_SUBJECT	
CERT_SUBJECT	

Table 3-3   The Authorization and Certification Variables

Name	Value
CONTENT_LENGTH	0
CONTENT_TYPE	
GATEWAY_INTERFACE	CGI/1.1
HTTPS	off
HTTPS_KEYSIZE	
HTTPS_SECRETKEYSIZE	
HTTPS_SERVER_ISSUER	
HTTPS_SERVER_SUBJECT	

Table 3-4   Content and HTTPS Variables

Name	Value
INSTANCE_ID	1
INSTANCE_META_PATH	/LM/W3SVC/1
LOCAL_ADDR	24.5.33.16
LOGON_USER	
PATH_INFO	/ASPBEG/CH03/script8.asp
PATH_TRANSLATED	e:\inetpub\wwwroot\ASPBEG\CH03\script8.asp
QUERY_STRING	fullname=&address=&phonenumber=
REMOTE_ADDR	24.5.33.16
REMOTE_HOST	24.5.33.16
REMOTE_USER	

Table 3-5 Instance, Address, Path, and Remote Variables

Name	Value
REQUEST_METHOD	GET
SCRIPT_NAME	/ASPBEG/CH03/script8.asp
SERVER_NAME	cx847962-a
SERVER_PORT	80
SERVER_PORT_SECURE	0
SERVER_PROTOCOL	HTTP/1.1
SERVER_SOFTWARE	Microsoft-IIS/5.0

Table 3-6 Request Method, Script Name, and Server Variables

Name	Value
URL	/ASPBEG/CH03/script8.asp
HTTP_ACCEPT	image/gif, image/x-xbitmap, image/jpeg, image/pjpeg, */*
HTTP_ACCEPT_LANGUAGE	en-us
HTTP_CONNECTION	Keep-Alive
HTTP_HOST	cx847962-a
HTTP_REFERER	http://cx847962-a/ASPBEG/CH03/default8.htm
HTTP_USER_AGENT	Mozilla/4.0 (compatible; MSIE 5.01; Windows NT 5.0)
HTTP_COOKIE	ASPSESSIONIDGQGQGLZQ=00DPIFCBBDGJKPJ0PMBPHLPA
HTTP_ACCEPT_ENCODING	gzip, deflate

Table 3-7 | **URL and More HTTP Variables**

Using ServerVariable Values

Use default8.htm on the Web site (click the Submit button on the
default8.htm form with nothing filled in in the text box) to generate
ServerVariables output. Have a look at the most useful of these values
to see what they can do for you. For starters, take a look at the
HTTP_REFERER value. It shows the URL and path of the file from
which you were referred to the current script. You can use that value to
direct the user back to the same page, depending upon the conditions you
find when processing the user's request (for example, a missing field in a
form). Remember, more than one form could be accessing the same
script, so it might be important to know which one is making the call.

Another useful value is the HTTP_USER_Agent, or the type and version
of the browser being used. Sniffing out this value allows you to produce
and send browser-specific pages back to the user based on this value. After
all, even though HTML is supposed to be platform independent, we're all
still very aware of the differences between browser types and versions, and
it's pretty common these days to produce several versions of a page for the
various browsers being used.

In conjunction with browser type, you may want to be aware of the HTTP_ACCEPT_LANGUAGE value. This value is supplied by the user's browser and specifies what language the browser is operating in. Like providing a browser-specific version of a page to the user, you can use this value to provide a language-specific page.

The HTTP_COOKIE value contains the values of any session cookies received. This information is very useful for tracking the movement of users across the site, as well as other things like establishing sessions each time the user connects.

The Cookies Collection

Cookies are small strings of data that a Web server can send to a browser and then retrieve at will. Cookies have attributes that can specify their lifetime and availability, which you would set with the Response object. The primary value in cookies is the value that can be set according to whatever scheme you choose, typically a unique identifier so you can tell one browser from others in a multitude of requests. Among the common values set in cookies are expiration date, domain and path, usernames and passwords, and just about anything else you can think of that you'd like to see the next time that browser connects.

Note

If the Expires property is not set, the cookies will expire when the browser is next closed. This property is convenient for setting cookies only for the time a user might be surfing on a given day.

Single-Value Cookies

Cookies can be either single value or multiple value (the syntax differences are explained in the Response object cookie section later in this module, "Sending Cookies"), and it is often important to determine the difference and extract all the values if a cookie has more than one. You can use the simple iteration routine to collect individual values:

```
For Each collItem In Request.Cookies
    Response.Write collItem & " = " & Request.Cookies(collItem) & "<BR>"
Next
```

Multiple-Value Cookies

Suppose one of the cookies has multiple values? You could use the HasKeys property of the Cookies collection in something like the following code to iterate through the multiple cookie values:

```
If Request.Cookies(collItem).HasKeys Then
    For Each collItemVal In Request.Cookies(collItem)
        Response.Write collItem & "(" & collItemVal & ")" & " = " &
Request.Cookies(collItem)(collItemVal) & "<BR>"
    Next
End If
```

Naturally, knowing the names and values of all cookies received in a request is the first step toward knowing what to do with the request if the functions being provided by the script depend on cookie values for conditional processing. You'll delve further into cookies and how to set their values in the upcoming Response object section (see "Writing Data to the Browser").

1-Minute Drill

- **What is the syntax for iterating through a collection, and how is the name of each item in the collection arrived at?**

- **A cookie can have a value, but how do you set a value within a multi-valued cookie?**

The ClientCertificate Collection

The ClientCertificate collection is primarily useful for assisting you in managing Web site security, by allowing you to force users to provide digital certificates to authenticate themselves. ASP provides a way to access the variables included with a certificate via the ClientCertificate collection,

---

- **For Each *XXX* In *YYY, Do Something,* Next is the syntax—where *XXX* is the name you've assigned for each item in the collection and *YYY* is the object containing the collection. The item name is simply whatever you assign.**
- **Assign a name to the attribute you want to attach to the cookie, and then assign a value for that attribute.**

and you can use the typical iteration methods to read out these variables. Once again, modify your script to display them, as shown here:

```
<CENTER>
<TABLE BORDER=1>
<% For Each collItem In Request.ClientCertificate() %>
<TR><TD><% Response.Write collItem & " = " &
Request.ClientCertificate(collItem) %></TD></TR>
<% Next %>
</TABLE>
</CENTER>
```

This code, properly inserted into a normal script page, produces such data values as the certificate issuer, the subject's name and company (subject being the person who registered the certificate), public key, validity (from and until) dates, and so forth.

Tip

Your server must be set up to accept personal certificates, or submitting a request with a personal certificate on your browser produces no results.

Ask the Expert

Question: There seems to be so much information coming from the user. Do I need all that information? Why are all those variables transmitted each time?

Answer: Server variables are an important part of the communication between browser and server, and maintaining the client/server relationship is their primary function. However, tapping into the values of those variables allows ASP to do some very interesting things. For example, one of the variables tells ASP what browser version is being used. This information allows ASP to programmatically assign special versions of your Web site pages according to browser type, meaning you can make pages that look good on a variety of browsers. That capability is covered in more detail in Module 8.

3

Question: **I'm not quite sure I understand how cookies work.
There seem to be several kinds, with possibly several values each.
Can you describe them in more detail?**

Answer: You'll learn more about session cookies in Module 5; but for
now, you should know that they play an important role in establishing
individual communication with a specific user. Ordinary cookies serve to
identify a particular client so ASP can track site usage from click to click.
You can make cookies multi-valued by adding keys, and you can retrieve
those values with the techniques described previously in this module.

Question: **How does authentication work? Is it hard to set up
certificates? Where do they come from?**

Answer: You can get certificates from certificate-issuing companies
such as Verisign, and there is a fairly simple procedure for placing them on
your server, in the IIS documentation. To authenticate themselves, users
must have a personal certificate installed on their browsers. The certificate
can be decoded only using a reference to other numbers stored by the
certificate authority, so certificate values not meeting this requirement are
considered false.

project3-2.zip

Project 3-2: Using the Request Object

The Request object is great for capturing form data for a multitude of
purposes, from checking to see if a user is already in your database to
validating form input, to conditionally redirecting a user, to setting
cookies.

You'll use the Request object extensively in your applications, so
let's put it to work in a simple but powerful way right off the bat,
checking to make sure a submission form is properly filled out and
complete prior to allowing the submission process to be completed.
First, you'll make a submission form in HTML, and then you'll make a
script that checks the value of each field and validates it.

To make the submission form, you can use Notepad (for you
hard-core HTML programmers out there) or some handy HTML-editing
program like Dreamweaver or FrontPage. Remember, if you use

FrontPage to create a form, you'll have to delete a few items from the form in order to use it with ASP.

Step-by-Step

Here's the HTML code for you to add to your submission form:

```html
<html><head>
<meta http-equiv="Content-Language" content="en-us">
<meta http-equiv="Content-Type" content="text/html; charset=windows-1252">
<meta name="GENERATOR" content="Microsoft FrontPage 4.0">
<meta name="ProgId" content="FrontPage.Editor.Document">
<title>In Practice Submission Form</title>
</head><body bgcolor="#99FFCC">
<H2>Please register using the following form:</H2>
<form method="POST" action="--WEBBOT-SELF--">
<!--webbot bot="SaveResults" U-File="fpweb:///_private/form_results.txt"
S-Format="TEXT/CSV" S-Label-Fields="TRUE" -->
<table border="1" width="100%"><tr>
<td width="50%" align="right"><b>First Name:</b></td>
<td width="50%"><input type="text" name="FirstName" size="20"
tabindex="1"></td></tr><tr>
<td width="50%" align="right"><b>Middle Initial:</b></td>
<td width="50%"><input type="text" name="MI" size="20" tabindex="2"></td>
</tr><tr>
<td width="50%" align="right"><b>Last Name:</b></td>
<td width="50%"><input type="text" name="LastName" size="20"
tabindex="3"></td></tr><tr>
<td width="50%" align="right"><b>Address 1:</b></td>
<td width="50%"><input type="text" name="Address1" size="20"
tabindex="4"></td></tr><tr>
<td width="50%" align="right"><b>Address 2:</b></td>
<td width="50%"><input type="text" name="Address2" size="20"
tabindex="5"></td></tr><tr>
<td width="50%" align="right"><b>City:</b></td>
<td width="50%"><input type="text" name="City" size="20" tabindex="6"></td>
</tr><tr>
<td width="50%" align="right"><b>State:</b></td>
<td width="50%"><input type="text" name="State" size="20" tabindex="7"></td>
</tr><tr>
<td width="50%" align="right"><b>Country:</b></td>
<td width="50%"><input type="text" name="Country" size="20"
tabindex="8"></td></tr><tr>
<td width="50%" align="right"><b>Zip or Postal Code:</b></td>
<td width="50%"><input type="text" name="PCode" size="20" tabindex="9"></td>
</tr><tr>
<td width="50%" align="right"><b>Home Phone:</b></td>
<td width="50%"><input type="text" name="HomePhone" size="20"
tabindex="10"></td></tr><tr>
<td width="50%" align="right"><b>Fax:</b></td>
<td width="50%"><input type="text" name="Fax" size="20" tabindex="11"></td>
</tr><tr>
<td width="50%" align="right"><b>Pager:</b></td>
<td width="50%"><input type="text" name="Pager" size="20"
tabindex="12"></td></tr><tr>
```

```
<td width="50%" align="right"><b>Mobile Phone:</b></td>
<td width="50%"><input type="text" name="Mobile" size="20"
tabindex="13"></td></tr><tr>
<td width="50%" align="right"><b>Email Address:</b></td>
<td width="50%"><input type="text" name="Email" size="20"
tabindex="14"></td></tr><tr>
<td width="50%" align="right"><b>Website URL:</b></td>
<td width="50%"><input type="text" name="WebsiteURL" size="20"
tabindex="15"></td></tr><tr>
<td width="50%" align="right"><input type="submit" value="Register Now"
name="B1"></td>
<td width="50%"><input type="reset" value="Start Over" name="B2"></td>
</tr></table>
</form>
</body></html>
```

Notice that FrontPage has inserted a few META tags that explain the generator used (FrontPage 4.0), as well as the language, content type, and character set. These won't hurt anything, but we can't use the form as is. FrontPage has inserted a reference to its own Web Bot named SaveResults.

1. Remove the preceding code (all code referencing WEBBOT), and replace it with the name of the script you're calling. Name the script **Project3-2.asp**. Then edit the FORM tag as follows:

```
<form method="POST" action="Project3-2.asp">
```

2. Don't forget to remove the two lines that follow the FORM tag as well. These set the parameters for the FrontPage Web Bot and are no longer needed. The finished form looks like that shown in Figure 3-2.

3. Because this module is divided into separate sections for the Request and Response objects, you'll split your validator script into two parts: the part that does the data capture and validation and the part that does the responding (this will be shown in the Project 3-3 section for the Response object). An easy way to capture the correct names for fields (as well as the look and feel of the submission form) is to copy the file with a new name and then proceed to modify it in a simple text editor such as Notepad or WordPad.

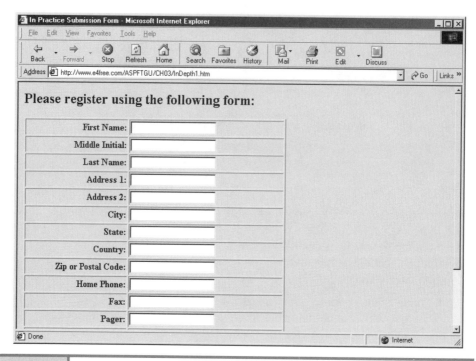

Figure 3-2 The Project 3-2 example registration form

4. Capture all the data sent by the user and insert it into variables. You can accomplish this simply by setting variables equal to Request.Form values, as follows (please note that the HMTL tags making up the return page have been omitted):

```
<%
fname = Request.Form("FirstName")
mi = Request.Form("MI")
lname = Request.Form("LastName")
addr1 = Request.Form("Address1")
addr2 = Request.Form("Address2")
cty = Request.Form("City")
st = Request.Form("State")
cntry = Request.Form("Country")
post = Request.Form("PCode")
hphn = Request.Form("HomePhone")
```

```
fphn = Request.Form("Fax")
pgr = Request.Form("Pager")
mphn = Request.Form("Mobile")
email = Request.Form("Email")
wURL = Request.Form("WebsiteURL")
%>
```

3

5. Following data acquisition, you can test each value to determine whether the field contains data and whether the data is the right kind and contains the right values. Test to make sure the fields contain data. Forms that include an e-mail field usually require that you provide this data, which makes sense because that is the most common communication method on the Internet. For the email field, you can test for data with the following code (note that this is *pseudo code*, not real code):

```
If email = "" Then
      send an error message
Else
      keep processing
End If
```

6. For validation, check to make sure the email field contains the @ sign, no spaces, and no special or escape characters that might break something. VBScript offers simple character-checking functions to assist you in this common task.

Once you have validated the data sent by the user, it's time to do something with it. Other processing you might perform and responses you might supply are covered in the Project 3-3 section for the Response object at the end of this module.

The Response Object

The Response object is your utility tool for responding to users' requests, but it serves other useful functions as well. For example, you can selectively direct users to other URLs or pages with the Redirect method. It also works with the buffering function (which stores the content of a returning page until all processing is complete) so you can send individual completed portions while the user is waiting for the other processing to get done.

Note

In ASP 2.0, buffering had to be explicitly set; while in ASP 3.0, buffering is the default, so you may find yourself using the buffering control functions in the Response object more frequently.

Response Object Collections

There is only one collection in the Response object, the cookies collection, which contains the values of all cookies that are to be sent to the browser in the current response. Cookie values must be created before they are made part of the response; once they are part of the response, they are write-only, which means you can determine their names from the Response object but not their values.

Response Object Properties

The Response object has nine properties, most of them readable and editable. They are created by the server, but you can change them to suit your needs.

- **Buffer**   This property can be either True or False, and specifies whether output being processed will be held in the buffer until all output is ready for delivery. Because you must set this property before any other output is sent, it is usually the first line in an ASP page. As mentioned previously, buffering is True by default in ASP 3.0 and False by default in earlier versions of ASP.

- **IsClientConnected**   This property is also True or False, depending upon whether the browser is still connected and loading a page. It is useful for initiating an action when the user goes to another page before finishing the current page's processing.

- **Expires**   The value of this property is a number representing the minutes for which a page is valid. If the user has this page cached for less than the value of Expires, the cached page will be displayed; otherwise, a new page will be generated.

- **ExpiresAbsolute**   This property is a specific date and time when the page expires, regardless of how old it is. It is expressed as a date/time value with the pound sign before and after the value.

● **Status**   This property contains the status value and message that will be sent to the browser in the event of an error, and can be used to indicate successful processing as well. It uses a string as the value and message.

● **CacheControl**   This property controls (or at least should control) whether proxy servers cache the page. Not all proxy servers honor this property. Set it to "Public" to allow caching, and "Private" to disallow caching. It is also a string value.

● **Charset**   This property adds the name of the character set in use to the HTTP Content-Type header, and is a string value.

● **ContentType**   This property can be used to set the HTTP content type for a response. If it is not used, the standard "text-html" is used. It is a string value.

● **PICS**   The PICS value, also a string, adds data to the header indicating whether the response contains content with adult themes, violence, and so forth.

Response Object Methods

The Response object is a workhorse, and it includes a number of useful methods that do the work. You've already used the Write method, and next you'll learn about the rest, including header and log methods and buffer control methods.

● **Write("string or other value")**   This method is used to write a string (or other value) into the overall response, and is typically inserted into the HTML code at the location where you want the response string to become part of the page.

● **Redirect("url")**   This method tells the browser to load the page or URL specified (as a string). The "302 Object Moved" HTTP header is used to accomplish this action.

● **Flush()**   This method forces an emptying of the buffer at the current stage of processing. It is useful for providing users a partial response, especially where the remaining processing may take quite some time, so they'll continue waiting for the rest of the page.

- **End()**   This method ends processing and returns whatever has been completed so far. It is useful when some process either is taking too long or cannot be completed normally.

- **Clear()**   This method simply erases the contents of the response buffer (but not the HTTP headers).

- **AddHeader("name," "content")**   This method adds a custom header to the response, with *name* and *content* values, and must be processed before any page content is sent.

- **AppendToLog("logentry")**   This method adds a string to the Web server log entry for the response when the W3C Extended Log File Format is used.

- **BinaryWrite(SafeArray)**   This method is used for writing the data contained in a Variant-type SafeArray into the output stream without character conversion occurring. As its name implies, it is useful for writing binary data such as that making up image files.

Writing Data to the Browser

You've already written data (received via the Request.Object's Form collection) back to the browser with the Response object. The syntax is pretty straightforward; just Request.Write and then the string, variable, or object reference you want to use as output. For example, the following code will write a message from you, the contents of a variable, and form entries back to a user (see Figure 3-3 for an example based on default10.htm on the Web site):

```
<CENTER>
<H2><% Response.Write "Thank you for responding" %></H2>
Today's Date is:
<% tDate = Date()
Response.Write tDate %><P>
Your personal data entries were:<BR>
<% Response.Write(Request.Form("fullname")) %><BR>
<% Response.Write(Request.Form("address")) %><BR>
<% Response.Write(Request.Form("phonenumber")) %><BR>
</CENTER>
```

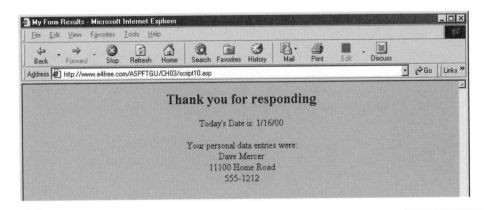

Figure 3-3   **Returning Request items and the current date using Response**

Sending Cookies

Cookies are a little more complex than strings and so forth, because there are more parts to them and because they may play a special role in your interactions with users. For example, some cookies spend quite a while on the user's machine, while others last only as long as a single session. And it's up to you to make sure you give each cookie a truly unique ID so you can always be sure which user you are dealing with.

For example, to write a single-valued cookie named "mycookie" with the value "MyCookie," you would use this:

```
Response.Write("mycookie") = "MyCookie"
```

To write a multiple-valued cookie with a primary name of "mycookie" and two subvalues named "mycookieA" and "mycookieB" with values "X" and "Y," respectively, you would code like this:

```
Response.Write("mycookie")("mycookieA") = "X"
Response.Write("mycookie")("mycookieB") = "Y"
```

Syntax and coding are very straightforward in ASP. Nothing magical; just write out a commonsense version of what you're trying to do and voilà, cookies of both kinds.

Cookie Constraints   Cookies, like the values in other collections, are read- and write-only. After receiving cookie values, you can't go back and change them, and this is good practice. Explicitly setting variables to cookie values and then processing the values means you can always rest assured that what was sent with the request is still intact, no matter how much processing you've done. The same goes for any cookies you're sending out.

In practice, this means that to update cookie values, you can't just reset some of them. You've got to completely rewrite the entire cookie, substituting the new values. That means, of course, that you must capture *all* cookie values each time you want to update *any* cookie values.

Another factor that comes into play is the placement of cookie values being sent in the output stream. They are part of the HTTP header, and as such, must be created before you send any other output back to the browser. However, they can be created anywhere in your page, as long as nothing is flushed back to the browser before cookie creation is accomplished.

Hint

With ASP 3.0, buffering is set to True by default, so you can completely process everything before creating your cookies, if you would prefer to do things that way. This comes in especially handy when the results of the processing affect cookie values in some way.

Writing Data with the BinaryWrite Method

As Web sites become more complex, interactive, and functional, you can expect to depend more heavily on methods such as BinaryRead and BinaryWrite. Dealing with binary data stored in a database, and perhaps gathering binary data occasionally, are powerful capabilities. For example, suppose you wanted to display employee pictures stored in database records. Pulling the record and outputting the bytes via BinaryWrite would do the trick.

3

To make the data ready for output, you would first have to construct Variant-type array (call it vArEmpImage) of the bytes pointed to by the database record. Overall, the process calls for accessing the database (perhaps selecting records by the username/password of an employer), retrieving the appropriate record of an individual employee, setting the value of vArEmpImage equal to the bytes that make up the image file pointed to by the EmployeePicture field, and then using the code as follows:

```
Response.BinaryWrite(vArEmpImage)
```

Redirecting the Browser

Have you ever been a victim of that little "prank" by which a Web site makes it impossible to back out using the Back button? Annoying, to say the least, but it's easy to do with browser redirection. Just make an ASP script that immediately redirects a person to another page; and each time that person presses the Back button, he or she will go to the ASP script, which immediately opens to the page the user just backed out of.

Browser redirection makes use of the "302 Object Moved" HTTP header, and is the same as creating a Refresh META tag in an HTML page. The META tag would look like this:

```
<META HTTP-EQUIV="REFRESH"
CONTENT="0;URL=someotherplace.htm">
```

In this case, content is the number of seconds before the refresh takes place; and the URL is, of course, where the user will end up after the refresh. When you send the "302 Object Moved" HTTP header, you're just telling the browser to update its location—you're not actually sending a new page, so the browser then sends a request for the new page.

Note

Refer to Module 4's discussion of the Server object for information about the new Transfer method in ASP 3.0. The Transfer method allows you to switch execution of processing from one page to another and is more suitable for many common tasks involving some form of redirection.

Page Buffering in ASP

Most ASP scripts that work within a single page or so of code will operate very quickly, producing results with little detectable lag or latency. But going into a database or performing complex processing can sometimes take quite a while, especially if the database must be accessed several times to complete processing.

For example, suppose you are searching for a value and, upon finding no values, search again for related values in the same database. This might happen when you build a directory of listings (of whatever your clients might want to list, such as dentists in a given region) for advertising purposes.

If a user searches for a dentist within his city, and the search finds none that match the specific criteria used, you might set the ASP script to return to the database using broader search criteria (the entire county, for instance). However, it would be nice to return a message to the user noting that although no records were found in the initial search area, your application is in the process of searching the surrounding area as well.

This is just good business practice and encourages users to wait for the finished search, rather than skipping to the next page or even away from the Web site altogether. The way you make this happen is by manipulating ASP's buffering feature.

To demonstrate, suppose you code your script to process a select query of the database and no records are found. You could use the following code to send a message back to the user:

```
Response.Write "No dentists matching your specifications
were found in the city you chose. We are now searching the
surrounding area and will provide these results shortly."
Response.Flush
```

You can also use the Response.End method to end all processing and send any buffered content to the user, or you can use the Response.Clear method to clear out the buffer. You might use these methods where partial processing has resulted in a complete response, or where partial processing has resulted in a response that must be erased (and presumably your script would then generate the correct response).

Hint

Use the IsClientConnected property of the Response object occasionally during consecutive processing efforts to determine whether the user is still connected, to prevent processing cycle waste when users get tired of waiting and click away. This can happen frequently, especially when a user has a low-speed connection, and there's no point in continuing processing if the user is already gone.

3

Setting Page Properties

The properties possessed by a Web page are defined in large measure by the content of the HTTP headers you send back with the page requested. Whether and when it is cached or expires, its MIME type and any PICs labels included can be specified using the CacheControl, Expires (and ExpiresAbsolute), Status, ContentType, and Pics properties of the Response object via the AddHeader method.

Caching   Most people are familiar by now with the fact that browsers cache Web pages in a temporary folder on the hard drive while they're surfing. I have a friend who, at one point, saved images from many of the sites he surfed simply by raiding his cache folder every so often. The purpose of caching, of course, is to speed up loading of pages you've recently visited. ISP proxy servers often cache as well (an important point to note for Web developers, as developers like to see the new look of pages they've just updated).

While the goal of caching is admirable, the effect is to dilute the "instantly updated" quality of Web material. After all, if you're looking for the latest price on an item, you don't want to be using yesterday's Web page. Users can play with their cache and update settings in the browser (in Internet Explorer 5.0, look in Tools | Internet Options; clicking the Setting button brings up the Settings dialog box), but you can also manipulate caching parameters by changing various Response object properties.

For example, if you would like to instruct proxy servers not to cache a page, you can set the CacheControl property to "Private" like so:

```
Response.CacheControl = "Private"
```

Setting the CacheControl property to "Public" has the opposite effect. Again, it's wise to understand that proxy servers are not bound to honor this setting and may still choose to cache if they want.

If caching occurs, the length of time in which a page remains cached can be affected with the Expires and ExpiresAbsolute properties. Expires contains the number of minutes since page acquisition before a page should be removed from the cache, and ExpiresAbsolute gives a fixed date and time for removal. Both properties are set using the same simple syntax as the Response.CacheControl property; but remember that the data type of Expires is a number, while the data type of ExpiresAbsolute is a date and time combination, so make the appropriate syntax adjustments when specifying them (no quotes for numbers, and the pound signs for dates and times).

The Status Property and Adding Headers   Status messages are like the server talking to the browser, telling the browser what has happened to its request for a page. HTTP 1.1 contains quite a few built-in status messages, and you can use the Response.Status property to generate or change them. For example, if a user has not been authenticated and you want to mislead the user into thinking the wrong URL was entered, you could generate an "HTTP 404 Not Found" message with the following code.

```
Response.Status = "HTTP 404 Not Found"
```

Not only can you generate status messages, but you can send them for use in conjunction with other headers, including ones you have generated or modified yourself. The following is a partial list of common HTTP status messages (for more information, see Module 2):

Section Reference	Meaning
400 Section 10.4.1	Bad Request
401 Section 10.4.2	Unauthorized
402 Section 10.4.3	Payment Required
403 Section 10.4.4	Forbidden
404 Section 10.4.5	Not Found
405 Section 10.4.6	Method Not Allowed
406 Section 10.4.7	Not Acceptable

Each of the section references just shown refers to areas online in which more information is available about that particular status message. The "404 Not Found" listing, for example, says that the server has not found anything matching the request and gives additional information about when and why this message is used and what it means.

Now, suppose you want to send a message back declaring that the user is unauthorized to access the page requested, and require the user to provide authentication. You can send a "401 Unauthorized" message with the Status property, and then add a header for authentication as follows:

```
Response.Status = "401 Unauthorized"
Response.AddHeader "WWW-Authenticate", "BASIC"
```

Using the ContentType Property

Content type refers to the kind of data (or file format) you are sending to the browser. The value of the ContentType property is a short text string of the form ("type"/"format"). An example would be "text/html." This example is the default for all ASP pages unless otherwise specified. Other common types are "text/text" for text files and "image/jpeg" for jpeg image files.

The technical term for these content type identifiers is *MIME-type*, or Multi-purpose Internet Mail Extensions. When sending content of a type other than HTML text files, make sure you include the ContentType property *before* sending any content.

1-Minute Drill

● **Name the types of responses you can produce with the Response object.**

● **How can you tell if a user has clicked away from your Web site while you are processing a request for him or her?**

● Write, Binary Write, Redirect, and flushing of processed content
● Examine the IsClientConnected property.

Ask the Expert

Question: What does it mean if a property of an object is read-only? For instance, cookies are read-only. How can they be changed if they are read-only?

Answer: Being read-only means that the value you retrieve cannot be changed as a property of the current Request object. However, if you reset the cookie using the Reponse.Write method, you are actually destroying the old cookie and creating a new one with the same name. Doing this means that the next time you retrieve that cookie, it will have the new value. Although it is read-only in the current Request object, you can still manipulate its value, just not directly.

Question: How does buffering work? Why would I use it, and what disadvantages are there to using it?

Answer: Scripts can sometimes take a while to process. Rather than have the processed contents dribble out to the user as they are processed, you can save them in a buffer on the server until they're all done. Of course, if you want the user to receive partial contents, you can use buffering, but also use the Flush method to send the currently complete results to the user. If the user has disconnected before processing is complete, you can check for that condition and use the End method to end unnecessary processing.

Question: How does caching work? Should I try to control caching?

Answer: Unfortunately, some servers are set up to cache content, so they can deliver it more quickly to their users. If a user is interacting with your Web site, the same URL might produce a different result each time the user clicks there. But if the server is caching, it will offer the same old page. Therefore, you should try to set caching attributes; but keep in mind that not all servers are smart enough to respect your caching settings, and it may still cause a problem.

Project 3-3: Using the Response Object

You've already created an HTML submission form for users to fill out when they want to enter your application, as well as the data capture scripting and validation scripting in the ASP script called. Now it's time to actually respond to the user. It would be easy to return the data they supplied; but how about if you return a page that lets them change the data if they desire, as well as pointing out any required fields they neglected to fill in? Here's how.

3

Step-by-Step

1. Open a Notepad window and write a validation routine for the email field, using a conditional statement to check the incoming value of the field.

2. If the value is null, send a message back to the user requesting that the user fills in the value.

3. If the email field is filled in, use a table structure (with HTML table tags) to display back to the user each value he or she filled in, plus the name of the field.

   Here is code similar to what you might use for these functions:

```
<%
If email = "" Then
    Response.Write("<H2>You must fill in your email address to submit
this form</H2>")
Else
%>
<H2>Thanks!</H2>
Here is the data you filled in.
<form method="POST" action="Project1a.asp">
<table border="1" width="100%"><tr>
<td width="50%" align="right">First Name:</td>
<td width="50%"><input type="text" value="<% Response.Write(fname)
%>" name="FirstName" size="20" tabindex="1"></td></tr><tr>
<td width="50%" align="right">Middle Initial:</td>
<td width="50%"><input type="text" value="<% Response.Write(mi) %>"
name="MI" size="20" tabindex="2"></td></tr><tr>
<td width="50%" align="right">Last Name:</td>
<td width="50%"><input type="text" value="<% Response.Write(lname)
%>" name="LastName" size="20" tabindex="3"></td></tr><tr>
<td width="50%" align="right">Address1:</td>
<td width="50%"><input type="text" value="<% Response.Write(addr1)
%>" name="Address1" size="20" tabindex="4"></td></tr><tr>
```

```
<td width="50%" align="right">Address2:</td>
<td width="50%"><input type="text" value="<% Response.Write(addr2)
%>" name="Address2" size="20" tabindex="5"></td></tr><tr>
<td width="50%" align="right">City:</td>
<td width="50%"><input type="text" value="<% Response.Write(cty) %>"
name="City" size="20" tabindex="6"></td></tr><tr>
<td width="50%" align="right">State:</td>
<td width="50%"><input type="text" value="<% Response.Write(st) %>"
name="State" size="20" tabindex="7"></td></tr><tr>
<td width="50%" align="right">Country:</td>
<td width="50%"><input type="text" value="<% Response.Write(cntry)
%>" name="Country" size="20" tabindex="8"></td></tr><tr>
<td width="50%" align="right">Zip or Postal Code:</td>
<td width="50%"><input type="text" value="<% Response.Write(post)
%>" name="PCode" size="20" tabindex="9"></td></tr><tr>
<td width="50%" align="right">Home Phone:</td>
<td width="50%"><input type="text" value="<% Response.Write(hphn)
%>" name="HomePhone" size="20" tabindex="10"></td></tr><tr>
<td width="50%" align="right">Fax:</td>
<td width="50%"><input type="text" value="<% Response.Write(fphn)
%>" name="Fax" size="20" tabindex="11"></td></tr><tr>
<td width="50%" align="right">Pager:</td>
<td width="50%"><input type="text" value="<% Response.Write(pgr) %>"
name="Pager" size="20" tabindex="12"></td></tr><tr>
<td width="50%" align="right">Mobile Phone:</td>
<td width="50%"><input type="text" value="<% Response.Write(mphn)
%>" name="Mobile" size="20" tabindex="13"></td></tr><tr>
<td width="50%" align="right">Email Address:</td>
<td width="50%"><input type="text" value="<% Response.Write(email)
%>" name="Email" size="20" tabindex="14">
</td></tr><tr>
<td width="50%" align="right">Website URL:</td>
<td width="50%"><input type="text" value="<% Response.Write(wURL)
%>" name="WebsiteURL" size="20" tabindex="15"></td></tr><tr>
<td width="50%" align="right"><input type="submit" value="Register
Now" name="B1"></td>
<td width="50%"><input type="reset" value="Start Over"
name="B2"></td>
</tr></table></form>
<%
End If
%>
```

☑ *Mastery Check*

3

1. When you write "Request.Form("fieldname")," what does the word *Form* represent?

   A. A built-in ASP object

   B. A method of the Request object

   C. A collection of the Request object

   D. A property of the Request object

2. What code could be used to send the message "Thank you!" back to the user, within the context of an HTML page?

   A. Response.Write("Thank you!")

   B. Response.Write "Thank you!"

   C. strThanks = "Thank you!" Response.Write strThanks

   D. All of the above

3. What object collection could you retrieve to get a cookie from the user?

   A. Request.ServerVariables("HTTP_COOKIE")

   B. Request.Cookie

   C. Both of the above

   D. Neither

☑ Mastery Check

4. When is it a good idea to buffer the results generated by your scripts?

   A. When you're using several scripting languages in one script

   B. When you're accessing a database

   C. When processing may take some time

   D. When you want to ensure all the content is ready before transmittal to the user

5. To immediately send processed results to the user, you would use the _____ method of the Response object. To stop processing, you would use the _____ method of the Response object. To send their browser to another location, you would use the _____ method of the Response object.

Module 4

The Server Object

The Goals of This Module

- Learn how to use server-side includes and server directives
- Set and change how long a script can run before timing out
- Transfer control and values from one script to another
- Create instances of components and practice using them
- Encode HTML and URLs into legal characters for transmission
- Capture error messages and build custom error pages

The Web server plays a central role in your ASP applications, and it's not surprising that ASP has a built-in Server object to make handling server characteristics convenient. There are some legacy capabilities you can use with the server, such as server-side includes, as well as specific functions you can call for moderating communications to and from the server. In addition, the Server object is used to create instances of components. Beyond the built-in ASP objects, components add the remaining functionality to your application.

The ASP Server Object

The ASP Server object has a kind of catchall role in the scheme of things. It assists with error handling, instantiating components, translating HTML tags into their proper codes for display, redirecting control, and other miscellaneous tasks. These topics will be discussed in the same fashion as the rest of the ASP objects, but first we need to lay the groundwork to make it easier to understand what the Server object does and why it is so important.

If you think about how typical application programs work, you will recognize that they manage functions and operational aspects that ordinary Web pages can't. Each screen within the program may contain controls that initiate actions through what's onscreen or through menus and toolbars. Other screens within the program can directly access the values or state of those controls, dialog boxes, and menu choices when it's their turn to appear or continue your processing.

If you should call a subprogram into being, it can run within the *context* of the current screen or application program, meaning it understands what is already going on and can provide services related to your existing processing environment or state. In addition, application programs encompass error-handling capabilities that provide specialized (although sometimes not very helpful) messages depending upon not just the error occurring but also the *context* in which the error occurred.

ASP Page and Object Context

ASP contains the ObjectContext object, which is available explicitly whenever you need to reference the context of a page (to retrieve the values associated with any of the ASP objects currently in it). The benefit inherent in this kind of capability is that the object itself (whether it is a component of some type, a connection object, or an instantiated custom object) can remain *stateless*, meaning that it does not have to hold its own references to the context after it finishes whatever it's doing. Instead, it can simply reference the context of a page whenever it needs to and get the latest data. The data will be unique to that page for any object created inside that page.

Note

In earlier versions of ASP, the method for referencing page context was to retrieve the ScriptingContext object via the OnStartPage event, triggered when the page was executed in ASP.

On the other hand, if you instantiate objects or components outside a page (using the VBScript Set and CreateObject commands, for example), you lose page context and the isolation and scalability provided by the server. Therefore, under most circumstances it's best to use the Server.CreateObject method to instantiate objects.

Server-Side Includes

Server-side includes (SSIs) offer another handy set of IIS (and ASP) capabilities. Server-side includes are directives that tell the server to perform certain actions while processing scripts. My first experience with one of these directives came when I was building a rather large and complex database-access script. The processing had become fragmented among several sets of conditions, and it was getting difficult to make sure my conditional statements matched, even with commenting and indenting. The script was just too large.

To make it easier to read, I cut out sections of the script between conditional statements where the processing was routine and placed those sections into text files of their own. Then I inserted include directives into the original script, like this:

```
<!-- #include file="script1.txt" -->
```

The resulting script was much easier to read and debug. As an added bonus, I could now reuse the script segment again wherever I wanted, while having to maintain or update it in only one file.

SSI Mapping

Some SSI directives must use file extensions that are mapped to SSI (by default, the extensions .stm, .shtm, and .shtml are mapped to the SSI interpreter Ssinc.dll). Directives that must use the SSI interpreter are #flastmod, #fsize, and #config. The #echo and #exec directives must run inside HTML pages, while the #include directive can run from HTML pages or ASP scripts.

SSI Directives

Server-side include directives provide more than just the ability to include scripts. There are six statements supported by IIS, as follows:

- **#include**   This directive allows the server to include the contents of a file in the response sent to the client. If it is used with an ASP script, the contents of the included file are interpreted by ASP (meaning you can use it for including processing segments).

- **#config**   This directive sets the format for dates, times, and file sizes that are returned when other directives (discussed next) are used. It can also be used to set the text of the standard SSI error message.

- **#flastmod**   This directive inserts the date and time the specified file was last modified into the response.

- **#fsize**   This directive inserts the size of the specified file into the response.

- **#echo**   This directive inserts an HTTP environment variable into the response.

- **#exec**   This directive executes a program or shell command on the server.

Hint

The data being inserted into a script completely replaces the include line. For example, if you insert an environment variable into the response stream, the directive line will not be found in the resulting HTML code on the browser, but the value of the environment variable will.

The #include Directive   If you've ever programmed a Perl script that must give a response to a user, you've probably written subroutines that produce standard beginnings and endings of HTML files for response pages, with logos and copyright notices. Whenever you need to include these sections in your response, you simply call the subroutine rather than rewrite all those print statements.

With ASP, you don't need to do this much, because you can mix in the HTML with your code directly. Once in a while, though, it may come in handy. For example, suppose you are building a Web site for a client consisting of multiple pages of text content. Suppose also that the structure of these pages doesn't change, but the text content changes frequently. Finally, suppose that the same content shows up in many different areas on the Web site. This is an ideal candidate for the #include directive.

Set up a simple page using includes. Start with a page called include1.asp, and then make a few text files to use with it, like this:

```
<!-- #include FILE="htmlheader.txt" -->
<!-- #include FILE="htmlbody.txt" -->      ◄──  Notice the HTML
<!-- #include FILE="aspprocessing.txt" -->      comment delimiters.
<!-- #include FILE="htmlending.txt" -->
```

You probably won't create too many files that include only #include directives, but it illustrates their usage nicely. Nothing in this file is ordinary HTML or ASP; everything is entirely made up of #include statements (notice they look just like HTML comments).

The files have all been given a .txt extension, but you could just as easily have given them an .asp extension. It's okay to use .txt extensions (even for files containing ASP) for your include files, but keep in mind that if someone happens to figure out the path and filename of one of your include files, it can be downloaded. If it happens to contain sensitive data (such as a user ID and password for access to a database), that could be a bad thing. Files with an .asp extension, on the other hand, would be processed rather than returned straight to the user.

Another thing to keep in mind is that you must place delimiters around code between #include statements. You can't allow processing to proceed into and through included files unless you put the <% and %> delimiters before and after the #include statement. Look at the contents of the beginning HTML file, named htmlheader.txt:

```
<HTML>
<HEAD>
<TITLE>Using Server-Side Includes - Include HTML Header</TITLE>
</HEAD>
```

Nothing surprising here. It's the same code you would have used on the page itself. The advantage is that if there were complex table structures or graphics to include, you wouldn't have to load your main page with them or rewrite or recopy them into each page you want to use them in. If you want to make a change, you can do it just once. The same goes for the body (named htmlbody.txt) and the ending, which follow here:

```
<BODY>
This text file creates the body of the document, before any ASP
processing is done.<BR>
```

Here's the ending HTML file (named htmlending.txt):

```
This text file creates the ending of the HTML document.<BR>
</BODY>
</HTML>
```

For the ASP processing page, the delimiters are shown inside the included code; but keep in mind that the ASP code must also be closed prior to the #include statement in the main script, and then reopened for processing to continue after the included file is done. The ASP processing code, named aspprocessing.txt, looks like this:

```
<%
Response.Write "This text was processed with ASP"
%>
```

Not much processing going on here, but it works just fine. Anything that can be processed ordinarily can be processed using an include file, just as though you had actually put that code into the main file. In fact, a major difference between the rest of the directives and the #include directive is that the contents of the included file are processed by ASP. While the other directives are processed by the server, the #include directive, when it occurs within an ASP script, inserts the content of the file into the main file and then it is processed by ASP as one big ASP script.

Tip

The reference to path and filename in the #include directive may be virtual rather than physical. To use a virtual relative or absolute path and filename, change the word "FILE" to "VIRTUAL" in the code, and then put in the virtual path you want to use.

Using the #confi, #flastmod, and #fsize Directives and Setting Error Messages

The #config directive is a utility directive and, according to Microsoft, can be used only in HTML. Although it is part of the server-side directives, it doesn't put anything in your pages. Instead, it tells the #fsize and #flastmod directives how to display their data. It can also be used to set the error message that is displayed if there is an SSI processing error. The allowable parameters for the #config directive are listed in Table 4-1.

The syntax of the #config directive for setting the date and time is as follows:

```
<!-- #config TIMFMT="%A, %B %d, %Y %H:%M" -->
```

This #config directive tells the server that when the #flastmod directive is used, it should display the full day of the week (%A) and then a comma; the full name of the month (%B), the numerical day of the month (%d), and then a comma; the full year (%Y), then a space and the hour of the day in 24-hour format (%H,), and then a colon and the minute of the hour (%M). To see this in action, you need to use the #flastmod directive to reference a file and display it the date and time it was last modified, as shown here:

```
<!-- #flastmod file = "somefile.txt" -->
```

Parameter Name	Parameter Function
ERRMSG	Sets the error message displayed when an error in SSI processing occurs, by means of a string.
TIMEFMT	Sets the format for the dates/times returned to the browser when the #flastmod directive is used, and the format for file size (bytes or kilobytes). Date and time values are specified by means of a token, for example:

Date Format	Date Format Definition
%a	Abbreviated name for day of the week
%A	Complete name for day of the week (Sunday)
%b	Abbreviated month name (Mar)
%B	Complete month name (March)
%c	Date and time appropriate for locale (07/06/00 12:51:32)
%d	Day of month as a decimal number (01–31)
%H	Hour in 24-hour format (00–23)
%I	Hour in 12-hour format (01–12)
%j	Day of year as a decimal number (001–366)
%m	Month as a decimal number (01–12)
%M	Minute as a decimal number (00–59)
%p	A.M./P.M. indicator for 12-hour format (AM)
%S	Second as a decimal number (00–59)
%U	Week of year as a decimal number (00–51)
%w	Day of week as a decimal number (0–6)
%W	Week of year as a decimal number starting with Monday (00–51)
%x	Date for the current locale (07/06/00)
%X	Time for the current locale (12:21:32)
%y	Year without the century as a decimal number (00)
%Y	Year with the century as a decimal number (2000)
%z, %Z	Time-zone name or abbreviation
SIZEFMT	Displays the file size in kilobytes (using the string "ABBREV") or bytes (using the string "BYTES").

Table 4-1 Parameters for the #config Directive

By the same token, you could use the following syntax to set the format of file size data with the #config directive:

```
<!-- #config SIZEFMT="BYTES" -->
```

This would make the #fsize directive return file size data in bytes, and you could use a similar syntax to produce that data, as shown here:

```
<!-- #fsize = "somefile.txt" -->
```

Finally, you could set the error message returned to the user when an SSI processing error is encountered with the following:

```
<!-- #config ERMSG="Whoops! SSI Processing Error" -->
```

The advantage of setting a custom error message is that it prevents the user from seeing the gory details of the error that occurred, which might help keep hackers from discovering the failure mode of your scripting mistakes.

The #echo Directive   In an ASP page, you can include HTTP header data using the Response object's ServerVariables collection. In an ordinary HTML page, you can provide the same data, if you choose, using the #echo directive. The permissible values are the same as those listed in Module 3, and the syntax for the #echo directive (for the request method, for instance) is

```
<!-- #echo VAR="REQUEST_METHOD" -->
```

To retrieve any of the other variables available, just exchange "REQUEST_METHOD" for the name of the variable you are interested in.

The #exec Directive   The #exec directive offers a means to run applications (such as CGI and ISAPI scripts) or shell commands. It is difficult to use and can present a security risk for your Web server, so we won't go into too much detail here except to say that you can invoke it (for a CGI script named perl.pl, for instance) with the following code (but only from an HTML page):

```
<!-- #exec CGI = "cgi-bin/perl.pl" -->
```

Proper Server-Side Include Usage

Server-side include technology is one of the older technologies still available for building Web sites. Before the days of ASP, plain HTML was used for everything, creating problems such as having to update many files with the same piece of footer information. SSI provided all of these functions:

● Ability to include one file into another

● Ability to execute a CGI script and show the results in an HTML page automatically

● Access to server variables that could be displayed on HTML pages

These functions are still available on IIS if you are using plain HTML pages or pages ending in .shtml, .shtm, or .stm. The ability to include a file is still available for ASP pages, which brings us to the next coding method.

When ASP developers "discover" server-side includes, they immediately start to figure out how to use them to save typing (their original purpose). Following this paragraph is an example of how some developers use SSI to include utility functions. The example uses the Dictionary object (explained in Module 6) and ADO (more on ADO in Modules 9-11):

```
<%
Subtotal = 0
for each key in dictCart
  sku = mid(key, 1, 7)
  color = mid(key, 8)
  SearchField = "sku"
  SearchData = sku
%>
<!--#include file="includes/dbopen.inc"-->
<%
if (IsNull(rstemp("bulkpriceqty")) or rstemp("bulkpriceqty")="") and
(IsNull(rstemp("bulkpriceamt")) or rstemp("bulkpriceamt")="") then
  LineTotal = FormatNumber(dictcart(key) * rstemp("price"),2)
  bulkitems = 0
else
  bulkitems = Int(dictcart(key)/rstemp("bulkpriceqty"))
```

```
  bulktotal = bulkitems * rstemp("bulkpriceamt")
  remainitems = dictcart(key) mod rstemp("bulkpriceqty")
  remaintotal = remainitems * rstemp("price")
  LineTotal = FormatNumber(bulktotal + remaintotal, 2)
  if bulkitems > 0 then
    BulkPricingApplied = True
  end if
end if
SubTotal = SubTotal + LineTotal
%>
```

This is the include file, dbopen.inc:

```
<%
set conntemp=server.createobject("adodb.connection")
' DSNless connection to Access Database
DSNtemp="DRIVER={Microsoft Access Driver (*.mdb)}; "
DSNtemp=dsntemp & "DBQ=" & server.mappath("data.mdb")
conntemp.Open DSNtemp
' DSNless connection to Access Database
If (SearchData <> "True" or SearchData <> "False") Then
  SearchData = "'" & SearchData & "'"
End If
if isnull(Sort) or Sort = "" then
  order = " ORDER BY sku"
else
  order = " ORDER BY " & sort
end if
sqltemp="select * from Main where " & SearchField & "=" & SearchData & Order
sqlcount="select count(*) from Main where " & SearchField & "=" & SearchData
set rstemp=conntemp.execute(sqltemp)
set cnttemp=conntemp.execute(sqlcount)
%>
```

In this file, the goal was admirable and partially realized. The programmer wanted to keep the database opening and searching code in a single file so that any changes would be reflected across the site.

The problem with this implementation, however, is that the developer has locked into a single method of retrieving data from the database. The data always has to come from the Main table. Two queries have to be executed every time data is needed so that the count of records is available. The calling code has to fill variables every time or the code won't work properly. Other than looking at the include file, there is no structured way to make sure that all variables have been supplied—at least not using this method.

The solution to this problem does not lie in removing the server-side include; in fact, server-side includes are a powerful part of the tools you'll use for writing good code. The method involves using VBScript's ability to create functions and subroutines. In this particular example, you should, at a minimum, create a function to open the database. With the database open, the calling code could create its own static recordset, which would make the record count available without having to do two queries. Alternatively, you could create another function that builds a SQL query based on input parameters, sends the query to the database, and returns a recordset to the caller. All of these functions would be stored in a common include file that would be used in all files needing these functions. I will typically include the common file in every ASP page, since the first line of my common file is Option Explicit.

Note

Using the Option Explicit parameter is highly recommended for every ASP page, because it forces you to dimension every variable rather than just pop up with variables any time you want them. It's just good coding practice and is discussed further in the next section.

1-Minute Drill

● **What is the syntax for an include file?**

● **What is the time format for the complete name of a day of the week?**

● **What file extensions denote include files?**

The Server Object

The server object is necessary because you must have some object or program capable of performing actions directly affecting the server and its operating environment. The following property (only one property is

---

● <!—— #include file="filename.txt" —>
● %A
● .txt

available) and methods (eight of them) are designed to give you the control you need on the server side:

- **The ScriptTimeout property**   Sets or returns the number of seconds a page can be processed before an error is generated.

- **The CreateObject("*identifier*") method**   Creates an instance of an object, which can be an application, a scripting object, or a component.

- **The Execute("*url*") method**   Halts the current page's execution and executes another page, after which execution on the current page is resumed.

- **The Transfer("*url*") method**   New in ASP 3.0, this method works like the Execute method (stopping execution of the current page and transferring execution to another page), but does not return control to the current page after the new page executes.

- **The MapPath("*url*") method**   Returns the physical path and filename of a file or resource.

- **The HTMLEncode("*string*") method**   Converts a string of HTML characters from ordinary characters to special characters (converts "<" to "&lt", for example).

- **The URLEncode("*string*") method**   Converts a string of characters making up a URL from non-legal characters (such as "?" to the legal characters "%3F").

- **The GetLastError() method**   Returns details of the last error that occurred, via the ASPError object.

Working with the Server Object

Among the things you want to be able to control at the server is the processing time allocated to each script. As a programmer, you are undoubtedly aware that poor programming can produce endless loops or even just excessive processing time. When you are hosting many scripts, and especially when many developers may be creating those scripts, it is important to have some kind of default timeout to halt execution and return an error message. This is the function of the ScriptTimeout property. The default is set at 90 seconds, but you can use the ScriptTimeout property to exceed that if you wish. If you create a buggy script, the timeout will at least prevent it from running on forever.

The ScriptTimeout Property

How long does it take to process a given script? Perhaps a better question would be this: is the time it takes to process a script fixed and determinable, does it always fall within a certain range, or is it highly variable or even random? The answer, of course, is that your scripts will not always take exactly the same time to process (because the processing time depends partly upon the current load on the server and its resources), but they should fall within a fairly predictable range. If they routinely exceed a reasonable amount of time, you should investigate creating faster-running components to handle some of the load.

Suppose you want to run a script beyond the default 90 seconds allowed by the server for ASP scripts? The ScriptTimeout property can be modified to enable scripts to run past the default. Scripts can run as long as 15 minutes for testing purposes, but longer than that is not advisable. You'll run into timeout functions in browsers or intermediate servers.

Here is a simple bit of code that sets the processing time for a script to five minutes:

```
<% ScriptTimeout = 300 %>
```

If you use this in a script, the script will keep processing until it is done or until it hits the five-minute mark, and then generate an error message. This is useful when you want to verify that processing was producing the correct results, even when the script runs beyond the default limit. However, if your script tends to run beyond the default limit, you need to investigate other ways of performing the processing, because 90 seconds is an awfully long time to keep your users waiting. By the way, even if you set processing for 10 or 15 minutes, you run the risk of the user's connection timing out.

The CreateObject Method

You can use the CreateObject method to create instances of objects within your ASP scripts, and these objects include applications (such as

Excel and other Office applications), components (such as page counters, ad rotators, and content rotators), and scripting objects (such as dictionaries and file objects). Some of these components (which will be covered in more detail in Modules 6, 7, and 8) provide the capability of persisting values beyond the scope of a session or application, even saving data in separate files on the server for use at any time.

The Page Counter Component   To demonstrate how object creation works, we'll create an instance of the Page Counter component. The Page Counter component counts the number of times a particular page is requested, and it saves that data in a text file on the server. Use code like the following to create an instance of the Page Counter:

```
<% Set objPageCounter = Server.CreateObject("MSWC.PageCounter") %>
```

Once you've created an instance of the Page Counter component, it's time to do something with it. The Page Counter component includes several methods to set the hit count, increment the hit count, and return the current hit count. They are

- **Reset()**   This method sets the hit count to zero for the current page, or you can include the path to another page to set that page's hit count to zero.

- **PageHit()**   This method increments the hit count for the current page.

- **Hits()**   This method returns the hit count for the current page, or for another page if you include the other page's path.

In practice, if you want to use this component to track visitors to a particular page, you could use code such as this (after creating the object):

```
<%
objPageCounter.PageHit()
vHits = objPageCounter.Hits()
Response.Write "You are visitor number " & vHits & "."
%>
```

Now proceed to the Execute and Transfer methods.

The Execute and Transfer Methods

The Execute and Transfer methods allow processes that were impossible with earlier versions of ASP—namely, transfer control and execution from one page to another without using the Response.Redirect method. The big benefit is that it is totally up to you, on the server side, how you want to accomplish the transfer. You don't have to go back to the user's browser and force it to another page to get the job done.

Hint

While Execute and Transfer are exciting and long-awaited methods, keep in mind that they do not work on previous versions. If you are using ASP 2.0 and IIS 4.0 or earlier, make sure you use the Response.Redirect method.

When you use the Execute method to transfer control to another page, execution on the current page stops and execution on the new page begins. The new page has control until execution finishes, at which time control passes back to the calling page. When you use the Transfer method, execution on the current page stops and control passes to the new page. When execution on the new page finishes, that's it. There is no further reference to the calling page unless you specifically include it (perhaps using another Transfer call).

Another benefit of using the Execute and Transfer methods is that the page context is transferred as well. All the variables that are available from the calling page are also available within the new page, and the browser doesn't recognize that it's working with a new page. The called pages work exactly the same as the calling pages, from the point of view of the browser.

To show how this works, let's build a few pages that transfer control back and forth a few times, while retaining the values passed to the first page by a form. Start by creating a simple form named index2.htm (use a clone of the form created in Module 3) with code like this:

```
<HTML><HEAD><TITLE>Using Execute and Transfer</TITLE></HEAD>
<BODY>
<FORM METHOD=POST ACTION="index2.asp">
Enter Your Name:<INPUT TYPE="text" NAME="yourname" SIZE=20>
<INPUT TYPE="submit" VALUE="Execute and Transfer">
<INPUT TYPE="reset" VALUE="Clear">
</FORM>
</BODY></HTML>
```

Next, create three scripts: one for processing the submission, and two more for demonstrating the Execute and Transfer methods, respectively. For processing the submission, make a file named index2.asp, using code like the following:

```
<%
vName = Request.Form("yourname")
Response.Write "Here is your original submission (your name): " & vName & "<P>"
Server.Execute("index2a.asp")
Server.Transfer("index2b.asp")
%>
```

This code writes back the original submission and then sends execution to the file named index2a.asp. This file is going to write back the original submission (even though it is another page, it still has access to the original submission data in the Request.Form collection) and then return control to the calling page (index2.asp). index2a.asp has code that looks like this:

```
<%
vNamea = Request.Form("yourname")
Response.Write "This is the second page to be executed, and here is your
original submission (your name) again: " & vNamea & "<P>"
%>
```

Notice that after index2a.asp executes, it automatically returns to index2.asp at the point where it left off, and then processes the next command in line—namely, the Transfer call to index2b.asp. index2b.asp then writes back the originally submitted data, and when it has finished execution, it dies right there. index2b.asp looks like this in code:

```
<%
vNameb = Request.Form("yourname")
Response.Write "This is the third page to be executed (using the Transfer
method) and after showing your name here execution will stop: " & vNameb & "<P>"
%>
```

1-Minute Drill

- **What is the syntax to create an instance of an object?**
- **In what version(s) of ASP does the Transfer method work?**
- **What does the Transfer method do that is so important?**

- **<% Set objname = Server.CreateObject("XXX.ObjectType") %>**
- **3.0 and above**
- **Transfers control of processing and variable values to another script**

The MapPath Method

Files inside an ASP application (the default virtual application) can be accessed by their virtual paths or URLs. Sometimes, though, you need to access files by their real (actual or physical) path. The MapPath method lets you get the physical path to a file from the server; this, in turn, lets you read and write files (using the proper built-in objects). I'm sure you're anxious to learn how to write files all over your server; but seriously, there are times when it is not only convenient but necessary.

For example, suppose you want to keep a set of text files related to your Web site outside the Web site itself, in a folder called WebsiteContentFiles. You might want to do this to keep them inaccessible to anyone who might try to guess their names, while making them accessible to properly authorized users via a URL (such as **http://mycomputer/webcontent**). At the same time, you might want to resolve the correct physical path to them for your own management purposes. If so, you can use code like the following to retrieve the physical path from the URL:

```
<%
vFilePath = "mycomputer/webcontent/webfile.htm"
Response.Write(Server.MapPath(vFilePath))
%>
```

The Response.Write method in the code just listed will display the physical path and filename of the file referenced by its URL. You'll put together a more elaborate and useful example in Module 6 when you use the FileSystemObject object and its colleagues.

The HTMLEncode Method

If you've ever written a Web page about HTML, or one that discusses HTML tags, you may have noticed that the code to produce the greater-than and less-than signs for display in a browser does not consist of the intended character, but rather a special character. Special characters direct the browser to display the correct character onscreen, instead of interpreting the character as the beginning of a new HTML tag.

For example, suppose you wanted to display the leading HTML tag in a page, the <HTML> tag. Use special characters to make the browser display the greater-than and less-than signs onscreen (like this: <HTML>).

4

Notice the use of the ampersand to start special characters and the use of the semicolon to end them.

Converting HTML Characters   Sometimes, when inserting data in the output stream, you want to display characters for HTML tags instead of letting the browser interpret them, and that is when the HTMLEncode method comes into play. Suppose you've set up a dictionary of HTML tags, and the person retrieving them can search by function to find the appropriate tag. You would want your output to consist of properly displayed HTML tags, and not have the browser interpret them. You might use code such as the following to produce this result (assume you've created a search form in HTML, pointed to the following script segment):

```
<%
vSearchFunctionText = Request.Form("searchentryfield")
%>
```

The code could then use the variable as a parameter to search your dictionary (a database) for the appropriate tag or tags. Next, you would include code to process the database output and return properly encoded HTML tags for display in the browser. Getting data from a database will be covered in later modules, so say a variable named vDatabaseOutput has been assigned a value from one of the records in the database. Subsequent code might look like this:

```
<%
Response.Write "The tag for that function is" &
Server.HTMLEncode(vDatabaseOutput)
%>
```

The URLEncode Method

Another encoding situation you might encounter (and perhaps more frequently than encoding HTML for display, depending upon your line of work) is encoding URLs. These days, URLs can include characters that are not legal within HTTP, such as spaces, exclamation points, and ampersands. Using the URLEncode method on a string representing a URL will remove illegal characters from the string and replace them with compliant characters. For example, suppose you want to place a link in your Web page that references another page with a name that contains a space. Perhaps the link reads **http://www.e4free.com/another page.htm**. You can't send this as is because the space will not be properly recognized. In this case, you could use the URLEncode method to properly encode the URL with a plus sign instead of the space. Examine some code to see how you would perform this conversion:

```
<A HREF="
<% Server.URLEncode("http://www.e4free.com/another page.htm") %>
">Click here to go to another page</A>
```

This method works in a straightforward manner. The output to the server from such a link would look like this:

```
http%3A%2F%2Fwww%2Ee4free%2Ecom%2Fanother+page%2Ehtm
```

You might ask, "What are these percent signs and numbers that have replaced the illegal characters in the URL?" The percent sign is an escape character. Illegal characters are represented by the percent sign followed by a hexadecimal number corresponding to the ANSI number of the illegal character. So if you have an exclamation point in your URL and you use Server.URLEncode to encode it, it will be converted to %21. You can find lists and further discussion of allowed and illegal characters at **http://www.ietf.org/rfc/rfc2396.txt**, or look for a discussion of HTTP 1.1 at **http://www.w3.org/**.

1-Minute Drill

- **With what does a special character start in HTML?**
- **What is the equivalent ANSI numerical special character for the special character >?**

The ASPError Object

The process of creating ASP applications inevitably involves errors, so there are error-handling features built into ASP (although they have been rather limited and crude in previous versions). The Server object has a

---

- &
- >

new method called GetLastError in ASP 3.0, and it provides fairly detailed information about errors encountered while processing your scripts. It works by creating and returning a reference to a new object called the ASPError object.

The ASPError object has nine properties, outlined here:

- **ASPCode**   This property is an integer value for the error number generated by ASP.

- **ASPDescription**   This property is a string value providing a description of the error.

- **Category**   This property is a string value showing the source of the error.

- **Column**   This property is an integer value for the character position within the file that generated the error.

- **Description**   This property is a string value consisting of a short description of the error.

- **File**   This property is a string value giving the name of the file that was being processed when the error occurred.

- **Line**   This property is an integer value for the line number within the file that generated the error.

- **Number**   This property is a number value that shows the standard COM error code.

- **Source**   This property is a string value returning the actual code that caused the error, if it is available.

IIS Error Handling

Trapping errors and generating error-specific feedback in response to them takes a little preliminary work on your part, due to the way the server processes ASP and IIS errors. Recall the familiar "404–File Not Found" error message? This message is displayed by the server when the page a user requested is not found (obviously), but the way this works may not be so obvious.

In fact, there are static HTML pages stored on the server that are mapped to each error status code returned, 404 being one of them. You can find them if you go to the folder WINNT\Help\iisHelp\common (there are other interesting HTML pages stored here as well; take a minute or two and review them while you're there). Most of them (and all of the status code error pages) can be located and opened in your browser, as Figures 4-1 and 4-2 show.

If you want to open the 404b.htm file in your browser, you will see the page depicted in Figure 4-2. This page opens automatically whenever IIS encounters this particular error; and because it is a plain HTML page, you can customize it to your heart's content. Many Web site hosting companies and ISPs customize these with company logos and custom messages; and, truthfully, some of these custom error pages provide better customer service in the form of more reassuring or understandable messages.

But these status codes do not become active when an ASP error occurs, except for the 500;100 error code. This code is mapped to a URL

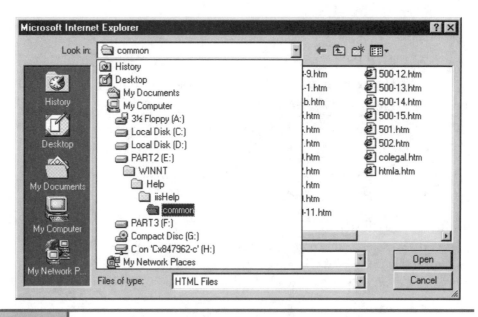

Figure 4-1 Finding error pages in Internet Explorer

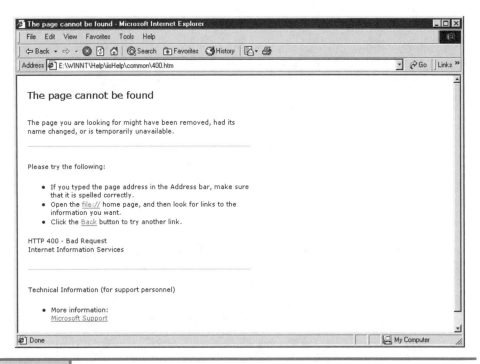

4

Figure 4-2 | **Opening the 404–File Not Found page**

rather than a file, and the default file there is named 500-100.asp. Notice the .asp extension. This is an ASP script, and you can replace this mapping with another pointing to a custom-made file of your own.

The exciting part of this mechanism is the way this mapping works. When an ASP error occurs, the file tied to the 500;100 error is activated and it receives the entire context (references to all variables) and a reference to the ASPError object *from the page where the error occurred.*

Note

ASP error file mapping can be set for your entire application or individually by folder within an application. You can set specific messages for any part of your application or a single set of messages for the entire thing.

Remapping the 500;100 File   To change the mapping of the
500;100 file, you'll need to use the Internet Services Manager. Open it
and find the Web site folder for which you want to change mappings.
Select that folder, and then open the Properties dialog box with the
Custom Errors tab showing, as in Figure 4-3.

Find and select the existing 500;100 HTTP error, and then click the
edit Properties button. The Error Mapping Properties dialog box will
appear (see the following illustration). Also shown is the new URL this
HTTP error is mapped to—namely, /ASPFTGU/CH04/AnError/
CustomError500-100.asp. Now you can place a customized error-trapping

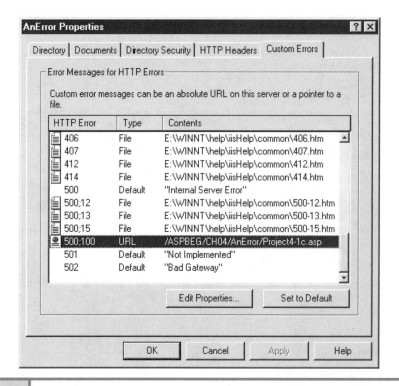

| **Figure 4-3** | The Properties dialog box showing the Custom Errors tab |

script in this folder and it will be activated whenever an ASP error is generated (but only for this folder).

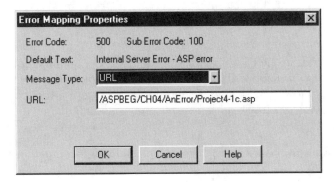

Trapping Errors

Now that you've set up a folder on the Web site for error handling, put a page in there to generate errors and demonstrate how they are trapped and handled. Start by making an HTML page named ErrorGeneratingPage2.htm, as follows:

```
<HTML><HEAD><TITLE>Custom ASP Error Page</TITLE></HEAD>
<BODY BGCOLOR="white" Text="black">
Click <A HREF="errormaker2.asp">here</A> to generate an error.
</BODY></HTML>
```

Next, build an ASP script page that contains some broken code to trigger an error when you reference it from the hyperlink. The code in it looks like this:

```
<HTML><HEAD><TITLE>Custom ASP Error Page</TITLE></HEAD>
<BODY BGCOLOR="white" Text="black">
<%
Response.Send "This makes an error"
%>
</BODY></HTML>
```

Since there is no collection, property, or method named "Send" for the Response object, this code generates an ASP error in the 500 group, with a subgroup of 100. When this error occurs, it is mapped to the 500;100 error message, and control is then transferred to the custom error script specified in the Internet Service Manager on the server.

Note

As it mentions in the IIS help files, Internet Explorer 5.0 will replace your custom error message with its own default message if your message is smaller than a certain file size. Make sure your custom error script is larger than 512 bytes, or it will not appear in the browser.

The code for your custom error script should look something like this (you can leave out the extra text about error file sizes):

```
<HTML><HEAD><TITLE>Custom ASP Error Page</TITLE></HEAD>
<BODY BGCOLOR="white" Text="black">
<H2>Whoops! Something went wrong. Talk to your system admin</H3>
An interesting note about custom error files is that Internet Explorer may
replace your custom files with its own error files if your files are smaller
than a certain size. The documentation says, "If you are using Internet
Explorer 5.0 with Windows, then Internet Explorer may replace the following
custom errors with its own HTTP error. If the file size of the custom error
is smaller than the size listed, the custom error will not be used:
403, 405, 410 - must be greater than 256 bytes
400, 404, 406, 408, 409, 500, 500.12, 500.13, 500.15, 501, 505 - must be
greater than 512 bytes"
</BODY></HTML>
```

Ask the Expert

Question: Server-side includes sound pretty good. Can I use them to build entire files? Can I use them to add repeating content to every page in a site, like Shared Borders in Microsoft FrontPage?

Answer: Yes, they can be used to build entire files; but a downside occurs for anyone coming after you who needs to interpret the file structure of your site: it will be more difficult than reading straight HTML. For recurring content, using include files makes your life much easier because you only have to change the content once, and it is automatically changed in every other place.

4

Question: Under what circumstances would I ordinarily use the config, flastmod, and fsize directives? They don't seem to offer too much for typical pages in an application.

Answer: You might find the other directives more useful within management pages, in which the site manager is interacting with the server, or for providing values for processing functions, rather than for providing information directly to users. If you are a programmer, you'll recognize the value of things like the echo directive and of being able to obtain the size and last modified date of files in your application.

Question: How long should I let my scripts run? Is it common to exceed the default 90 seconds? What happens if I accidentally create an infinite loop?

Answer: Unfortunately, it is possible to create infinite loops, just like with any programming language. That's why there is a built-in limit. However, it is bad form to make users wait at their browser for your scripts to complete processing for a minute or more. Most people will just click away, which is why it's a good idea to build in a check or two to see if the user is still connected. If you allow things to process for too long, such as when retrieving large amounts of data from a database, you could overload the user's browser. Unless it is critical, make sure your scripts all run under a minute, and preferably within a few seconds. Get a faster server if necessary.

Question: What's the advantage of using customer error messages? Aren't the standard error-page messages sufficient?

Answer: The error pages included with IIS are just a standard, and may not be the type of communication you want your users to see. For example, the standard error messages have no formatting that indicates what site they belong to; but you can customize them with your logo and layout, so at least they'll look more like the rest of your site. In addition, the standard error-page messages are designed to give clues about the nature of the problem, such as filenames and line numbers. First of all, showing these error messages to users is bad form; and second, sophisticated users may be able to use them as clues for hacking your site.

project4-1.zip

Project 4-1: Using SSI, the Server Object, and Errors

You've seen how some of the server-side include directives and Server object methods work, so let's go into detail on the more common ones. You'll now build a page that lets you display the output of the #config directive (used with the #flastmod directive), the output of the #echo directive, and generate errors and display all the ASPError properties.

Step-by-Step

1. Start with the HTML page that lets you perform these actions. Name it **Project4-1.htm**. Here is the code:

```
<HTML><HEAD><TITLE>Revealing SSI, the Server object, and Errors</TITLE>
</HEAD>
<BODY>
<H2>Server-side Includes</H2>
<H3>Showing the #config directive ouput for #flastmod</H3>
Click <A HREF="Project1a.shtm">here</A> to show #config directive output
formatting for #flastmod.
<H3>Showing the #echo directive output values</H3>
Click <A HREF="Project1b.shtm?MyString=This is it">here</A> to show HTTP
header info with #echo.
<H3>Showing values of the ASPError object</H3>
Click <A HREF="errormaker2.asp">here</A> to generate an ASP error and show
what's captured using the Project1c.asp file as a custom error message.
</BODY></HTML>
```

The code above builds three simple links referencing three different scripts, each of which demonstrates in detail how a directive or object works. The code underneath the three pages shows how they work. The Project4-1c.asp page is activated when the user clicks the third link, as the 500;100 error mapping has been changed to reflect the new filename. Figure 4-4 shows the browser view.

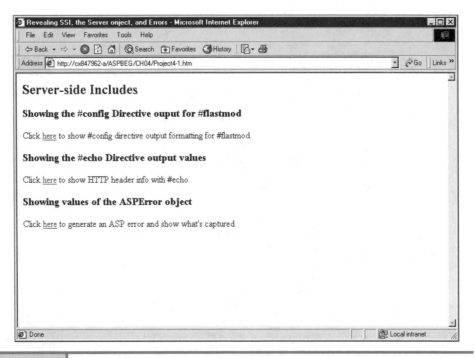

Figure 4-4   The HTML page referencing SSI and errors

2. You'll see the code for the first of the three links, Project4-1a.shtm. Notice that the filename has an .shtm extension rather than just plain .htm. This is because it uses a server-side include directive that must be of this type:

```
<HTML><HEAD><TITLE>The #config Directive ouput</TITLE></HEAD>
<BODY>
<TABLE border=1 cellpadding=5>
<TR><TD><B>Formatted Item</B></TD>
<TD><B>Value</B></TD><TD><B>Token</B></TD></TR>
<TR><TD>The abbreviated day is</TD><TD>
<B><!-- #config TIMEFMT="%a" --><!-- #flastmod FILE="Project4-1.htm" --></B>
</TD><TD><B>%a</B></TD></TR>
<TR><TD>The full day is</TD><TD>
<B><!-- #config TIMEFMT="%A" --><!-- #flastmod FILE="Project4-1.htm" --></B>
</TD><TD><B>%A</B></TD></TR>
<TR><TD>The abbreviated name of the month is </TD><TD>
<B><!-- #config TIMEFMT="%b" --><!-- #flastmod FILE="Project4-1.htm" --></B>
</TD><TD><B>%b</B></TD></TR>
<TR><TD>The full name of the month is </TD><TD>
```

```
<B><!-- #config TIMEFMT="%B" --><!-- #flastmod FILE="Project4-1.htm" --></B>
</TD><TD><B>%B</B></TD></TR>
<TR><TD>The current date and time is </TD><TD>
<B><!-- #config TIMEFMT="%c" --><!-- #flastmod FILE="Project4-1.htm" --></B>
</TD><TD><B>%c</B></TD></TR>
<TR><TD>The day of the month as a number is </TD><TD>
<B><!-- #config TIMEFMT="%d" --><!-- #flastmod FILE="Project4-1.htm" --></B>
</TD><TD><B>%d</B></TD></TR>
<TR><TD>The current hour in 24-hour format is </TD><TD>
<B><!-- #config TIMEFMT="%H" --><!-- #flastmod FILE="Project4-1.htm" --></B>
</TD><TD><B>%H</B></TD></TR>
<TR><TD>The current hour in 12-hour format is </TD><TD>
<B><!-- #config TIMEFMT="%I" --><!-- #flastmod FILE="Project4-1.htm" --></B>
</TD><TD><B>%I</B></TD></TR>
<TR><TD>The day of the year as a number is </TD><TD>
<B><!-- #config TIMEFMT="%j" --><!-- #flastmod FILE="Project4-1.htm" --></B>
</TD><TD><B>%j</B></TD></TR>
<TR><TD>The month as a number is </TD><TD>
<B><!-- #config TIMEFMT="%m" --><!-- #flastmod FILE="Project4-1.htm" --></B>
</TD><TD><B>%m</B></TD></TR>
<TR><TD>The current minute as a number is </TD><TD>
<B><!-- #config TIMEFMT="%M" --><!-- #flastmod FILE="Project4-1.htm" --></B>
</TD><TD><B>%M</B></TD></TR>
<TR><TD>The current designation AM or PM is </TD><TD>
<B><!-- #config TIMEFMT="%p" --><!-- #flastmod FILE="Project4-1.htm" --></B>
</TD><TD><B>%p</B></TD></TR>
<TR><TD>The current second as a number is </TD><TD>
<B><!-- #config TIMEFMT="%S" --><!-- #flastmod FILE="Project4-1.htm" --></B>
</TD><TD><B>%S</B></TD></TR>
<TR><TD>The week of the year as a number (starting with Sunday) is </TD><TD>
<B><!-- #config TIMEFMT="%U" --><!-- #flastmod FILE="Project4-1.htm" --></B>
</TD><TD><B>%U</B></TD></TR>
<TR><TD>The day of the week as a number (starting with Sunday as 0) is
</TD><TD>
<B><!-- #config TIMEFMT="%w" --><!-- #flastmod FILE="Project4-1.htm" --></B>
</TD><TD><B>%w</B></TD></TR>
<TR><TD>The week of the year as a number (starting with Monday as the first
day of the week) is </TD><TD>
<B><!-- #config TIMEFMT="%W" --><!-- #flastmod FILE="Project4-1.htm" --></B>
</TD><TD><B>%W</B></TD></TR>
<TR><TD>The current date is </TD><TD>
<B><!-- #config TIMEFMT="%x" --><!-- #flastmod FILE="Project4-1.htm" --></B>
</TD><TD><B>%x</B></TD></TR>
<TR><TD>The current time is </TD><TD>
<B><!-- #config TIMEFMT="%X" --><!-- #flastmod FILE="Project4-1.htm" --></B>
</TD><TD><B>%X</B></TD></TR>
<TR><TD>The year number without the century is </TD><TD>
<B><!-- #config TIMEFMT="%y" --><!-- #flastmod FILE="Project4-1.htm" --></B>
</TD><TD><B>%y</B></TD></TR>
<TR><TD>The year number with the century is </TD><TD>
<B><!-- #config TIMEFMT="%Y" --><!-- #flastmod FILE="Project4-1.htm" --></B>
</TD><TD><B>%Y</B></TD></TR>
<TR><TD>The time zone abbreviation is </TD><TD>
<B><!-- #config TIMEFMT="%z" --><!-- #flastmod FILE="Project4-1.htm" --></B>
</TD><TD><B>%z</B></TD></TR>
</TABLE>
</BODY></HTML>
```

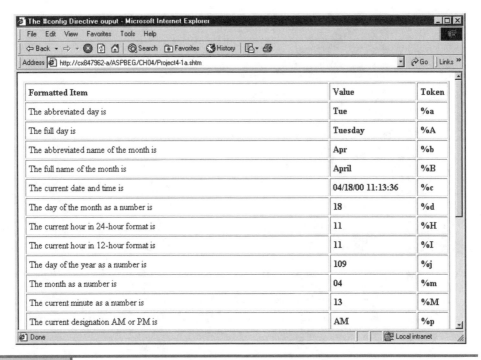

Figure 4-5 **Date and time formats using #config tokens**

Each row of the table shows a single date/time formatting style and its associated description and token. Figure 4-5 shows the browser view.

3. View the code for displaying HTTP header information. It looks like this:

```
<HTML><HEAD><TITLE>The #echo Directive ouput</TITLE></HEAD>
<BODY>
<TABLE border=1 cellpadding=5>
<TR><TD><B>HTTP Header Variable</B></TD>
<TD><B>Value</B></TD><TD><B>Token</B>
</TD></TR>
<TR><TD>The Authentication type is </TD><TD>
<B><!-- #echo VAR="AUTH_TYPE" --></B>
</TD><TD><B>AUTH_TYPE</B></TD></TR>
<TR><TD>The Authentication password is </TD><TD>
<B><!-- #echo VAR="AUTH_PASSWORD" --></B>
</TD><TD><B>AUTH_PASSWORD</B></TD></TR>
<TR><TD>The Authentication user is </TD><TD>
```

```
<B><!-- #echo VAR="AUTH_USER" --></B>
</TD><TD><B>AUTH_USER</B></TD></TR>
<TR><TD>The number of bytes in the body of the request is
</TD><TD>
<B><!-- #echo VAR="CONTENT_LENGTH" --></B>
</TD><TD><B>CONTENT_LENGTH</B></TD></TR>
<TR><TD>The MIME type for data sent as a POST request is
</TD><TD>
<B><!-- #echo VAR="CONTENT_TYPE" --></B>
</TD><TD><B>CONTENT_TYPE</B></TD></TR>
<TR><TD>The full physical path and filename of the document requested is
</TD><TD>
<B><!-- #echo VAR="DOCUMENT_NAME" --></B>
</TD><TD><B>DOCUMENT_NAME</B></TD></TR>
<TR><TD>The full virtual path and filename of the document requested is
</TD><TD>
<B><!-- #echo VAR="DOCUMENT_URI" --></B>
</TD><TD><B>DOCUMENT_URI</B></TD></TR>
<TR><TD>The date and time (unadjusted from Greenwich Mean Time) on the
server is </TD><TD>
<B><!-- #echo VAR="DATE_GMT" --></B>
</TD><TD><B>DATE_GMT</B></TD></TR>
<TR><TD>The date and time (adjusted from Greenwich Mean Time) is </TD><TD>
<B><!-- #echo VAR="DATE_LOCAL" --></B>
</TD><TD><B>DATE_LOCAL</B></TD></TR>
<TR><TD>The type of interface handling the request is </TD><TD>
<B><!-- #echo VAR="GATEWAY_INTERFACE" --></B>
</TD><TD><B>GATEWAY_INTERFACE</B></TD></TR>
<TR><TD>The list of MIME types the browser can handle is </TD><TD>
<B><!-- #echo VAR="HTTP_ACCEPT" --></B>
</TD><TD><B>HTTP_ACCEPT</B></TD></TR>
<TR><TD>The date and time when the file requested was last modified is
</TD><TD>
<B><!-- #echo VAR="LAST_MODIFIED" --></B>
</TD><TD><B>LAST_MODIFIED</B></TD></TR>
<TR><TD>The full virtual path and filename of the document requested is
</TD><TD>
<B><!-- #echo VAR="PATH_INFO" --></B>
</TD><TD><B>PATH_INFO</B></TD></TR>
<TR><TD>The full physical path and filename of the document requested is
</TD><TD>
<B><!-- #echo VAR="PATH_TRANSLATED" --></B>
</TD><TD><B>PATH_TRANSLATED</B></TD></TR>
<TR><TD>The value of any query string appended to the URL of the document
requested is </TD><TD>
<B><!-- #echo VAR="QUERY_STRING" --></B>
</TD><TD><B>QUERY_STRING</B></TD></TR>
<TR><TD>The value of any query string (unescaped) appended to the URL of the
document requested is </TD><TD>
<B><!-- #echo VAR="QUERY_STRING_UNESCAPED" --></B>
</TD><TD><B>QUERY_STRING_UNESCAPED</B></TD></TR>
<TR><TD>The IP address of the remote machine is </TD><TD>
<B><!-- #echo VAR="REMOTE_ADDR" --></B>
</TD><TD><B>REMOTE_ADDR</B></TD></TR>
<TR><TD>The host name or IP address of the network the request was made from
is </TD><TD>
<B><!-- #echo VAR="REMOTE_HOST" --></B>
```

```
</TD><TD><B>REMOTE_HOST</B></TD></TR>
<TR><TD>The name of the remote machine that made the request is
</TD><TD>
<B><!-- #echo VAR="REMOTE_USER" --></B>
</TD><TD><B>REMOTE_USER</B></TD></TR>
<TR><TD>The request method is </TD><TD>
<B><!-- #echo VAR="REQUEST_METHOD" --></B>
</TD><TD><B>REQUEST_METHOD</B></TD></TR>
<TR><TD>The full virtual path and filename of the script being run is
</TD><TD>
<B><!-- #echo VAR="SCRIPT_NAME" --></B>
</TD><TD><B>SCRIPT_NAME</B></TD></TR>
<TR><TD>The name of the server receiving the request is </TD><TD>
<B><!-- #echo VAR="SERVER_NAME" --></B>
</TD><TD><B>SERVER_NAME</B></TD></TR>
<TR><TD>The port number the request was received at is </TD><TD>
<B><!-- #echo VAR="SERVER_PORT" --></B>
</TD><TD><B>SERVER_PORT</B></TD></TR>
<TR><TD>The port number if the request used a secure protocol is
</TD><TD>
<B><!-- #echo VAR="SERVER_PORT_SECURE" --></B>
</TD><TD><B>SERVER_PORT_SECURE</B></TD></TR>
<TR><TD>The HTTP protocol used is </TD><TD>
<B><!-- #echo VAR="SERVER_PROTOCOL" --></B>
</TD><TD><B>SERVER_PROTOCOL</B></TD></TR>
<TR><TD>The name and version of the Web server is </TD><TD>
<B><!-- #echo VAR="SERVER_SOFTWARE" --></B>
</TD><TD><B>SERVER_SOFTWARE</B></TD></TR>
<TR><TD>The URL requested is </TD><TD>
<B><!-- #echo VAR="URL" --></B>
</TD><TD><B>URL</B></TD></TR>
<TR><TD>The name and value pairs for all HTTP environment variables not
included previously is </TD><TD>
<B><!-- #echo VAR="ALL_HTTP" --></B>
</TD><TD><B>ALL_HTTP</B></TD></TR>
</TABLE>
</BODY></HTML>
```

Each of the rows of the table displays a different HTTP header variable through the #echo directive, as shown in Figure 4-6.

4. Finally, use the same error-generator page used previously to generate an ASP error, but this time use the Server.GetLastError method to obtain all the properties in the ASPError object and display them in the browser. Remember, you're using a different ASP script than you did earlier in the module, so you must remap

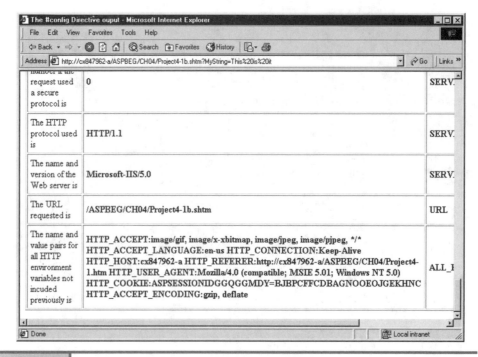

Figure 4-6 The #echo directive HTTP header data

that URL path and filename in the Properties dialog box of the folder you're using before this new file will work. You can see the browser view in Figure 4-7, and here's the code:

```
<HTML><HEAD><TITLE>Custom ASP Error Page</TITLE></HEAD>
<BODY BGCOLOR="white" Text="black">
<H2>Error!</H2>
An error was generated by the script you just tried to run, and here are the
details:<P>
<%
Set objASPError = Server.GetLastError()
%>
<TABLE border=1 cellpadding=5>
<TR><TD><B>Description</B></TD><TD><B>Property</B></TD><TD>
<B>Value</B></TD></TR>
<TR><TD>The error code is</TD><TD>ASPError.ASPCode</TD><TD>
<b><% Response.Write(objASPError.ASPCode) %></B></TD></TR>
<TR><TD>The error number is</TD><TD>ASPError.Number</TD><TD>
<b><% Response.Write(objASPError.Number) %></B></TD></TR>
<TR><TD>The error source is</TD><TD>ASPError.Source</TD><TD>
```

```
<b><% Response.Write(objASPError.Source) %></B></TD></TR>
<TR><TD>The error category is</TD><TD>ASPError.Category</TD><TD>
<b><% Response.Write(objASPError.Category) %></B></TD></TR>
<TR><TD>The error file is</TD><TD>ASPError.File</TD><TD>
<b><% Response.Write(objASPError.File) %></B></TD></TR>
<TR><TD>The error line is</TD><TD>ASPError.Line</TD><TD>
<b><% Response.Write(objASPError.Line) %></B></TD></TR>
<TR><TD>The error column is</TD><TD>ASPError.Column</TD><TD>
<b><% Response.Write(objASPError.Column) %></B></TD></TR>
<TR><TD>The error description is</TD><TD>ASPError.Description</TD><TD>
<b><% Response.Write(objASPError.Description) %></B></TD></TR>
<TR><TD>The error ASP descripton is</TD><TD>ASPError.ASPDescription</TD><TD>
<b><% Response.Write(objASPError.ASPDescription) %></B></TD></TR>
</TABLE>
</BODY></HTML>
```

4

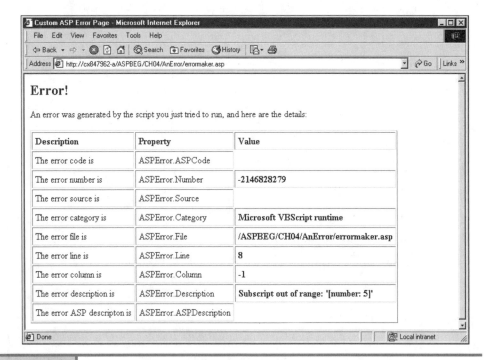

Figure 4-7   The ASPError object browser view

☑ *Mastery Check*

1. Server-side includes are a legacy technology. Besides the include directive, what other directives are there?

   A. Config, flastmod, fsize, echo, exec

   B. Config, flastmod, error, modify, exec

   C. Config, fsize, echo, exec, error

   D. None of the above

2. What is the proper extension for an included file that contains ASP code?

   A. .asp

   B. .txt

   C. .htm

   D. .shtm

3. What is the default timeout for ASP scripts, and what is the syntax for resetting the timeout property to 100 seconds?

   A. 1.5 minutes, and <% ScriptTimeout = 100 %>

   B. 900 seconds, and <% Set ScriptTimeout = 100 %>

   C. 90 seconds, and <% ScriptTimeout = 100 secs %>

   D. None of the above

4. Why is it sometimes necessary to encode HTML characters?

   A. Different browsers map HTML characters in different ways.

   B. Some browsers cannot process images correctly.

   C. HTML characters are sometimes part of a string, and will be misinterpreted by the browser if not encoded.

   D. All HTML characters must be encoded when coming from the server.

☑ Mastery Check

5. How can you, as the developer, change error messages the server generates?

A. Modify and recompile the source code.

B. Substitute edited HTML pages for the existing error pages.

C. Modify the existing error pages.

D. Map errors to pages outside the application to the operating system.

4

Module 5

The Application and Session Objects

The Goals of This Module

- Understand state and scope
- Understand application and session events and event handlers
- Learn how to code and work with application and session variables
- Review and practice using the collections of the Application and Session objects
- Create and modify the global.asa file for applications and sessions

163

Writing a single program or function becomes fairly routine after awhile. You decide what the function is supposed to do, declare your variables and build your logic, debug it, and it works. But suppose you must break the processing into several functions. This is a very common scenario in ASP, because often your scripts will need additional data from the user or from a database. Writing several scripts means there must be some way of keeping track of an individual user, as well as a means of storing values across the entire Web site application. This module covers the Application and Session objects, ASP's mechanism for establishing such control.

Visitor Status and State

After the Request and Response objects, the next two most important objects in ASP are the Application and Session objects. These objects do much of the work that allows you to set up your Web site as a real, application-style program, rather than just dynamic pages.

As a Web site application developer, one of your primary concerns is managing how your application deals with visitors. A prerequisite to dealing effectively with visitors is knowing who they are, and the status of their overall interaction with your application. The ASP Application and Session objects provide the information you need to continually gauge their status and create appropriate responses/processes to their inputs and actions.

The concept of *state* may seem a little fuzzy, so let's see if we can clarify it with an example or two. Suppose you run a convenience store and people show up, buy things, and leave without you ever knowing who they are. Although you could sell products this way, suppose someone came into the store and claimed they'd been there an hour ago and bought a product that is now on sale, and they want a discount. If you had no way to tell that this was true, you could call your situation stateless. Every visitor to your store is for all intents and purposes anonymous. On your Web site, even if you have hit-tracking statistics, you can't be sure it's the same computer hitting your site each time, much less the same person.

On the other hand, suppose every person swipes a club card when they enter your store (not just when they make a purchase) and your closed-circuit camera watches them as they browse through your store. If you can make a connection between who they are and what they do when in your store, you are cognizant of state. This puts you in a much better position to deal effectively with your customers. It works the same on the Web. If visitors must log in when they enter your site, or if you can capture a long-duration cookie, you can reference data from all their previous visits. Even if they don't have a cookie already set from a previous visit, you can still manage all their interactions if they'll let you set a cookie for the duration of their current visit.

ASP contains two state-related objects (Application and Session) because there are basically two kinds of state you want your Web application to be cognizant of at all times. One is the state of an individual user's visit, and the other is the state of all current users' visits. For example, if a person is on your site filling out a survey and he or she submits survey answers, you may want to provide the number of other folks who are currently also filling out and submitting survey forms, as well as the average responses. Therefore, you would need to know both the individual answers and the overall answers. Typical Web applications are constantly using variables like these. When the first page of your ASP Web application is requested for the first time, the Application object is created; and when an individual user first requests a page, an individual Session object is created.

Maintaining State with Cookies

When a visitor to your site first requests a page, ASP attempts to set a special cookie that lasts only the length of the visit (until the visitor goes to another site or closes his or her browser). You've seen this cookie (called ASPSESSIONID) in the HTTP headers shown in Module 3. It only lasts the current session because it has no Expires date, and it isn't visible in the Request or Response Cookies collections.

ASP generates this cookie automatically to support state within your application for each user session. Of course, if the user's browser doesn't allow cookies (if the cookie is too old), you won't be able to track interactions with them, and you'll be less capable of dealing effectively with them.

---**Hint**------------------------------------

The automatically created ASPSESSIONID cookies only provide state for the current session, not multiple sessions over time. You'll want to set up longer duration cookies with the Request and Response Cookies collections, with an expiration date fairly far into the future, to track users across several sessions.

Scope

Web applications often need data available that encompasses all current users, as well as individual users. If you've ever programmed, you understand the concept of global (public) and local (private) scope. Global variables make their values available to everything in an application, while local variables are only available within their own procedure.

In a similar fashion, data residing in the Application object is available across the entire Web application, while data residing in an individual Session object is only available to that individual session. The Application object is created once as soon as the first user requests a page, and Session objects are created for the first and every subsequent user. Session objects are closed when users leave the site or close their browsers, while the Application object only closes after all active Sessions are closed or the server is shut down.

Default and Virtual ASP Applications

Upon installation of Windows 2000, IIS, and ASP, a default Web site is created, and it is set up as a Web application (see Figure 5-1). In the Default Web Site Properties dialog box, on the Home Directory tab, the name given this application is Default Application. Within the default application on the root folder you can also set up virtual applications in subfolders. Virtual applications are able to access variables in the default application, but not vice versa.

If a virtual application happens to store a variable with the same name as an existing variable in the default application, it can only see its own variable (for that name). Other virtual applications in the default application can still see the original global variable for that name. It's probably best in most situations to use different names for variables in the default and related virtual applications.

5

Figure 5-1   The Default Web Site Properties dialog box

As mentioned in Module 1, the Internet Services Manager can be used to create virtual applications, remove virtual applications, and set properties for virtual applications (and the default application as well). Application and Session objects are created when a page is first requested, and the Request and Response objects operate within their individual sessions, as well as within the overall application. The Server, Application, Session, Request, and Response objects all work together to provide true application-style functionality at your Web site. Understanding the collaborative roles of these objects is key to understanding ASP in general.

The Application Object

The Application object has no properties, but it does have collections, methods, and events. It provides a global storage space for variables (all of type Variant, with subtypes for each data type) that can house text, numbers, dates, arrays, and pointers to COM objects. Within the root folder of an application you will place a special file named global.asa. This file has several functions, including initialization of Application and Session variables. We'll discuss (and provide examples of) global.asa as we progress through the module.

The Application Object's Events

Events are like triggers. They are simply a way of defining things that can happen to objects. For example, you are probably familiar with the onClick event for buttons in many programming environments. It occurs whenever the user clicks a button. The Application object is associated with two events, providing a means of initiating actions whenever an application starts or ends. The events are

- **onStart** This event occurs when the application starts, before the first requested page is executed and before any sessions are created.

- **onEnd** This event occurs when the application ends and after any sessions have ended.

You'll put these two events to work in a global.asa file to set up some objects and variables in the Application object, and you'll also use similar events to do the same kinds of things with the Session object.

Application Collections

The Application object offers two collections:

- **Contents** This collection consists of the variables in the Application object that are not specified using the <OBJECT> tag.

- **StaticObjects** This collection consists of the variables in the Application object specified using the <OBJECT> tag.

The global.asa File

For our next exercise, let's create a global.asa file in the default root directory of your Web site and put some example objects and variables in it. The global.asa file is at the root of your default directory because its role is to manage the operating environment of your application. Although you don't have to have a global.asa file in your application to run ASP code, and although you're starting with a very simple global.asa file, you'll find that this file can be used for many important management tasks and can become fairly complex.

In the global.asa file, you'll use the MyInfo component (we'll delve into components more in Modules 7 and 8) and a simple variant containing a string. To create the global.asa file, you can simply open Notepad and begin writing code like this:

```
<OBJECT ID="objMyInfo" RUNAT="server" SCOPE="Application"
PROGID="MSWC.MyInfo">
</OBJECT>
<SCRIPT Language="VBScript" RUNAT="server">
Sub Application_onStart()

objMyInfo.vDailyBanner = "The Big News Today is..."

Dim vMyVar
vMyVar = "Some text stored in the Application"
Application("storedtext") = vMyVar

End Sub
</SCRIPT>
```

> **Starts Application and creates object, creates variable, and stores text string.**

In the start of the global.asa file, you have placed the <OBJECT> tag, to instantiate the MyInfo component. Whenever your application starts, it will build the MyInfo component with an ID of objMyInfo. Next, you insert some script to run at the server that includes a subroutine triggered when the onStart event occurs for the Application object. You can add properties to the instance of MyInfo you've created by simply naming them and adding values, as you did in the line that starts with objMyInfo.vDailyBanner. This line creates a property named vDailyBanner and sets it equal to a string of text whenever the application starts. You can find the properties and their values in an XML file under your WINNT\system32\inetserv folder, named MyInfo.xml (but it won't be there until you run the component at least once).

The next step is to create a variable named vMyVar and then fill it with a short string. You can add the contents of this variable to the application under the name "storedtext" using the line Application("storedtext") = vMyVar.

After that, just end the subroutine and then end the script section and you're good to go. You now have data inside your global.asa file that is available globally, but can be changed (in the MyInfo component), and also a simple variable (vMyVar) that can be read out.

To see how these objects and variables can provide their data or allow their data to be changed, let's use a couple of simple ASP files to retrieve and change them. First, use Notepad to create the following file and name it index.asp:

```
<HTML>
<HEAD><TITLE>Showing Application Variables</TITLE></HEAD>
<BODY>
<H2>The Daily Banner Headlines</H2>
<%
objMyInfo.vDailyBanner = "My Personal News is"
vDayBan = objMyInfo.vDailyBanner
Response.Write(vDayBan) & ": "
vMVr = Application.Contents("storedtext")
Response.Write(vMVr) & "<BR>"

%>
</BODY>
</HTML>
```

Retrieves value of Application variable in Contents collection.

The first line of ASP scripting writes a new value to the vDailyBanner property of the MyInfo object named objMyInfo. This new value is then available to any other pages that reference the value of that object, unless they change it themselves, in which case the value they insert is available to all other pages. In practical terms, if there is a value that simply accumulates for all users referencing it (such as total number of visitors to a given page), this would work well for keeping that sort of information.

The next lines collect the value of the vDailyBanner property from the objMyInfo object and write it back to the user, demonstrating that the value has been set and then referenced. Following that, you also gather and write back the value of the storedtext variable from the Contents collection of the Application object.

If there were more than one variable in the Contents collection of the Application object, you could use code such as the following to iterate through those variables and write out their names and values:

```
For Each collItem in Application.Contents
Response.Write "The variable name is '" & collItem & "'and the value in it
is: "
vMVr = Application.Contents(collItem)
Response.Write(vMVr) & "<BR>"
Next
```

1-Minute Drill

- **What does the Application.Contents collection contain?**
- **What does the Application.StaticObjects collection contain?**

Application Methods

The Application object also includes several methods that are very handy for managing the Contents collection. As you've seen, you can add a variable to the Contents collection by giving it a name and a value (like this: Application("*variablename*") = *value*). Suppose you want to get rid of a variable? There are a couple of methods you can use to do that, discussed shortly.

Another issue that arises with Application variables, because of their global nature, is who has control. If user1 accesses the value of a variable and, after some processing, tries to reset the value, what happens if user2 is trying to do the same thing at the same time? The Application object has two methods that help you manage concurrency in a simple but effective way.

Here are the methods of the Application object:

- **Contents.Remove("variablename")**   This method lets you remove a variable by name.

- **Contents.RemoveAll()**   This method lets you remove all the variables in the Contents collection.

- **The variables that are not specified using the <OBJECT> tag**
- **The variables that are specified using the <OBJECT> tag**

● **Lock()**   This method lets you lock the Application object so that only the current page can access the Contents collection.

● **Unlock()**   This method unlocks the Application object.

Removing variables is pretty straightforward; just type **Application. Contents.Remove** followed by the variable name, or simply use the RemoveAll method to remove all variables. Of course, it helps to know the name of the variable if you want to remove a specific one. Locking the Application object is also pretty straightforward; but like any system of locking and unlocking, it is possible to get users into a situation in which each is waiting for the other to release a variable. Therefore, it's important to always use the Lock and Unlock methods together, and only perform actions on one variable at a time.

Let's try removing variables and locking/unlocking the Application object. First you'll create a simple form for entering new variables names and values, and then you'll create a script to respond to the request. Use the following code to create the form:

```
<HTML><HEAD><TITLE>Showing Application Variables</TITLE></HEAD>
<BODY>
<H2>Creating Messages Accessible to Everyone</H2>
<B>Add a variable and value to the Application object</B><P>
<FORM ACTION="index2.asp" METHOD=POST>
<TABLE><TR><TD>
Name Your Variable:</TD><TD><INPUT TYPE="text" SIZE=20
NAME="newvariable"></TD></TR>
<TR><TD>Enter Your Value:</TD><TD><INPUT TYPE="text" SIZE=50
NAME="newvalue"></TD></TR>
<TR><TD><BR></TD><TD><INPUT TYPE="submit" VALUE="Add Variable and Value">
<INPUT TYPE="reset" VALUE="Clear"></TD></TR></TABLE>
</FORM>
</BODY></HTML>
```

The HTML code just builds a simple page and puts a form inside a table to arrange it nicely on the page. The form contains two text boxes: one for the name of the variable and one for the message you want to insert into the variable. Naturally, each text box has a distinct name, so the script on the other end can process them into the new variable. The Web page is shown in Figure 5-2.

Now let's build a script that creates the new variable and then shows it has been created by telling what the name and value are. Use the following code:

```
<HTML><HEAD><TITLE>Showing Application Variables</TITLE></HEAD>
<BODY>
<H2>The New Application Variable and Its Value</H2>
<%
vNewVariable = Request.Form("newvariable")
vNewValue = Request.Form("newvalue")
Application.Lock
Application(vNewVariable) = vNewValue
Application.Unlock
For Each collItem in Application.Contents
    If collItem = vNewVariable Then
          Response.Write "Your new variable is named '" &
collItem & "'and the value in it is: "
          vNVal = Application.Contents(collItem)
          Response.Write(vNVal) & "<BR>"
    End If
    Next
    %>
</BODY></HTML>
```

> Locks the Application to set a new value for **vNewVariable**.

Figure 5-2 | HTML form for creating a new Application variable

The responding script starts with ordinary HTML code to create a page, and then sets a couple of variables (vNewVariable and vNewValue) to the value of the text boxes coming from the form. Once these values are set, the Application is locked, the new variable is created, and the new value is added, then the Application is unlocked. Following that, the ASP script iterates through the Application Contents collection until it finds the one whose name matches the name given by the user (using a For Each...Next loop and the If...Then conditional processing). The next lines respond to the user with the name of the variable and the value assigned by the user.

project5-1.zip

Project 5-1: Using The Application Object

The Application object is very useful for holding variables and values that are accessible to every page/user in an application, and at some point you may like to have an easy way of finding out what these variables/values are and removing some of them. As the application manager, it's easy to create a page for yourself that lets you see what is currently available and remove those you'd like to remove. These are called application management pages.

Step-by-Step

1. Making an application management page means you'll be creating a page that gives you capabilities other users might not have. In this case, you're going to make the management page display all current variables and easily remove those you choose. The code looks like this (see Figure 5-3 for a view of the application management page in the browser):

```
<HTML><HEAD><TITLE>Application Management</TITLE>
<META http-equiv="Content-Type" content="text/html; charset=iso-8859-1">
</HEAD>
<BODY BGCOLOR="#EEFFFF">
<FONT SIZE="+2" face="Arial, Helvetica, sans-serif"><b>An Application
Management Page</b></FONT>
<HR ALIGN="left" WIDTH="50%">
<TABLE BORDER=1 cellpadding=10><TR><TD COLSPAN=2 ALIGN=center><B>Current
Variables and Values</B></TD></TR>
<TR><TD><B>Variable</B></TD><TD><B>Value</B></TD></TR>
<% For Each collItem in Application.Contents
```

```
vVVal = Application.Contents(collItem)
Response.Write "<TR><TD>" & collItem & "</TD>"
Response.Write"<TD>" & vVVal & "</TD></TR>"
Next
%>
</TABLE>
<br>
<FORM METHOD="POST" ACTION="appman1.asp">
Remove Value from Application
<SELECT NAME="select" size="1" MULTIPLE>
<%
For Each collItem in Application.Contents
            Response.Write "<OPTION>" & collItem & "</OPTION>"
Next
%>
</SELECT>
<INPUT TYPE="submit" VALUE="REMOVE">
</FORM>
<HR WIDTH="50%" ALIGN="left">
</BODY></HTML>
```

5

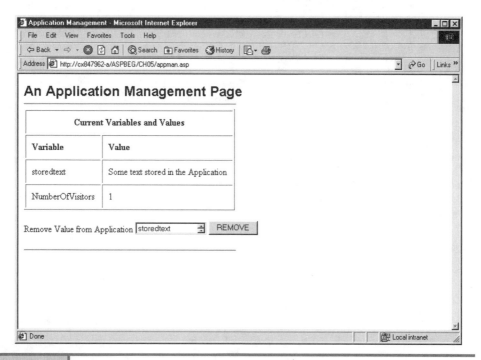

Figure 5-3   An application management page

2. The page that actually does the removing will have a section in it (inside the typical HTML code) that looks like this (see Figure 5-4 for a page view):

```
<%
Application.Lock
Application.Contents.Remove(Request.Form("select"))
Application.Unlock
%>
The variable has been removed. Click
<A HREF="appman.asp">here</A> to go back to the Application Management page.
```

3. The main application management page begins with a table listing all current Application variables and their values. This table list includes variables that were initialized when the application was first started, as well as any variables that have been added by users along the way. Each variable/value row of the table was created using the familiar iteration procedure through each item in the Application.Contents collection.

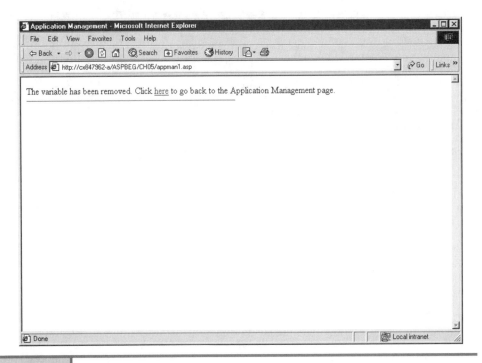

Figure 5-4   The removal response

4. Below the variable/value table is a control comprised of a drop-down box or menu that contains, as the name of each option, the name of each variable in the Application.Contents collection.

5. When the REMOVE button is clicked, the name of that option is sent back to the appman1.asp script. The appman1.asp script locks the application, removes the variable named in Request.Form("select"), and unlocks the application. It then displays a message to the user that the variable has been removed and a link pointing back to the application management page (appman.asp). When the user returns to the application management page, the table list is refreshed (and the drop-down menu as well).

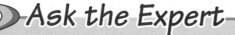

Ask the Expert

Question: I understand the concepts of applications and sessions as a means of making a collection of scripts work together, but I'm not so sure about the global.asa file. What is the basic role of the global.asa file, and are there any other weird files like this in ASP?

Answer: I felt the same way about the global.asa file when I first discovered it. In fact, it didn't occur to me that there was even a need for this cohesiveness until I'd built a few scripts and then wondered how I was going to get them to "talk" to each other.

The global.asa file is the only one of its kind, and it serves as a central point of contact for all the scripts in your application's root directory. When the application is first started (upon the first request for a page when the server is started), the global.asa file is activated. If you have no code attached to the OnStart and OnEnd events, of course, nothing exciting happens. But if you do, you can set initial conditions for Application and Session variables, as well as provide a common ground for further application and session interactions. Think of it as providing the same kind of control that is taken for granted on application programs you run from your desktop computer.

Question: I'm somewhat new to programming, but I've run into events more than once. What exactly are they, and how do they differ from old-style programming?

Answer: In traditional programming, a single, monolithic program would contain all the code required to run the application, including all interactions with users. This could be incredibly difficult to construct and debug, especially if several programmers worked on a project, because there might be connections between many parts of the program that worked, but made no logical sense. If one part were changed slightly, it could have unforeseen and disastrous effects on other parts of the program.

Object-oriented programming builds functions into small modules that can operate on their own in response to events. Each object contains the code it needs to accomplish its functions, as well as the data required. It watches for things to happen that initiate its functions, by way of events. For instance, if an object must respond when it is clicked, it must have a built-in event (typically called onClick) that watches for the mouse to be over it and recognizes when the user clicks the mouse button. Then the object's code runs.

In the same way, the onStart and onEnd events watch for the beginning and ending of applications and sessions, and run the appropriate code when these events occur. The big benefit of programming in this fashion is that it is much easier to program and debug applications when each object is small and independently operated.

ASP Sessions

Like the Application object, the Session object exists to make variables available and to perform functions such as initializing those variables when a session is started. The primary difference between a session and an application is that the application is global, while the session is local to its user. Variables found in the session are accessible only by the user who started the session.

ASP creates sessions by default whenever a user first requests a page (and does so automatically for each user who requests a page). Upon reflection you will see that this implies some exchange of identifying information between the server and the user, so the server can identify each individual user from the others. The identifying information that is passed is a special cookie, as mentioned previously. If cookies are disabled, no session can be established.

Enabling and Disabling Sessions

Processing cookies each time a page is requested consumes server resources and can be disabled if you choose. If you happen to know that some of your pages perform actions that require no sessions to get the job done, you can turn off sessions for those pages with a processing directive, like so:

```
<% ENABLESESSIONSTATE=False %>
```

You can also turn off sessions for the entire application by changing the Enable Session State setting. To perform this action, start the Internet Services Manager (by clicking Start|Programs|AdministrativeTools| InternetServices Manager) and open the Default Web Site Properties dialog box, as shown in Figure 5-5.

Next, click the Configuration button and click the App Options tab to open the Application Configuration dialog box, shown in Figure 5-6.

Figure 5-5   The Default Web Site Properties dialog box

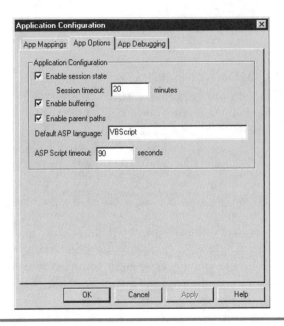

Figure 5-6   The Application Configuration dialog box

You should be able to enable or disable session state by selecting or deselecting the check box, and you should also be able to change the default session timeout.

The Session Object

Like the Application object, the Session object has several events associated with it that allow you to initiate actions when a session starts or ends. Sessions start with the first page requested and end under the following circumstances:

- The session times out before the page is loaded.

- The Session.Abandon method is called.

You can set the timeout period using the Application Configure dialog box, or you can set it for individual pages using the Session.Timeout property. Either way, it provides a convenient way of managing user sessions within your application.

Session Event Handlers

The two session event handlers are onStart and onEnd. They work in the same fashion as the Application object onStart and onEnd events, and are utilized from the global.asa file. To illustrate how they work, you can build in a useful little function that counts the total number of visitors to the site during the current run of the application. Start by making some modifications to the global.asa file, with code like this inserted into the Application_onStart subroutine to initialize the global counter variable:

```
Application("NumberOfVisitors") = 0
```

This just adds a variable named "NumberOfVisitors" to the Application.Contents collection when the application starts and sets the value to zero. To make the counter variable count, you'll also need to add some code to the global.asa file such as the following:

```
Sub Session_onStart()
Application.Lock
nVisitors = Application("NumberOfVisitors") + 1
Application("NumberOfVisitors") = nVisitors
Application.Unlock
End Sub
```

This code locks the application and increments the counter variable's value by one, and then unlocks the application. Last, you'll make a page for users that tells them the current total number of visitors, using code like this:

```
<HTML><HEAD><TITLE>Session Events</TITLE></HEAD>
<BODY>
<FONT SIZE="+2" face="Arial, Helvetica, sans-serif"><b>Your
Session</b></FONT><P>
There are currently
<%
objVarVal = Application("NumberOfVisitors")
Response.Write(objVarVal)
%>
 visitors in this Web site.<BR>
</BODY>
</HTML>
```

5

This code retrieves the current value of the "NumberOfVisitors" variable and displays it on the page, inside a text message describing the value they are seeing.

Session Properties

The Session object includes four properties:

- **CodePage**   This property sets the code page as a number representing the character set that will be used in the browser when displaying the page. For example, ANSI code page 1252 is used to display pages in American English.

- **LCID**   This property sets the locale identifier. Each locale has a unique identifier number that refers to such things as the type of currency symbol to use with a page.

- **SessionID**   This property contains the session identifier number (of type *long*) that is generated by the server upon creation of the session. All SessionIDs are unique within an instance of the Application object, but may be used repeatedly across consecutive instances of an application.

- **Timeout**   This property can be used to set or retrieve the time a session will last before automatically timing out if no actions are performed.

Knowing the SessionID of a user will come in very handy as your applications get more complex, and it can also be useful to know the code page, LCID, and timeout he or she is using. Let's make your user session page display these values.

Create a new ASP page and call it session2.asp. Put code like the following in it (inside the usual beginning and ending HTML tags):

```
<FONT SIZE="+2" face="Arial, Helvetica, sans-serif"><b>Your Session
Properties</b></FONT><P>
<TABLE><TR>
<%
vCodePage = Session.CodePage
vLCID = Session.LCID
vSessionID = Session.SessionID
vTimeout = Session.Timeout
```

```
Response.Write "<TD>The Code Page you are using is: </TD><TD><B>" &
vCodePage & "</B></TD></TR>"
Response.Write "<TD>Your Locale Identifier is: </TD><TD><B>" & vLCID &
"</B></TD></TR>"
Response.Write "<TD>Your Session ID is: </TD><TD><B>" & vSessionID &
"</B></TD></TR>"
Response.Write "<TD COLSPAN=2>Your Session will time out in <B>" & vTimeout
& "</B> minutes with no further use.</TD></TR>"
%>
</TABLE>
```

This code lays out the variables and their values in a borderless table by setting the value of variables equal to the value of the session properties for code page, LCID, SessionID, and Timeout, as shown in Figure 5-7.

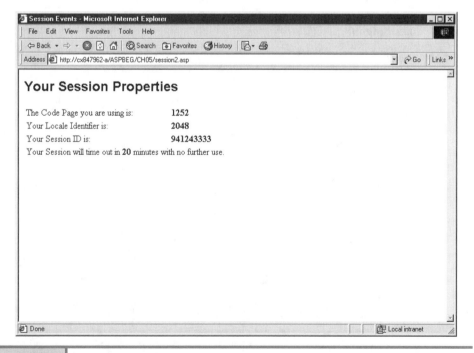

| **Figure 5-7** | Session properties displayed |

1-Minute Drill

● **What is the Session.LCID used for?**

● **What is the Session.CodePage used for?**

Session Collections

Like the Application object, the Session object has two collections: the Contents collection and the StaticObjects collection. The Contents collection contains all the variables and their values that are generated in a given session, but are not defined by the <OBJECT> tag. The StaticObjects collection contains all the variables that are generated in a given session and are defined by the <OBJECT> tag. The values in the variables can be read using any of the methods we discussed for the Application object. The values in the Contents collection can be changed, while the values in the StaticObjects collection remain static (no surprise there).

Session Methods

Finally, the Session object also has methods for removing variables and for ending the session. They are

● **Contents.Remove("variablename")**   This method removes the variable you have named.

● **Contents.RemoveAll()**   This method removes all variables from the Contents collection.

● **Abandon()**   This method ends the current user session and destroys the Session object when the page has finished executing.

The usage of the Contents.Remove and Contents.RemoveAll methods is the same as for the Application object, while the code for using the Abandon method is simply

```
<% Session.Abandon %>
```

● **The locale identifier, a unique identifier number that refers to such things as the type of currency symbol**
● **The code page, a number representing the character set that will be used in the browser**

Hint

Making a call to the Session.Abandon method works, but only after the calling page finishes executing. To ensure that it works properly, make it the last call on a page or exit the page after the call.

project5-2.zip

Project 5-2: Using the Session Object in an Application

Although we haven't covered common components or databases in detail, the ASP objects discussed so far can still provide quite a bit of functionality. In this project, we'll go a little further than we have with other project sections, in that we'll end up with a functional application.

5

Step-by-Step

You're going to make a rudimentary e-commerce shopping-cart application, with a management area to place products online and check current orders; a process for users to become shoppers; and the capability for users to add items to their baskets, remove items from their baskets, calculate their total at any time, and place their orders. It won't be secure (or very fancy, either), but we'll get to those things in later modules.

Note

After you've read this script from beginning to end and tested it out, you'll notice that it doesn't save the contents of the variables (products or orders) from one running of the application to the next—a major weak point. Another limitation of this shopping cart application is that it allows only one product to be ordered per order. We'll examine how to save the contents of variables across sessions and application instances (as well as add more than one product to an order) in the modules on components (Modules 7 and 8), and how to insert values directly into a database in Modules 9, 10, and 11).

1. The only changes you'll need to make to your global.asa file are the following, inside the Application_onStart and Session_onStart event, respectively:

```
vMyVar = Now()
Application("startdate") = vMyVar

vMySVar = Now()
Session("startdate") = vMySVar
Session("ordercounter") = 1
```

2. To begin your little e-commerce adventure, let's make a management page on which you (the store manager) can

   ● Put products online.

   ● Remove products.

   ● Check to see how many orders are posted.

   ● Check the current value of those orders.

   Since this is a rather long file, we'll break it into sections and describe the functions of each one.

3. The first section of code begins the management page and immediately looks for any submissions from the management page itself (in case you have added or removed a product, which you'll be doing further along). It checks for a value of Add in the Request.Form collection member AddProduct. AddProduct is the name of the button used to add products, and when it is clicked it returns a value of Add.

4. It does the same for the button named RemoveProduct, and then uses the VBScript flow control structure Select Case to determine the actions to take in either case. If a product is to be added, it creates an Application variable of type Variant with the appropriate product name and assigns the posted values (again taken from the Request.Form collection) to it. If a product is to be removed, it removes the Variant variable using the product identified in the drop-down list (which we will also come to later in this script).

```
<html><head><title>The Ecommerce Adventure Store</title>
<meta http-equiv="Content-Type" content="text/html; charset=iso-8859-1">
</head>
<body bgcolor="#CCFFCC">
```

```
<%
If Request.Form("AddProduct") = "Add" Then
     vButtonPressed = "AddProduct"
Else
     If Request.Form("RemoveProduct") = "Remove" Then
          vButtonPressed = "RemoveProduct"
     End If
End If
Select Case vButtonPressed
     CaCase "AddProduct"
     Dim vArProd(2)
     vArProd(0) = Request.Form("pname")
     vArProd(1) = Request.Form("pprice")
     vArProd(2) = Request.Form("pshipping")
     Application(Request.Form("pnumber")) = vArProd
     Case "RemoveProduct"
     Application.Contents.Remove(Request.Form("product"))
End Select
%>
```

5. Next, the page continues with a welcoming statement and begins a table that shows current conditions such as the current date and start time of the application:

```
<p><font size="+1"><b><font face="Arial, Helvetica, sans-serif"
size="+2">Welcome to the Ecommerce Adventure shopping cart
manager!</font><font face="Arial, Helvetica, sans-serif"><br>
</font></b></font><font face="Arial, Helvetica, sans-serif"><i><b><font
color="#333399">We make managing your shopping cart a real
adventure!!</font></b></i></font></p>
<hr>
<p>     The Ecommerce Adventure store shopping cart
manager provides a variety of tools to manage your online store and shopping
cart:</p>
<table border=1 cellpadding=5>
<tr><td align=center colspan=4><B>Statistics</b></td></tr>
<tr><td>Today's Date</td><td><b><% Response.Write(Date) %></b></td>
<td>Application Start Date/Time</td><td><b>
<% Response.Write(Application("startdate")) %></b></td></tr>
```

6. The vital statistics of the application are displayed each time the management page is opened or refreshed. These include the current number of orders and the total value of those orders, displayed in table form by the next portion of the script:

```
<tr><td>Total Orders</td><td>
<%
ordercntr = 0
pricecntr = 0
For Each collItem in Application.Contents
     If Mid(collItem,1,1) = "O" Then
          ordercntr = ordercntr + 1
          vArcosts = Application(collItem)
          pricecntr = pricecntr + vArcosts(1)
          pricecntr = pricecntr + vArcosts(2)
     End If
Next
Response.Write(ordercntr)
%>
</td>
<td>Total Sales</td><td>
<%
Response.Write(pricecntr)
%>
</td></tr>
```

7. The current products on the list are taken from existing Application variables with this next script segment:

```
<tr><td align=center colspan=4><b>Current List of
Products</b></td></tr>
<tr><td><b>ProductID</b></td><td><b>Name</b></td><td><b>Price</b></td><td><b>Shipping Cost</b></td></tr>
<%
For Each collItem in Application.Contents
     If Mid(collItem,1,7) = "Product" Then
          vPnumber = Application(collItem)
          vPname = vPnumber(0)
          vPprice = vPnumber(1)
          vPshipping = vPnumber(2)
          Response.Write "<tr><td>" & collItem & "</td><td>"
          & vPname & "</td><td>" & vPprice & "</td><td>" &
          vPshipping & "</td></tr>"
     End If
Next
%>
```

8. To add products to the existing products, you must provide a means to create new Application variables and insert the proper data in them. This next script section displays text boxes (and their respective labels) in table format and submits them to the same script (see the If...Then and Select Case in the Shopping Manager Initial Processing code for the corresponding processing statements) when the Add button is clicked:

```
<td colspan=4><b>Add a Product</b></td></tr>
<tr><td><b>ProductID</b></td><td><b>Name</b></td><td><b>Price</b></
td><td><b>Shipping Cost</b></td></tr>
<tr><td><form method=post action="shopman1.asp">
<input type="text" name="pnumber" size=10 value="ProductXX"></td>
<td><input type="text" name="pname" size=20></td>
<td><input type="text" name="pprice" size=10></td>
<td><input type="text" name="pshipping" size=10></td></tr>
<tr><td colspan=4><input type="submit" name="AddProduct"
value="Add"></td></tr>
```

9. Like the previous segment, the following script segment uses form elements to accomplish its work. It creates a drop-down box built from the appropriate Application variables (which it finds by keying on the first 7 characters of the variable name: Product) and then submits that value to the same script for removal:

```
<tr><td colspan=2>Remove a Product</td><td colspan=2>
<select name="product">
<%
For Each collItem in Application.Contents
    If Mid(collItem,1,7) = "Product" Then
        vPnumber = Application(collItem)
        vPname = vPnumber(0)
        Response.Write "<option>" & collItem & "</option>"
    End If
Next
%>
</select>
<input type="submit" name="RemoveProduct" Value="Remove">
</td></tr>
</form>
```

10. Finally, a link is provided to the shopper's page (in case you want to test your handiwork), and the page is closed with ordinary HTML:

```
</table>
<p>     Please click <a
href="shopper1.asp">here</a>
to go to our easy-to-use shopping cart, starting on our
catalog.</p>
<hr>
<p><b><font face="Arial, Helvetica, sans-serif">Thanks for using
the Ecommerce Adventure shopping cart manager!!</font></b></p>
</body></html>
```

Figure 5-8 shows what the shopping cart page looks like with a few products added, but no orders yet.

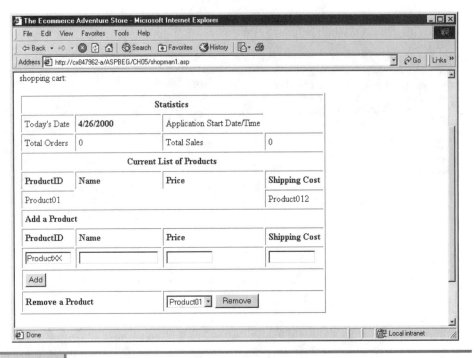

Figure 5-8 The shopping cart page

11. Next, let's make a nice page welcoming folks to the store and asking if they'd like to shop from your catalog. You can do this with any competent HTML editor (I've used Dreamweaver 2.0 for this example). The code for your first page is as follows:

```
<html><head><title>Untitled Document</title>
<meta http-equiv="Content-Type" content="text/html; charset=iso-8859-1">
</head>
<body bgcolor="#CCFFCC">
<p><font size="+1"><b><font face="Arial, Helvetica, sans-serif"
size="+2">Welcome to our Ecommerce Adventure store!</font><br>
</b><font face="Arial, Helvetica, sans-serif"><i><b><font color="#333399">We

make finding what you want a real adventure!!</font></b></i></font></p>
<hr>
<p>     The Ecommerce adventure store specializes in
```

```
hard-to-find goods for the adventurous at heart. We update our catalog daily,
and because we leave out the fancy graphics you'll find our store always
easy-to-download, easy-to-shop. We offer:</p>
<ul>
  <li>Free Shipping</li>
  <li>Next-Day Service</li>
  <li>Low Prices</li>
  <li>Broad Selection</li>
  <li>Privacy Guaranteed</li>
  <li>Excellent Warranties</li>
</ul>
<p>     Please click <a href="shopper1.asp">here</a>
to
go to our easy-to-use shopping cart, starting on our catalog.</p>
<hr>
<p><b><font face="Arial, Helvetica, sans-serif">Thanks for Shopping with
Ecommerce Adventure!!</font></b></p>
</body></html>
```

This is just an ordinary HTML page. The real fun starts happening when the link is clicked and the user goes to shopper1.asp. However, accessing this page is the start of a session for each user (and the start of the application if he or she got there first), so it is important to have some kind of entry page.

12. The page used for shopping is called shopper1.asp, and it functions in a similar manner as the shopping management page, except that it makes heavy use of the Session ID property. It's also rather long, and we'll break it up into sections as with the management page script.

13. The shopper1.asp script opens with the typical HTML header information and an immediate set of processing instructions. These initial processing instructions look for any submitted orders to add or remove, using a mechanism similar to the one used in the shopping manager (If...Then and Select Case). Notice that each individual order is marked by the Session ID property, begins with an O, and uses the pnumber value to distinguish between successive orders:

```
<html><head><title>The Ecommerce Adventure Store</title>
<meta http-equiv="Content-Type" content="text/html; charset=iso-8859-1">
</head>
<body bgcolor="#CCFFCC">
<%
If Request.Form("OrderProducts") = "Order" Then
```

```
        vButtonPressed = "OrderProducts"
Else
        If Request.Form("RemoveOrder") = "Remove" Then
             vButtonPressed = "RemoveOrder"
        End If
End If
Select Case vButtonPressed
        Case "OrderProducts"
             If Request.Form("pnumber") = "" Then
             messagestring = "Sorry, you didn't select a product to order.
Please try again."
Else
             vFn = Request.Form("pnumber")
             vPnm = "pname" & vFn
             vPprc = "pprice" & vFn
             vPshp = "pshipping" & vFn
             Dim vArProdOrder(3)
             vArProdOrder(0) = Request.Form(vPnm)
             vArProdOrder(1) = Request.Form(vPprc)
             vArProdOrder(2) = Request.Form(vPshp)
             vArProdOrder(3) = "O" & Session.SessionID
             Application("O" & Session.SessionID & "-" &
             Session("ordercounter")) = vArProdOrder
             Session("ordercounter") = Session("ordercounter") + 1
             End If
        Case "RemoveOrder"
             For Each collItem in Application.Contents
                  If collItem = Request.Form("removethisorder") Then
                       Application.Contents.Remove(collItem)
                  End If
             Next
End Select
%>
```

14. In the next section, the script code presents a few welcoming messages and then begins a table. The first few cells of the table show the current date and the session start time, retrieved from the global.asa file:

```
<p><font size="+1"><b><font face="Arial, Helvetica, sans-serif"
size="+2">Welcome to the Ecommerce Adventure shopping cart!</font><font
face="Arial, Helvetica, sans-serif"><br>
</font></b></font><font face="Arial, Helvetica, sans-serif"><i><b><font
color="#333399">We make shopping a real
adventure!!</font></b></i></font></p>
<hr>
<p>     The Ecommerce Adventure store shopping cart
provides a variety of informtation to conduct your shopping adventure:</p>
```

```
<table border=1 cellpadding=5>
<tr><td align=center colspan=4><B>Order Information</b></td></tr>
<tr><td>Today's Date</td><td><b><% Response.Write(Date) %></b></td>
<td>Shopping Session Start Date/Time</td><td><b>
<% Response.Write(Session("startdate")) %></b></td></tr>
```

15. The current orders count and total price (if any) are displayed by the following code segment, retrieving them from among the existing Application variables that have the correct Session ID property values inside their name:

```
<tr><td>Your Current Orders</td><td>
<%
ordercntr = 0
pricecntr = 0
For Each collItem in Application.Contents
     If Mid(collItem,2,9) = Session.SessionID Then
          ordercntr = ordercntr + 1
          vArcosts = Application(collItem)
          pricecntr = pricecntr + vArcosts(1)
          pricecntr = pricecntr + vArcosts(2)
     End If
Next
Response.Write(ordercntr)
%>
</td>
<td>Current Orders Total Price</td><td>
<%
Response.Write(pricecntr)
%>
</td></tr>
```

16. A list of all products available for ordering is next, created by placing a radio button next to the contents of existing product values (from among Application variables whose names begin with the word "Product"):

```
<tr><td align=center colspan=4><b>Order the Following Product<br>
<font size=-1><i>One Product Per Order, Please</i></font></b></td></tr>
<tr><td><b>ProductID</b></td><td><b>Name</b></td><td><b>Price</b></td>
<td><b>Shipping Cost</b></td></tr>
<tr><td><form method=post action="shopper1.asp">
<%
vFieldNumber = 1
For Each collItem in Application.Contents
     If Mid(collItem,1,7) = "Product" Then
          vPnumber = Application(collItem)
```

```
                vPname = vPnumber(0)
                vPprice = vPnumber(1)
                vPshipping = vPnumber(2)
%>
<tr><td><input type="radio" name="pnumber" size=10 value="<%
Response.Write(vFieldNumber) %>">
<input type="hidden" name="<% Response.Write "pname" & vFieldNumber %>"
value="<% Response.Write(vPname) %> ">
<input type="hidden" name="<% Response.Write "pprice" & vFieldNumber %>"
value="<% Response.Write(vPprice) %> ">
<input type="hidden" name="<% Response.Write "pshipping" & vFieldNumber %>"
value="<% Response.Write(vPshipping) %> ">
<% Response.Write collItem & "</td><td>" & vPname & "</td><td>" & vPprice &
"</td><td>" & vPshipping & "</td></tr>"
End If
vFieldNumber = vFieldNumber + 1
Next
%>
```

17. Any current orders the shopper has placed appear in the
following list:

```
<tr><td colspan=4 align=center><B>Your Current Orders</B></td></tr>
<tr><td><b>OrderID</b></td><td><b>Name</b></td><td><b>Price</b></td>
<td><b>Shipping Cost</b></td></tr>
<% For Each collItem in Application.Contents
    If Mid(collItem,2,9) = Session.SessionID Then
    vPnumber = Application(collItem)
    vPname = vPnumber(0)
    vPprice = vPnumber(1)
    vPshipping = vPnumber(2)
    Response.Write "<tr><td>" & collItem & "</td><td>" & vPname &
        "</td><td>" & vPprice & "</td><td>" & vPshipping & "</td></tr>"
End If
Next
%>

<tr><td colspan=4><input type="submit" name="OrderProducts"
value="Order">  <b><% Response.Write(messagestring) %>
</b></td></tr>
```

18. To remove an order, the following code segment creates a
drop-down box filled with any current orders the shopper
has placed:

```
<tr><td colspan=2><b>Remove an Order</b></td><td colspan=2>
<select name="removethisorder">
<%
```

```
For Each collItem in Application.Contents
     If Mid(collItem,2,9) = Session.SessionID Then
          Response.Write "<option>" & collItem & "</option>"

     End If
Next
%>
</select>
<input type="submit" name="RemoveOrder" Value="Remove">
</td></tr>
</form>
</table>
```

19. Finally, the script uses ordinary HTML to place a link to a function
    that terminates the session, puts the shopper back at the
    Ecommerce Adventure welcome page, and closes out the
    existing page:

```
<p>     Please click <a
href="shopend1.asp">here</a> to go end your shopping session without further
ordering.</p>
<hr>
<p><b><font face="Arial, Helvetica, sans-serif">Thanks for using the
Ecommerce Adventure shopping cart manager!!</font></b></p>
</body>
</html>
```

20. The script to terminate the session uses some very simple code that
    ends the session (using Session.Abandon) and redirects the user to
    the welcome page:

```
<%
Session.Abandon
Response.Redirect "shop1.htm"
%>
```

Figure 5-9 shows the shopper's page with a few products ordered
and the current products list.

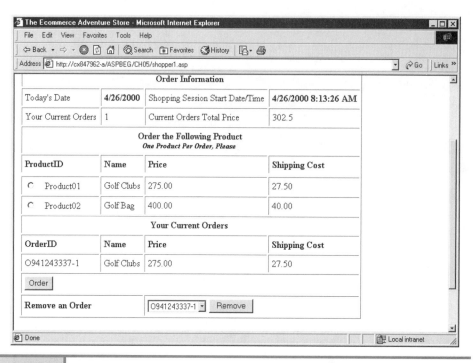

Figure 5-9 The shopper's page

☑ *Mastery Check*

1. What does scope mean, in the context of ASP?

    A. Defines the audience for your script

    B. Allows every script to see the variables of every other script

    C. Defines which variables can be seen by which scripts

    D. None of the above

2. What is the difference between application and session scope?

    A. Only application managers can use application scope.

    B. Only users can use session scope.

☑ Mastery Check

C. Application scope maintains variables that can be seen by any script running within the application, while session scope maintains variables that can be seen only by scripts running within the session of that individual user.

D. There is no functional difference.

3. By what mechanism does the global.asa file permit you to run code when your applications and session's start or finish?

A. Global parameters

B. Scope settings

C. Cookies

D. Events

4. How does your application identify an individual user and establish a session?

A. The user must log in.

B. By the user's IP address

C. Using a session cookie

D. None of the above

5. The code to add a variable to the application is _____.
The code to abandon a session is _____.
The code to remove all variables from a session is

_____.

5

Part 2

Active Server Components and ADO

Module 6

The Scripting Object Model and SOM Objects

The Goals of This Module

- Learn the relationships between the members of the Scripting Object Model
- Create and use the Dictionary object
- Create a FileSystemObject object and navigate the file system with it
- Create a Drive object and list drives and their properties with it
- Create a Folder object and move files from folder to folder
- Create files with a File object and list their properties
- Create and read from files with a TextStream object

If you've already done application programming, you're probably used to being able to read and write files from and to the drives. If you've done JavaScript and VBScript programming in Web pages, you may have noticed these capabilities are absent. Naturally, because JavaScript and VBScript run on download, these capabilities have been left out so malicious programmers cannot write Web pages that destroy user's machines simply on downloading a Web page.

On the server, however, at times you'll want to have the capability to read from or write to the drives. Module 6 covers the objects available to ASP that allow these functions to be performed. But, remember to proceed carefully; this is very important, so you don't destroy your own machine accidentally!

The Scripting Object Model

Active Server Pages 3.0 supports the use of objects installed on the server to enhance the capabilities inherent in ASP. The Request and Response objects are built-in (or intrinsic) objects. Components are objects as well. We've already used the MyInfo component to store data between pages and sessions, and quite a few other components/objects are available. In fact, objects exist for manipulating the file system, for managing common Web site tasks, and even for changing registry settings and uploading files. Think of objects as reusable application program components that provide specific functionality in a way that is easy to use inside your ASP applications, without having to reinvent the wheel.

An *object model* is simply a description of how available objects fit together and are related to one another in function. In ASP 3.0, three objects are available via the Scripting Runtime Library. They are

- **The Dictionary object** This object can store name/value pairs you can create, set, and retrieve.

- **The FileSystemObject** This object gives you access to the underlying file system (via drive, folder, and file objects) on the server, and also in IE 5.0 on the client.

- **The TextStream object** This object enables you to create, read, and write to text files.

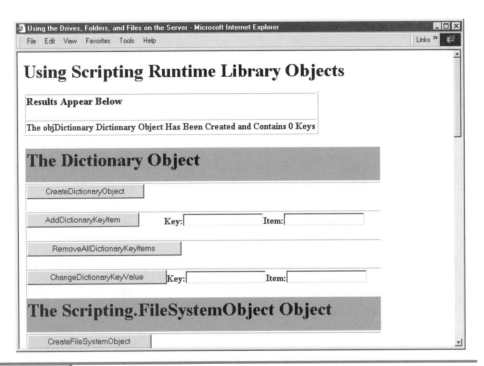

Figure 6-2 | Dictionary object created with zero keys

Listing Dictionary Names/Values

Just for fun, name/value pairs in the Dictionary object are called keys and items, respectively. In the next code segment, you create an instance of a Dictionary object with session-level scope (so it will retain values across successive pages in our application) in the global.asa file:

```
<OBJECT ID="objDictionarySes" RUNAT="server" SCOPE="Session"
PROGID="Scripting.Dictionary">
</OBJECT>
```

Next, you put together some code to access that Dictionary object from an ASP script in your application. This code dimensions a few variables (for holding name/value pair data, a counter, and a reference to the Dictionary object), sets the value of some of those variables to the values received from the requesting form page, and iterates through the name/value pairs created (as shown in Figure 6-3):

```
Dim vKey
Dim vItem
Dim arKeys
Dim arItems
Dim intI
Dim objDictionaryS
Set objDictionaryS = Session("SessionDictionary")
vKey = Request.Form("key")
vItem = Request.Form("item")
objDictionaryS.Add vKey, vItem
arKeys = objDictionaryS.Keys
arItems = objDictionaryS.Items
Response.Write "<B>Session Dictionary Object Created</B><BR>"
Response.Write "<B>The Dictionary Key/Item Pairs You Added Are:</B><P>"
    For intI = 0 to objDictionaryS.Count - 1
        Response.Write "<B>Key = </B>" & arKeys (intI)
        Response.Write " and <B>Item = </B>" & arItems (intI) & "<BR>"
    Next
```

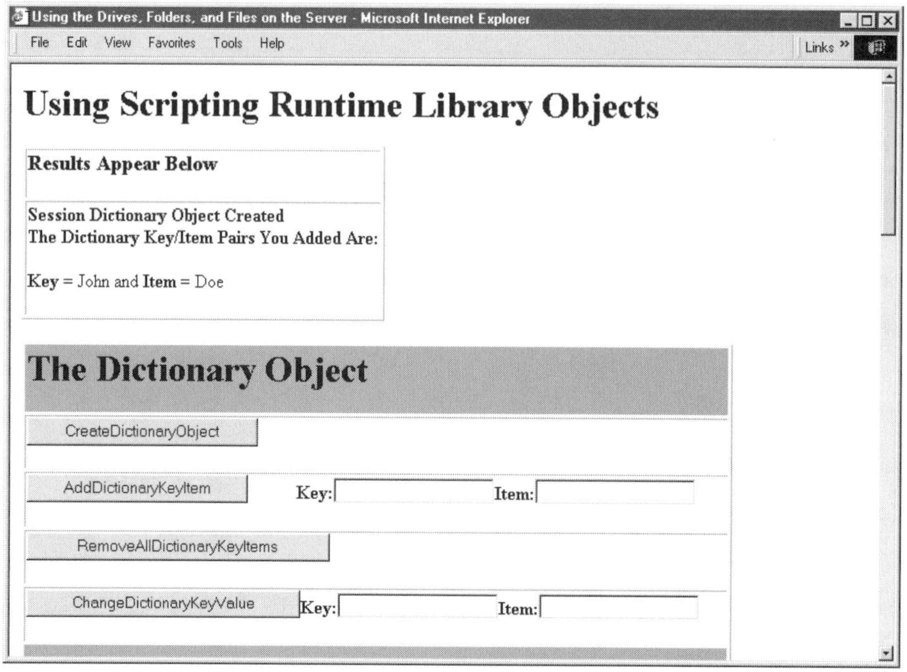

Figure 6-3   Global Dictionary object created with key/item

As an experiment to try on your own, add a name/value pair to the Dictionary, and then try to add the same name to the Dictionary again. You should get an error message stating that key already exists.

Removing Dictionary Name/Value Pairs

To remove name/value pairs from the Dictionary object, you can use a built-in Remove method. Figure 6-4 shows it removing key/value pairs. When referencing the session-level Dictionary object created in global.asa from our page, you also need to set the session-level Dictionary equal to the object in your page for the change to take effect, as shown in the following code in line 3:

```
Set objDictionaryS = Session("SessionDictionary")
objDictionaryS.RemoveAll
Set Session("SessionDictionary") = objDictionaryS
```

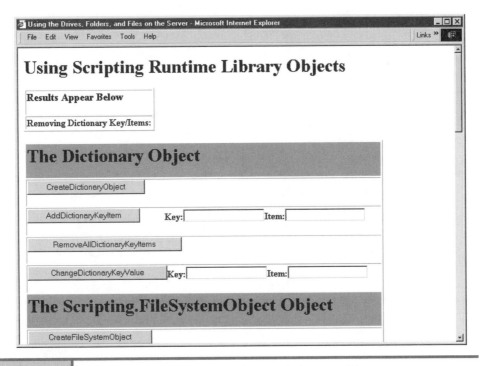

Figure 6-4 | Removing key/value pairs from Dictionary object

Changing Dictionary Object Names/Values

Once created, Dictionary object names and values can be changed at the page level. You might want to do this so a particular user can play a game with other users online—some kind of simple word game, wherein one user creates a name/value pair, another user changes that name/value pair, and the first user tries to guess what was changed.

These kinds of changes can be made with code such as the following, as shown in Figure 6-5:

```
Set objDictionaryS = Session("SessionDictionary")
vKey = Request.Form("key")
vItem = Request.Form("item")
objDictionaryS.Item(vKey) = vItem
Set Session("SessionDictionary") = objDictionaryS
Response.Write "<B>Dictionary Key Item Value Has Been
Changed To:</B><P>"
arKeys = objDictionaryS.Keys
arItems = objDictionaryS.Items
    For intI = 0 to objDictionaryS.Count - 1
            Response.Write "<B>Key = </B>" & arKeys (intI)
            Response.Write " and <B>Item = </B>" & arItems
(intI) & "<BR>"
    Next
```

This code references the session-level Dictionary object, sets the value of a couple of variables according to Form elements in the requesting page, changes the value of existing Dictionary object name/value pairs, and then lists the name/value pairs for review to show the changes made.

1-Minute Drill

- **The Dictionary object contains name/value pairs. What is the Dictionary object name for a name?**
- **What is the Dictionary object name for a value?**

- Key
- Item

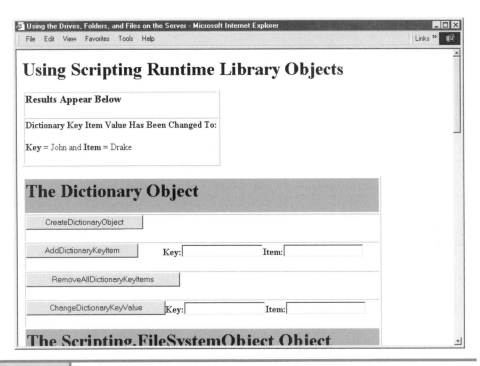

Figure 6-5 Changing item values for a Dictionary object

The Scripting.FileSystemObject Object

Warning! Using the FileSystemObject object improperly can potentially damage your system because the FileSystemObject object can access and make changes to any folder or file on your system.

That said, the FileSystemObject object and its subsidiary objects are among the most valuable tools in your toolbox, precisely because of their power. The demonstration ASP page with buttons for creating and displaying info about the FileSystemObject object is shown in Figure 6-6.

Just remember, any access you provide to the server's drives, folders, and files could mess up your operations, so be extremely careful what you do. Although in these examples, the user is allowed to choose any folder or file for modification, this is one time when it might be best to

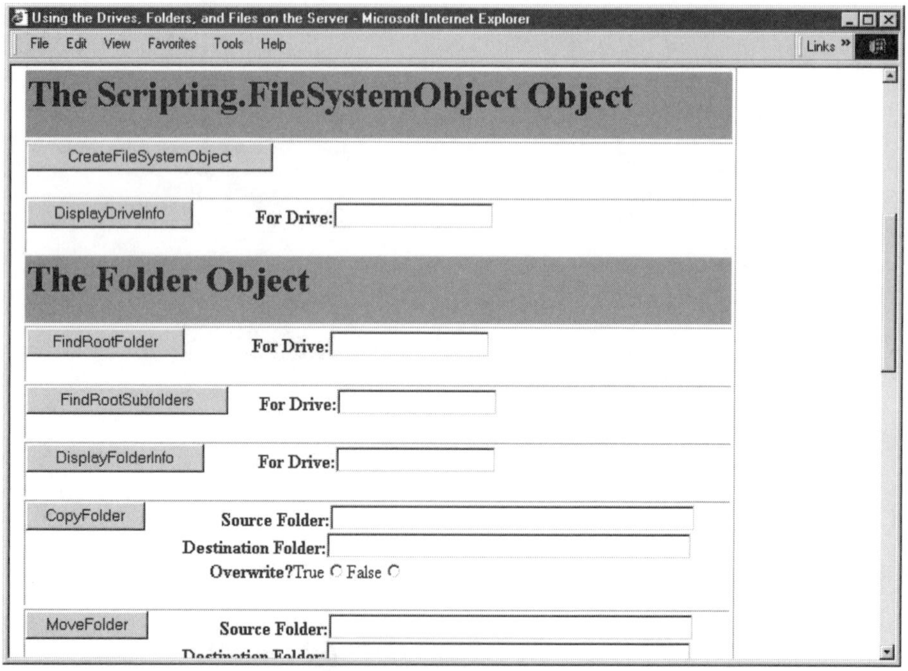

Figure 6-6   The FileSystemObject section

hard-code in folder and file references, rather than to provide unlimited access through variables.

FileSystemObject Properties

The FileSystemObject object provides only one property—Drives—and this property returns a collection of all the Drives available on the system, and also any network drives mapped to it. You can set an object of your choice equal to this property, and then the Drives are accessible through the Drive object properties and methods (in the upcoming section).

FileSystemObject Methods

The FileSystemObject has quite a few methods, some pertaining to drives, some pertaining to folders, and some pertaining to files. A number of ways exist to navigate to and alter folders and files, and they are useful under different circumstances. For instance, if you happen to have the entire path to a file, you might want to use the FileSystemObject to retrieve and modify it. Or, if you are in the folder already, you might want to use the folder object to reference and change the file. It just depends on where in the file system you are and what information you have available. In any case, here are the methods of the FileSystemObject:

- **DriveExists(driveletter)** This method returns True if the drive letter specified exists and False if it doesn't.

- **GetDrive(driveletter)** This method returns a Drive object equivalent to the drive letter specified.

- **GetDriveName(driveletter)** This method returns the name of the drive specified by driveletter as a string.

- **BuildPath(path, name)** This method adds the file or folder specified by name to the current path and adds a separator character ("\") as necessary.

- **CopyFolder(source,destination,overwrite)** This method copies a folder from one location (the source) to another (the destination), overwriting by default unless the overwrite parameter is explicitly set to False.

- **CreateFolder(foldername)** This method creates a folder named foldername at the path specified in foldername.

- **DeleteFolder(folderpathname,force)** This method deletes a folder residing at folderpathname and can even delete read-only folders if the overwrite parameter is set to True.

- **FolderExists(folderpathname)** This method returns True if the folder specified in folderpathname exists and False if it doesn't.

- **GetAbsolutePathName(path)** This method returns a path based on the current folder's path and the path specified.

- **GetFolder(folder)** This method returns a folder object equivalent to the folder specified.

6

- **GetParentFolderName(path)**   This method returns the name of the parent folder for the folder or file specified in path.

- **GetSpecialFolder(folder)**   This method returns a folder object equivalent to the special folder specified, such as a Windows folder, a System folder, or a Temporary folder.

- **MoveFolder(source,destination)**   This method moves a folder specified in source (the complete path including folder name) to the location specified in destination (the complete path including the folder name).

- **CopyFile(source,destination,overwrite)**   This method copies a file specified in source to the location specified in destination, overwriting any existing file with the same path and name unless the overwrite parameter is set to False.

- **CreateTextFile(filepath,overwrite,unicode)**   This method creates a text file specified in filepath, overwriting an existing file of the same path and name unless the overwrite parameter is set to False and as ASCII unless the optional Unicode parameter is set to True.

- **DeleteFile(filepath,force)**   This method deletes the file specified in filepath, even read-only files if the force parameter is set to True

- **FileExists(filepath)**   This method returns True if the specified file exists

- **GetBaseName(filepath)**   This method returns the name of the file specified in filepath, removing the drive, folder, and extension data.

- **GetExtensionName(filepath)**   This method returns the extension for a given file.

- **GetFile(filepath)**   This method returns a File object equivalent to the file specified in filepath.

- **GetFileName(path)**   This method returns the name portions of the path and filename specified by path.

- **GetTempName**   This method generates a random filename for use when generating temporary files or folders.

- **MoveFile(source,destination)**   This method moves a file specified in source to the location specified in destination.

- **OpenTextFile(filename,iomode,create,format)**   This method either creates or opens a text file named filename (depending on whether the create parameter is set to True), using an iomode for reading, writing, or appending and formatted as ASCII, Unicode, or system default format.

Creating a FileSystemObject Object

The following code can be used to create a FileSystemObject object and iterate through the drives available on your local machine:

```
Dim objFileSysOb
Dim collObj
Set objFileSysOb = Server.CreateObject("Scripting.FileSystemObject")   ←——
Response.Write "<B>The FileSystemObject Has Been Created and the Server
Drives Are:</B>"
      For Each collObj in objFileSysOb.Drives
            Response.Write "<BR>Drive = " & collObj
      Next
```

> Code to create an object
> and set it to a variable.

The code simply dimensions a couple of variables, sets objFileSysOb to a server-created FileSystemObject object, and then writes back an iterated list of all the drives on the server (see Figure 6-7).

The Drive Object

Once you create a FileSystemObject object, you can easily get your hands on a Drive object, and then you can start retrieving information about the available drives. Drive objects have the following properties:

- **AvailableSpace**   This property returns the amount of space available on the drive.

- **DriveLetter**   This property returns the drive letter.

- **DriveType**   This property returns the drive type as unknown, removable, fixed, network, CD-ROM, or RAMDisk.

- **FileSystem**   This property returns the file system type of the drive as FAT, NTFS, or CDFS, as long as the type is recognizable.

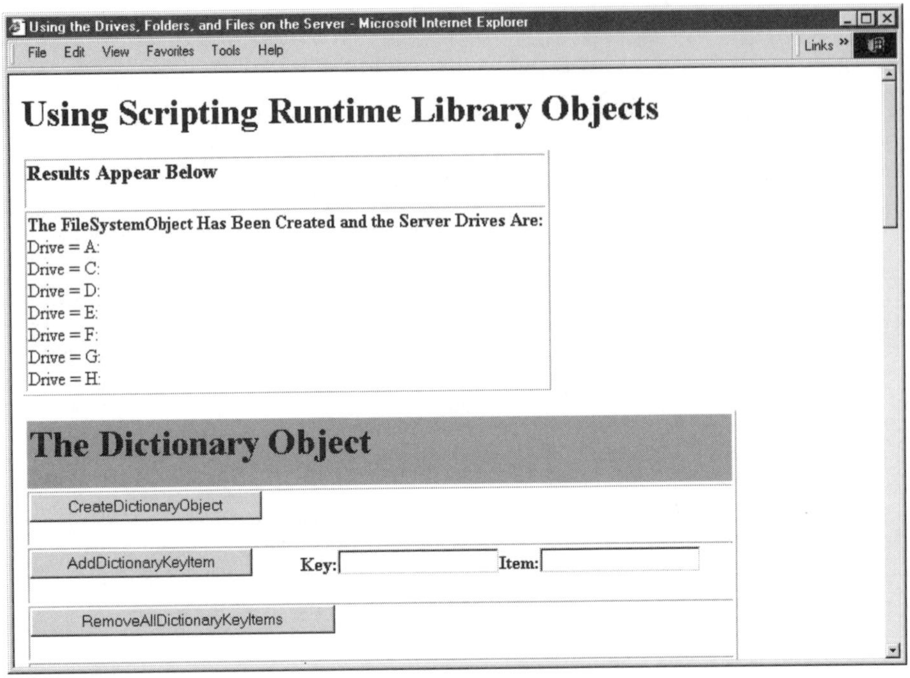

Figure 6-7   All the drives on the server

- **FreeSpace**   This property returns the total free space available on the drive.

- **IsReady**   This property is True if the drive is ready and false if it isn't.

- **Path**   This property returns the drive letter specification for the drive (C:, for instance).

- **RootFolder**   This property returns a Folder object equivalent to the root folder for the drive.

- **SerialNumber**   This property returns the serial number that identified the disk volume.

- **ShareName** This property returns the network name for a shared drive.

- **TotalSize** This property returns the total size of the drive.

- **VolumeName** This property sets or returns the volume name for local drives.

Iterating Drive Properties

You can set up a listing of all available drives and their properties with the Drive object, using code such as the following:

```
Dim vDrive
vDrive = Request.Form("drive")
Set objFileSysOb = Server.CreateObject("Scripting.FileSystemObject")
Response.Write "<B>The Drive Info Is:</B><P>"
Response.Write "Drive Letter = " & objFileSysOb.GetDrive(vDrive).DriveLetter
& "<BR>"
Response.Write "Drive Type = " & objFileSysOb.GetDrive(vDrive).DriveType &
"<BR>"
Response.Write "File System = " & objFileSysOb.GetDrive(vDrive).FileSystem &
"<BR>"
Response.Write "AvailableSpace = " &
objFileSysOb.GetDrive(vDrive).AvailableSpace & "<BR>"
Response.Write "Free Space = " & objFileSysOb.GetDrive(vDrive).FreeSpace &
"<BR>"
Response.Write "Is Ready = " & objFileSysOb.GetDrive(vDrive).IsReady &
"<BR>"
Response.Write "Path = " & objFileSysOb.GetDrive(vDrive).Path & "<BR>"
Response.Write "Root Folder = " & objFileSysOb.GetDrive(vDrive).RootFolder &
"<BR>"
Response.Write "Serial Number = " &
objFileSysOb.GetDrive(vDrive).SerialNumber & "<BR>"
Response.Write "Share Name = " & objFileSysOb.GetDrive(vDrive).ShareName &
"<BR>"
Response.Write "Total Size = " & objFileSysOb.GetDrive(vDrive).TotalSize &
"<BR>"
Response.Write "Volume Name = " & objFileSysOb.GetDrive(vDrive).VolumeName &
"<BR>"
```

6

This code dimensions a variable named vDrive to hold a drive letter specification supplied by the user and sets it equal to that value using the Request object. It then creates a FileSystemObject and retrieves a Drive object and corresponding drive properties with the FileSystemObject.GetDrive(vDrive) property references. Figure 6-8 shows the resulting list of Drive properties.

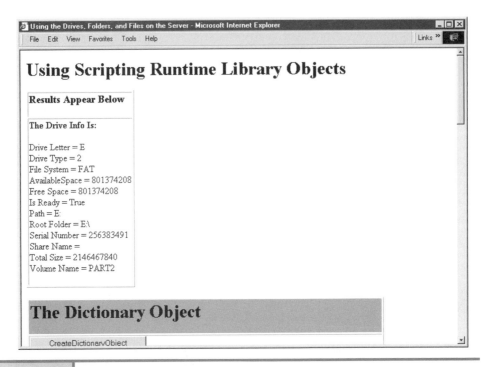

Using Scripting Runtime Library Objects

Results Appear Below

The Drive Info Is:

Drive Letter = E
Drive Type = 2
File System = FAT
AvailableSpace = 801374208
Free Space = 801374208
Is Ready = True
Path = E:
Root Folder = E:\
Serial Number = 256383491
Share Name =
Total Size = 2146467840
Volume Name = PART2

The Dictionary Object

CreateDictionaryObject

Figure 6-8 Drive properties listed

1-Minute Drill

● **List three Drive object properties.**
● **List three types of Drive objects.**

The Folder Object

Although you can get folder and files with the FileSystemObject, the Folder object can also be used to retrieve and work with files. You can use the Folder object's Subfolders property to retrieve a Folders collection and the Files property to retrieve a Files collection, and you can even create text files with the Folder object.

● **Available Space, Drive Letter, Drive Type**
● **Removable, Fixed, CD-ROM**

Folder Object Properties

The Folder object exposes the following properties:

- **Attributes**   This property returns attributes such as normal, read-only, hidden, system, volume, directory, archive, alias, and compressed.

- **DateCreated**   This property returns the date and time the folder was created.

- **DateLastAccessed**   This property returns the date and time the folder was last accessed.

- **DateLastModified**   This property returns the date and time the folder was last modified.

- **Drive**   This property returns the drive letter for the folder.

- **Files**   This property returns a Files collection of the File objects equivalent to all the files in the folder.

- **IsRootFolder**   This property returns True if the folder is the root folder of the drive.

- **Name**   This property sets or returns the name of the folder.

- **ParentFolder**   This property returns a Folder object equivalent to the parent folder for the current folder.

- **Path**   This property returns the absolute path for the current folder.

- **ShortName**   This property returns the DOS version of the folder name.

- **ShortPath**   This property returns the DOS version of the path for the folder.

- **Size**   This property returns the size for the files and folders in the current folder.

- **Subfolders**   This property returns a Folders collection for all the folders in the current folders.

- **Type**   This property returns a description of the current folder as a string, if the description is available.

6

Folder Object Methods

Once you have a Folder object available, you can directly copy, move, delete, and so on, but without having to specify a full path because you're already there. You can also create a text file. The methods to accomplish these actions are

- **Copy(destination,overwrite)** This method copies the current folder to the location specified in destination, overwriting an existing folder of the same name unless the overwrite parameter is set to True.

- **Delete(force)** This method deletes the current folder and its contents; and, if the force parameter is set to True, it deletes even read-only folders.

- **Move(destination)** This method moves the current folder to the location specified in destination, but generates an error if a folder is already in that location with the same name.

- **CreateTextFile(filepath,overwrite,unicode)** This method creates a text file using the specified file path and name, overwriting existing files of that name if the overwrite parameter is set to True and in the Unicode format if unicode is set to True.

Finding the Root Folder   Being able to locate and return a reference to the root folder is often a useful capability, and the following code does just that:

```
vDrive = Request.Form("drive")
Set objFileSysOb =
Server.CreateObject("Scripting.FileSystemObject")
Response.Write "<B>The Root Folder Is:</B><P>"
Response.Write "Root Folder = " &
objFileSysOb.GetDrive(vDrive).RootFolder & "<BR>"
```

The code uses the already-dimensioned vDrive variable to retrieve and hold the Drive specification supplied by the user, and then looks up the root folder (see Figure 6-9) for the specified drive using the RootFolder property for that drive from the FileSystemObject object.

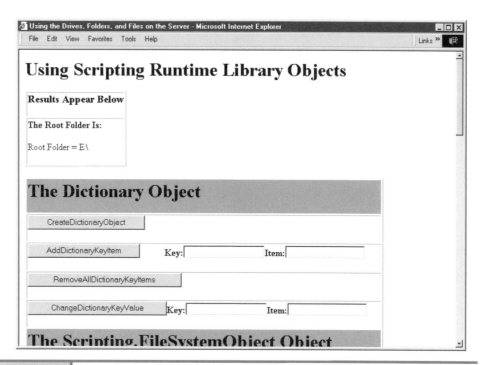

Figure 6-9 Finding the root folder

Finding Subfolders from a Root Folder The next code
example retrieves subfolders from the root folder for a drive, and then lists
them, another nice capability. Notice in the following code, you need to
set a reference to the Root Folder object, and then retrieve the subfolders
from that, rather than doing all the referencing in one step, as you have in
previous examples:

```
Dim colFolder
Dim colSubFolders
Dim colSubFolderItem
vDrive = Request.Form("drive")
Set objFileSysOb = Server.CreateObject("Scripting.FileSystemObject")
Set colFolder = objFileSysOb.GetDrive(vDrive).RootFolder
Set colSubFolders = colFolder.SubFolders
Response.Write "<B>The Root Subfolders Are:</B>"
For Each colSubFolderItem in colSubFolders
    Response.Write "Root SubFolder = " & colSubFolderItem & "<BR>"
Next
```

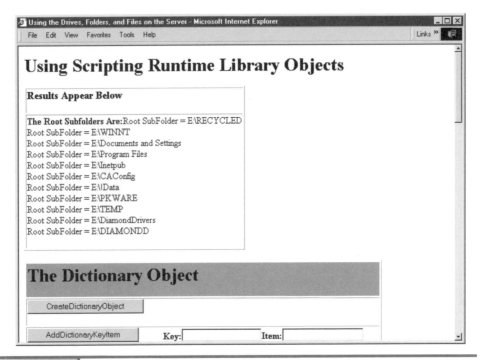

Also, notice in the code that a few additional variables were dimensioned to handle the extra collections being used, such as Folder and SubFolders. Figure 6-10 shows the listed subfolders.

Displaying Folder Information   Each folder in the collection has its own set of data values, including date created, date last modified, size, type, path, and so forth. These values can be displayed using a reference to the subfolder and the usual For Each . . . Next loop, as shown in Figure 6-11 and the code here:

```
Dim vSubFolder
vDrive = Request.Form("drive")
vSubFolder = Request.Form("subfolder")
Set objFileSysOb = Server.CreateObject("Scripting.FileSystemObject")
Set colFolder = objFileSysOb.GetDrive(vDrive).RootFolder
Set colSubFolders = colFolder.SubFolders
Response.Write "<B>The SubFolder Info Is:</B><P>"
```

```
For Each colSubFolderItem in colSubFolders
     Response.Write "<B>Folder Drive is: " & colSubFolderItem.Drive &
"</B><BR>"
   Response.Write "Folder Name is: " & colSubFolderItem.Name & "<BR>"
   Response.Write "Folder Attributes = " & colSubFolderItem.Attributes &
"<BR>"
   Response.Write "Folder Parent Folder is: " &
colSubFolderItem.ParentFolder & "<BR>"
     Response.Write "Folder Date Created is: " &
colSubFolderItem.DateCreated & "<BR>"
   Response.Write "Folder Date Last Accessed is: " &
colSubFolderItem.DateLastAccessed & "<BR>"
     Response.Write "Folder Date Last Modified is: Attributes = " &
colSubFolderItem.DateLastModified & "<BR>"
     Response.Write "Folder Size is: " & colSubFolderItem.Size & "<BR>"
     Response.Write "Folder Type is: " & colSubFolderItem.Type & "<BR>"
     Response.Write "Folder Path is: " & colSubFolderItem.Path & "<BR>"
     Response.Write "Folder Short Name is: " & colSubFolderItem.ShortName &
"<BR>"
     Response.Write "Folder Short Path is " & colSubFolderItem.ShortPath &
"<BR>"
     Response.Write "Folder is Root? " & colSubFolderItem.IsRootFolder &
"<P>"
```

6

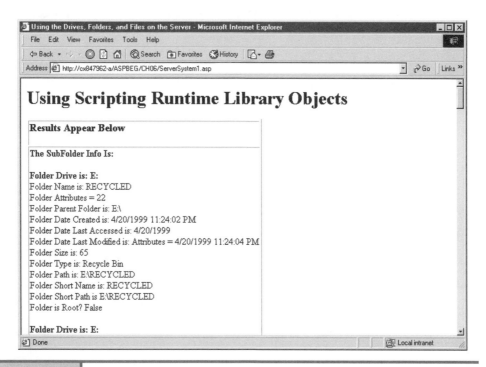

Figure 6-11   Folder info for the E: drive

Copying, Moving, and Deleting Folders With a reference to a particular folder, you can then copy, move, and delete folders (carefully, of course), as shown in the following three code examples (and in Figure 6-12):

```
Dim vSFolder
Dim vDFolder
Dim vOverwrite
Dim colFolderName
vSFolder = Request.Form("Sfoldername")
vDFolder = Request.Form("Dfoldername")
vOverwrite = Request.Form("overwrite")
Response.Write "<B>The Folder Has Been Copied To:</B><P>"
Set objFileSysOb = Server.CreateObject("Scripting.FileSystemObject")
Set colFolderName = objFileSysOb.GetFolder(vSFolder)
colFolderName.Copy vDFolder,vOverwrite
Response.Write vDFolder
```

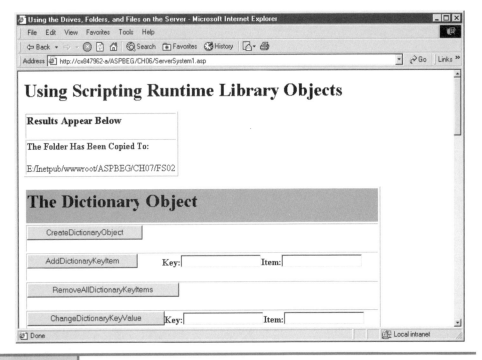

Figure 6-12 Copying a folder

Notice you first dimension more variables to retrieve the source folder, destination folder, and overwrite parameters from the user, and then create a FileSystemObject object to get to the correct folder object (specified in vSFolder). The last step is to use the Copy method of the Folder object with the VDFolder and VOverwrite parameters to perform the copy and use the Response object to tell the user what has been copied.

For moving a folder the code is similar:

```
vSFolder = Request.Form("Sfoldername")
vDFolder = Request.Form("Dfoldername")
Response.Write "<B>The Folder Has Been Moved To:</B><P>"
Set objFileSysOb = Server.CreateObject("Scripting.FileSystemObject")
Set colFolderName = objFileSysOb.GetFolder(vSFolder)
colFolderName.Move vDFolder
Response.Write vDFolder
```

For deleting a folder, the code is also similar. The primary difference is the addition of the "force" parameter (also retrieved from the user with the Request object and the vForce variable):

```
Dim vForce
vSFolder = Request.Form("Sfoldername")
vForce = Request.Form("force")
Response.Write "<B>The Following Folder Has Been Deleted:</B><P>"
Set objFileSysOb = Server.CreateObject("Scripting.FileSystemObject")
Set colFolderName = objFileSysOb.GetFolder(vSFolder)
colFolderName.Delete vForce
Response.Write vSFolder
```

Showing Files in a Folder   Naturally, having a reference to a folder is only a starting point. The next obvious thing you want to do is to access the files in the folder. One of the first requirements for doing this is to be able to list those files. This example (illustrated in Figure 6-13) shows how to list all the files in the folder, using a couple of variables and the standard For Each . . . Next loop:

```
Dim vFileItem
Dim vFiles
vSFolder = Request.Form("Sfoldername")
Set objFileSysOb = Server.CreateObject("Scripting.FileSystemObject")
Set colFolderName = objFileSysOb.GetFolder(vSFolder)
Set vFiles = colFolderName.Files
Response.Write "<B>The Files In The Folder Are:</B><P>"
For Each vFileItem in vFiles
      Response.Write vFileItem & "<BR>"
Next
```

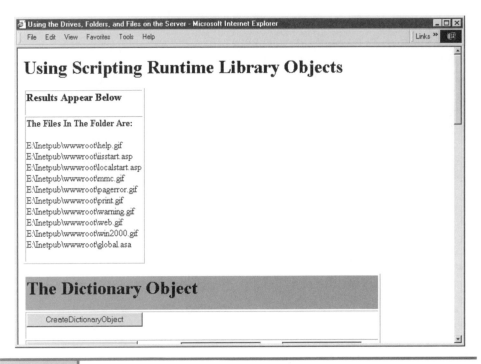

Figure 6-13 Listing the files in a folder

The vFiles variable is actually a collection of files that can be listed using the For loop, using the Response object to write out the name of each file.

Creating Text Files In Figure 6-14, the rest of the folder section of the ASP demonstration page is shown; and, as you can see, it provides the opportunity to create text files. To create a text file, you need to get the correct folder name in which to create the file, and the name of the file you want to create. Also, decide whether you want to overwrite an existing file of the same name, and whether you want the file to have the Unicode format.

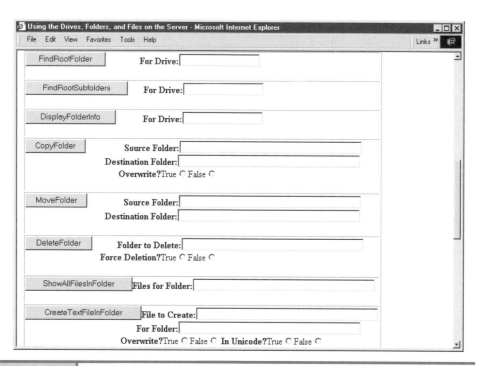

Figure 6-14 The remainder of the folder section controls

The following code example shows how to retrieve these values from a user and specify them to create a text file. The results are shown in Figure 6-15:

```
Dim vFilename
Dim vUnicode
vFilename = Request.Form("filename")
vSFolder = Request.Form("Sfoldername")
vOverwrite = Request.Form("overwrite")
vUnicode = Request.Form("unicode")
Set objFileSysOb = Server.CreateObject("Scripting.FileSystemObject")
Set colFolderName = objFileSysOb.GetFolder(vSFolder)
colFolderName.CreateTextFile vFilename,vOverwrite,vUnicode
Response.Write "<B>The Text File You Created Is:</B><P>"
Response.Write vSFolder & vFilename
```

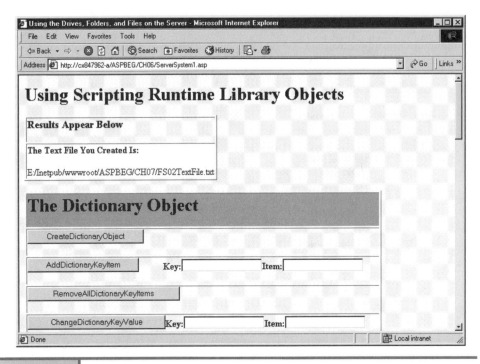

Figure 6-15 Creating a text file

The File Object

The *File* object is the next-to-last object in the hierarchy of file system objects, and has properties and methods quite similar to the Folder object. The File object creation and manipulation area of the ASP page is shown in Figure 6-16. You can display file information such as date created and last modified, size, and so forth; and you can copy, move, and delete files. You can also create text files or open them as TextStream objects.

File Object Properties

The File Object has the following properties:

- **Attributes** This property returns attributes such as normal, read-only, hidden, system, volume, directory, archive, alias, and compressed.

- **DateCreated**   This property returns the date and time the file was created.

- **DateLastAccessed**   This property returns the date and time the file was last accessed.

- **DateLastModified**   This property returns the date and time the file was last modified.

- **Drive**   This property returns the drive letter for the file.

- **Name**   This property sets or returns the name of the file.

- **ParentFolder**   This property returns a Folder object equivalent to the parent folder for the current file.

- **Path**   This property returns the absolute path for the current file.

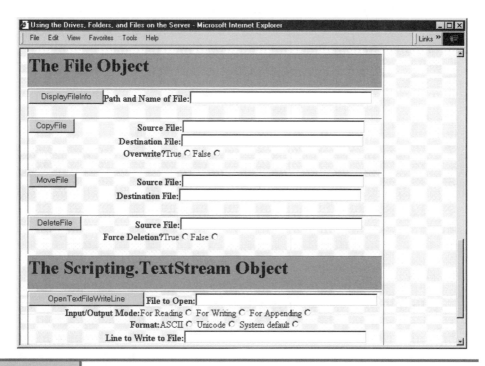

Figure 6-16   The File object section

- **ShortName**   This property returns the DOS version of the filename.

- **ShortPath**   This property returns the DOS version of the path for the file.

- **Size**   This property returns the size for the file in bytes.

- **Type**   This property returns a description of the current file as a string, if the description is available.

File Object Methods

The File object also has methods similar to Folder methods, as listed here:

- **Copy(destination,overwrite)**   This method copies the current file to the location specified in destination, overwriting an existing file of the same name unless the overwrite parameter is set to True.

- **Delete(force)**   This method deletes the current file and its contents, and if the force parameter is set to True, it deletes even read-only files.

- **Move(destination)**   This method moves the current file to the location specified in destination, but generates an error if a file in that location already exists with the same name.

- **CreateTextFile(filepath,overwrite,unicode)**   This method creates a text file using the specified file path and name, overwriting existing files of that name if the overwrite parameter is set to True and in the Unicode format if unicode is set to True.

- **OpenAsTextStream(iomode,format)**   This method opens a file in the specified mode (reading, writing, appending) depending on the value of the iomode parameter, and as ASCII, Unicode, or system default, depending on the value of the format parameter.

Displaying File Information   Once you have a reference to a file, you can display data about that file with code, such as the following:

```
Dim vFilePathname
Dim colFileName
vFilePathname = Request.Form("filepathname")
Set objFileSysOb = Server.CreateObject("Scripting.FileSystemObject")
```

```
Set colFileName = objFileSysOb.GetFile(vFilePathname)
Response.Write "<B>The File Info Is:</B><P>"
Response.Write "<B>File Name is: " & colFileName.Name & "</B><BR>"
Response.Write "File Drive is: " & colFileName.Drive & "<BR>"
Response.Write "File Attributes = " & colFileName.Attributes & "<BR>"
Response.Write "File Parent Folder is: " & colFileName.ParentFolder & "<BR>"
Response.Write "File Date Created is: " & colFileName.DateCreated & "<BR>"
Response.Write "File Date Last Accessed is: " & colFileName.DateLastAccessed
& "<BR>"
Response.Write "File Date Last Modified is: Attributes = " &
colFileName.DateLastModified & "<BR>"
Response.Write "File Size is: " & colFileName.Size & "<BR>"
Response.Write "File Type is: " & colFileName.Type & "<BR>"
Response.Write "File Path is: " & colFileName.Path & "<BR>"
Response.Write "File Short Name is: " & colFileName.ShortName & "<BR>"
Response.Write "File Short Path is " & colFileName.ShortPath & "<P>"
```

In this code, you pull the file starting with the FileSystemObject
object, so the user must supply the entire path to the file. Once you have
a reference to the file, you can use the Response object and the File
properties to display each individual property of the file, as shown in
Figure 6-17.

6

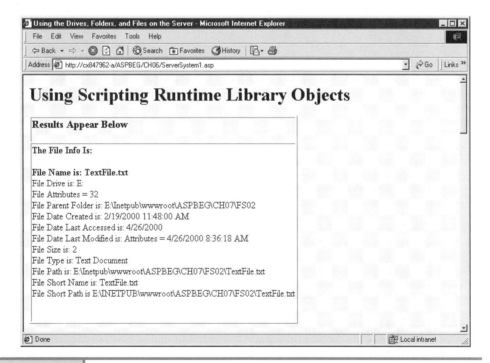

| **Figure 6-17** | File info displayed |

Copying, Moving, and Deleting Files   Files can be copied, moved, and deleted just like folders, and the following code examples demonstrate how to do this, starting with copying a file:

```
Dim vSFile
Dim vDFile
vSFile = Request.Form("Sfilename")
vDFile = Request.Form("Dfilename")
vOverwrite = Request.Form("overwrite")
Response.Write "<B>The File Has Been Copied To:</B><P>"
Set objFileSysOb = Server.CreateObject("Scripting.FileSystemObject")
Set colFileName = objFileSysOb.GetFile(vSFile)
colFileName.Copy vDFile,vOverwrite
Response.Write vDFile
```

You need to know the name of the file to copy, where to copy it to, and whether to overwrite it; so you first retrieve these values from the user, and then use them with the File object and the Copy method to perform the job. Figure 6-18 shows how this works.

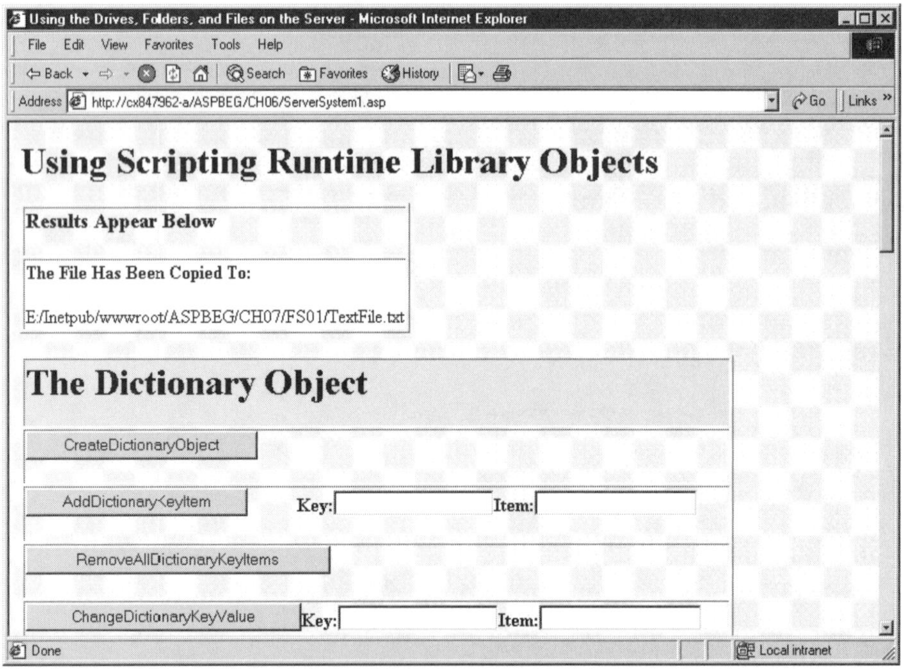

Figure 6-18   Copying a file

For moving a file, the code is similar:

```
vSFile = Request.Form("Sfilename")
vDFile = Request.Form("Dfilename")
Response.Write "<B>The File Has Been Moved To:</B><P>"
Set objFileSysOb = Server.CreateObject("Scripting.FileSystemObject")
Set colFileName = objFileSysOb.GetFile(vSFile)
colFileName.Move vDFile
Response.Write vDFile
```

And to delete files, you can use code like this:

```
vSFile = Request.Form("Sfilename")
vForce = Request.Form("force")
Response.Write "<B>The Following File Has Been Deleted:</B><P>"
Set objFileSysOb = Server.CreateObject("Scripting.FileSystemObject")
Set colFileName = objFileSysOb.GetFile(vSFile)
colFileName.Delete vForce
Response.Write vSFile
```

Here you retrieve a File object from the FileSystemObject object and get the filename to delete from the user, as well as the value of the force parameter. Then simply perform the action on the File object.

6

The Scripting.TextStream Object

Although TextStream objects are separate entities, they can only be created using the CreateTextFile, OpenTextFile, and OpenAsTextStream methods of the FileSystemObject object, the Folder object, and the File object. Any of these objects can use CreateTextFile, while only the FileSystemObject can use the OpenTextFile method and only the File object can use the OpenAsTextStream method. Figure 6-19 shows the TextStream object section of your ASP page.

TextStream Object Properties

The TextStream object exposes the following properties to tell us about itself:

- **AtEndOfLine**   This property returns True if the file pointer is at the end of a line in a file.

- **AtEndOfStream**   This property returns True if the file pointer is at the end of the file.

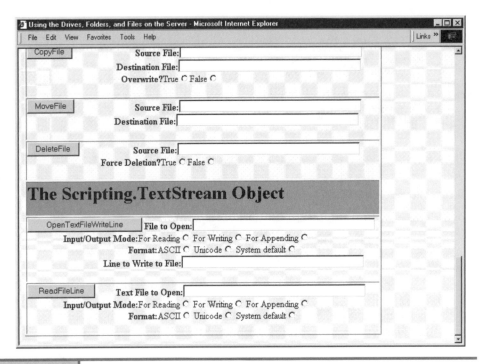

Figure 6-19 | The TextStream object section

- **Column**   This property returns the column number of the current character.

- **Line**   This property returns the line number for the current line.

TextStream Object Methods

The TextStream object supplies methods for navigating files, as well as reading from and writing to files. They are

- **Close**   This method closes the current file.

- **Read(numberofcharacters)**   This method reads the specified number of characters from a file.

- **ReadAll**   This method reads all the characters in a file.

- **ReadLine**   This method reads a line from a file as a string.

- **Skip(numberofcharacters)**   This method skips over the specified number of characters while reading.

- **SkipLine**   This method skips the next line while reading.

- **Write(string)**   This method writes a string into a file.

- **WriteLine**   This method writes a string (if specified) and a newline character to a file.

- **WriteBlankLines(number)**   This method writes the specified number of newline characters to a file.

Creating and Writing to a File   The File object can be used to create a new file as a TextStream object, and then the TextStream object can be manipulated with the WriteLine method to insert a line within that new file, all at once, as the following code (and Figure 6-20) shows.

6

```
Dim vIomode
Dim vFormat
Dim vLinetowrite
Dim objTextStream
vSFile = Request.Form("Sfilename")
vIomode = Request.Form("iomode")
vFormat = Request.Form("format")
vLinetowrite = Request.Form("linetowrite")
Response.Write "<B>The Line You Have Written Is:</B><P>"
Set objFileSysOb = Server.CreateObject("Scripting.FileSystemObject")
Set colFileName = objFileSysOb.GetFile(vSFile)
Set objTextStream = colFileName.OpenAsTextStream(vIomode, vFormat)
objTextStream.WriteLine vLinetowrite
Response.Write vLinetowrite
```

Again, you retrieve the name of the file to create, its iomode, and format from the users via some variables you dimension, and then you retrieve a File object from the FileSystemObject and create a new text file as a TextStream object with the OpenAsTextStream method. Finally, you write a line to the new file with the WriteLine method.

Reading a Line from a File   To read a line from a file, all you have to do is get a reference to that file, and then use the ReadLine method to retrieve the line and show it to the user. Of course, you have to ask how

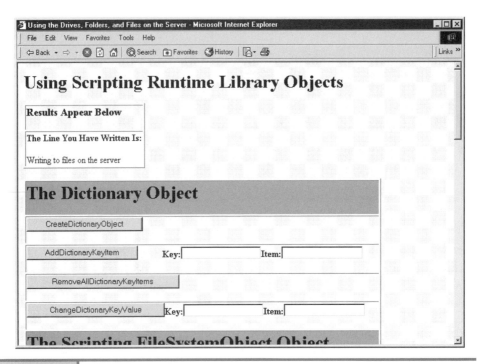

Figure 6-20   Creating a TextStream object and writing a line

the file should be opened; but, in practice, you might not leave that up to the user. For demonstration purposes, however, how this could be done is shown here. Figure 6-21 shows the results:

```
Dim vReadline
vSFile = Request.Form("Sfilename")
vIomode = Request.Form("iomode")
vFormat = Request.Form("format")
Response.Write "<B>The First Line in the File Is:</B><P>"
Set objFileSysOb = Server.CreateObject("Scripting.FileSystemObject")
Set colFileName = objFileSysOb.GetFile(vSFile)
Set objTextStream = colFileName.OpenAsTextStream(vIomode, vFormat)
vReadline = objTextStream.ReadLine
Response.Write vReadline
```

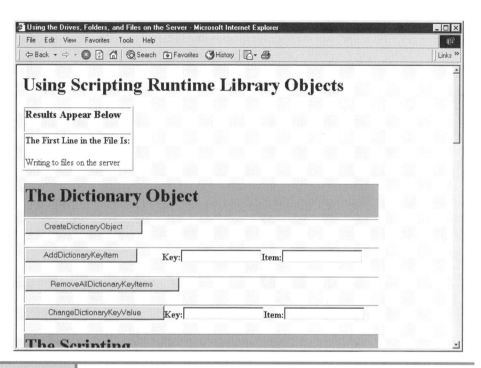

Figure 6-21   Reading a line from a file

Ask the Expert

Question: I've heard of object models before, but I'd like a better explanation of what they are and what they apply to. Can I create my own? Under what circumstances are they useful and how can they help me?

Answer: Object models are first and foremost models, like any other kind of model. At the most basic level, all models are conceptual representations of things, some more realistic than others. For example, a model railroad contains itty bitty railroad cars, people, tracks, and so forth, hooked together in a representation of a real railroad.

In programming, models are often used to represent how ideas or structures are related to each other. The relationship of database data in tables can be depicted via lines going from one table to the next (and you see examples of this in later modules). For the Scripting Library objects, the relationships are relatively simple ones—primarily which objects can create or navigate to others, and what collections they have.

Question: The FileSystemObject object seems to possess many of the capabilities of a File Manager–type program. Could I develop my own with ASP? If I am in the server anyway, why do I need these capabilities in ASP?

Answer: Developing online applications for clients is common, and it's also common for clients to want certain management-type functions automated. This means you will probably develop a set of functions for users and also another set of functions for client employees who are going to manage the application.

Within your user functions, FileSystem capabilities will likely be hidden or tightly controlled, to keep users from breaking your server. Within client employee management functions, FileSystem capabilities will probably be more flexible, with a lesser amount of control, although you will probably build in enough control to prevent breaking the server unless the client employee is warned first.

Either way, much of the use and management of your applications is likely to be online, rather than directly at the server. Therefore, you need the capability to get in and work with the file system from a browser.

project6-1.zip

Project 6-1: Pulling Together These Examples

In the following example, all the code examples used in this module are pulled together and displayed as one comprehensive example page that could be used to do typical file management functions remotely. Each object or component created and manipulated has its own section in the page; and for everything being done, the page references itself. Notice, to use the FileSystemObject effectively, you supply a reference to the FileSystemObject type library near the top of your script as well, using the METADATA tag. Using the METADATA tag to reference type libraries for COM objects is discussed in more detail in later modules.

Step-by-Step

1. The first set of examples for this page work with the Dictionary object. Although you can create a Dictionary object with page-level scope, for several of these examples, you need a Dictionary object with session-level scope. You must remember to add that object with the global.asa file, as covered earlier in the module.

2. Documenting and commenting your code thoroughly is always a good idea, but I've left off the commenting here because fairly good comments are provided in the text of the module and further commenting would clutter up the code.

3. The entire code for the examples used in this module, as well as the HTML that produces the user interface, is as follows:

```
<%
Option Explicit
Dim btnClicked
%>
<!-- METADATA TYPE="typelib" FILE="E:\WINNT\System32\scrrun.dll" -->
<html><head>
<title>Using the Drives, Folders, and Files on the Server</title>
<meta http-equiv="Content-Type" content="text/html; charset=iso-8859-1">
</head>
<body bgcolor="#77FF77">
<H2>Using Scripting Runtime Library Objects</H2>
<TABLE border=1>
<TR><TD><H3>Results Appear Below</H3></TD></TR><TR><TD bgcolor="white">
<%
btnClicked = Request.Form("btnval")
Select Case btnClicked
 Case "CreateDictionaryObject"
%><OBJECT RUNAT="SERVER" SCOPE="PAGE" ID="objDictionary"
PROGID="Scripting.Dictionary"></OBJECT>
<%
Response.Write "<B>The objDictionary Dictionary Object Has Been Created and
Contains " & objDictionary.Count & " Keys</B>"
Case "AddDictionaryKeyItem"
Dim vKey
            Dim vItem
            Dim arKeys
            Dim arItems
            Dim intI
```

```
        Dim objDictionaryS
        Set objDictionaryS = Session("SessionDictionary")
        vKey = Request.Form("key")
        vItem = Request.Form("item")
        objDictionaryS.Add vKey, vItem
        arKeys = objDictionaryS.Keys
        arItems = objDictionaryS.Items
        Response.Write "<B>Session Dictionary Object Created</B><BR>"
        Response.Write "<B>The Dictionary Key/Item Pairs You Added
Are:</B><P>"
        For intI = 0 to objDictionaryS.Count - 1
            Response.Write "<B>Key = </B>" & arKeys (intI)
            Response.Write " and <B>Item = </B>" & arItems (intI) &
"<BR>"
        Next
    Case "RemoveDictionaryKeyItem"
        Set objDictionaryS = Session("SessionDictionary")
        Response.Write "<B>Removing Dictionary Key/Items:</B>"
        objDictionaryS.RemoveAll
        Set Session("SessionDictionary") = objDictionaryS
    Case "ChangeDictionaryKeyValue"
        Set objDictionaryS = Session("SessionDictionary")
        vKey = Request.Form("key")
        vItem = Request.Form("item")
        objDictionaryS.Item(vKey) = vItem
        Set Session("SessionDictionary") = objDictionaryS
        Response.Write "<B>Dictionary Key Item Value Has Been Changed
To:</B><P>"
        arKeys = objDictionaryS.Keys
        arItems = objDictionaryS.Items
        For intI = 0 to objDictionaryS.Count - 1
            Response.Write "<B>Key = </B>" & arKeys (intI)
            Response.Write " and <B>Item = </B>" & arItems (intI) &
"<BR>"
        Next
    Case "CreateFileSystemObject"
        Dim objFileSysOb
        Dim collObj
        Set objFileSysOb =
Server.CreateObject("Scripting.FileSystemObject")
        Response.Write "<B>The FileSystemObject Has Been Created and the
Server Drives Are:</B>"
        For Each collObj in objFileSysOb.Drives
            Response.Write "<BR>Drive = " & collObj
        Next
    Case "DisplayDriveInfo"
        Dim vDrive
        vDrive = Request.Form("drive")
        Set objFileSysOb =
Server.CreateObject("Scripting.FileSystemObject")
        Response.Write "<B>The Drive Info Is:</B><P>"
        Response.Write "Drive Letter = " &
objFileSysOb.GetDrive(vDrive).DriveLetter & "<BR>"
        Response.Write "Drive Type = " &
objFileSysOb.GetDrive(vDrive).DriveType & "<BR>"
        Response.Write "File System = " &
objFileSysOb.GetDrive(vDrive).FileSystem & "<BR>"
        Response.Write "AvailableSpace = " &
objFileSysOb.GetDrive(vDrive).AvailableSpace & "<BR>"
```

```
            Response.Write "Free Space = " &
objFileSysOb.GetDrive(vDrive).FreeSpace & "<BR>"
            Response.Write "Is Ready = " &
objFileSysOb.GetDrive(vDrive).IsReady & "<BR>"
            Response.Write "Path = " & objFileSysOb.GetDrive(vDrive).Path &
"<BR>"
            Response.Write "Root Folder = " &
objFileSysOb.GetDrive(vDrive).RootFolder & "<BR>"
            Response.Write "Serial Number = " &
objFileSysOb.GetDrive(vDrive).SerialNumber & "<BR>"
            Response.Write "Share Name = " &
objFileSysOb.GetDrive(vDrive).ShareName & "<BR>"
            Response.Write "Total Size = " &
objFileSysOb.GetDrive(vDrive).TotalSize & "<BR>"
            Response.Write "Volume Name = " &
objFileSysOb.GetDrive(vDrive).VolumeName & "<BR>"
        Case "FindRootFolder"
            vDrive = Request.Form("drive")
            Set objFileSysOb =
Server.CreateObject("Scripting.FileSystemObject")
            Response.Write "<B>The Root Folder Is:</B><P>"
            Response.Write "Root Folder = " &
objFileSysOb.GetDrive(vDrive).RootFolder & "<BR>"
        Case "FindRootSubfolders"
            Dim colFolder
            Dim colSubFolders
            Dim colSubFolderItem
            vDrive = Request.Form("drive")
            Set objFileSysOb =
Server.CreateObject("Scripting.FileSystemObject")
            Set colFolder = objFileSysOb.GetDrive(vDrive).RootFolder
            Set colSubFolders = colFolder.SubFolders
            Response.Write "<B>The Root Subfolders Are:</B>"
            For Each colSubFolderItem in colSubFolders
                Response.Write "Root SubFolder = " & colSubFolderItem &
"<BR>"
            Next
        Case "DisplayFolderInfo"
            Dim vSubFolder
            vDrive = Request.Form("drive")
            vSubFolder = Request.Form("subfolder")
            Set objFileSysOb =
Server.CreateObject("Scripting.FileSystemObject")
            Set colFolder = objFileSysOb.GetDrive(vDrive).RootFolder
            Set colSubFolders = colFolder.SubFolders
            Response.Write "<B>The SubFolder Info Is:</B><P>"
            For Each colSubFolderItem in colSubFolders
                Response.Write "<B>Folder Drive is: " &
colSubFolderItem.Drive & "</B><BR>"
                Response.Write "Folder Name is: " & colSubFolderItem.Name
& "<BR>"
                Response.Write "Folder Attributes = " &
colSubFolderItem.Attributes & "<BR>"
                Response.Write "Folder Parent Folder is: " &
colSubFolderItem.ParentFolder & "<BR>"
                Response.Write "Folder Date Created is: " &
colSubFolderItem.DateCreated & "<BR>"
```

```
                    Response.Write "Folder Date Last Accessed is: " &
colSubFolderItem.DateLastAccessed & "<BR>"
                    Response.Write "Folder Date Last Modified is: Attributes =
" & colSubFolderItem.DateLastModified & "<BR>"
                    Response.Write "Folder Size is: " & colSubFolderItem.Size
& "<BR>"
                    Response.Write "Folder Type is: " & colSubFolderItem.Type
& "<BR>"
                    Response.Write "Folder Path is: " & colSubFolderItem.Path
& "<BR>"
                    Response.Write "Folder Short Name is: " &
colSubFolderItem.ShortName & "<BR>"
                    Response.Write "Folder Short Path is " &
colSubFolderItem.ShortPath & "<BR>"
                    Response.Write "Folder is Root? " &
colSubFolderItem.IsRootFolder & "<P>"
            Next
        Case "CopyFolder"
            Dim vSFolder
            Dim vDFolder
            Dim vOverwrite
            Dim colFolderName
            vSFolder = Request.Form("Sfoldername")
            vDFolder = Request.Form("Dfoldername")
            vOverwrite = Request.Form("overwrite")
            Response.Write "<B>The Folder Has Been Copied To:</B><P>"
            Set objFileSysOb =
Server.CreateObject("Scripting.FileSystemObject")
            Set colFolderName = objFileSysOb.GetFolder(vSFolder)
            colFolderName.Copy vDFolder,vOverwrite
            Response.Write vDFolder
        Case "MoveFolder"
            vSFolder = Request.Form("Sfoldername")
            vDFolder = Request.Form("Dfoldername")
            Response.Write "<B>The Folder Has Been Moved To:</B><P>"
            Set objFileSysOb =
Server.CreateObject("Scripting.FileSystemObject")
            Set colFolderName = objFileSysOb.GetFolder(vSFolder)
            colFolderName.Move vDFolder
            Response.Write vDFolder
        Case "DeleteFolder"
            Dim vForce
            vSFolder = Request.Form("Sfoldername")
            vForce = Request.Form("force")
            Response.Write "<B>The Following Folder Has Been
Deleted:</B><P>"
            Set objFileSysOb =
Server.CreateObject("Scripting.FileSystemObject")
            Set colFolderName = objFileSysOb.GetFolder(vSFolder)
            colFolderName.Delete vForce
            Response.Write vSFolder
        Case "ShowAllFilesInFolder"
            Dim vFileItem
            Dim vFiles
            vSFolder = Request.Form("Sfoldername")
            Set objFileSysOb =
Server.CreateObject("Scripting.FileSystemObject")
```

```
                Set colFolderName = objFileSysOb.GetFolder(vSFolder)
                Set vFiles = colFolderName.Files
                Response.Write "<B>The Files In The Folder Are:</B><P>"
                For Each vFileItem in vFiles
                        Response.Write vFileItem & "<BR>"
                Next
        Case "CreateTextFileInFolder"
                Dim vFilename
                Dim vUnicode
                vFilename = Request.Form("filename")
                vSFolder = Request.Form("Sfoldername")
                vOverwrite = Request.Form("overwrite")
                vUnicode = Request.Form("unicode")
                Set objFileSysOb =
Server.CreateObject("Scripting.FileSystemObject")
                Set colFolderName = objFileSysOb.GetFolder(vSFolder)
                colFolderName.CreateTextFile vFilename,vOverwrite,vUnicode
                Response.Write "<B>The Text File You Created Is:</B><P>"
                Response.Write vSFolder & vFilename
        Case "DisplayFileInfo"
                Dim vFilePathname
                Dim colFileName
                vFilePathname = Request.Form("filepathname")
                Set objFileSysOb =
Server.CreateObject("Scripting.FileSystemObject")
                Set colFileName = objFileSysOb.GetFile(vFilePathname)
                Response.Write "<B>The File Info Is:</B><P>"
                Response.Write "<B>File Name is: " & colFileName.Name &
"</B><BR>"
                Response.Write "File Drive is: " & colFileName.Drive & "<BR>"
                Response.Write "File Attributes = " & colFileName.Attributes &
"<BR>"
                Response.Write "File Parent Folder is: " &
colFileName.ParentFolder & "<BR>"
                Response.Write "File Date Created is: " &
colFileName.DateCreated & "<BR>"
                Response.Write "File Date Last Accessed is: " &
colFileName.DateLastAccessed & "<BR>"
                Response.Write "File Date Last Modified is: Attributes = " &
colFileName.DateLastModified & "<BR>"
                Response.Write "File Size is: " & colFileName.Size & "<BR>"
                Response.Write "File Type is: " & colFileName.Type & "<BR>"
                Response.Write "File Path is: " & colFileName.Path & "<BR>"
                Response.Write "File Short Name is: " & colFileName.ShortName &
"<BR>"
                Response.Write "File Short Path is " & colFileName.ShortPath &
"<P>"
        Case "CopyFile"
                Dim vSFile
                Dim vDFile
                vSFile = Request.Form("Sfilename")
                vDFile = Request.Form("Dfilename")
                vOverwrite = Request.Form("overwrite")
                Response.Write "<B>The File Has Been Copied To:</B><P>"
                Set objFileSysOb =
Server.CreateObject("Scripting.FileSystemObject")
                Set colFileName = objFileSysOb.GetFile(vSFile)
```

6

```
                    colFileName.Copy vDFile,vOverwrite
                    Response.Write vDFile
        Case "MoveFile"
                    vSFile = Request.Form("Sfilename")
                    vDFile = Request.Form("Dfilename")
                    Response.Write "<B>The File Has Been Moved To:</B><P>"
                    Set objFileSysOb =
Server.CreateObject("Scripting.FileSystemObject")
                    Set colFileName = objFileSysOb.GetFile(vSFile)
                    colFileName.Move vDFile
                    Response.Write vDFile
        Case "DeleteFile"
                    vSFile = Request.Form("Sfilename")
                    vForce = Request.Form("force")
                    Response.Write "<B>The Following File Has Been Deleted:</B><P>"
                    Set objFileSysOb =
Server.CreateObject("Scripting.FileSystemObject")
                    Set colFileName = objFileSysOb.GetFile(vSFile)
                    colFileName.Delete vForce
                    Response.Write vSFile
        Case "OpenTextFile"
        Dim vIomode
        Dim vFormat
        Dim vLinetowrite
        Dim objTextStream
                    vSFile = Request.Form("Sfilename")
                    vIomode = Request.Form("iomode")
                    vFormat = Request.Form("format")
                    vLinetowrite = Request.Form("linetowrite")
                    Response.Write "<B>The Line You Have Written Is:</B><P>"
                    Set objFileSysOb =
Server.CreateObject("Scripting.FileSystemObject")
                    Set colFileName = objFileSysOb.GetFile(vSFile)
                    Set objTextStream = colFileName.OpenAsTextStream(vIomode,
vFormat)
                    objTextStream.WriteLine vLinetowrite
                    Response.Write vLinetowrite
        Case "ReadFileLine"
        Dim vReadline
                    vSFile = Request.Form("Sfilename")
                    vIomode = Request.Form("iomode")
                    vFormat = Request.Form("format")
                    Response.Write "<B>The First Line in the File Is:</B><P>"
                    Set objFileSysOb =
Server.CreateObject("Scripting.FileSystemObject")
                    Set colFileName = objFileSysOb.GetFile(vSFile)
                    Set objTextStream = colFileName.OpenAsTextStream(vIomode,
vFormat)
                    vReadline = objTextStream.ReadLine
                    Response.Write vReadline
End Select
%>
<BR></TD></TR></TABLE>
<P>
<TABLE border=1><TR><TD>
<H3>The Dictionary Object</H3></TD></TR><TR>
<TD><FORM METHOD=POST ACTION="ServerSystem1.asp"><INPUT TYPE="submit"
```

> **The HTML page actually displayed begins here.**

```
NAME="btnval" VALUE="CreateDictionaryObject">
<B>Creates a Dictionary object with page level scope.</B></FORM></TD>
</TR><TR>
<TD><FORM METHOD=POST ACTION="ServerSystem1.asp">
<B>Key:</B><INPUT TYPE="text" NAME="key"><B>Item:</B><INPUT TYPE="text"
NAME="item"><BR>
<INPUT TYPE="submit" NAME="btnval" VALUE="AddDictionaryKeyItem">
<B> Adds a key (name) and item (value) to the Dictionary object and lists
them.</B>
</FORM></TD>
</TR><TR>
<TD><FORM METHOD=POST ACTION="ServerSystem1.asp"><INPUT TYPE="submit"
NAME="btnval" VALUE="RemoveDictionaryKeyItem">
<B>Removes a key/item pair.</B></FORM></TD>
</TR><TR>
<TD><FORM METHOD=POST ACTION="ServerSystem1.asp">
<B>Key:</B><INPUT TYPE="text" NAME="key"><B>Item:</B><INPUT TYPE="text"
NAME="item"><BR>
<INPUT TYPE="submit" NAME="btnval" VALUE="ChangeDictionaryKeyValue">
<B>Changes the value of an Item for a Key.</B></FORM></TD>
</TR>
<TR><TD>
<H3>The Scripting.FileSystemObject Object</H3></TD></TR><TR>
<TD><FORM METHOD=POST ACTION="ServerSystem1.asp"><INPUT TYPE="submit"
NAME="btnval" VALUE="CreateFileSystemObject">
<B>Creates a FileSystemObject object with page level scope and lists the
Server Drives</B></FORM></TD>
</TR><TR>
<TD><FORM METHOD=POST ACTION="ServerSystem1.asp">
<B>For Drive:</B><INPUT TYPE="text" NAME="drive"><BR>
<INPUT TYPE="submit" NAME="btnval" VALUE="DisplayDriveInfo">
<B>Displays information about a specific drive on the server</B></FORM></TD>
</TR>
<TR><TD>
<H3>The Folder Object</H3></TD></TR><TR>
<TD><FORM METHOD=POST ACTION="ServerSystem1.asp">
<B>For Drive:</B><INPUT TYPE="text" NAME="drive"><BR>
<INPUT TYPE="submit" NAME="btnval" VALUE="FindRootFolder">
<B>Finds the root folder for a specific drive</B></FORM></TD>
</TR><TR>
<TD><FORM METHOD=POST ACTION="ServerSystem1.asp">
<B>For Drive:</B><INPUT TYPE="text" NAME="drive"><BR>
<INPUT TYPE="submit" NAME="btnval" VALUE="FindRootSubfolders">
<B>Shows the subfolders of the root folder</B></FORM></TD>
</TR><TR>
<TD><FORM METHOD=POST ACTION="ServerSystem1.asp">
<B>For Drive:</B><INPUT TYPE="text" NAME="drive"><BR>
<INPUT TYPE="submit" NAME="btnval" VALUE="DisplayFolderInfo">
<B>Displays information about subfolders</B></FORM></TD>
</TR><TR>
<TD><FORM METHOD=POST ACTION="ServerSystem1.asp">
<B>Source Folder:</B><INPUT TYPE="text" SIZE=50 NAME="Sfoldername"><BR>
<B>Destination Folder:</B><INPUT TYPE="text" SIZE=50 NAME="Dfoldername"><BR>
<B>Overwrite?</B>True<INPUT TYPE="radio" NAME="overwrite"
VALUE="True">False<INPUT TYPE="radio" NAME="overwrite" VALUE="False"><BR>
<INPUT TYPE="submit" NAME="btnval" VALUE="CopyFolder">
<B>Copies a folder from one location to another</B></FORM></TD>
```

```
</TR><TR>
<TD><FORM METHOD=POST ACTION="ServerSystem1.asp">
<B>Source Folder:</B><INPUT TYPE="text" SIZE=50 NAME="Sfoldername"><BR>
<B>Destination Folder:</B><INPUT TYPE="text" SIZE=50 NAME="Dfoldername"><BR>
<INPUT TYPE="submit" NAME="btnval" VALUE="MoveFolder">
<B>Moves a folder from one location to another</B></FORM></TD>
</TR><TR>
<TD><FORM METHOD=POST ACTION="ServerSystem1.asp">
<B>Folder to Delete:</B><INPUT TYPE="text" SIZE=50 NAME="Sfoldername"><BR>
<B>Force Deletion?</B>True<INPUT TYPE="radio" NAME="force"
VALUE="True">False<INPUT TYPE="radio" NAME="force" VALUE="False"><BR>
<INPUT TYPE="submit" NAME="btnval" VALUE="DeleteFolder">
<B>Deletes a folder</B></FORM></TD>
</TR><TR>
<TD><FORM METHOD=POST ACTION="ServerSystem1.asp">
<B>Files for Folder:</B><INPUT TYPE="text" SIZE=50 NAME="Sfoldername"><BR>
<INPUT TYPE="submit" NAME="btnval" VALUE="ShowAllFilesInFolder">
<B>Shows all the files in a folder</B></FORM></TD>
</TR><TR>
<TD><FORM METHOD=POST ACTION="ServerSystem1.asp">
<B>Name of File to Create:</B><INPUT TYPE="text" SIZE=50
NAME="filename"><BR>
<B>For Folder:</B><INPUT TYPE="text" SIZE=50 NAME="Sfoldername"><BR>
<B>Overwrite?</B>True<INPUT TYPE="radio" NAME="overwrite"
VALUE="True">False<INPUT TYPE="radio" NAME="overwrite" VALUE="False"><BR>
<B>In Unicode?</B>True<INPUT TYPE="radio" NAME="unicode"
VALUE="True">False<INPUT TYPE="radio" NAME="unicode" VALUE="False"><BR>
<INPUT TYPE="submit" NAME="btnval" VALUE="CreateTextFileInFolder">
<B>Creates a text file within a specified folder</B></FORM></TD>
</TR>
<TR><TD>
<H3>The File Object</H3></TR><TR>
<TD><FORM METHOD=POST ACTION="ServerSystem1.asp">
<B>Path and Name of File:</B><INPUT TYPE="text" SIZE=50
NAME="filepathname"><BR>
<INPUT TYPE="submit" NAME="btnval" VALUE="DisplayFileInfo">
<B>Displays information about a file</B></FORM></TD>
</TR><TR>
<TD><FORM METHOD=POST ACTION="ServerSystem1.asp">
<B>Source File:</B><INPUT TYPE="text" SIZE=50 NAME="Sfilename"><BR>
<B>Destination File:</B><INPUT TYPE="text" SIZE=50 NAME="Dfilename"><BR>
<B>Overwrite?</B>True<INPUT TYPE="radio" NAME="overwrite"
VALUE="True">False<INPUT TYPE="radio" NAME="overwrite" VALUE="False"><BR>
<INPUT TYPE="submit" NAME="btnval" VALUE="CopyFile">
<B>Copies a file to another location</B></FORM></TD>
</TR><TR>
<TD><FORM METHOD=POST ACTION="ServerSystem1.asp">
<B>Source File:</B><INPUT TYPE="text" SIZE=50 NAME="Sfilename"><BR>
<B>Destination File:</B><INPUT TYPE="text" SIZE=50 NAME="Dfilename"><BR>
<INPUT TYPE="submit" NAME="btnval" VALUE="MoveFile">
<B>Moves a file to another location</B></FORM></TD>
</TR><TR>
<TD><FORM METHOD=POST ACTION="ServerSystem1.asp">
<B>Source File:</B><INPUT TYPE="text" SIZE=50 NAME="Sfilename"><BR>
<B>Force Deletion?</B>True<INPUT TYPE="radio" NAME="force"
VALUE="True">False<INPUT TYPE="radio" NAME="force" VALUE="False"><BR>
<INPUT TYPE="submit" NAME="btnval" VALUE="DeleteFile">
```

```
<B>Deletes a file</B></FORM></TD>
</TR>
<TR><TD>
<H3>The Scripting.TextStream Object</H3></TR><TR>
<TD><FORM METHOD=POST ACTION="ServerSystem1.asp">
<B>Text File to Open:</B><INPUT TYPE="text" SIZE=50 NAME="Sfilename"><BR>
<B>Input/Output Mode:</B>For Reading<INPUT TYPE="radio" NAME="iomode"
VALUE="1">
For Writing<INPUT TYPE="radio" NAME="iomode" VALUE="2">
For Appending<INPUT TYPE="radio" NAME="iomode" VALUE="8"><BR>
<B>Format:</B>ASCII<INPUT TYPE="radio" NAME="format" VALUE="0">
Unicode<INPUT TYPE="radio" NAME="format" VALUE="-1">
System default<INPUT TYPE="radio" NAME="format" VALUE="-2">
<BR>
<B>Line to Write to File:</B><INPUT TYPE="text" SIZE=50
NAME="linetowrite"><BR>
<INPUT TYPE="submit" NAME="btnval" VALUE="OpenTextFile">
<B>Opens a text file and writes a line</B></FORM></TD>
</TR><TR>
<TD><FORM METHOD=POST ACTION="ServerSystem1.asp">
<B>Text File to Open:</B><INPUT TYPE="text" SIZE=50 NAME="Sfilename"><BR>
<B>Input/Output Mode:</B>For Reading<INPUT TYPE="radio" NAME="iomode"
VALUE="1">
For Writing<INPUT TYPE="radio" NAME="iomode" VALUE="2">
For Appending<INPUT TYPE="radio" NAME="iomode" VALUE="8"><BR>
<B>Format:</B>ASCII<INPUT TYPE="radio" NAME="format" VALUE="0">
Unicode<INPUT TYPE="radio" NAME="format" VALUE="-1">
System default<INPUT TYPE="radio" NAME="format" VALUE="-2">
<BR>
<INPUT TYPE="submit" NAME="btnval" VALUE="ReadFileLine">
<B>Reads a line from a file</B></FORM></TD>
</TR></TABLE>
</BODY>
</HTML>
```

6

☑ *Mastery Check*

   1. What is an Object model?

     A. A model of the functions each object performs in your application

     B. A model of the objects with which users are allowed to interact

     C. A description of illustration of the relationships of objects to each other

     D. None of the above

☑ Mastery Check

2. What does the Dictionary object contain, and how can they be changed?

   A. Variables, and they can be changed by assigning new values.

   B. Name/value pairs, and they can be changed by using Dictionary object properties.

   C. Folder objects, and they can be changed by removing them.

   D. The Dictionary object contains nothing that can be changed.

3. In the File object, what attributes can be set when using the CreateTextFile method?

   A. filepath, overwrite, unicode

   B. filename, filesize, filepath

   C. filepath, filename, filesize

   D. Overwrite, Unicode, filesize

4. Which Scripting Library objects can be used to create text files?

   A. Only the File object

   B. Only the TextStream object

   C. All of them

   D. Only the FileSystemObject object, Folder object, File object, and TextStream object

5. Working with files sometimes requires navigating within them to find and edit particular sections of text. To move from one line to the next within a file, you would use the _____ method of the _____ object. To write a blank line into a file, you would use the _____ method of the _____ object. To determine what column you are in within a text file, you would use the _____ property of the _____ object.

Module 7

Major Active Server Components

The Goals of This Module

- Set up the Ad Rotator component and associated image files
- Review the Browser Capabilities component and capabilities storage text file
- Link content into Web pages using the Content Linking component
- Rotate content through Web pages with the Content Rotator component

249

Built-in ASP objects—such as the Request and Response objects, and objects included in the Scripting Runtime Library—are not the only objects or components available to ASP. There is a set of objects called ActiveX Data Objects that are extremely useful for accessing and working with databases, and we'll cover them in great detail in Modules 9 through 11. Another type of components (and the focus of this module) are referred to simply as server components, and they are installed as part of the basic installation of ASP and IIS in Windows 2000.

Active Server Components

Server components are very handy for performing functions that would otherwise take quite a bit of programming to accomplish with ASP, as well as running more quickly than plain script. In fact, it's important to use them under the appropriate circumstances because not only do they run more quickly, they can also save you a fair amount of development time. Also, they've been tested and debugged, and you can feel confident that they will work as advertised.

Within the ASP environment, scripting languages are available for use (notably VBScript and JScript) via their Dynamic Link Library (DLL) files. There is a DLL file installed and registered for VBScript and for JScript. If you intend to run other scripting languages, you must install and register their DLLs as well. Server components have DLL files also, and the ones we discuss in this module should already be installed and registered. In Module 8, we'll discuss third-party components you can buy, install, and register. By the way, you can also make and install your own components, and sell them to the public if you like.

Naturally, the first server components to be written were aimed at the most common or frequently used functions for Web site applications. For example, the Page Counter component (discussed in Module 8) counts (and records) the number of times a given page has received a hit, and it can do so for any page on your site. Tracking the number of hits a page receives provides information that can be used to analyze the layout of a Web site, and this capability has been around in various incarnations for a long time. Building this functionality into an ASP server component was an obvious step.

Creating Server Components with ASP

There are two methods you can use to create server components for your ASP pages:

- The Server.CreateObject method

- The <OBJECT> tag set

These methods are identical to the process for creating Scripting Runtime Library objects that we use in Module 6, so there's no need to do too much rehashing here. Suffice it to say, either method works fine, but only the <OBJECT> tag method within the global.asa file will create objects with application- or session-level scope.

Checking Object Instantiation

If you attempt to create a component and it isn't installed or registered, or if it is not created for any reason, your application will be damaged and perhaps unable to perform its function. Fortunately, there is a way to check whether the object exists, called the IsObject function. It can work for you like this:

```
On Error Resume Next
Set objComponent = Server.CreateObject("MSWC.ServerComponent")
If IsObject(objComponent) Then
    On Error Goto 0
Else
    Response.Write "No data available. Please try again later."
End If
```

To use this code, you would have to substitute a valid component ID, but the remaining code could be used as is. The first action is to shut off normal error handling. Next, the code instantiates the component and checks to see whether it was actually created. If so, normal error handling is turned back on and you can insert whatever scripting you'd like. If not, an error message is sent back to the user via the Response.Write method. You might also provide a Back button to take the user back to the previous page at that point.

The components we cover in this module should already be properly installed and registered, so we won't need to bother with the details of those processes here. When we get to the installation of third-party components in Module 9, we'll walk through the installation and registration process to give you a feel for what you'll encounter if you buy and install non-Microsoft components.

The Ad Rotator Component

Ah, yes—rotating ads on a Web page, such a lovely function. As you can probably tell, I have mixed feelings about this one. While click-through rates for banner ads seem to be steadily dropping, chances are you'll often find it necessary to include them in your pages, and the Ad Rotator function makes this pretty easy. As a matter of fact, a simple version of this function (called the Banner Ad Manager) is built into Microsoft FrontPage and can be used by anyone familiar with the program, without any programming. It works a little differently than the Ad Rotator component, as it rotates banner ads in the same page, rather than changing them each time the page receives a hit.

My feeling is that you'll get more mileage from building target-specific ads (or even small sections or come-ons) into a page rather than building typical banner ads. In any case, since the Ad Rotator component has the capability to display different ads each time the page receives a hit, you can use it to produce any kind of rotation schedule you like, for any image size you like.

The Schedule File

The Ad Rotator component depends on a file called the schedule file to know what ad images to display, what links to attach to them, and how frequently each one should come up. The schedule file also contains data that can send information to a redirection file (discussed in the next section) so the links can be properly formatted. Here's the schedule file for this example. Note the asterisk separating the first block of text from the rest of the file. We'll discuss the purpose of the asterisk in just a few more paragraphs:

```
REDIRECT AdRotator/RedirectionFile/RedirectFile.asp
*
AdRotator\banner1.gif
http://www.e4free.com
E4free.com
1
AdRotator\banner2.gif
http://www.acs-isad.com
Advanced Computer Services Webhosting
1
AdRotator\banner3.gif
http://www.zipwell.com
Zipwell Online Webhosting
1
```

Path and name of image file. Place to link image to ALT text to display Impression Ratio number.

Notice the first line uses the REDIRECT command to redirect the contents of the file to another file that will properly insert links and images for you. We'll cover this other file (called the redirection file) in a moment. First, let's talk about the other things that can be included in the schedule file.

Although you're only using the REDIRECT command in this example, there are some other commands you can use in the schedule file. They are

● **Width(*pixels*)**   This command sets the width of the displayed ad in pixels. If it is not included, the default of 440 pixels is used.

● **Height(*pixels*)**   This command sets the height of the displayed ad in pixels, and the default of 60 pixels is used if it is not included.

● **Border(*pixels*)**   This command sets the width of the border around the image in pixels. You can set it to 0 so no border will show.

7

Now, about the asterisk. After you enter these lines, you would put an asterisk (*) as a separator character before the individual settings for each ad are entered. Each ad setting consists of the following:

- **imageURL**   This setting points to the location of the ad image. It can be on your server or at another location entirely (for example, the Web site of the advertiser).

- **advertiserLink**   This setting points to the place to which the user is taken when the image is clicked. If no link is specified, a hyphen should be inserted here.

- **Text(*string*)**   This setting makes your page display a line of text as an alternative if the image will not display.

- **ImpressionRatioNumber**   This setting is simply a number that, when added to all the other ImpressionRatioNumbers for ads in the schedule file, represents the percentage of time this particular ad will appear on the page. For example, you have three ads in this schedule file, each of which has been assigned a 1 for its ImpressionRatioNumber. Adding these numbers together totals 3, and 1 divided by the total (3) gives 0.33 or 33 percent. So each ad will appear 33 percent of the time. By the way, there is no set order in which the ad images will appear. The Ad Rotator component generates a random selection process, but ensures that each ad shows up the appropriate number of times.

The Redirection File

The redirection file can be any valid script/file that produces the redirection effect. For this example, you'll use an ASP script using the Response.Redirect method to perform the redirection action. Your example file looks like this:

```
<% Option Explicit
Dim vSendToURL
vSendToURL = Request.QueryString("url")
Response.Redirect vSendToURL
%>
```

The sole function of this redirection file is to capture the selected redirection URL and image URL from the current schedule file ad settings. As you can see, you only capture the redirection URL in your example, as the image files are located on your own server. It is often more efficient to allow advertisers' image files to remain on their own servers and just get a reference to them from the schedule file.

Ad Rotator Methods and Properties

The Ad Rotator component has a single method and three properties, as follows:

- **GetAdvertisement(*scheduletextfile*)**   This method gets the currently selected image and URL settings (based on the impression ratio) from the schedule text file, and, in the process, creates the appropriate HTML tags to encase the image file path and name and the redirection URL.

- **Border**   This property allows you to set the size of the border around the image. If it is not specified, either the default or the BORDER command setting in the header of the schedule file will be used.

- **Clickable**   This property is either True or False, and tells the component whether the image will function as a hyperlink (using the advertiser URL specified in the schedule file). If unset, this property defaults to True.

- **TargetFrame**   This property contains the name of the frame in which to display the image. It can also be set to the standard HTML frame names, such as _child, _self, and _blank.

`project7-1.zip`

Project 7-1: An Example of Rotating Ads

It's very common to have rotating ads on your Web site, and you can pay lots of money to third-party companies for ad rotation services—so perhaps it would be a good idea to develop the capability for yourself. In this project, you'll put together a very rudimentary ad rotation service.

Step-by-Step

1. The following code is similar to previous pages you've done for
server components and objects. It brings up a button you can
use to initiate rotating ads; and after the first page load, it will
rotate the ads randomly each time the button is pressed:

```
<%
Option Explicit
Dim btnClicked
%>
<html><head><title>Using IIS Server Components</title>
<meta http-equiv="Content-Type" content="text/html; charset=iso-8859-1">
</head>
<body bgcolor="#77FF77">
<H2><font size="6">Using ASP Server Components</font></H2>
<TABLE border=1>
<TR><TD><H3>The Ad Rotator Component</H3></TD></TR><TR><TD bgcolor="white">
<%
btnClicked = Request.Form("btnval")
Select Case btnClicked
    Case "RotateAd"
        Dim objAdRotator
        Dim vAd
        Set objAdRotator = Server.CreateObject("MSWC.AdRotator")
        vAd =
objAdRotator.GetAdvertisement("AdRotator\AdRotatorTextFile.txt")
        Response.Write vAd
    End Select
%>
</TD></TR></TABLE>
<P>
<TABLE border=1><TR><TD bgcolor="#00CC99">
<H3><font size="6">The Ad Rotator Component</font></H3></TD></TR><TR>
<TD><FORM METHOD=POST ACTION="ServerComponents1.asp">
<INPUT TYPE="submit" NAME="btnval" VALUE="RotateAd">
</FORM></TD>
</TR>
</TABLE>
</BODY></HTML>
```

2. Figures 7-1 and 7-2 show the Ad Rotator component in use in
Internet Explorer 5.0, before the button is pressed and after the
button is pressed. When the button is pressed, the proper case is
selected and an Ad Rotator component is instantiated.

3. Next, a variable is set to the value of the GetAdvertisement method
for the AdRotator component, returning the proper HTML string.

4. Finally, the contents of the variable are inserted into the proper area
of the page with the Response.Write method.

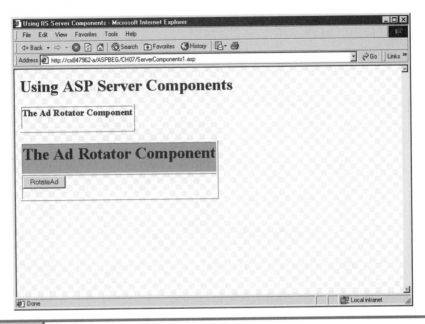

Figure 7-1   The Ad Rotator component in the browser before instantiation

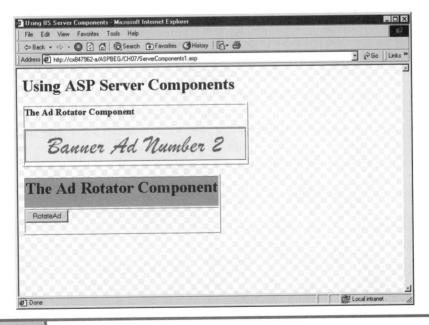

Figure 7-2   The Ad Rotator in use

The Browser Capabilities Component

Another very useful capability to add to your Web site applications is the ability to detect a user's browser type. From the early days of the Web, we've all been told what a wonderful thing it is that the Web and HTML are platform independent; but the reality is slipping ever closer to the proprietary, platform dependent nature of traditional applications programs. Every new version of browser seems to add new, nonstandard features that other browser brands don't (and won't) support, and it's not uncommon to code several versions of a page to be compliant with the majority of browser types currently in use.

Adding the Browser Capabilities component means you can at least detect and respond with appropriate Web pages to most of the browsers out there. Although it won't rewrite your pages for you yet, the time is approaching when you'll be able to build in the logic to automatically redefine your Web pages on the fly to be compliant with whatever browser the user happens to be using. This kind of user-based response system will make the Web much more user friendly, so expect developers to adopt these capabilities very rapidly as they become more mainstream.

The browscap.ini File

On your server there is a file named browscap.ini, probably in the WINNT\System32\inetsrv folder. If you're not sure where it is, use the search function in Windows Explorer to find it by name. This file holds the capabilities of browsers for which it has been most recently updated. To keep up with the capabilities of new browsers and versions as they appear, you'll want to perform regular maintenance to this file and make sure it is updated often. There are Web sites where updated versions of browscap.ini are made available, including Microsoft's own Web site.

Like other text files holding data for use by a component, the browscap.ini file has its own special syntax and data elements. Here's a small section from the browscap.ini file installed with Windows 2000:

```
;;;;;;;;;;;;;;;;;;;;;;;;;;;;;;;;;;;;;;;;;;;; IE 5.0
[IE 5.0]
browser=IE
Version=5.0
majorver=5
minorver=0
frames=True
```

```
tables=True
cookies=True
backgroundsounds=True
vbscript=True
javaapplets=True
javascript=True
ActiveXControls=True
```

Comments can be added anywhere with the semicolon, as you can see on the first line, and individual browser sections are headed by the name and version of the browser encased in brackets, as shown on the second line. Following that, each property defined by this file has its own line with the name of the property set equal to the value of the property for this browser/version. Although several of the values are strings, most of them are simply True or False Boolean values. These initial sections are called the parent browser sections, and they are followed by smaller sections that contain properties of specific minor versions or nongeneric versions for that browser type.

Displaying Browser Capabilities

Any ASP page can display the user's browser capabilities using the code shown after this paragraph; and if you can capture browser capabilities with an ASP page, you can easily redirect users to an appropriate version of the file to which they are connecting. Here's the example ASP page code:

```
<%
Option Explicit
Dim btnClicked
%>
<html><head><title>Using IIS Server Components</title>
<meta http-equiv="Content-Type" content="text/html; charset=iso-8859-1">
</head>
<body bgcolor="#77FF77">
<H2><font size="6">Using ASP Server Components</font></H2>
<TABLE border=1>
<TR><TD><H3>The Browser Capabilities Component</H3></TD></TR><TR><TD
bgcolor="white">
<%
btnClicked = Request.Form("btnval")
Select Case btnClicked
     Case "DisplayBrowserCapabilities"
          Dim objBrowserCap
          Dim colBrowserCap
          Set objBrowserCap = Server.CreateObject("MSWC.BrowserType")
          colBrowserCap = objBrowserCap("browser")
          Response.Write "<B>Your Browser Is " & colBrowserCapcolBrowserCap
=objBrowserCap("Version")
```

7

```
         Response.Write colBrowserCap & "</B><BR>"
         colBrowserCap = objBrowserCap("majorver")
         Response.Write "<B>The major version is " & colBrowserCap &
"</B><BR>"
         colBrowserCap = objBrowserCap("minorver")
         Response.Write "<B>The minor version is " & colBrowserCap &
"</B><BR>"
         colBrowserCap = objBrowserCap("frames")
         Response.Write "<B>It is " & colBrowserCap & " that your browser
supports frames</B><BR>"
         colBrowserCap = objBrowserCap("tables")
         Response.Write "<B>It is " & colBrowserCap & " that your browser
supports tables</B><BR>"
         colBrowserCap = objBrowserCap("cookies")
         Response.Write "<B>It is " & colBrowserCap & " that your browser
supports cookies</B><BR>"
         colBrowserCap = objBrowserCap("backgroundsounds")
         Response.Write "<B>It is " & colBrowserCap & " that your browser
supports background sounds</B><BR>"
         colBrowserCap = objBrowserCap("vbscript")
         Response.Write "<B>It is " & colBrowserCap & " that your browser
supports VBScript</B><BR>"
         colBrowserCap = objBrowserCap("javaapplets")
         Response.Write "<B>It is " & colBrowserCap & " that your browser
supports javaapplets</B><BR>"
         colBrowserCap = objBrowserCap("javascript")
         Response.Write "<B>It is " & colBrowserCap & " that your browser
supports javascript</B><BR>"
         colBrowserCap = objBrowserCap("ActiveXControls")
         Response.Write "<B>It is " & colBrowserCap & " that your browser
supports ActiveX controls</B><BR>"
         End Select
%>
</TD></TR></TABLE>
<P>
<TABLE border=1><TR><TD bgcolor="#00CC99">
<H3><font size="6">The Browser Capabilities
Component</font></H3></TD></TR><TR>
<TD><FORM METHOD=POST ACTION="ServerComponents2.asp">
<INPUT TYPE="submit" NAME="btnval" VALUE="DisplayBrowserCapabilities">
</FORM></TD>
</TR>
</TABLE>
</BODY></HTML>
```

This page dimensions a couple of variables and then uses one to create a Browser Capabilities component instance. Next, it makes a variable equal to the "browser" property value and writes that back to the user. Then it makes the variable equal to the "version" property value and writes that back to the user, and so on and so forth, until it has gone through most of the properties available. You can see the results in Figure 7-3.

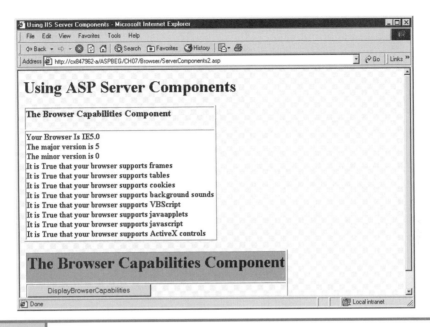

Figure 7-3   Browser capabilities listed

1-Minute Drill

- **How are click-throughs enabled with the Ad Rotator component?**
- **In the browscap.ini file, what delimiters contain the browser name?**

The Content Linking Component

Those of us born back in the age of books are familiar with the traditional, linear way of reading through material from front to back, and a standard part of most books is the table of contents. For those born into the information age, the table of contents may seem somewhat archaic, approaching obsolescence. For myself, it's hard to imagine reading material

---

- **The URL is specified after the path and name of the image file.**
- **[and]**

without a table of contents, and so it's not surprising that I've created hypertext classroom materials (static Web pages) that include tables of contents.

A table of contents is actually meta-data about the contents of a work (whether book, magazine, Web site, or whatever) that provides an easy way to skim and find information of interest. In the case of the Content Linking component, the purpose of this component is to create an easy way to access table of contents, as well as a set of navigable links through that content. The Content Linking component has a set of methods (listed next) that allows you not only to find out how much content (how many files) you're dealing with, but to return a description and link to each, as well as move among the pages with ease.

Now, you might think the average person could just as easily use the Back and Forward buttons on his or her browser to perform these actions; and in many cases, you'd be right—but there are also many circumstances in which you'll find it convenient to control the movement of a user through your site. The Content Linking component offers that kind of control.

The Content Linking List File

Like the other components you've encountered, the Content Linking component depends on an external file kept on the server for its list of navigable content. A typical Content Linking list file will be a text file looking somewhat like the following example:

Tab-delimited text file

```
ScannerClass/Section1.html    Scanner Class Introduction    Includes
introduction, Image acquisition, Digitizing
ScannerClass/Section1-Software.html    Scanner Software    Includes typical
software for scanners
ScannerClass/Section1-ColorPrinters.html    Color Printers    Includes color
printer data
ScannerClass/Section1-BuildingQuality.htm    Getting Good Results    Tells
how to properly scan
ScannerClass/Section1-Shopping.html    Shopping for Scanners    Tells what
to look for when shopping for scanners
```

Although it may not be easy to tell from the file just listed, the Content Linking list file is just a plain text file, each line of which includes three things: the relative URL of the content page of interest, the display text, and a comment describing the content. Each of the three sections of a line must be separated by a tab character (not spaces). Wherever the file is saved, the URL must, of course, be appropriate to point to the content files.

The Content Linking Component Methods

The Content Linking component has no properties, only the following methods:

- **GetListCount(*contenttextfile*)**   This method returns the number of file listings in the content text file.

- **GetListIndex(*contenttextfile*)**   This method returns the index number of the current page in the content text file.

- **GetNextURL(*contenttextfile*)**   This method returns the URL for the next page in the content text file list.

- **GetNextDescription(*contenttextfile*)**   This method returns the description for the next page in the content text file.

- **GetPreviousURL(*contenttextfile*)**   This method returns the URL for the previous page in the content text file.

- **GetPreviousDescription(*contenttextfile*)**   This method returns the description for the previous page in the content text file.

- **GetNthURL(*contenttextfile,number*)**   This method return the URL for the page indicated by number in the content text file.

- **GetNthDescription(*contenttextfile,number*)**   This method returns the description for the page indicated by number in the content text file.

project7-2.zip

Project 7-2: Using the Content Linking Component

The Content Linking component is useful for creating tables of contents and providing navigation links across the site. This example uses a mechanism similar to that used in previous examples to provide the user with the ability to activate an instance of the Content Linking

7

component. It also displays a series of links to content listed in the Content text file. Here's an easy exercise to do on your own.

Step-by-Step

1. Navigation buttons on each page can be created using the GetNext and GetPrevious methods of the Content Linking component. Here's the example code:

```
<%
Option Explicit
Dim btnClicked
%>
<html><head><title>Using IIS Server Components</title>
<meta http-equiv="Content-Type" content="text/html; charset=iso-8859-1">
</head>
<body bgcolor="#77FF77">
<H2><font size="6">Using ASP Server Components</font></H2>
<TABLE border=1>
<TR><TD><H3>The Content Linking Component</H3></TD></TR><TR><TD
bgcolor="white">
<%
btnClicked = Request.Form("btnval")
Select Case btnClicked
    Case "DisplayLinkList"
        Dim objContent
        Dim intI
        Dim intC
        Dim vURL
        Dim vDesc
        Set objContent = Server.CreateObject("MSWC.NextLink")
        intI = 1
        intC = objContent.GetListCount("ScannerContent.txt")
        Response.Write "<OL>"
        For intI = 1 to intC
            vURL = objContent.GetNthURL("ScannerContent.txt", intI)
            vDesc = objContent.GetNthDescription("ScannerContent.txt",
intI)
            Response.Write "<LI><B><A HREF= """
            Response.Write vURL
            Response.Write """">"
            Response.Write vDesc
            Response.Write "</A></B>"
        Next
            Response.Write "</OL>"
End Select
%>
</TD></TR></TABLE>
<P>
<TABLE border=1><TR><TD bgcolor="#00CC99">
<H3><font size="6">The Content Linking Component</font></H3></TD></TR><TR>
<TD><FORM METHOD=POST ACTION="ServerComponents3.asp">
<INPUT TYPE="submit" NAME="btnval" VALUE="DisplayLinkList">
```

> **Counting through the list using the GetListCount method.**

```
</FORM></TD>
</TR>
</TABLE>
</BODY></HTML>
```

2. This code creates an instance of the Content Linking component and iterates through all the pages of content listed in the Content Linking list file with a numbered list (the <OL> and <LI> tags).

3. For each content file listed, it retrieves the URL and the description with the GetNthURL and GetNthDescription methods, using the counter intI to count each time through the loop. The variable intC is just used to hold the number of items in the list, which it retrieves with the GetListCount method. Figure 7-4 shows the linked list of files onscreen.

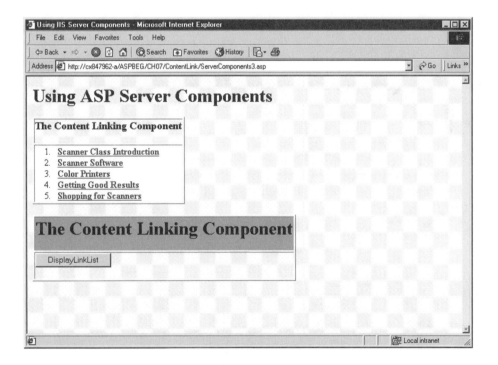

Figure 7-4   Results of the Content Linking component

The Content Rotator Component

The Content Rotator component is similar to the Ad Rotator component in that it displays selected content according to a preset ratio (not a schedule or timetable). Like the Ad Rotator component, it uses a schedule file to list the content to be included in the rotation, but the only thing you can set (other than the content to display) is the rotation ratio. Again, you simply use a number to indicate the ratio, based on the total of all included numbers for each set of content you wish to display.

Content Rotator Methods

The content Rotator component has two methods:

- **GetAllContent(***contentlistfile***)**   This method displays all the content entries in the schedule file.

- **ChooseContent(***contentlistfile***)**   This method retrieves the next selected content listing from the schedule file according to the ratio you set.

The Content Rotator Schedule File   The Content Rotator schedule file does not display content on a schedule, as its name implies, but rather displays content according to the ratio you've set. Each content item starts with two percent signs (%%) and then the schedule ratio number. Following that are some comments (following the two slashes) and then the lines of content, which can be whatever you like until the next set of percent signs are encountered:

```
%% 1 //This text will display five percent of the time
For excellent web hosting and construction services,
please visit <A HREF="www.zipwell.com">Zipwell Online</A>

%% 3 //This text will display fifteen percent of the time
For unique Web graphics design and artistry,
please visit <A HREF="www.allwebworks.com">All Web Works</A>

%% 5 //This text will display twenty-five percent of the time
For full-featured web hosting, including collaboration services,
please visit <A HREF="www.acs-isad.com">Advanced Computer Services</A>

%%11 //This text will display 55 percent of the time
For discrete application services please visit
<A HREF="www.e4free.com">E4free</A>
```

Rotating Content

This example uses code like the other examples you've used for working with components. After the initial page load you'll be able to rotate content each time you click the button provided, as shown in Figure 7-5. The example code is as follows:

```
<%
Option Explicit
Dim btnClicked
%>
<html><head><title>Using IIS Server Components</title>
<meta http-equiv="Content-Type" content="text/html; charset=iso-8859-1">
</head>
<body bgcolor="#77FF77">
<H2><font size="6">Using ASP Server Components</font></H2>
<TABLE border=1>
<TR><TD><H3>The Content Rotator Component</H3></TD></TR><TR><TD
bgcolor="white">
<%
btnClicked = Request.Form("btnval")
Select Case btnClicked
     Case "DisplayContent"
          Dim objContentRotator
          Dim vCont
          Set objContentRotator = Server.CreateObject("MSWC.ContentRotator")
          vCont = objContentRotator.ChooseContent("ContentRotator.txt")
          Response.Write vCont
End Select
%>
</TD></TR></TABLE>
<P>
<TABLE border=1><TR><TD bgcolor="#00CC99">
<H3><font size="6">The Content Rotator Component</font></H3></TD></TR><TR>
<TD><FORM METHOD=POST ACTION="ServerComponents4.asp">
<INPUT TYPE="submit" NAME="btnval" VALUE="DisplayContent">
</FORM></TD>
</TR>
</TABLE>
</BODY></HTML>
```

7

1-Minute Drill

- **What method is used to get the number of files in the content linking text file?**

- **What notation is used to specify the percentage of time content items are rotated?**

- **GetListCount**
- **%% and then the number**

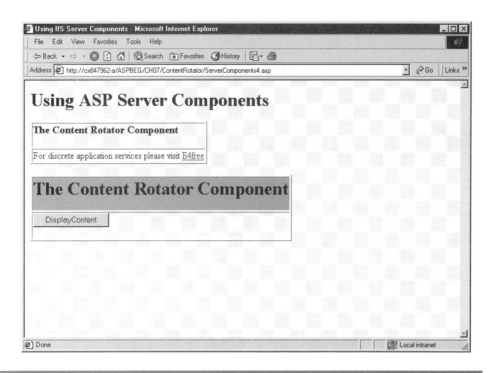

Figure 7-5 Rotating content

Ask the Expert

Question: It sounds like these components are actually little programs that run on my server. Is this the case? How many can I run? Should I pay for them or create them myself? Where can I get them?

Answer: Yes, you're right. Components are compiled programs that run on your server when they are instantiated using one of the two methods described at the beginning of this module. Since they are compiled, they run faster than script would; and since they are prebuilt and pretested, the bugs have been worked out. You don't have to buy the ones discussed in this module (or in the beginning of the next module); but typically, you would buy components made by third parties, unless they are giving away time-limited demos or "light" versions.

You can run as many as your system resources will allow, meaning you are constrained by the amount of memory and processor capability, just like any other programs. You can find third-party components on most Web sites related to ASP, and we'll cover some of them in the next module.

Question: **These components make use of text files on the server. Is this a security risk? Will people be loading things on my server and perhaps compromising security?**

Answer: Users of your site will be activating components via ASP; so as long as those script files are secure, there's not much they can do other than overload your system if too many of them hit your site at once. However, if you happen to be developing sites for other people, it is probable they will want to manage their sites from their locations. This means you will have to allow access to some sensitive areas on your server, so it is a good idea to build management pages for them that will allow them to do what they need to do without having full access to the server. Since you're going to be developing management pages, take the time to set up appropriate users and groups, and limit the actions client-users can take on your server. It's worth the effort to preserve your peace of mind.

`project7-3.zip`

Project 7-3: Beginning Your Web Site Application

In this project, you'll begin to arrange pages in a fashion similar to what you might use for a normal Web site application, although yours will undoubtedly be much more complex. Please note that your first script will probably be named index.asp or default.asp, rather than the descriptive name (detect.asp) given here, unless you reset the server to go to a beginning page of another name by default.

Step-by-Step

1. We've covered the Browser Capabilities component in this module because what it can do makes it an obvious candidate for a first page, although people will never see it on their screen. With the following code, you'll create the structure for a browser detection page that will determine what browser people are using and then redirect them to the appropriate version of your Web pages, each stored in a separate folder of its own on your Web site.

2. The page contains no ordinary HTML, because it should never be seen. However, you may want to add some very basic HTML to accommodate those cases in which no browser type can be determined:

```
<%
Option Explicit
Dim objBrowserCap
Dim vBrowserCapType
Dim vBrowserCapVersion
Set objBrowserCap = Server.CreateObject("MSWC.BrowserType")
vBrowserCapType = objBrowserCap("browser")
vBrowserCapVersion = objBrowserCap("version")
If vBrowserCapType = "IE" Then
    Select Case vBrowserCapVersion
        Case "5.0"
            Response.Redirect "IE5/start.asp"
        Case "4.0"
        Case "3.0"
        Case "2.0"
        Case "1.5"
    End Select
End If
%>
```

3. Notice the example includes an If statement to determine whether the browser type is Internet Explorer, and then a Select statement to find which version it is. You can add as many If statements as you like to determine browser type, and then Select statements for each version within that type. Following the If statements would be an appropriate place for any plain HTML that might be required to service unknown browser types.

4. For your first page, use the name start.asp and insert it into a folder named IE5 (users are redirected there by detect.asp). Of course, you could use home.asp, or first.asp, or whatever you wish. I created the structure of this example page in about three minutes using FrontPage 2000, and you can certainly use whatever tool is handy and then copy and paste your ASP script into it. The start.asp code looks like this:

```
<%
Option Explicit
%>
<html><head><title>Our Site for IE 5.0 Browsers</title>
<meta http-equiv="Content-Type" content="text/html; charset=iso-8859-1">
</head>
<body bgcolor="#FFFFFF">
<div align="center">
<center>
<table border="0" cellpadding="6" width="96%">
<tr>
<td colspan=3>
<%
Dim objAdRotator
Dim vAd
Set objAdRotator = Server.CreateObject("MSWC.AdRotator")
objAdRotator.TargetFrame="Target=" & Chr(34) & "_blank" & chr(34)
vAd = objAdRotator.GetAdvertisement("AdRot.txt")
Response.Write vAd
%>
</td>
</tr>
<tr>
<td width="15%">
</td>
<td colspan="2" nowrap>
<p align="center"><font size="6">Welcome!!</font></td>
<td width="15%"></td>
</tr>
<tr>
<td valign="top" width="15%"><font size="2"><strong></strong></font><font
size="3"><br>
</font><font size="2"></font>
<p><font size="2"><strong>SECTION 1</strong></font><font size="4"><br>
</font><font size="2">
<%
Dim objContent
Dim intI
Dim intC
Dim vURL
Dim vDesc
Set objContent = Server.CreateObject("MSWC.NextLink")
intI = 1
intC = objContent.GetListCount("ContLink.txt")
For intI = 1 to intC
    vURL = objContent.GetNthURL("ContLink.txt", intI)
    vDesc = objContent.GetNthDescription("ContLink.txt", intI)
    Response.Write "<A HREF= """
    Response.Write vURL
    Response.Write """>"
    Response.Write vDesc
    Response.Write "</A><P>"
```

```
Next
%>
</font></p>
        <p><font size="2"><strong>SECTION 2</strong></font><font
size="3"><br>
        </font><font size="2">Title  1<br>
        Title  2<br>
        Title  3<br>
        Title  4<br>
        Title  5</font></p>
        </td>
<td valign="top" width="30%"><font size="2">Lorem ipsum dolor sit amet,
consectetuer adipiscing elit, sed diem nonummy nibh euismod tincidunt
ut lacreet dolore magna aliguam erat volutpat. Ut wisis enim ad minim
veniam, quis nostrud exerci tution ullamcorper suscipit lobortis nisl
ut aliquip ex ea commodo consequat. Duis te feugifacilisi. Duis autem
dolor in hendrerit in vulputate velit esse molestie consequat, vel
illum dolore eu feugiat nulla facilisis at vero eros et accumsan et
iusto odio dignissim qui blandit praesent luptatum zzril delenit au
gue duis dolore te feugat nulla facilisi.</font>
<p><font size="2">Ut wisi enim ad minim veniam, quis nostrud exerci
taion ullamcorper suscipit lobortis nisl ut aliquip ex en commodo
consequat. Duis te feugifacilisi per suscipit lobortis nisl ut
aliquip ex en commodo consequat.Lorem ipsum dolor sit amet,
consectetuer adipiscing elit, sed diem nonummy nibh euismod tincidunt
ut lacreet dolore magna aliguam erat volutpat. Ut wisis enim ad minim
veniam, quis nostrud exerci tution ullamcorper suscipit lobortis nisl
ut aliquip ex ea commodo consequat.</font></td>
<td valign="top" width="30%"><font size="2">Ut wisis enim ad minim
veniam, quis nostrud exerci tution ullamcorper suscipit lobortis nisl
ut aliquip ex ea commodo consequat. Duis te feugifacilisi. Duis autem
dolor in hendrerit in vulputate velit esse molestie consequat,
vel illum dolore eu feugiat nulla facilisis at vero eros et accumsan
et iusto odio dignissim qui blandit praesent luptatum zzril delenit
au gue duis dolore te feugat nulla facilisi.</font>
<p><font size="2">Ut wisis enim ad minim veniam, quis nostrud exerci
tution ullamcorper suscipit lobortis nisl ut aliquip ex ea commodo
consequat.</font></p>
<p><font size="2">Lorem ipsum dolor sit amet, consectetuer adipiscing
elit, sed diem nonummy nibh euismod tincidunt ut lacreet dolore magna
aliguam erat volutpat.</font></td>
<td width="15%"><font size="1">
<%
Dim objContentRotator
Dim vCont
Set objContentRotator = Server.CreateObject("MSWC.ContentRotator")
vCont = objContentRotator.ChooseContent("ContRot.txt")
Response.Write vCont
%>
</td>
</tr>
</table>
</center>
</div>
</BODY></HTML>
```

Filler Text to make
the page look normal

5. The code in this example first rotates in a banner ad, a common practice on commercial Web pages. It pulls the information for the banner ad from both the Ad Rotator schedule file and the Ad Rotator redirection file. Figure 7-6 shows the finished product.

6. Within the body of the page, the code places a table with three columns and several rows. The first row displays a Welcome message in the center column. The second row displays, in the left column, a table of contents or menu selection using the Content Linking component; in the center two columns, some fake text; and in the right column, a sidebar that changes each time the page is accessed. The sidebar uses the Content Rotator component to switch out text content.

Figure 7-6   **Your IE 5.0 Web page with rotating content and ads**

7. Let's look at the Ad Rotator schedule file first:

```
REDIRECT AdRotRed.asp
*
E4free1.gif
http://www.e4free.com
E4free.com
1
header1.jpg
http://www.acs-isad.com
Advanced Computer Services Webhosting
1
topleft1.jpg
http://www.zipwell.com
Zipwell Online Webhosting
1
```

8. The rotation schedule file displays images according to the impression ratio set, and inserts the HTML for links according to data contained in the redirection file, as follows:

```
<% Option Explicit
Dim vSendToURL
vSendToURL = Request.QueryString("url")
Response.Redirect vSendToURL
%>
```

9. For the menu in the left column, use the Content Linking component to insert a list of links from the content link text file, as shown here:

```
ScannerClass/Section1.html    Scanner Class Introduction
Includes introduction, Image acquisition, Digitizing
ScannerClass/Section1-Software.html    Scanner Software
Includes typical software for scanners
ScannerClass/Section1-ColorPrinters.html    Color Printers
Includes color printer data
ScannerClass/Section1-BuildingQuality.htm    Getting Good
Results    Tells how to properly scan
ScannerClass/Section1-Shopping.html    Shopping for
Scanners    Tells what to look for when shopping for
scanners
```

10. Again, this text file simply contains three pieces of information separated by tab characters: the path and filename where the page is located, the display text for the hyperlink, and a short description of the content of the page for your own use.

11. Finally, the page pulls text content rotated randomly from the content rotation schedule file as follows:

```
%% 2 //This text will display twenty percent of the time
<FONT COLOR="red">Duis te feugifacilisi. Duis autem dolor in
hendrerit in vulputate velit esse molestie consequat, vel illum dolore
eu feugiat nulla facilisis at vero eros et accumsan et iusto odio
dignissim qui blandit praesent luptatum zzril delenit au gue duis dolore
te feugat nulla facilisi.</font>
%% 3 //This text will display thirty percent of the time
<FONT COLOR="green">Duis te feugifacilisi. Duis autem dolor in
hendrerit in vulputate velit esse molestie consequat, vel illum dolore
eu feugiat nulla facilisis at vero eros et accumsan et iusto odio
dignissim qui blandit praesent luptatum zzril delenit au gue duis dolore
te feugat nulla facilisi.</font>
%% 5 //This text will display fifty percent of the time
<FONT COLOR="blue">Duis te feugifacilisi. Duis autem dolor in
hendrerit in vulputate velit esse molestie consequat, vel illum dolore
eu feugiat nulla facilisis at vero eros et accumsan et iusto odio
dignissim qui blandit praesent luptatum zzril delenit au gue duis dolore
te feugat nulla facilisi.</font>
```

12. The rotation ratio has been modified in the code here to display one set 20 percent of the time, the next set 30 percent of the time, and the last set 50 percent of the time. Also, to make it more noticeable that the text is changing, the color of the text is different for each block displayed.

7

☑ *Mastery Check*

1. What capabilities does the Ad Rotator component offer?

   A. It stores banner ads for display.

   B. It provides a means of accessing banner ads for scheduled rotation display.

   C. It provides a means of accessing banner ads for random rotation according to a set percentage for display.

   D. None of the above.

☑ *Mastery Check*

2. Why is the Browser Capabilities component so important, and where is the content it uses kept?

A. It detects browser types, providing a means to display customized Web content based on browser type and version. The content it uses to accomplish this is kept in a text file named browscap.ini.

B. It can automatically refer to a browscap.ini file located on the sites of the major browser manufacturers, and make sure your content is always compatible with the latest browser types and versions.

C. It checks the browser you currently have installed to make sure it is the most up-to-date version, so your pages will always be compatible with the latest browser types and versions.

D. None of the above.

3. How does the Content Linking component perform its job?

A. It links the content of your Web site for you, without the traditional hyperlinks.

B. It refers to a content linking text file for information about path, name, and description of the files in your Web site, and uses methods and properties to assist the user in navigating the site.

C. It links the content of your site with the content of other sites automatically, generating more traffic through reciprocal links.

D. None of the above.

4. What is one of the primary advantages of using the Content Rotator component?

A. You can set the rotation schedule and forget it, meaning you have less management to do.

B. You can rotate text and hyperlinks across your pages according to the percentage paid for by advertisers.

C. Rotating content in 3-D is a cool effect to add to your site.

D. Rotating content in 3-D is hard to do manually, and the Content Rotator does it for you.

Module 8

More Active Server Components

The Goals of This Module

- Use the Counters component for general tracking
- Create a Page Counter component and track page hits
- Set permissions and check them with the Permission Checker component
- Examine and use the tools in the Tools component
- Create log records with the Logging Utility component
- Install and use Infomentum's ActiveFile component for uploading/downloading

In Module 7, we made a good dent in testing out some of the most commonly used Active Server components. In this module, we'll cover the rest of the available components, as well as some of the third-party components that can be installed and run—specifically a well-made component for uploading and downloading files.

More Active Server Components

A good place to look for third-party components is **http://www.15seconds.com**, a Web site devoted to the construction of ASP Web sites and ASP applications. If you visit **http://www.15seconds.com/component/default.htm**, you'll find tons of free, shareware, and commercial components for evaluation and operational use, as well as plenty of reviews and documentation. You can also find many other sites where ASP is the main topic of discussion and where third-party components are available. Simply go to your favorite search engine and enter "Active Server Pages," "ASP Components," "Microsoft IIS Server Components," and so forth.

More Microsoft IIS Server Components

We covered how to create server components in the previous module, so we won't discuss it further here. In Module 5, we covered the MyInfo component, so that is also omitted here. There are some issues concerning third-party components (such as installation, registration, documentation, and support) that will be covered later in this module. For now, let's just jump right into the rest of the installed components and their usefulness. In addition to what we have covered in other modules, the following server components are available with a standard installation of Windows 2000:

● The Counters component, for counting anything you want to track

● The Page Counter component, for tracking page hits

● The Permission Checker component, for checking authorization levels

● The Tools component, a set of ASP tools for common functions

● The Logging Utility component, for managing log files

These components should already be installed and ready for use when you install IIS 5.0.

The Counters Component

The Counters component is a single component that can easily be used to create any number of individual counters for an application. Since you create the Counters component from within the global.asa file, these counters are accessible from any page in your application; but by the same token, this component does not scale very well. However, it is easy to use and can be quite helpful in a pinch.

Each counter you create holds a number (an integer) in a text file named counter.txt. Please note that this text file is not updated until the application ends or the server is stopped. It is not a good reference for existing counter values in real time.

Counters Component Methods

The Counters component has methods for creating counters and retrieving their values, as well as incrementing or setting values, and removing counters altogether (there are no properties). The methods are

● **Get(*counter*)**   This method returns the current value of whatever counter you specify. If the counter doesn't exist, it creates it and returns zero as the value.

● **Increment(*counter*)**   This method increases the value of the specified counter by one. If the counter doesn't exist, it also creates the counter and sets the value to 1.

● **Remove(*counter*)**   This method removes the specified counter.

● **Set(*counter,value*)**   This method sets the value of the specified counter to *value*. If the counter doesn't exist, it also creates the counter and sets the value to *value*.

8

Project 8-1: Using the Counters Component

To make a Counters component part of an application, there are several things you must do. The methods available are fairly straightforward, but put you in the position of performing some activities in a slightly convoluted way. This project takes you through the basic construction of a Counters component and demonstrates its usage.

Step-by-Step

1. The first step is to add some code to the global.asa file.

As mentioned earlier, to use the Counters component, you'll need to instantiate it from the global.asa file. You can perform this operation by placing code like the following in your global.asa file:

```
<OBJECT ID="objCounter" RUNAT="server" SCOPE="Application"
PROGID="MSWC.Counters">
</OBJECT>
```

All you did was use the <OBJECT> tags, and give your component a name and "Application" scope. The program ID is simply "MSWC.Counters."

2. Now that you have a Counters component ready, you can make counters on any page of your application, just by naming them and using one of the Counters component methods. In this example, you'll use the familiar Select statement to create, increment, set, and remove counters according to the contents of a fill-out form. Here goes:

```
<%
Option Explicit
Dim btnClicked
%>
<html><head><title>Using IIS Server Components</title>
<meta http-equiv="Content-Type" content="text/html; charset=iso-8859-1">
</head>
<body bgcolor="#77FF77">
<H2><font size="6">Using ASP Server Components</font></H2>
<TABLE border=1>
<TR><TD><H3>The Counters Component</H3></TD></TR><TR><TD bgcolor="white">
<%
btnClicked = Request.Form("btnval")
Select Case btnClicked
```

```
     Case "CreateCounter1"
          Dim vCounterName
          vCounterName = Request.Form("CounterName")
          objCounter.Get(vCounterName)
          Response.Write "You have created " & vCounterName & " and it's
value is: "
          Response.Write objCounter.Get(vCounterName)
     Case "IncrementCounter1"
          vCounterName = Request.Form("IncrementName")
          objCounter.Increment(vCounterName)
          Response.Write "You have incremented " & vCounterName & " and it's
value is: "
          Response.Write objCounter.Get(vCounterName)
     Case "SetCounter1"
          Dim vSetCounterValue
          vCounterName = Request.Form("CounterName")
          vSetCounterValue = Request.Form("SetCounterValue")
          objCounter.Set vCounterName, vSetCounterValue
          Response.Write "You have set " & vCounterName & " and it's value
is now: "
          Response.Write objCounter.Get(vCounterName)
     Case "RemoveCounter1"
          vCounterName = Request.Form("CounterName")
          objCounter.Remove vCounterName
          Response.Write "You have removed " & vCounterName
End Select
%>
</TD></TR></TABLE>
<P>
<TABLE border=1><TR><TD bgcolor="#00CC99" COLSPAN=3>
<H3><font size="6">The Counters Component</font></H3></TD></TR><TR>
<TD><FORM METHOD=POST ACTION="ServerComponents5.asp">
Enter a Counter Name:</TD><TD><INPUT TYPE="text" NAME="CounterName"
SIZE="20"></TD><TD>
<INPUT TYPE="submit" NAME="btnval" VALUE="CreateCounter1"></TD></TR>
</FORM>
<TR>
<TD><FORM METHOD=POST ACTION="ServerComponents5.asp">
Increment a Counter:</TD><TD><INPUT TYPE="text" NAME="IncrementName"
SIZE="20"></TD><TD>
<INPUT TYPE="submit" NAME="btnval" VALUE="IncrementCounter1"></TD></TR>
</FORM>
<TR>
<TD><FORM METHOD=POST ACTION="ServerComponents5.asp">
Set a Counter:</TD><TD><INPUT TYPE="text" NAME="CounterName" SIZE="20"> to
<INPUT TYPE="text" NAME="SetCounterValue" SIZE="2"></TD><TD>
<INPUT TYPE="submit" NAME="btnval" VALUE="SetCounter1"></TD></TR>
</FORM>
<TR>
<TD><FORM METHOD=POST ACTION="ServerComponents5.asp">
Remove a Counter:</TD><TD><INPUT TYPE="text" NAME="CounterName"
SIZE="20"></TD><TD>
<INPUT TYPE="submit" NAME="btnval" VALUE="RemoveCounter1"></TD></TR>
</FORM>
</TABLE>
</BODY></HTML>
```

8

3. You've named this file ServerComponents5.asp, so each time the form is filled out and submitted, it submits to itself. The page in the browser is shown in Figure 8-1.

4. The first form allows the user to enter a name for a counter to create. The first case of the Select statement creates the counter and gets the value of that counter for display in the response. Technically, it's not necessary to use the Get method twice; but logically, it is more intuitive.

5. There is no Create method, so creation and value retrieval are combined in Get, and we use the method twice here to illustrate both creating the counter and getting its value.

6. The next two forms allow the user to increment the counter and set the value of the counter, with the work being done by the Select statement cases, respectively. Incrementing the counter is accomplished by entering the name of the counter in the form and using the Increment method for that case.

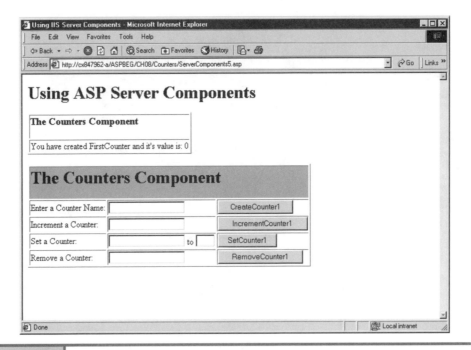

Figure 8-1 The Counters page in the browser

─Hint─────────────────────────────────────

Please keep in mind that if the user enters a counter name that does not exist, a new counter of that name will be created and set to a value of 1. The Set method works in a similar fashion, except that the user can specify the value to be set for the counter specified.

7. The last form and case pair in your code simply removes the specified counter entirely. However, there is no method that will check for the existence of a counter without creating that counter and setting its value to zero at least. So if a counter is removed but then checked with any of the other methods available, it will be immediately re-created.

The Page Counter Component

The Page Counter component is a special kind of counter specifically designed to help track the number of hits a page gets. Unlike the Counters component, it makes use of an internal Central Management object to write page hit counts to a text file periodically, so that if the server is shut down, the data isn't lost.

Page Counter Methods

Like the Counters component, the Page Counter component has no properties, only methods. They are

- **Hits(*pagepath*)**   This method returns the hit count for the specified page; but if the *pagepath* argument is left out, it returns the hit count for the current page.

- **PageHit()**   This method increments the hit count for the current page.

- **Reset(*pagepath*)**   This method resets the hit count to zero for whatever page is specified, or for the current page if *pagepath* is left out.

Working with Page Hits

Typically, the Webmaster will be interested in the number of hits a page has gotten, and there was a time when it was common to display the

8

number of page hits on the page itself. The Page Counter component can be used for either of these purposes, but you should keep in mind that there are very elaborate, well-done, and graphical page hit counting services and software available, so you might not want to reinvent the wheel. Also, displaying the number of hits on a page has become pretty dated. Here is an example of using the Page Counter, and even a way to set your page hit count to whatever number you like. Here's the code:

```
<%
Option Explicit
Dim btnClicked
Dim objPageCounter
Set objPageCounter = Server.CreateObject("MSWC.PageCounter")
%>
<html><head><title>Using IIS Server Components</title>
<meta http-equiv="Content-Type" content="text/html; charset=iso-8859-1">
</head> ·
<body bgcolor="#77FF77">
<H2><font size="6">Using ASP Server Components</font></H2>
<TABLE border=1>
<TR><TD><H3>The Page Counter Component</H3></TD></TR><TR><TD
bgcolor="white">
<%
btnClicked = Request.Form("btnval")
Select Case btnClicked
    Case "GetHits"
        Dim vPagePath
        vPagePath = Request.Form("PagePath")
        objPageCounter.PageHit()
        Response.Write "This page has gotten " &
objPageCounter.Hits(vPagePath) & " so far."
    Case "IncrementPageCount"
        Dim vIncrementAmount
        Dim intI
        intI = 1
        vIncrementAmount = Request.Form("IncrementAmount")
        For intI = 1 to vIncrementAmount
            objPageCounter.PageHit()
        Next
        Response.Write "This page has gotten " &
objPageCounter.Hits(vPagePath) & " so far."
    Case "ResetPageCount"
        vPagePath = Request.Form("PagePath")
        objPageCounter.Reset(vPagePath)
        Response.Write "This page now has " &
objPageCounter.Hits(vPagePath) & " hits."
End Select
%>
</TD></TR></TABLE>
<P>
```

```
<TABLE border=1><TR><TD bgcolor="#00CC99" COLSPAN=3>
<H3><font size="6">The Page Counter Component</font></H3></TD></TR><TR>
<TD><FORM METHOD=POST ACTION="ServerComponents6.asp">
Get the number of hits for a page (leave blank for current
page):</TD><TD><INPUT TYPE="text" NAME="PagePath" SIZE="20"></TD><TD>
<INPUT TYPE="submit" NAME="btnval" VALUE="GetHits"></TD></TR>
</FORM>
<TR>
<TD><FORM METHOD=POST ACTION="ServerComponents6.asp">
Increment the Page Count by:</TD><TD><INPUT TYPE="text"
NAME="IncrementAmount" SIZE="5"></TD><TD>
<INPUT TYPE="submit" NAME="btnval" VALUE="IncrementPageCount"></TD></TR>
</FORM>
<TR>
<TD><FORM METHOD=POST ACTION="ServerComponents6.asp">
Reset the Page Count to Zero:</TD><TD><BR></TD><TD>
<INPUT TYPE="submit" NAME="btnval" VALUE="ResetPageCount"></TD></TR>
</FORM>
</TABLE>

</BODY></HTML>
```

This file is named ServerComponents6.asp, and again it references itself each time the form is submitted. The first case just retrieves the current number of hits for whatever page the user enters. It's pretty easy to see how this might be combined with the Scripting.Dictionary objects covered earlier in the book to produce a list of Web site page files and then list the current number of hits for each one. See Figure 8-2 for a screen shot.

The next form/case pair is our little cheater. It lets you increment the hit count for the current page by any number, simply by looping through a For…Next loop whatever number of times is entered. Each trip through the loop uses the PageHit() method to raise the number of hits by one.

The last form/case pair sets the hit count of the current page or the specified page back to zero, using the Reset method. Just specify the page or leave the form field blank, and it will do the job.

The Permission Checker Component

The Permission Checker component is a little more complex to set up and use, because its function is to help you manage restricted areas on your system. It has only one method and no other attributes. The method is HasAccess(*filepath*), and this method checks to see if the current user has the appropriate permissions to use the resource named in *filepath*. There

8

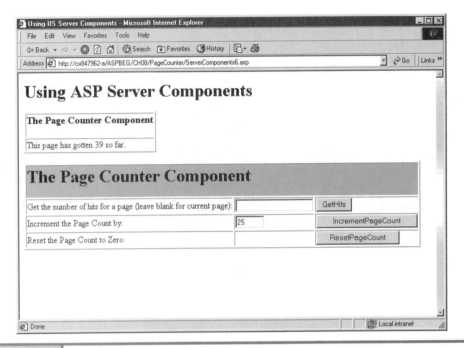

Figure 8-2   The Page Hits page

are a few things you'll need to check or set up before this component will perform the functions you want it to. They are

- Check disk format for NTFS

- Make a virtual Web site

- Turn off anonymous access

- Create users

- Set access requirements

In the next few sections, we'll cover these steps in detail.

Formatting for NTFS

Primarily, the Permission Checker is useful for checking to see whether a user has the correct permissions to use a particular resource. Therefore, you have to be running the area in question on hard drive space formatted as NTFS, rather than FAT. You can check the current format of the default Web site by opening Windows Explorer and right-clicking the drive letter in which the default Web site resides (see Figure 8-3 for an example). If you need to, you can reformat the drive, but be very careful that you understand what you are doing before you do this, as all data on that drive will be lost!

─┤Note ─────────────

Changing the format of a drive is easy to do, but it is also potentially disastrous. Make sure you are aware of all the implications for your server before you attempt this operation.

8

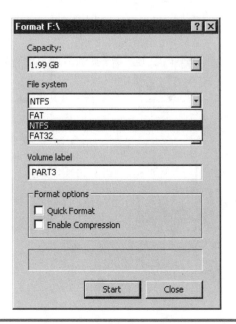

Figure 8-3 | **F: drive in Windows Explorer, showing format**

To give you a real-life example, I originally installed Windows 2000 on my E: drive using the FAT format. I wanted to keep this drive in the FAT format, but fortunately I had already partitioned off an F: drive (on the same physical hard drive). I had no data on the F: drive, so there was nothing to lose when I reformatted it to NTFS. It was a one-step operation, but Windows did warn me that all data would be lost during the reformat operation.

Once I had the F: drive formatted as NTFS (it took about five minutes), I then needed to make a virtual Web site on the F: drive. To do this, I opened the Internet Services Manager, created a new folder in the default Web site, and then right-clicked that folder and chose New | Virtual Directory from the shortcut menu. Figure 8-4 shows this being done. I named my folder ASPVirtual.

Turning Off Anonymous Access

In my virtual Web site folder, I placed my ASP page for this example using the Permission Checker, and then I turned off anonymous access to the

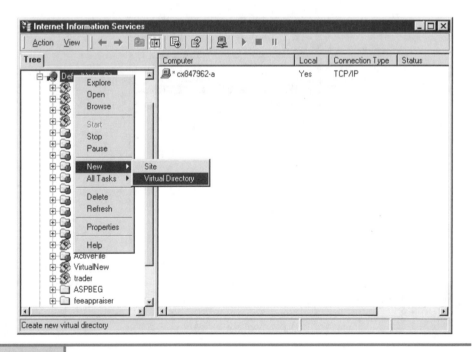

Figure 8-4   Creating a virtual Web site

virtual Web site folder (see next paragraph for details). Taking this action makes IIS display a prompt asking for username and password when the user tries to access this page (instead of using its own IUSR_ computername account to let everyone have anonymous access).

You can turn off anonymous access for a given Web site, folder, or file with the Internet Services Manager. Just open it up, right-click the folder or file of interest, and choose Properties. In the Properties dialog box, select the Directory Security tab, click the Edit button, and then deselect the check box for Anonymous Access, as shown in Figure 8-5. Click OK to get out of the dialog boxes, and anonymous access is off.

Creating Users

To restrict anonymous users and allow authorized users access to a given restricted file, you'll need to create a special user account. To do so, click Start | Settings | Control Panel from the Desktop and open Administrative Tools (as shown in Figure 8-6).

8

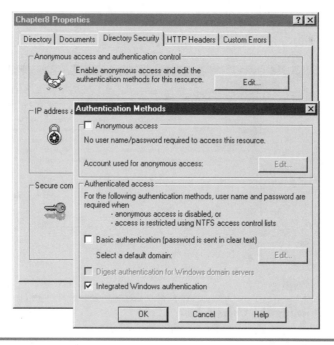

Figure 8-5 Turning off anonymous access

Figure 8-6 Opening Administrative Tools

Double-click the Computer Management icon, and then open the Local Users and Groups folder. Click the Users folder (see Figure 8-7).

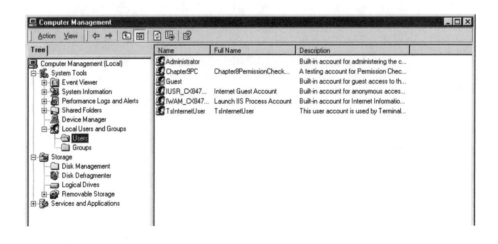

Figure 8-7 Opening the Users folder

A dialog box will open allowing you to create new users with
whatever username and password you choose (as shown in Figure 8-8).

For this example, a user named Chapter8PC is created (shown in
Figure 8-9), and this is the user account that is given access to a particular
file on the server.

Setting Access Requirements for the Virtual Web Site

The easiest way to set permissions for a file is to open Windows Explorer,
right-click the file, and choose Properties. In the Properties dialog box,
you will see a Security tab, and on that page of the dialog box you will
have the opportunity to select which users have access to the file and what
they can do with it. If the file is not stored on an NTFS-formatted hard
disk area, you will not see any user/group or permissions setting available.

Now you're ready to set up the virtual Web site.

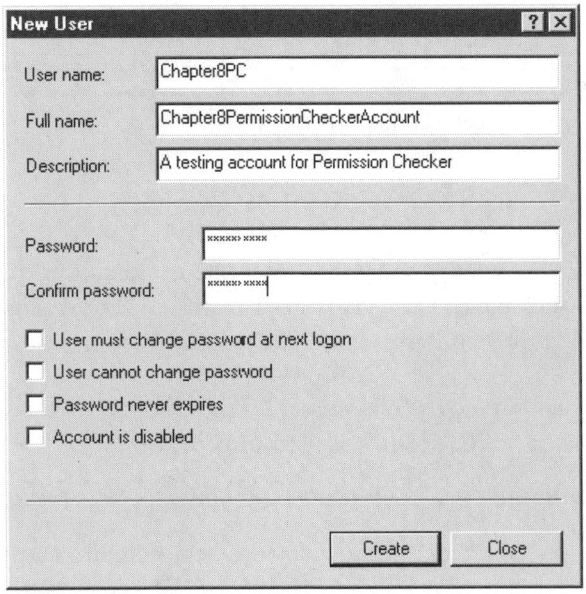

Figure 8-8   Creating new users

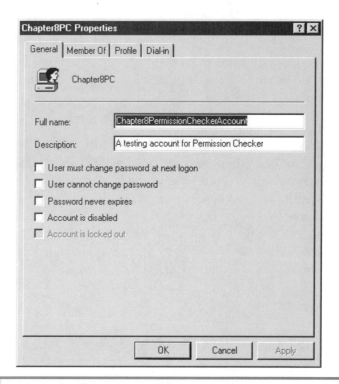

Figure 8-9 The Chapter8PC user account

Create a folder in the virtual Web site to hold your demo files, and then create a file to place access restrictions on. For this example, you'll use a folder named PermissionChecker, and a file named SCPC7.asp.

1. Open Windows Explorer and right-click the virtual Web site folder on the NTFS-formatted hard drive space.

2. Open the Properties dialog box, and select the Security tab.

3. In the tab, click Add to add your new user and set permissions for access in the Permission Entry dialog box (Figure 8-10). Click OK.

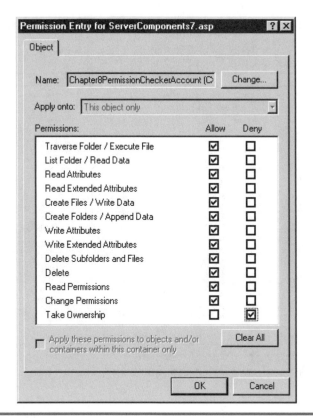

Figure 8-10	**Adding specific user permissions**

4. In the Access Control Settings dialog box, select Everyone, and then
   click Remove to remove the Everyone account.

5. Deselect the Allow Inheritable Permissions to Propagate to this
   Object check box, so that no one but your special user will be able
   to access the resource. Figure 8-11 shows the screen before Everyone
   is removed and with inheritable permissions selected. Do the same
   for the files inside the folder (in this example, you're using both the
   demonstration ASP file and the file named previously, SCPC7.asp).

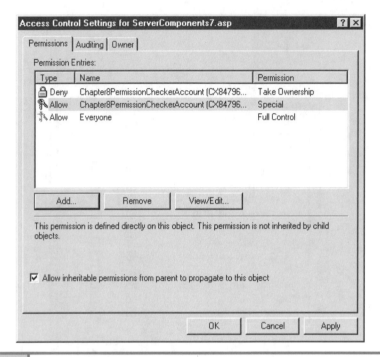

Figure 8-11 Access Control Settings dialog box

Demonstrating the Permissions Checker

The Permissions Checker works by allowing or disallowing access to a particular resource based on the permissions set for that resource, so we'll demonstrate it in action using a file named ServerComponents7.asp, as shown in Figure 8-12. This file is located in your virtual Web site; so before the user can even access the file, the proper username and password for that area must be given.

In the previous section, you set that area so that only the Chapter8PC user has access. The following code works from inside the restricted area, and it displays a link to SCPC7.asp if the user has the correct permissions

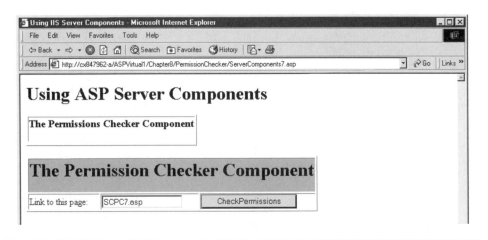

Figure 8-12   Browser view of the Permissions Checker page

(see Figure 8-13), but displays a "not found" type message if the user doesn't have the appropriate permissions (see Figure 8-14):

8

```
<%
Option Explicit
Dim btnClicked
Dim objPermissionChecker
Set objPermissionChecker = Server.CreateObject("MSWC.PermissionChecker")
%>
<html><head><title>Using IIS Server Components</title>
<meta http-equiv="Content-Type" content="text/html; charset=iso-8859-1">
</head>
<body bgcolor="#77FF77">
<H2><font size="6">Using ASP Server Components</font></H2>
<TABLE border=1>
<TR><TD><H3>The Permissions Checker Component</H3></TD></TR><TR><TD
bgcolor="white">
<%
btnClicked = Request.Form("btnval")
Select Case btnClicked
    Case "CheckPermissions"
        Dim vPagePath
        vPagePath = Request.Form("PagePath")
        If objPermissionChecker.HasAccess(vPagePath) Then
            Response.Write "Click <A HREF=""" & vPagePath & """> here
```

```
</A> for access to " & vPagePath
        Else
            Response.Write "That page does not exist, or you do not have
access to it."
        End If
    End Select
%>
</TD></TR></TABLE>
<P>
<TABLE border=1><TR><TD bgcolor="#00CC99" COLSPAN=3>
<H3><font size="6">The Permission Checker
Component</font></H3></TD></TR><TR>
<TD><FORM METHOD=POST ACTION="ServerComponents7.asp">
Link to this page:</TD><TD><INPUT TYPE="text" NAME="PagePath"
SIZE="20"></TD><TD>
<INPUT TYPE="submit" NAME="btnval" VALUE="CheckPermissions"></TD></TR>
</FORM>
</TABLE>
</BODY></HTML>
```

The preceding code creates an instance of the Permission Checker component with the context of the page, and submitting the form activates a condition-testing routine (using If. . .Then) that checks permissions for the resource requested. If the resource doesn't exist or the user doesn't have the correct permissions (and remember the user had to log in as Chapter8PC before even opening ServerComponents7.asp), the link will not be displayed.

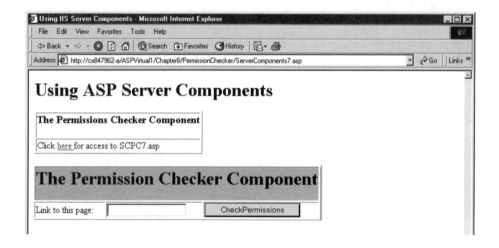

Figure 8-13   User gains access

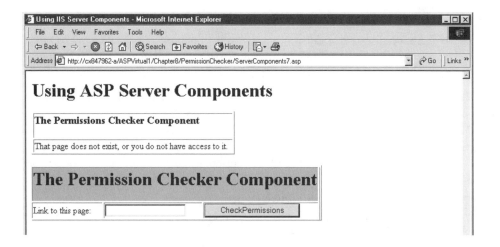

Figure 8-14 User is denied access

Hint

The response message doesn't tell an unqualified user whether a resource actually exists, because you may not want a user without the proper permissions to have this information. Sometimes, an ambiguous answer is appropriate.

The way the ASP file and permissions are currently set up, the user would gain access to the restricted file. To demonstrate the opposite, change the permissions for the individual file so that only the Administrator account (or any other account) has access to the file, and then run the operation again. The negative answer will appear.

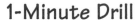

1-Minute Drill

● **What do three of the four Counter component methods have in common?**

● **To use the Permission Checker component, the restricted resources must reside on what type of hard drive partition?**

● They create a counter if it does not exist.
● NTFS

8

The Tools Component

The Tools component is a kind of multipurpose, catch-all component that contains several useful functions. It can be used to verify whether a file exists, it can generate random numbers, and it can also be used to create customized pages. None of these functions seems to have an obvious association, although it's easy to see how they might come in handy in a typical Web site application. In fact, there are even a couple of Macintosh-only methods exposed by the Tools component; but, of course, we won't be using them here.

Tools Component Methods

Like the other components we've seen in this module, the Tools component has only methods, no properties. They are

- **FileExists(*pathname*)**   This method will check for the existence of any file residing within the Web site folder, and *pathname* must be a virtual relative path and filename.

- **Random()**   This method generates a random number between –32768 and 32767.

- **ProcessForm(*output,template,insertionpoint*)**   This method retrieves the file specified as *template*, inserts whatever values are passed by the initiating page into the template file at *insertionpoint*, and writes the file to the *output* path and filename on the server.

Demonstrating the Tools Component

The next code example demonstrates the simpler Tools component functions, checking for the existence of a file and generating random numbers. Then it creates a customized page, combining input from the user with an existing template page and providing a link to the output file. You'll need to use several files to accomplish the full effect. Here's the code for the template file, named toolstemplate.asp:

```
<HTML>
<HEAD><TITLE>Your Customized Page</TITLE></HEAD>
<BODY>
<H2>Your Full Name Is: <%% =Request.Form("fullname") %%>
</BODY>
</HTML>
```

Notice the use of double percent signs (%%) in this file. This allows the ProcessForm method of the Tools component to insert a value into this page, so the output will contain content retrieved from the user on the original page.

Now let's go over the code in the main Tools component page:

```
<%
Option Explicit
Dim btnClicked
Dim objTool
Set objTool = Server.CreateObject("MSWC.Tools")
%>
<html><head><title>Using IIS Server Components</title>
<meta http-equiv="Content-Type" content="text/html; charset=iso-8859-1">
</head>
<body bgcolor="#77FF77">
<H2><font size="6">Using ASP Server Components</font></H2>
<TABLE border=1>
<TR><TD><H3>The Tools Component</H3></TD></TR><TR><TD bgcolor="white">
<%
btnClicked = Request.Form("btnval")
Select Case btnClicked
    Case "CheckFile"
        Dim vFileName
        vFileName = Request.Form("FileName")
        If objTool.FileExists(vFileName) Then
            Response.Write "Click <A HREF=""" & vFileName & """>here </A>
to go to " & vFileName
        Else
            Response.Write "Sorry, that page does not exist."
        End If
    Case "GenerateRandomNumber"
        Dim vRandomNumber
        vRandomNumber = objTool.Random()
        Response.Write "Your random number is " & vRandomNumber
    Case "BuildPage"
        Dim vToolsOutput
        Dim vFullname
        vToolsOutput = Request.Form("ToolsOutput")vFullname =
Request.Form("fullname")
        objTool.ProcessForm vToolsOutput, "toolstemplate.asp", "[target]"
        Response.Write "Click <A HREF=""" & vToolsOutput & """> here</A>
to see your customized page."
End Select
%>
</TD></TR></TABLE>
<P>
<TABLE border=1><TR><TD bgcolor="#00CC99" COLSPAN=3>
<H3><font size="6">The Tools Component</font></H3></TD></TR><TR>
<TD><FORM METHOD=POST ACTION="ServerComponents8.asp">
Check this File Name:</TD><TD><INPUT TYPE="text" NAME="FileName"
SIZE="20"></TD><TD>
<INPUT TYPE="submit" NAME="btnval" VALUE="CheckFile"></TD></TR>
</FORM>
<TR>
<TD><FORM METHOD=POST ACTION="ServerComponents8.asp">
```

8

```
Generate a Random Number:</TD><TD><BR></TD><TD>
<INPUT TYPE="submit" NAME="btnval" VALUE="GenerateRandomNumber"></TD><TD>
</TR>
</FORM>
<TR>
<TD><FORM METHOD=POST ACTION="ServerComponents8.asp">
Build a Customized Page:</TD><TD><INPUT TYPE="text" NAME="ToolsOutput"
SIZE="20"><BR>
Enter your Full Name: <INPUT TYPE="text" NAME="fullname" SIZE="30"></TD><TD>
<INPUT TYPE="submit" NAME="btnval" VALUE="BuildPage"></TD></TR>
</FORM>
</TABLE>
</BODY></HTML>
```

The first case/form pair works in a pretty straightforward way; it simply
tests whether the file named by the user exists; and if so provides a link to
it, and if not says so. The second case/form pair generates and displays a
random number using the Random method of the Tools component, as
shown in Figure 8-15 in the small Tools component box at the top.

The last case/form pair allows the user to enter a name for an output
file and the user's full name, and then inserts the name into the output file,

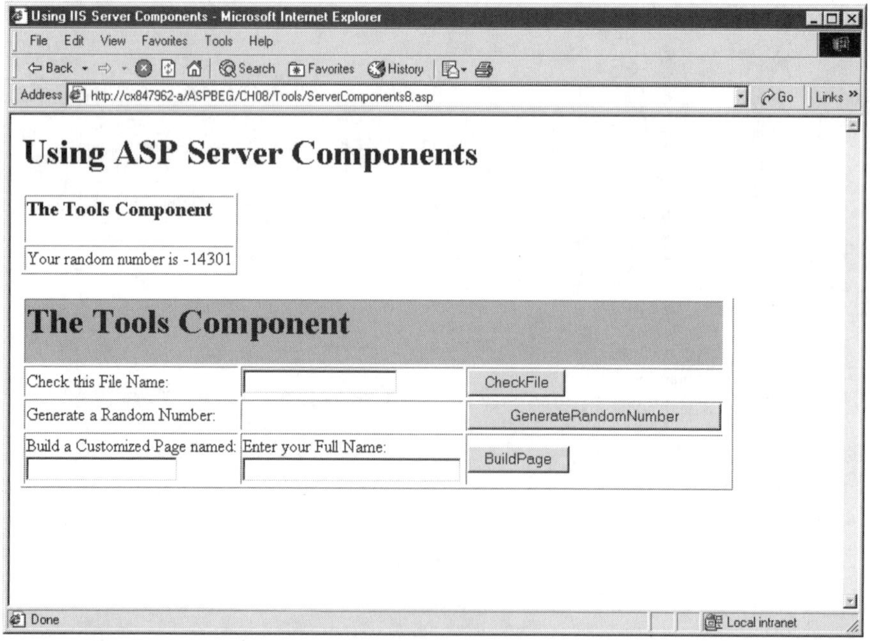

Figure 8-15 The Tools page

while providing a link to the output file back to the user. The screen display is shown in Figure 8-16, again in the small Tools component box at the top.

The contents of the output file are shown in the following illustration. Note that each time this method runs it rewrites the contents of the output file without giving any warning.

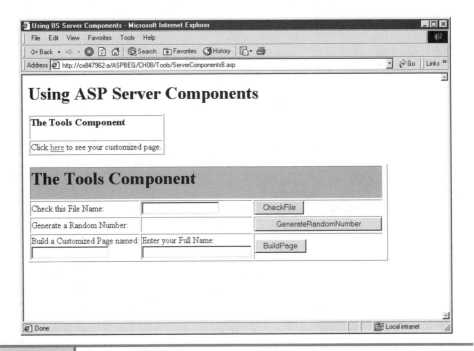

Figure 8-16   The link to the output file

The Logging Utility Component

The Logging Utility component is a new arrival with ASP 3.0, and it provides a convenient way to read and write to log files, something you may have to do if you're the Webmaster for your site. Its use is restricted to authenticated administrators or operators on the server on which IIS is running. If anyone else attempts to use this component, the script instantiating the Logging Utility component simply won't work.

Logging Utility Component Methods and Properties

The Logging Utility component makes the following methods available, allowing authenticated users to open, read, and close log files; select certain records from those files; write to log files; and tell when they're at the end of a log file:

- **OpenLogFile(*filename,iomode,servicename,serviceinstance, outputformat*)**   This method opens the log file (or set of log files) specified in *filename*, using either ForReading or ForWriting as the *iomode*, for the service specified by *servicename* and *serviceinstance* (W3SVC, for example), and with an optional format for writing specified with *outputformat*.

- **CloseLogFiles(*iomode*)**   This method closes log files that are open, either with *iomode* ForReading or ForWriting, or AllOpenFiles.

- **ReadFilter(*start,end*)**   This method selects records returned based on *start* and *end* data. If *start* and *end* are left out, the method starts with the first record and ends with the last record.

- **ReadLogRecord()**   This method reads the next record in the current log file.

- **WriteLogRecord(*loggingutilityobject*)**   This method writes log records from a log file opened for reading to a log file opened for writing, using an object you create that references the Logging Utility component.

- **AtEndOfLog()**   This method returns True if you are at the end of records in a log file.

Once you've got a log file open for reading, you can access the values of any of the following properties (provided extended logging has been properly set up, which is discussed in the next section):

- **BytesReceived**   This property tells how many bytes were received from the browser in the request.

- **BytesSent**   This property tells how many bytes were sent to the browser in a response.

- **ClientIP**   This property tells what the Client IP address is, or what the IP address of their proxy server is.

- **Cookie**   This property shows the contents of cookies sent by the browser with the request.

- **CustomFields**   This property provides an array consisting of custom headers that were added to the request.

- **DateTime**   This property is the date and time of the request.

- **Method**   This property is the method used, such as Get or Post.

- **ProtocolStatus**   This property shows the status message that went to the browser, such as "404 Not Found."

- **ProtocolVersion**   This property shows the protocol type and version, such as HTTP 1.1.

- **Referer**   This property shows the URL of the page containing the link the user clicked to make the request.

- **ServerIP**   This property shows the server's IP address.

- **ServerName**   This property shows the name of the server.

- **ServerPort**   This property shows the port number on which the request was received, typically 80.

- **ServiceName**   This property shows the name of the running service, such as W3SVC.

- **TimeTaken**   This property shows the time spent to process the request.

8

- **URIQuery**   This property shows parameters, if any, attached to the query string of the request.

- **URIStem**   This property shows the target Uniform Resource Identifier (URI) of the request.

- **UserAgent**   This property shows the user agent string, meaning the type of browser being used.

- **UserName**   This property shows the logon name used to access the server when the user is not anonymous.

- **Win32Status**   This property shows the Win32 status code returned by the server after processing the request.

Enabling the Logging Utility Component

There are several things you'll need to do to get ready to use the Logging Utility component. As mentioned earlier, you must be logged on as an administrator or operator to gain access to the log files through this component, so you'll want to place your script in a folder on the Web site to which you can restrict access, much the same as you did for the Permission Checker component. You'll also need to check the structure of your log files for the Web service. You should be able to find a folder on your server called W3SVC (meaning WWW service), and inside that folder you should find plenty of log files. On my system this folder is located in E:\WINNT\system32\LogFiles. If you know the file naming convention being used, you can program your scripts to pick out a particular file, or you can just open the folder and iterate through or filter the files to find the records of interest.

Chances are, you already have extended logging turned on; but if you need to turn it on, check it, or increase the number of fields being logged, open the Internet Services Manager, select the default Web site by right-clicking it, open the Properties dialog box, and then click the Properties button of the Active Log Format to change log field settings. See Figure 8-17 for a view of the pertinent dialog boxes, and note the format of the log files at the bottom of the Extended Logging Properties dialog box.

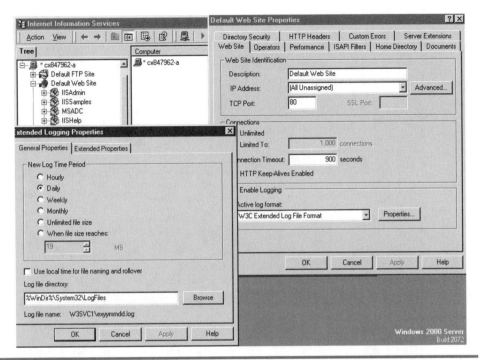

Figure 8-17 | The Internet Services Manager and Extended Logging Properties dialog box

A Logging Utility Component Example

Once you've got everything properly set up, it's a fairly straightforward exercise to put the Logging Utility component to work for you. The following code uses the familiar Select. . .Case structure to provide the user some control over the log file readouts, and the results of using this page are shown in Figure 8-18:

```
<%
Option Explicit
Dim btnClicked
%>
<html><head><title>Using IIS Server Components</title>
<meta http-equiv="Content-Type" content="text/html; charset=iso-8859-1">
<!-- METADATA TYPE="typelib" FILE="E:\WINNT\system32\inetsrv\logscrpt.dll"
-->
```

```
</head>
<body bgcolor="#77FF77">
<H2><font size="6">Using ASP Server Components</font></H2>
<TABLE border=1>
<TR><TD><H3>The Logging Utility Component</H3></TD></TR><TR><TD
bgcolor="white">
<%
btnClicked = Request.Form("btnval")    ◄────  Hard-coded
Select Case btnClicked                        reference to
     Case "ReadLog"                           log file
          Dim objLog
          Set objLog = Server.CreateObject("MSWC.IISLog")
          objLog.OpenLogFile
"E:\WINNT\system32\LogFiles\W3SVC1\ex000228.log", ForReading, "W3SVC1", 1, 0
          objLog.ReadLogRecord
          Response.Write "Bytes received = " & objLog.BytesReceived & "<BR>"
          Response.Write "Bytes sent = " & objLog.BytesSent & "<BR>"
          Response.Write "Client IP = " & objLog.ClientIP & "<BR>"
          Response.Write "Cookie value = " & objLog.Cookie & "<BR>"
          Response.Write "Custom fields = " & objLog.CustomFields & "<BR>"
          Response.Write "Date and time = " & objLog.DateTime & "<BR>"
          Response.Write "Method used = " & objLog.Method & "<BR>"
          Response.Write "Protocol status = " & objLog.ProtocolStatus &
"<BR>"
          Response.Write "Protocol version = " & objLog.ProtocolVersion &
"<BR>"
          Response.Write "Referer = " & objLog.Referer & "<BR>"
          Response.Write "Server IP = " & objLog.ServerIP & "<BR>"
          Response.Write "Server name = " & objLog.ServerName & "<BR>"
          Response.Write "Server port = " & objLog.ServerPort & "<BR>"
          Response.Write "Service name = " & objLog.ServiceName & "<BR>"
          Response.Write "Processing time taken = " & objLog.TimeTaken &
"<BR>"
          Response.Write "URI query parameters = " & objLog.URIQuery &
"<BR>"
          Response.Write "Target URI = " & objLog.URIStem & "<BR>"
          Response.Write "Browser type (user agent) = " & objLog.UserAgent &
"<BR>"
          Response.Write "User name = " & objLog.UserName & "<BR>"
          Response.Write "Win32 status = " & objLog.Win32Status & "<BR>"
          objLog.CloseLogFiles(ForReading)
End Select
%>
</TD></TR></TABLE>
<P>
<TABLE border=1><TR><TD bgcolor="#00CC99" COLSPAN=2>
<H3><font size="6">The Logging Utility Component</font></H3></TD></TR><TR>
<TD><FORM METHOD=POST ACTION="ServerComponents9.asp">
Read the Most Recent Log File Entry</TD><TD>
<INPUT TYPE="submit" NAME="btnval" VALUE="ReadLog"></TD></TR>
</FORM>
</TABLE>
</BODY></HTML>
```

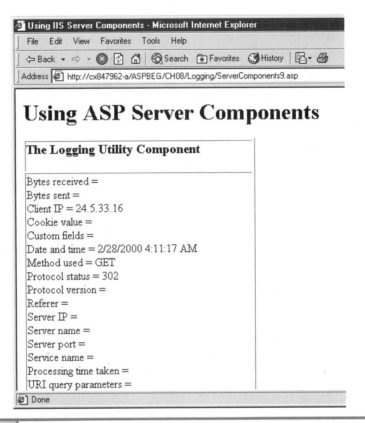

Figure 8-18	The log files values

Please note the inclusion of the METADATA tag containing the reference to the type library file logscrpt.dll. This allows you to use the constants ForReading and ForWriting without having to declare them in your script. For this example, the name of the log file to review has been hard-coded in, but it will often be more convenient to build a variable allowing the user to select files or records from a particular time frame for review. Also notice that because, in this example, Windows 2000 is installed on the E: drive, the entire path to the log file had to be included to get it to open.

1-Minute Drill

- **What component can be used both to check the existence of a given file and to generate random numbers?**
- **What property of the Logging Utility component reveals how long it took to process a request?**

Third-Party Components for ASP

Microsoft is not the only company making components that will work with ASP; and, in fact, Microsoft promotes the production of components by third parties as a means of expanding the appeal of ASP and IIS. You can find third-party components by going to your favorite search engine and entering the phrase "ASP Components," or go to one of the well-known ASP developer sites such as **http://www.15seconds.com, http://www.4guysfromrolla.com, http://www.aspwatch.com,** or **http://www.activeserverpages.com**.

There are many third-party components available, and one very appealing function that several components can perform is file uploading and downloading. Microsoft makes a component of this type called the Posting Acceptor (you can find it at **http://microsoft.com/windows/ software/webpost/post_accept.htm**), but for this exercise we'll use a third-party component called ActiveFile, made by Infomentum **(http://www.infomentum.com)**.

Getting and Installing Third-Party Components

The component we're using for this section is easy to get and easy to install. If you go to the Infomentum home page and choose ActiveFile, you'll find a selection on the menu offering a free demo version that is fully functional for the trial period. Like the other file upload components available, ActiveFile is compliant with RFC 1867, and version 2.2 can not only upload and download files, but also automatically allows users to browse for the files they want to upload. In addition, ActiveFile 2.2 has an extensive set of methods and properties to make it easier to detect Macintosh files, work with compressed files, make directories, and check file types.

- **The Tools component**
- **TimeTaken**

Installing ActiveFile 2.2 is easy as well. The installation follows a standard installation process. Some third–party components can only be installed manually, meaning you have to put the files in the correct folders yourself and make changes to the registry. Manual installation can be time consuming and just a bit technical, so it's best to avoid it if possible.

ActiveFile Methods and Properties

The ActiveFile component has quite a few objects, properties, and methods available, but we're only going to cover a couple of them here. For a more detailed explanation and graphical guide, take a look at the Component Manual at **http://www.infomentum.com/activefile/ doc**. For this example, you'll be using the Post object and the FormInputs object (which is a collection of the Post object). The only method you'll use is the Upload method of the Post object, and the only properties will be the Name and Value properties of the FormInputs object. Let's review the code and see what's happening:

```
<%
Option Explicit
%>
<html><head><title>Using Third-Party IIS Server Components</title>
<meta http-equiv="Content-Type" content="text/html; charset=iso-8859-1">
</head>
<body bgcolor="#77FF77">
<H2><font size="6">Using Third-Party ASP Server Components</font></H2>
<TABLE border=1>
<TR><TD><H3>The ActiveFile Component</H3></TD></TR><TR><TD bgcolor="white">
<%
Dim Post
Dim FormInput
Set Post = Server.CreateObject("ActiveFile.Post")
Post.Upload "E:\Inetpub\wwwroot\ASPFTGU\CH09\ThirdPartyComponents\Temp"
For Each FormInput in Post.FormInputs
    Response.Write FormInput.Name & " = " & FormInput.Value & "<BR>"
Next
%>
</TD></TR></TABLE>
<P>
<TABLE border=1><TR><TD bgcolor="#00CC99" COLSPAN=3>
<H3><font size="6">The ActiveFile Component</font></H3></TD></TR><TR>
<TD><FORM METHOD=POST ACTION="ServerComponents10.asp"
enctype="multipart/form-data">
Upload this File:</TD><TD><INPUT TYPE="file" NAME="UploadedFile"
SIZE="20"></TD><TD>
<INPUT TYPE="submit" NAME="btnval" VALUE="PostFile"></TD></TR>
</FORM>
</TABLE>
</BODY></HTML>
```

8

In this script, you're not allowed to use the Request object's methods to capture any values from the form; so you remove the references to the name of the submit button that activates the Select. . .Case statement, and in doing so, you also remove the entire Select. . .Case structure. What's left is simply an ASP script that instantiates the ActiveFile component when called, uploads whatever file you've chosen, places it in the folder you've chosen, and responds with a notice saying what was uploaded. Checking the specified folder shows that the file was actually uploaded. Note that if you use the browse function, it will insert the entire physical path and the filename; but you can also use the relative path and filename and it will work just as well.

The ActiveFile product seems to work quite well with the installation of the OS currently being used, and having this capability working will add some nice application functions to your site. For example, not only can you upload files, but you can place them into a database as well. Therefore, you can allow your users to upload and post images as well as text (or other binary file types).

Ask the Expert

Question: Microsoft has provided a number of installed components, and these components provide quite a few basic functions that come in handy in applications. I can also program my own components or make scripts that do the required functions. How can I tell when it's time to buy third-party components?

Answer: Buying third-party components is a decision you can make based on money, time, and projected future usage. For example, suppose you have plenty of money, but little time. You might want to buy third-party components to speed up your development process. By the same token, if you have little money but plenty of time (and enough programming expertise), you might want to create your own components. An added benefit of creating your own components is that you can then sell them to other folks, although you should understand that this is essentially a business itself (meaning that while it's easy to create components, you should not assume that it will be as easy to market and sell them competitively). Last, if you expect to use many variations of the component in your future applications, it may be better to develop your own, so you have the source code and can modify them as you please.

Question: **The Permission Checker and Logging Utility components seem to perform functions that only an administrator can usually perform. Why are they included?**

Answer: Sometimes you want to automate administrative functions, and these components will assist you with that effort. The Permission Checker component is useful for checking conditions to allow or disallow access to resources based on permissions. You can always assign guests a particular status at login, thereby relieving yourself of manually managing permissions for each and every user. The Logging Utility component provides similar management capability based on application conditions.

project8-2.zip

Project 8-2: Using These ASP Components

8

Continuing with previous projects' efforts to create a working Web application that contains common useful functions, this project places a few of the components you've worked with in this module into a single page as a set of management functions. Several additional pages are also included as examples of how you might display the file upload and download capabilities to your users.

Step-by-Step

1. The following code not only allows you to create counters, you can list them as well—at least after you've shut down the application and then restarted it. It's too bad the component doesn't allow you to read an active list of counters at any time, but there are other ways to do such things. This code uses the Counters component to create counters (the Counters object is instantiated in global.asa, of course), but it uses the TextStream object to read the contents of counter.txt (the file carrying counter data for the Counters component):

```
<%
Option Explicit
Dim btnClicked
%>
<html><head><title>Using IIS Server Components</title>
<meta http-equiv="Content-Type" content="text/html; charset=iso-8859-1">
<!-- METADATA TYPE="typelib" FILE="E:\WINNT\System32\scrrun.dll" -->
</head>
<body bgcolor="#77FF77">
<H2><font size="6">Management Page 1</font></H2>
<TABLE border=1>
<TR><TD><H3>Displaying Counters</H3></TD></TR><TR><TD bgcolor="white">
<%
btnClicked = Request.Form("btnval")
Select Case btnClicked
     Case "CreateCounters"
          Dim vCounterName
          vCounterName = Request.Form("CounterName")
          objCounter.Get(vCounterName)
          Response.Write "You have created " & vCounterName & " and its
value is: "
          Response.Write objCounter.Get(vCounterName)
     Case "DisplayCounters"
          Dim objFileSysOb
          Dim colFileName
          Dim objTextStream
          Dim vReadline
          Response.Write "<B>The Available Counters and Their Values
Are:</B><P>"
          Set objFileSysOb =
Server.CreateObject("Scripting.FileSystemObject")
          Set colFileName =
objFileSysOb.GetFile("E:\WINNT\system32\inetsrv\counters.txt")
          Set objTextStream = colFileName.OpenAsTextStream(ForReading)
          Do While Not objTextStream.AtEndOfStream
               vReadline = objTextStream.ReadLine
               Response.Write "The counter is: " & vReadline & "<BR>"
          Loop
          objTextStream.Close
End Select
%>
</TD></TR></TABLE>
<P>
<TABLE border=1><TR><TD bgcolor="#00CC99" COLSPAN=3>
<H3><font size="6">Creating and Displaying
Counters</font></H3></TD></TR><TR>
<TD><FORM METHOD=POST ACTION="Management1.asp">
Enter a Counter Name:</TD><TD><INPUT TYPE="text" NAME="CounterName"
SIZE="20"></TD><TD>
```

```
<INPUT TYPE="submit" NAME="btnval" VALUE="CreateCounters"></FORM></TD></TR>
<TR>
<TD><FORM METHOD=POST ACTION="Management1.asp">
Increment a Counter:</TD><TD><INPUT TYPE="text" NAME="IncrementName"
SIZE="20"></TD><TD>
<INPUT TYPE="submit" NAME="btnval" VALUE="DisplayCounters"></FORM></TD></TR>
</TABLE>
</BODY></HTML>
```

   2. After getting a new counter, which both creates it and sets its
   value to zero, you can look up all the counters currently in the
   counters.txt file using the next function provided by this page.
   Figure 8-19 shows what the output looks like.

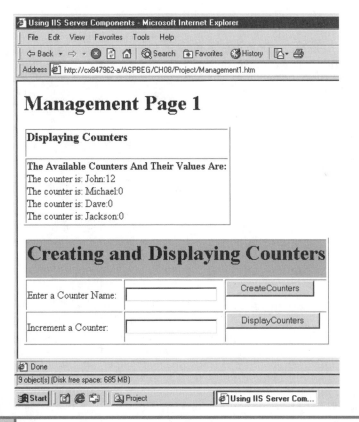

Figure 8-19   The contents of counters.txt

3. The next sample application page uses both the third-party ActiveFile component and the Microsoft Tools component together to allow users to upload image files to your server, and then see a custom page created that shows their name and the image they uploaded. It does this by using the ActiveFile upload capability to place their image files in a folder (Pictures) you've set aside for this purpose. It then uses the Tools ProcessForm method to insert their names and a reference to their image files into your template file, finally providing them with a link to the custom page they created. To make it work effectively, you'll separate the ASP scripting from the initial upload page form.

4. Here's the code for the upload page:

```
<html><head><title>Creating a Customized Web Page</title>
<meta http-equiv="Content-Type" content="text/html; charset=iso-8859-1">
</head>
<body bgcolor="#77FF77">
<H2><font size="6">Create Your Own Web Page</font></H2>
<TABLE border=1><TR><TD bgcolor="#00CC99" COLSPAN=3>
<H3><font size="6">Enter Data</font></H3></TD></TR><TR>
<TD><FORM METHOD=POST ACTION="CustomUpload.asp"
enctype="multipart/form-data">
Build a Customized Page Named:</TD><TD><INPUT TYPE="text" NAME="ToolsOutput"
SIZE="20"></TD></TR>
<TR><TD>
Enter the Full Name to Appear on Your Page:</TD><TD><INPUT TYPE="text"
NAME="fullname" SIZE="30"></TD></TR>
<TR><TD>
Browse to Find the Image File to Upload:</TD><TD><INPUT TYPE="file"
NAME="UploadedFile" SIZE="20">
<INPUT TYPE="submit" NAME="btnval" VALUE="PostFile"></TD></TR>
</FORM>
</TABLE>
</BODY></HTML>
```

5. As you can see in Figure 8-20, this form allows the user to enter the name of the file he or she wants to create, the user's own name, and the image file the user wants to upload. The following code shows how the ActiveFile and Tools components respond to the request:

```
<%
Option Explicit
Dim objTool
Set objTool = Server.CreateObject("MSWC.Tools")
%>
```

```
<html><head><title>Creating a Customized Web Page</title>
<meta http-equiv="Content-Type" content="text/html; charset=iso-8859-1">
</head>
<body bgcolor="#77FF77">
<TABLE border=1>
<TR><TD><H3>Find Your Page Here</H3></TD></TR><TR><TD bgcolor="white">
<%
Dim Post
Dim FormInput
Dim vToolsOutput
Dim vFullName
Dim vFileName
Set Post = Server.CreateObject("ActiveFile.Post")
Post.Upload "E:\Inetpub\wwwroot\ASPFTGU\CH09\InDepth\Pictures"
vToolsOutput = Post.FormInputs("ToolsOutput")
vFullName = Post.FormInputs("fullname")
vFileName = Post.FormInputs("UploadedFile")
objTool.ProcessForm vToolsOutput, "customtemplate.asp", "[target]"
Response.Write "Click <A HREF=""" & vToolsOutput & """> here</A> to see your
customized page."
%>
</TD></TR></TABLE>
</BODY></HTML>
```

6. Notice the use of Post.FormInputs rather than Request.Form to
capture data submitted by the user. With ActiveFile, you cannot use
Request.Form to capture user data. The last chunk of code is the
template file, and it shows how to insert the correct information
into the output file so the user's name and image file will be
displayed properly:

```
<HTML>
<HEAD><TITLE>Your Customized Page</TITLE></HEAD>
<BODY>
<center>
<H2>My Name Is: <%% =vFullName %%></H2>
<H4>and here's my picture</H4>
<IMG SRC="pictures/<%% =vFileName %%>">
</center>
</BODY>
</HTML>
```

In this template file, you're using the <%% and %%> delimiters to
insert ASP code for processing before the final version of the output
file is created. This means the values you're referencing will be
inserted, not plain ASP code.

8

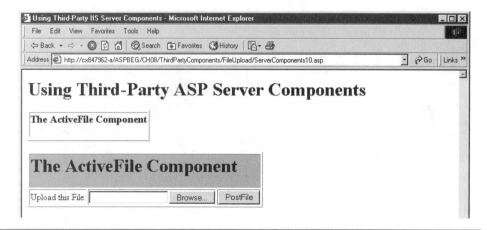

Figure 8-20 The upload form

✓ Mastery Check

1. What is the difference between the Counters component and the Page Counter component?

   A. The Counters component can't store page hits.

   B. The Page Counter component is not a separate component, but an object within the Counter component.

   C. The Counters component can create as many counters as you want.

   D. None of the above.

2. What are some of the steps you must take to use the Permission Checker component?

   A. Make sure the partition type is FAT, set permissions on the resource, and allow anonymous access.

   B. Set permissions on the resource, make sure the partition type is NTFS, and disallow anonymous access.

☑ *Mastery Check*

    C. Make sure the partition type is NTFS, set permissions on the resource, and create the Administrator user.

    D. None of the above.

3. Using the OpenLogFile method of the Logging Utility, you can specify the log file to open with the _____ attribute, set the reading or writing attribute with _____, and set the format for the output with the optional _____ attribute.

4. What does the ProcessForm method of the Tools component use to build new customized files?

    A. Templates

    B. Templates and insertion points

    C. Templates, insertion points, and the output path and filename

    D. None of the above

5. What is the correct syntax for including the DLL file when using the Logging Utility ForReading and ForWriting attributes?

    A. <!— METADATA TYPE="typelib"
       FILE="C:\WINNT\system32\inetsrv\logscrpt.dll" —>

    B. <!— METADATA TYPE="typelib"
       FILE="D:\WINNT\system32\inetsrv\logscrpt.dll" —>

    C. <!— METADATA TYPE="typelib"
       FILE="E:\WINNT\system32\inetsrv\logscrpt.dll" —>

    D. You must use the path and filename that are appropriate for your system.

8

Module 9

ActiveX Data Objects and SQL Overview

The Goals of This Module

- Discuss reverse engineering and understand how it is performed

- Examine various database designs

- Review relational database design and what makes a database relational

- Learn about Structured Query Language (SQL) and practice writing SQL statements

- See what Microsoft Access 2000 can do, and where Data Access Pages (DAP) fit in

- Review the capabilities of ActiveX Data Objects (connections, commands, and recordsets)

As you are no doubt beginning to realize, modern Web sites are made with a mixture of languages, including HTML, JavaScript, VBScript, and so forth. SQL is one of the languages commonly used in Web sites to communicate with databases, and ActiveX Data Objects (ADOs) are used to run SQL statements against a database or other data source and manipulate the records found. It's very important that you understand how each of the languages assists in the process of working with databases connected to your Web site. This module examines the relationships between these languages and their components, and focuses on SQL statements as the key to opening up various databases.

Using Databases in ASP Applications

In this module and the next two, we'll be discussing how to create, install, and interact with databases behind the scenes of your ASP Web site or application. As you are surely aware, databases play a special role in many applications, because of their ability to store and manipulate data in very effective ways. While data can be stored in arrays for limited purposes, you'll often find that the ability to access a database makes building particular functions into your applications much easier, and the tools for doing it are legion.

Best of all, since many Web site applications are going to be based on existing data stores, you shouldn't have to reinvent the wheel. There will be many cases in which you can import from or connect directly to working legacy databases using ADO, thereby speeding the overall development process and easing integration of online functionality into existing business processes.

In the next section, we briefly cover database design, to lay the groundwork for some examples and to illustrate the connection between database structure and interactions with your Web pages. We'll use Microsoft Access 2000 as a simple prototyping tool, and we'll also demonstrate using SQL Server once your initial design is firmed up. Access is great for smaller, simpler Web applications, but SQL Server and the other industrial-strength DBMSs are appropriate for larger and more heavily used applications. Later in the module, we'll cover the object model of ADO and the mechanics of making a connection and using either kind of database.

Database Design

If you've already worked with databases extensively, you may want to skip over this section, as it covers many of the basics of good database design. Or you might want to review design principles and learn more about how database design affects the performance of your ASP applications. We'll also take a look at how the incorporation of a well-designed database can improve the functionality and decrease the maintenance requirements of your Web site.

Database Construction and Objects

A database is, for the most part, an information container. It will usually consist of the following objects, and perhaps a few more depending upon specific application requirements:

- **Tables**   Data is stored in tables, as records (each row is a record) of information related to a single subject. Records store pieces of information as fields, and each field may have a specific data type associated with it.

- **Queries**   Queries are general-purpose utility tools—not just for selectively retrieving data from tables, but for a variety of other functions as well, such as updating or deleting specific records. Although queries are often used for retrieving or modifying many records at once, they are just as useful for working with individual records.

- **Forms**   Forms are the user interface of database applications, generally being used either to directly access data residing in a table (adding, editing, deleting, or searching for individual records) or as a navigation device. On a Web site, HTML-based forms substitute for the forms you might use to work with a database application through the DBMS in which it was created.

- **Reports**   Reports are primarily used for printing specific records or groups of records for specific purposes. On a Web site, you will most likely not generate printable reports, but will use data-display Web pages instead.

9

Design Parameters

Since you'll probably be called upon to design databases from scratch or integrate existing databases into Web site applications, it's important to have some requirements analysis tools handy. If you've ever done any software development, you understand that bottom-line results are what the client is interested in, and before you begin designing you should have a clear idea what those results must show. A detailed and specific requirements list should be in hand before any design or development takes place. The client should sign off on it or at least be given the chance to review it before you invest many hours on the project.

Hint

It's very common that the client doesn't have a real grasp of each requirement or even each result they'd like to see. Therefore, your interview may be the first time the client has given serious thought to their own business processes. Be careful to tread softly here, because deciding what they want to leave in the project (their requirements) is also the process of deciding what to leave out (everything they can't afford to do at present), and that can be painful. That said, you should also remind them that it's likely their requirements will change as the project progresses, adding more time and expense. This occurs because everything happens on the Web at light speed (including the emergence of new software capabilities or the addition of features to competitors' Web sites), and also because it's very common for customers to be unable to understand or convey their requirements clearly until the project is underway and they have something to point to.

Reverse Engineering

Developing a database can be thought of as a process of reverse engineering. You have to know what you want the database to do for you (the requirements) *before* you can begin programming it to do those functions. You can ask your clients, managers, and colleagues what they want to accomplish, or what processes the database must support. From those answers comes the information you need to begin constructing the database objects that will perform those functions.

For example, if you want to produce a database to track incoming orders, you need to build tables (several tables) that hold the following fields:

- **OrderID**   A unique number for each order

- **Customer information**   Name, Address, Phone Number, and E-mail Address

- **Billing information**   Credit Card Number, and Expiration Date

- **Product information**   Product ID, Product Name, and Price

- **Order information**   Qty Ordered, Shipping, Taxes, and Order Date

Most likely, you'd build a table to hold all the customer information in one place, another table to hold data relating to each individual order, and yet another table to hold the data for each individual order item. This probably seems like a lot of tables, but it actually reduces the total amount of data stored, as well as reducing the likelihood of data-entry errors and the amount of time necessary to search records. Creating multiple tables brings us to our next subject, relational databases.

Relational Databases

A database is said to be relational when it meets several criteria, notably when data for each entity of interest is allocated a table of its own, when the data in each field is discrete (not a mixture of first and last names, for example), and so forth. In fact, there are what are called *normal forms*. Normal forms begin at 1 (first normal form) and go to 5 and beyond. Each level of normal form means the database conforms more and more to relational database standards. In practice, most databases are third normal form.

So, in a relational database, how would the data in the Customers table be related to the data in the Orders table? Let's go over the construction of a table and the special fields inside it that can be linked to other tables.

Table Structure

The basic unit of storage in a database is a *table*. Data is stored in a table in the form of *records*, and inside the records individual items of data are stored in *fields*. The key thing to keep in mind is that tables are best constructed to contain data about one general class of thing (customers, for instance), with the exception of tables that mainly serve to link other tables.

Each record in a table will contain data about one of the class of things (a single customer, for instance), while the fields store various important attributes of that one individual thing (a customer's name, address, and so forth). The attributes stored in a record depend on what *you* think is important or essential for fulfilling the purpose of the database. For example, if you want to be able to bill your customers, you would keep data about their addresses (so you can send them a bill), but you wouldn't need to know the names of their pets (although if you were a veterinarian, that might be useful data).

Primary Key Fields   A special field that is commonly included in a table is a *primary key* field. A primary key field always contains a unique value for each record, so that each individual record can be unambiguously distinguished from every other record in the table. These fields are used to link (or relate) tables to each other.

Why link the tables? Suppose you have a bunch of customers, and they each make hundreds of orders. You could keep all that data in one table, with fields for all the customer data plus fields for all the ordering data (items, quantity, price, description, and so on). But then you'd have to store massive quantities of repetitive data (each order repeats all the customer data), not to mention running a big risk of entering customer information incorrectly, making it extremely difficult to research old orders.

So instead of repeating customer data for each order, a link is created between the Customers table and the Orders table, based on the value of the Customers table's primary key field. For example, customer number 11 will have one entry in the Customers table. This entry will be a single record with a CustomerID number (the primary key) of 11, and other fields for important data such as name, address, phone number, and so on. In the Customers table, there will be only one record with a CustomerID number of 11, and no other CustomerID numbers can duplicate this.

In the Orders table, each record will contain an OrderID number (the primary key) to distinguish it from all the other orders, and each record will contain data such as order date, total due, and so forth. In addition, each order will contain a field called CustomerID. This field is of the same data type (see the next section for a discussion of data types) as the CustomerID field in the Customers table, but in the Orders table

CustomerIDs may be duplicated. In the Orders table, CustomerID is referred to as the *foreign key*.

For each customer record in the Customers table, there may be many records in the Orders table that contain an identical CustomerID number. In practice, this means that a single customer (represented by their record in the Customers table) may have many orders (represented by their multiple records in the Orders table). For each order for the same customer, the only data that is duplicated is the CustomerID number, rather than the entire name, address, phone number, and so on. Moreover, today's DBMSs deal very effectively and automatically with tables in relational structures, making it easy to create primary and foreign keys, and link tables together. Figure 9-1 shows the relationships between customers and orders in a sample Access 2000 database named OrderEntry. Notice the number 1 on the Customers table end of the line linking the Customers table and the Orders table, and notice the infinity symbol (∞) on the Orders table end. This depicts a one-to-many relationship between these tables, meaning one customer can have many orders.

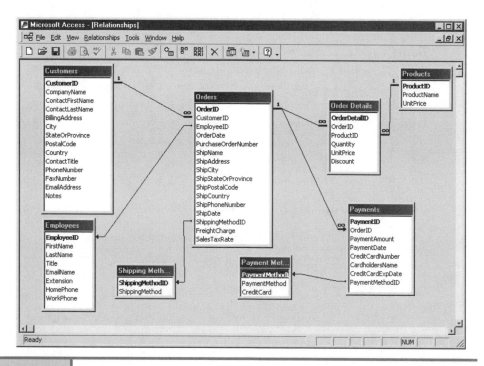

Figure 9-1   Relationships between Customers and Orders tables (and others)

Ask the Expert

Question: I understand how to create relational databases, but do I need to create a primary key for every table?

Answer: Primary keys need to be created only for those tables that link to other tables from the "1" (or "parent") side, but it's still a good habit to create them for most of your tables anyway. It is not uncommon to find a need to perform this kind of linking later on in the game, and it is more convenient if you already have records with a primary key.

Question: How do I make a many-to-many relationship?

Answer: To make a many-to-many relationship, you'll have to create a junction table. This is a special table that serves as a link between two tables that are parents in their own right (both on the "1" side). Since you can't connect them directly to each other, you make a junction table containing both of their primary keys as foreign keys, and connect them to the junction table. Try it, it works!

Data Types *Data type* refers to the kind of data stored in a field in a database, or in a variable when you are programming. VBScript uses a variant as the primary data type, with subtypes that change to suit the needs of your programs. In a database, there are typically five to seven types of data kept in tables:

- **Text** Name, address, phone number, and so on
- **Number** Numbers that can be manipulated with arithmetic
- **Date/Time** Dates and times
- **Yes/No** Logical yes or no, on or off, and so forth
- **Hyperlink** Web addresses, URLs
- **Memo** Large, unstructured text data
- **BLOB** Binary large objects, such as image or application files

It is important to choose the correct data type for each field when creating a Web database, as you need to make sure the right data is being input or queried to get the right answers. For online databases, it's easiest to keep data as Text, Numbers, and Dates. The Microsoft Access hyperlink data type will not work easily online.

Building Microsoft Access Tables

If you are using Access, you have the opportunity to specify data type when creating fields within tables. As you name each field, you will also be selecting the data type, with Text as the default.

Another thing to keep in mind when creating fields is that you should strive to keep each field specific and unique for the data it contains. For example, you could put street address, city, state, and zip code all in one field. However, doing this makes it difficult to retrieve records by zip code later, because the field contains not only the zip code but also all that other data. For the same reason, it is usually best to split name fields into separate fields for first name and last name, because it is very common to retrieve records by last name only. Keeping this in mind makes your design cleaner from the beginning, and easier to work with down the road.

Queries and SQL

Desktop DBMSs, such as Microsoft Access 2000, come with plenty of tools to make life easier for the typical user. In fact, the database used as an example for relationships between Customers and Orders was created in about two minutes using the built-in wizards in Access 2000. Both Access 97 and Access 2000 are easy to use and create very nice databases automatically.

One of the tools that comes with Access 2000 is used for making queries, and it uses an interface called Query-By-Example (QBE). The QBE interface gives users a visual view of the columns or fields of data they are retrieving, and makes it easy to specify the criteria used to select records. Figure 9-2 shows a simple query created in the QBE interface, using the example OrderEntry database. Notice both the Customers and Orders tables are included (with the join line), and the fields are arrayed in a row. Also notice that there are selection criteria present for the

9

CompanyName and OrderDate fields. Only records having a company name of ShopHere.com and an order date later than 1/1/2000 will be retrieved.

It should be clear that CompanyName is a field of data type Text, while OrderDate is a field of data type Date/Time; and an important distinction between the two is the way they are entered in the query. Text data types are delimited by quotes, while date/time data types are delimited by the pound sign. You'll find this convention in use throughout scripting and programming languages.

Setting up a query in Access 2000 is simply a matter of choosing what tables play a role in the results, adding those tables to the query, and then choosing the fields from those tables. Clicking and dragging them into the query grid makes them part of the results.

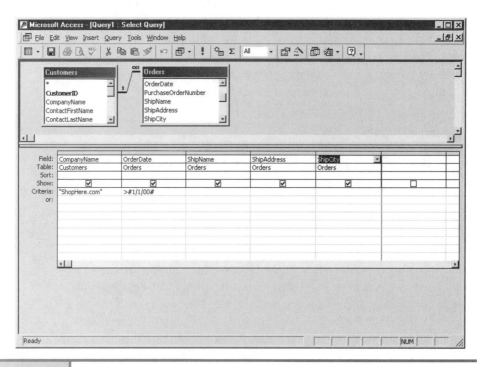

Figure 9-2 A query in the QBE interface

After choosing the tables and fields, you have several options for query types. They are

- **Select Query**   This query selects records based on the criteria you enter in the criteria row. The results contain every record matching those criteria with the fields you include.

- **Delete Query**   This query deletes records matching the criteria you specify.

- **Append Query**   This query appends records matching your criteria from the tables you include to another table.

- **Update Query**   This query updates all records matching your criteria from their existing value (for a given field) to a new value you enter.

- **Make-Table Query**   This query makes a new table from all the records matching your criteria with the fields you include.

Access 2000 also lets you build several other types of query, but let's concentrate on those we've listed. It's easy to make them in Access 2000, and they work well there, but how do you translate them for your ASP scripting applications? The answer is SQL.

Access and Structured Query Language (SQL)

SQL stands for Structured Query Language, and it is the industry-standard method for accessing databases. SQL is a set of English-language statements that specify the query to be performed. Although each DBMS seems to support its own particular version of SQL, the differences are slight and the commonalities are great, so knowing SQL is indispensable.

Fortunately, Access 2000 (and Access 97) contains a simple method for converting from the QBE interface to SQL. As a matter of fact, you can write SQL statements and then switch to QBE, or vice versa, quite easily. Access is actually writing SQL behind the scenes as you create your queries in the QBE interface, much the same way FrontPage writes HTML in the background as you create Web pages visually.

9

The following illustration shows the SQL view of the query we just created in Access 2000. This view can be reached by selecting View | SQL View from the menu when designing a query in Access.

The SQL is also shown here:

```
SELECT Customers.CompanyName, Orders.OrderDate, Orders.ShipName,
Orders.ShipAddress, Orders.ShipCity
FROM Customers INNER JOIN Orders ON Customers.CustomerID = Orders.CustomerID
WHERE (((Customers.CompanyName)="ShopHere.com") AND
((Orders.OrderDate)>#1/1/2000#));
```

As you can see, SQL is made up of fairly easy-to-understand statements that are highly structured for initiating specific actions upon tables in a database. They can also perform many other actions in a database, and the SQL language has evolved far enough to allow complete control of databases.

The preceding SQL code above starts out with the SELECT statement, meaning the action to be performed in the selection of records. The next portion of the code specifies the names of the fields to be selected, combined with the table to select them from (Customers.CompanyName, Orders.OrderDate, and so on).

The FROM statement specifies which tables to select records from and how they are related (INNER JOIN specifies the relationship ON the CustomerID fields of both tables). The WHERE statement specifies the criteria by which to select records.

It's tempting to think that using Access is an easy way to create valid SQL statements for ASP scripts; but, unfortunately, it's not quite that easy. The syntax and structure of SQL statements for ASP scripts are not identical to the syntax and structure of SQL statements that work inside Access. You can use Access to build SQL statements that almost work, but there is usually a little bit of refining that needs to be done. We'll discuss the exact changes required as we get further into building queries for ASP in

Modules 10 and 11, and at the end of this module is a whole section devoted to nothing but coding SQL properly.

Forms as a User Interface

Forms are used primarily for two purposes: entering and editing data in tables and navigating your application. Access 2000 has several methods for creating forms, and also includes a utility called the Switchboard Manager that makes creating navigation forms easy. The most important thing to keep in mind when creating forms is to make them easy to understand and use for the specific task at hand. There's no need to include every field from a table in a form, if only three of the fields will allow the user to do the job.

We won't be covering forms in great detail here, at least not the forms you can create in a DBMS, because you will most likely be developing those forms as Web pages. HTML forms with links and command buttons contain many of the same capabilities as typical database forms, so you might want to develop a process flow for your applications first in the DBMS.

Online and Offline Processes and Forms   Ordinarily, you will be creating very different forms for each application (online versus offline) because each has very different business processes to support. Online, you might want to take orders. Offline, you might want to process orders. Online, users will be customers placing orders, while offline users will be employees processing those orders.

You can use Microsoft FrontPage 2000 or any production HTML-editing tool to create forms for your application. It can be helpful to use the same names for fields on your HTML forms as for the fields in the tables in your database, and make sure to leave out spaces and special characters in field names and table names. Other than that, common sense will guide you in the construction of your forms. Make your forms easy to understand and use, and you will do fine.

Reports and Data Access Pages (DAPs)

Microsoft Access 2000 contains wizards that make it easy to produce reports, so you shouldn't have any major problems building printable, presentable reports in just a few simple steps. Access 2000 also contains a new facility that creates what are called Data Access Pages (DAPs). These are separate

9

HTML files that link directly to online database tables. DAPs are a wonderful method for quickly creating online database access forms. If they are in the standard format (list of records), they can be used to enter and edit data; but if they are grouped and summarized, they are more like a report and are read-only. The biggest drawback is that they only work with Internet Explorer 5.0 and above. If you have control over the user's browser choice (as in an intranet environment), they can make a very nice addition to your database access tools.

1-Minute Drill

● **What fields provide the data for linking tables in a relational format?**

● **QBE uses what format to build queries?**

ActiveX Data Objects

ActiveX Data Objects (ADO) is a special class of ASP components specifically designed with database and data store support in mind. They work well with ASP by design, because so many applications require database support. Behind the scenes you can use just about any database you like, whether it's Microsoft Access 2000, SQL Server, or any other ODBC-compliant database. There are also quite a few proprietary database and online database access technologies, if you care to investigate or have a special need.

While databases might be the most familiar data containers for most of us, there are many containers of data, from spreadsheets and word processing documents to e-mail clients and the newer directory services. In fact, just about any bits or bytes on- or offline can be thought of as a store of data. In addition, online applications are stateless, meaning ADO must work well with a lack of persistent connections to the data source.

● **Key fields, primary and foreign**
● **A visual format, with included tables or queries on top and a grid for columns and criteria on the bottom**

Data Consumers and Data Providers

Any object that stores data can be thought of as a data provider, while any application that uses that data can be thought of as a data consumer. Microsoft has created a two-layer architecture for retrieving data, consisting of ADO and OLE DB. OLE DB is the mechanism for interacting directly with the data store, whatever it might be, and ADO interacts with OLE DB. This means you can program for ADO, and OLE DB will take care of all the technical stuff behind the scenes for you (well, almost).

OLE DB Providers

When you install Windows 2000, ADO is installed, and with it comes a set of OLE DB providers:

- **Jet OLE DB 4.0**   Used to access Microsoft Access databases

- **DTS Packages**   Used for SQL Server Data Transformation Services

- **Internet Publishing**   Used to access Web servers

- **Indexing Service**   Used for index catalogs

- **Site Server Search**   Used for the Site Server search catalog

- **ODBC drivers**   Used for accessing ODBC data sources

- **OLAP services**   Used for the Microsoft OLAP server

- **Oracle**   Used to access Oracle databases

- **SQL Server**   Used to access Microsoft SQL Server databases

- **Simple Provider**   Used to access simple text files

- **MSDataShape**   Used to access hierarchical data

- **Microsoft Directory Services**   Used for the Windows 2000 Directory Services

- **DTS Flat File**   Used for the SQL Server Data Transformation Services flat file manager

9

The ADO 2.5 Object Model

ADO 2.5 consists of a number of objects for connecting to and working with the data you retrieve. Like other components, there is a fairly simple syntax for using them; and once you've made your connection, it's pretty straightforward to work with the data they gather.

The objects in ADO are the Connection and Command objects, the Recordset and Record objects, and the Stream object. The Connection object has an Errors collection, the Command object has a Parameters collection, and the Recordset and Record objects have a Fields collection. Each type of Provider also exposes to the objects just listed a unique Properties collection. The reason for a unique Properties collection for each Provider is that Providers can be just about anything, and some Providers require properties that others don't need. For example, a database may have special security settings that a simple text file doesn't need.

The Connection Object

Let's discuss the workings of each of the objects in the ADO 2.5 object model. We'll start with the Connection object. The primary function of the Connection object is to allow you to connect to data stores via OLE DB. You can specify the provider to use, security parameters, and other parameters. Although it is common to create a Connection object in the course of accessing data, Connection objects are implicitly created whenever you use the other ADOs. Even though there is a separate Command object, you can use the Connection object to run commands against a data store.

The Command Object

The Command object is specifically designed to run commands against a data store, and is more flexible and capable in this regard than the Connection object. In fact, when you run commands using the Connection object, a limited Command object is implicitly created to perform those commands. The Command object is more powerful than the Connection object in that it allows you to be very specific about how the commands you are running are formed, as well as providing a more intuitive interface and programming structure for those commands.

The Recordset Object

If you've ever done any database programming with DBMSs such as Microsoft Access or Paradox for Windows, you've probably used recordsets. The Recordset object is kind of like a table in your hands. You can retrieve recordsets from a table, and then manipulate those recordsets in a fashion similar to having a table open in front of you.

For example, you can navigate around a recordset, going to the first, last, previous, or next record. You can add, edit, and delete records. And you can filter or find and change records based on values in individual fields.

The Record Object

The Record object is new and was added to handle data not formatted in structured rows and columns. Data in databases and spreadsheets is nicely formatted, but other data sources may only be somewhat structured. For example, suppose your data is in an e-mail program within mailboxes and folders, some messages containing attachments, hyperlinks, or embedded images. The structure of the mailboxes and folders may be uniform, but the properties of each e-mail message may differ significantly. The Record object is designed to cope with differences in structure between one record and the next. You won't be using the Record object for much of your work with this book; but as your applications begin to use more and varied data providers, your use of the Record object will also grow.

The Stream Object

If the contents of a field is a binary large object (BLOB) or some other type of data that does not fit well into the common data types, you can use the Stream object to retrieve and manipulate it.

1-Minute Drill

- **What ADO is like a table in a database?**
- **What ADO is best for running commands against a database?**

- **The Recordset object, because it allows you to manipulate individual records as though the table were open in front of you**
- **The Command object, although you can also use the Connection object in a limited way**

Coding Structured Query Language (SQL)

In Module 2, we mention SQL and its role in working with databases and ASP scripting. The following section covers the major SQL commands and syntax, with the objective of familiarizing you with SQL enough to build confidence when scripting SQL commands.

Although I'm sure it's not the case for everyone, I find SQL easy to understand and use, because the syntax is fairly simple and the commands so English-like. However, I should warn you that the structure of some of the commands is highly dependent upon the structure of whatever database you are accessing. You would be well advised to learn about relational database structure in general before trying to write complex table joins from scratch. That said, always remember that DBMS programs such as Microsoft Access have built-in SQL generators, and these can be a great help in properly formatting SQL commands quickly. Osborne/McGraw-Hill also publishes an excellent SQL reference book entitled (appropriately enough) *SQL, The Complete Reference*, by James R. Groff and Paul N. Weinberg (ISBN 0-07-211845-8).

SQL Statements

Writing SQL code is just a little bit different from writing scripting language code or using ASP, in that the code tends to have a query-like flavor. For example, a very common SQL statement is the SELECT statement (by convention, this book will list SQL commands as uppercase, although it is not required). The SELECT statement retrieves data from a database by specifying the columns (or fields) to retrieve, the table or tables from which to retrieve data, and any criteria limiting the records retrieved.

In SQL, you can use SELECT to retrieve data, INSERT to add records (or rows), DELETE to remove records, and UPDATE to edit or modify data in records. The SQL statement performing any of these actions would begin with one of these verbs and be followed by additional details about which tables and records are to be affected.

SQL also contains a variety of commands that affect the structure of the database or tables. These include CREATE TABLE, ALTER TABLE, and DROP TABLE, as well as similar commands affecting VIEWs, INDEXes, SCHEMAs, and DOMAINs. There are also a few statements for controlling access privileges, and transactions, and for defining programmatic SQL functions such as using cursors and conducting dynamic operations.

SQL Keywords and Table/Field Names

There are quite a number of reserved keywords in SQL, and additional keywords may exist in the various flavors of SQL available. Naturally, you want to avoid using these keywords as table or field names. Fortunately, they are usually similar to reserved keywords in scripting languages, and it's not too hard to remember what words to avoid. For example, DATE, DAY, DELETE, DESC, ELSE, GET, GOTO, and IN are all SQL keywords. Many of these are also keywords in VBScript, but I've found a few ACCESS databases in which the Description field (for a product record, for instance) has been shortened to Desc. SQL doesn't work well with this, so keep an eye out for this and other conflicting field names.

project9-1.zip

Project 9-1: Using SQL

For this module, we've devoted an entire Project section to SQL queries, with the differences between what Microsoft Access generates and the standard ANSI/SQL explained. This will be a good reference for constructing your own SQL queries quickly, as your applications become more and more database dependent.

Step-by-Step

Let's start with the simpler queries and build from there. We'll use Access to construct the queries, and then look at the SQL Access generates. After that, we'll construct the query in ordinary SQL to illustrate the differences.

Simple SELECT Queries

1. The first step in this project is to use the QBE interface to build a query. We start with a SELECT query using several variations.

9

2. Figure 9-3 shows an example of a very simple SELECT query on the Customers table of our example database, using Access's QBE interface. Following is the SQL code as Access has generated it.

```
SELECT Customers.CustomerID, Customers.CompanyName,
Customers.ContactFirstName, Customers.ContactLastName,
Customers.BillingAddress, Customers.City,
Customers.StateOrProvince, Customers.PostalCode,
Customers.Country, Customers.ContactTitle,
Customers.PhoneNumber, Customers.FaxNumber,
Customers.EmailAddress, Customers.Notes
FROM Customers;
```
Here's the reference to the table.

3. There are only two SQL commands, SELECT and FROM, in this code. The rest of the code consists of the field names (qualified by the table they reside in) and the name of the table itself. The result of this query is a table consisting of all rows and columns in the original tables. In effect, this query creates a complete snapshot of the original table.

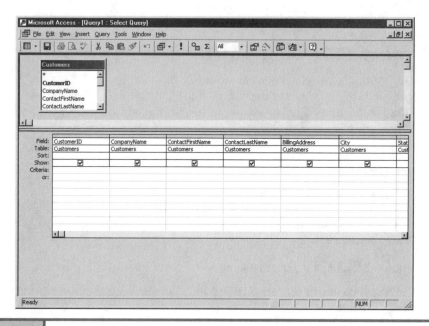

Figure 9-3   A SELECT query on the Customers table

4. To make this code simpler, SQL also includes a coding convention whereby a single asterisk can be substituted for the names of all the fields in the table (this works for Access also), so the code would be

```
SELECT Customers.*
FROM Customers;
```

5. Figure 9-4 shows the addition of a single criterion in the ContactLastName column, making the query only return rows (records) in which the value of the ContactLastName field is exactly equal to Johnson. The SQL code follows:

```
SELECT Customers.*
FROM Customers
WHERE (((Customers.ContactLastName)="Johnson"));
```

6. Notice the way Access has organized the WHERE clause. ANSI SQL doesn't require all the parentheses and the semicolon. Also, ANSI SQL uses single apostrophes rather than the quotes Access uses around the specified text value.

9

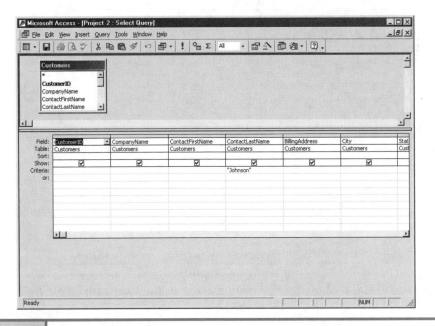

Figure 9-4   Selecting for records with ContactLastName = "Johnson"

7. Figure 9-5 shows sorting by the CompanyName field added to the returning results, and I deliberately used descending order so the DESC keyword would be included in the ORDER BY clause. If ascending order is desired, the sort order indicator is omitted.

```
SELECT Customers.* FROM Customers
WHERE (((Customers.ContactLastName)="Johnson"))
ORDER BY Customers.CompanyName DESC;
```

8. Figure 9-6 shows a modification to the query we've been building that allows the query to retrieve any record that starts with the first four characters "John" and then contains any number of characters after that as the value of the field named ContactLastName. Pattern-matching expressions of this type use the Like keyword, and in Microsoft Access the asterisk is used as the wildcard character, meaning any character any number of times.

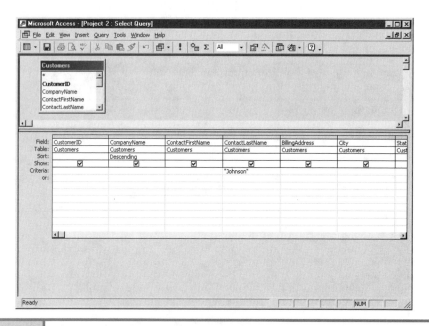

Figure 9-5   Query showing descending order in the CompanyName field

9. In Access, the question mark is used to match a single character. In ANSI SQL, the wildcard characters with the same meanings are the percent sign and the underscore, respectively.

```
SELECT Customers.*
FROM Customers
WHERE (((Customers.ContactLastName) Like "John*"))
ORDER BY Customers.CompanyName DESC;
```

10. Like most languages, SQL can use comparison operators in expressions. Equal, not equal to, greater-than, less-than, and so forth, can all be used in arithmetical operations, string comparisons, and date comparisons. If the comparison is true, the record is retrieved; but if the comparison is false or null, the record is not retrieved (we'll discuss null values shortly). The next figure (Figure 9-7) and code show how Access queries compare date values in a field to the specified date, to find all records with a date

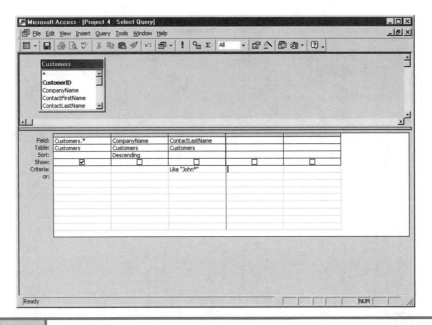

Figure 9-6 | Query using wildcard characters for "John" and any characters

later than 1/1/2000. (We've switched from using the Customers table to the Orders table.)

```
SELECT Orders.*, Orders.OrderDate
FROM Orders
WHERE (((Orders.OrderDate)>#1/1/2000#));
```

11. The BETWEEN keyword can also be used to make a simpler version of two separate comparison tests, to find values between a low and high value set. For example, if you wanted to find orders dated between 1/1/2000 and 3/1/2000, rather than forming two individual WHERE clauses you could use the following code:

```
SELECT Orders.*, Orders.OrderDate
FROM Orders
WHERE (((Orders.OrderDate) Between #1/1/2000# And #3/1/2000#));
```

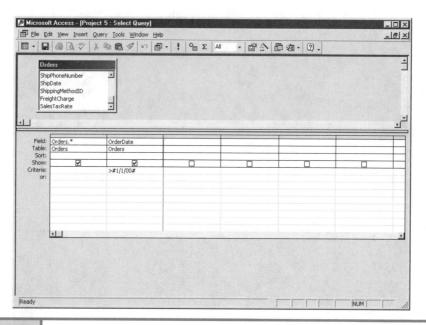

Figure 9-7 Query finding all records in the Orders table after 1/1/2000

12. The term "null values" is actually a misnomer, as null means there is no value in a field. Technically, null means that the value is unknown, whereas a zero-length string means the value is "nothing." Finding null values in records becomes important under fairly common circumstances. For example, if you count all your customers in California by zip code, your count result may be 1,000; but suppose 15 of your customers in California have nothing entered for zip code? The real total of 1,015 would not be the result you get. So to find null values, you would specify Is Null in your query. Figure 9-8 and the following code show the use of Is Null in Access SQL in the Orders table, for finding all records in which no freight charge was applied.

```
SELECT Orders.*, Orders.FreightCharge
FROM Orders
WHERE (((Orders.FreightCharge) Is Null));
```

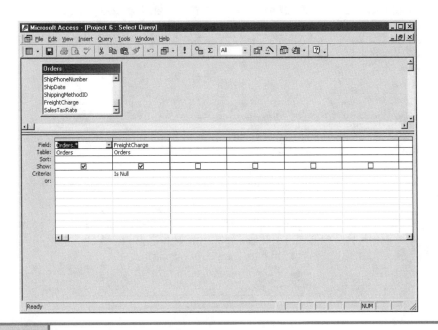

Figure 9-8   Query finding records without freight charges

13. You will often require a query to SELECT records based on criteria in two or more fields, or based on two or more conditions for a single field. You can use the logical operators AND, OR, and NOT to find records in this fashion, as Figure 9-9 and the following code illustrate:

```
SELECT Orders.*
FROM Orders
WHERE (((Orders.OrderDate)>#1/1/2000#) AND ((Orders.ShipDate)<#1/1/2000#));
```

14. This query finds orders in which there is obviously an error, indicated by order dates after shipping dates. To be retrieved, a record must have an order date greater than 1/1/2000 and a shipping date prior to 1/1/2000.

15. If you changed the AND to an OR, this query would retrieve all orders made after 1/1/2000,44 as well as all records with a shipping date before 1/1/2000. If you further changed this query so that only the OrderDate field was used as part of the criteria, all records not

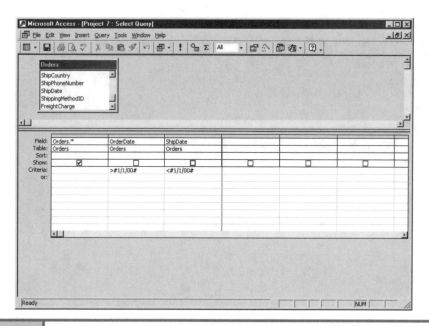

| Figure 9-9 | Query using Boolean operators |

ordered on 1/1/2000 would be retrieved, because you would be requesting all records with an order date before or after 1/1/2000.

16. Finally, if you further changed this query so that instead of OR the condition used the NOT operator (all order dates after 1/1/2000 but not before 1/1/2000), we would get only those orders dated after 1/1/2000. A more useful query might be all records with an order date after 1/1/2000 where payment has not yet been received; but, of course, you would then have to include the Paid field or something to that effect.

17. When building your database, you will encounter field values that can be calculated based on other field values. Sales tax due, for example, is the result of a calculation multiplying the total cost of products ordered (individual product cost times the quantity ordered, added up) times the applicable sales tax rate.

18. The question is, do you add a field to your table for this amount, or do you just let the other fields hold the data and then calculate the total sales tax due whenever you need it? You will frequently just perform the calculation whenever you need to view sales tax due or other calculated values. You can use SQL to calculate values during queries, as shown in Figure 9-10.

```
SELECT Orders.OrderID, [OrderProductCost]*[SalesTaxRate] AS SalesTaxDue
FROM Orders;
```

19. Another common occurrence is the duplication of values for a given field. For example, if you wanted to find all employees who have placed orders for customers, you could search the Orders table under the EmployeeID field. However, you would want to produce a list of the employees by ID number in which duplicate entries have been removed. The SQL DISTINCT keyword accomplishes this. Although inserting this keyword in the SQL shows no differences in Access's QBE example (Figure 9-11) it eliminates duplicate EmployeeID records in the result set. The syntax is shown in the code

```
SELECT DISTINCT Orders.EmployeeID
FROM Orders;
```

9

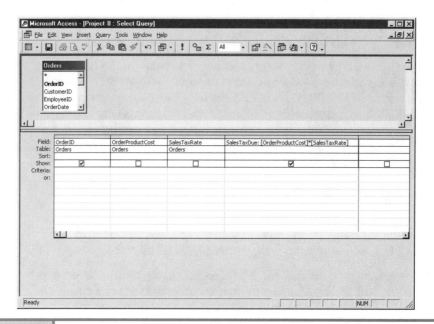

Figure 9-10   Query creating a calculated field

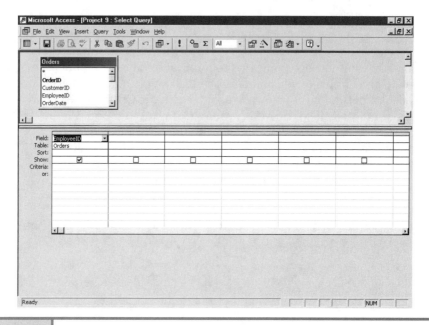

Figure 9-11   Query using the DISTINCT keyword

SQL Table Joins

In a relational database, data is kept in individual tables that keep track of a single subject, item, or thing. Customers, employees, orders, inventory items, and so on, are all examples of things that might have their own tables. Relationships between tables can be defined using key fields (primary and foreign keys). To express a relationship between two or more tables in a SQL query, joins are used.

Joins come in several flavors:

- **Equi-join**   This type of join results in recordsets where the values of the joined fields are exactly equal. All records in either table not matching joined field values in the other table do not appear in the results. This type of join is also referred to as an inner join. In SQL, the notation for this type of join is an equal sign (=) between the matching fields from each table.

- **Outer-join**   This type of join results in recordsets where the values of the joined fields may be equal, but may also *not* have a matching value in the other table. Therefore, all records that match and all records that don't match will be included, with null values where unmatched fields occur. In SQL, the notation for this type of join is an asterisk, an equal sign, and another asterisk (*=*).

- **Left and right outer joins**   These types of join result in recordsets where all records that match are included, but only the nonmatching records of one or the other table are included, not both. In SQL, the notation for this type of join is an asterisk on the side of the equal sign indicating the table from which nonmatching records are to be included (*=) or (=*).

Figure 9-12 shows an Access query using an inner join to connect the Customers and Orders tables, to produce a listing of the orders for each customer.

The Access code to produce such a listing is

```
SELECT Customers.CustomerID, Customers.CompanyName,
Orders.OrderID, Orders.OrderDate, Orders.OrderProductCost
FROM Customers INNER JOIN Orders ON Customers.CustomerID =
Orders.CustomerID;
```

9

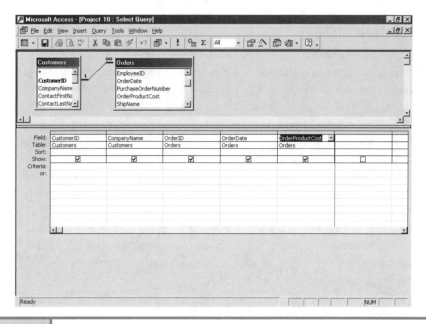

Figure 9-12 Query relating two tables (Customers and Orders) via the primary key

The standard SQL code to produce the same result is just

```
SELECT Customers.CustomerID, Customers.CompanyName,
Orders.OrderID, Orders.OrderDate, Orders.OrderProductCost
FROM Customers, Orders
WHERE Customers.CustomerID = Orders.CustomerID
```

To produce a left or right join in Access for this query, simply substitute the word LEFT or RIGHT for the word INNER in the code.

Summary Queries

SQL contains a number of functions that allow you to summarize field values. For example, you can compute the sum of all OrderProductCost fields from the Orders table for each individual customer. You can also ascertain the average, minimum value, maximum value, total number of values, and total number of records. The keywords for these functions are SUM, AVG, MIN, MAX, COUNT, and COUNT*. Figure 9-13 shows our Access query redesigned once again, so it will produce the sum of all orders from the Orders table, using the summary function SUM.

The following code shows the way this is done in SQL:

```
SELECT Sum(Orders.OrderProductCost) AS SumOfOrderProductCost
FROM Orders;
```

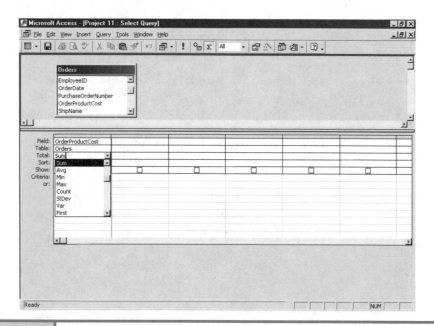

Figure 9-13 Query using aggregation or grouping to produce totals

Ask the Expert

Question: SQL seems to be the standard language for working with databases, as you've mentioned. What relationship does SQL have with Microsoft products, other vendors' products, and Web sites in general?

Answer: Although there are many variations of SQL, they tend to be pretty slight variations, usually just subtle differences in the reserved words, special characters (such as wildcard characters), and delimiters. Each version of SQL is appropriate for the type of database it is accessing or the circumstances under which it is used. For example, if you insert a parameter in a SQL statement being used within Microsoft FrontPage, the delimiters will be different from those used with ASP to achieve the same result. Keep in mind that SQL is central to database access no matter what program or environment you are using, but be prepared to do some research (and a little trial and error) to get your SQL statements to work.

Question: I'm not quite sure I understand the concept of relational database design. How important is it, and can I get along without it?

Answer: You might want to do further research into relational database design, but I'm afraid it doesn't get much easier than this. There are actually several levels of relational structure (called the normal forms), and most designers use the third normal form for their designs. This means that no fields have more than one piece of data in them (no city-state-zip fields, for example), each trackable entity has its own table, and data is only stored once per entity. However, depending upon the use to which your database will be put, it may be expedient to break some of these rules. Good designers know when to break them.

Since there are basically three types of relationships between tables (one-to-one, one-to-many, and many-to-many), I usually just ask myself what the relationship is. For example, if you have employees in a company and you want to track them, that means one table for them. However, if an employee can be on several teams, while teams can have several employees on them, then the relationship between employees and teams can be stated as, "An employee may be on many teams, and a team may have many employees; therefore, the relationship is many-to-many." Talking it out is helpful.

☑ *Mastery Check*

1. What is the process of determining the end result and working backward to determine requirements called?

   A. From-the-ground-up engineering

   B. Backward engineering

   C. Reverse engineering

   D. None of the above

2. What is the SQL command for specifying criteria in a SELECT statement?

   A. WITHIN

   B. WHERE

   C. FROM

   D. None of the above

3. What are the SQL text field delimiters?

   A. Single-quote marks

   B. Double-quote marks

   C. The percent sign

   D. None of the above

4. What takes the place of traditional DBMS navigational forms on a Web site?

   A. Queries

   B. Reports

   C. HTML forms

   D. Data Access Pages (DAPs)

9

Module 10

The ADO Connection-Related Objects

The Goals of This Module

- Connect to databases with the Connection object
- Examine the functions the Command object can perform
- Run action commands with the Command object
- Set various cursor types
- Create and run stored procedures
- Insert parameters into connections

The first step in establishing access to a database is the creation of a connection. In this module, you learn how to illustrate how the basic connection and command methods work, as well as some of the things you can do with a connection once you establish it. Because ASP is a flexible technology, it gives you the option of using several objects to work with databases and database records, not only the Recordset. In this module, you build knowledge of the Connection and Command objects, and factors affecting their use.

Interactivity and Latency

ASP is all about providing data to users, as well as gathering data from users or, more plainly, interactivity. *Latency* is the term for the waiting time users endure while they interact with your site. Latency is greatly affected by your ability to optimize the structure of your database and the connection methods you employ. How you make connections and what you can do with them are restricted by a range of factors, including server capability, bandwidth available, both server and database software (and drivers), and the requirements of your application. This means making good connections and using them appropriately is important. A number of subjects are covered in this chapter as you are encouraged to develop good structural skills. This module contains further explanation of how to create and use connections effectively.

Optimizing Database Interactions

Working with a database behind the scenes makes your applications lively, but it can slow things down considerably if you don't take steps to optimize your applications' database interactions. In this section, you'll learn a few ideas to keep your applications speedy.

Opening and Closing Connections

You should know and practice a few things when you open a connection to keep your applications running efficiently. Opening a connection is a time-consuming operation, so you should do it as infrequently as possible. Fortunately, OLE DB has connection pooling built in, which means after you close a connection, it goes into a pool of inactive connections. If another connection of the same type is required by your application, the inactive connection is made active again, rather than reestablishing a whole new connection.

To optimize connection pooling, open your connections as late in your application as possible, and close it as quickly as possible. This means fewer whole new connections will be opened, and your application then runs faster for more users. Remember to insert the connection close method after you finish using each connection. The connection is then available for the next user.

Using Stored Procedures

You can code your processing to run within your scripts, and you can sometimes code your processing to run as a stored procedure within the database itself. Wherever you can run stored procedures, you should, because they are precompiled and run much faster. Stored procedures are discussed more in just a bit.

Use Required Data Only

When you retrieve data, you don't always need to create a Recordset and, if you do create one, you don't always need every field in a table or the capability to modify records. Limit what you retrieve to required data and functionality only. Less functionality translates to less processing overhead and less data transmitted back and forth.

10

The Connection Object

The Connection object can be used to make a connection to a database, and it can also be used to run SQL statements against a database. The SQL statements can be ordinary SELECT queries or they can insert, update, or delete records. Differences in the functionality are provided by various data providers and, with some providers, some of the collections, methods, and properties discussed in the following may not be available.

---*Hint*---

When making a connection, you can often apply constants (ADO Constants) that define the type of locking or cursor to be used. These constants take the form of various values. The constant names themselves—and the values to which they are equivalent—can be found in a file named adovbs.inc in the Program Files\CommonFiles\ System\ado subfolder of the drive on which the operating system is installed. Copy that file into the folder in which your scripts are running, and then you can reference the file as an include file to make the constant names available within your connection strings, and so forth.

Connecting to a data source can be accomplished using a complete connection string, a separate file that contains the connection information, or via a *Data Source Name (DSN)*. I prefer to use DSNs, but sometimes you don't have that luxury.

Storing and Accessing Connection Information

A connection string typically contains the name and path of the database file, user ID and password, and a reference to the driver to be used with the data provider. The syntax isn't too difficult; but if you're using a connection string in several places or pages of your ASP application and some detail changes, it can make more work to change each instance. Better to store the connection details in an include file or as an Application variable, so you only have to change the details in one place.

---*Hint*---

If you store the connection details as an Application variable in your global.asa file, you must start and stop the Application each time you modify the connection details. As mentioned in earlier modules, this can be extra work.

Connection Strings   Following are several examples of acceptable connection strings:

Microsoft Access

```
Driver={Microsoft Access Driver (*.mdb)}; DBQ=the path and file name
Provider=Microsoft.Jet.OLEDB.4.0; Data Source=the path and file name
```

Microsoft SQL Server

```
Driver={SQL Server}; Server=the server name; Database=the database name;
UID=the user ID; PWD=the password
```

Data Link Files   A *data link* file is another method you can use
to connect to a database. It stores additional information about the
connection, but you must have either a DSN or a connection string ready
to use a data link file. Essentially, you create the DSN or connection sting,
and then create a blank text file with a name of your choice. Rename the
file extension to .udl, and then open the files' properties by right-clicking
the file. You get several screens, as shown in the following figures, starting
with Figure 10-1.

The Microsoft OLE DB Provider for ODBC Drivers is chosen here.
Click Next to go to the next screen, or click the Connection tab. On
the next screen (Figure 10-2), you see you have a choice between using a
data source name (how to set one up is discussed in a moment) and using
a connection string.

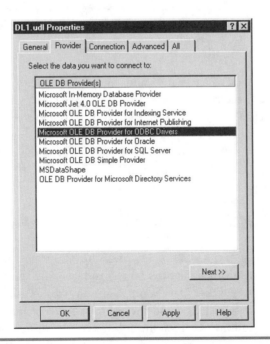

10

| **Figure 10-1** | The Provider screen of a .udl file properties dialog box |

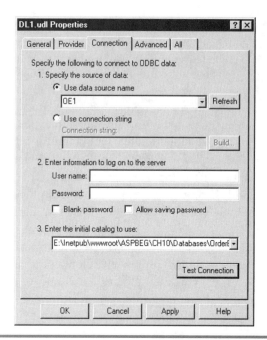

Figure 10-2 The Connection tab of a .udl file properties dialog box

Choose data source name, and then choose the only catalog that is available, the filename and path to your DSN's database file. You can skip the Advanced screen and go straight to the All tab to see the results of your choices before you close the dialog box, as in Figure 10-3.

If you open the .udl file in Notepad, you can see it is storing the same information as a connection string. To reference it in your ASP scripts, use the following syntax:

```
MyConn.Open "File Name=the path and file name"
```

DSNs   To set up a DSN, go to the Administrative Tools section of the Programs menu (from the Start menu) and choose Data Sources (ODBC). This opens the ODBC Data Source Administrator, as shown in Figure 10-4.

Choose System DSN, and then choose Add to add a new one. You get a single additional screen listing the types of drivers available, and you should choose the Access driver to go along with the Access database being used. Click Finish, and you get the screen shown in Figure 10-5.

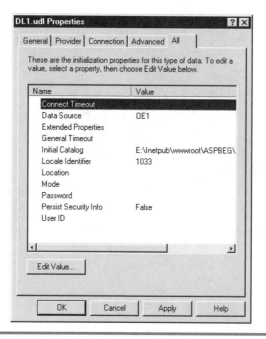

Figure 10-3   The All tab of a .udl file properties dialog box

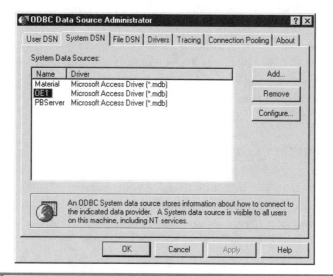

Figure 10-4   The ODBC Data Source Administrator

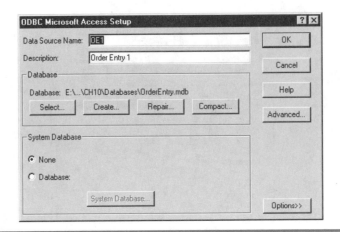

Figure 10-5 The DSN configuration screen

Name your new connection whatever you like (OE1, if you're following along with the examples in the book) and choose the path and file to the appropriate database file. That's it!

After setting up a DSN, you can access it from your ASP scripts when opening a connection with the following syntax:

```
MyConn.Open "theDSNname"
```

This follows the typical syntax for the Connection object, which is the name of the object (for this example, the name used is MyConn); the Open method; and either the DSN or the Connection string, followed by the UserID, the Password, and any options you want to set. The simpler syntax with a DSN is used for most of these examples.

Connection Object Methods

The Connection object is associated with a number of useful properties. Some of them are primarily useful if you intend to manage transactions; others you use in most of your database operations. In this module, the more common Connection methods are covered and, in Module 12, the transaction-related Connection methods are reviewed. To whet your appetite, transactions enable you to control the execution of changes to a data source so, if part of the changes fail, the entire set of changes is reversed, leaving your data intact—an important consideration in critical operations. In any case, here's a list of them all:

- **Open**   This method opens a connection to a data source and accepts arguments such as a ConnectionString, a UserID, and a Password.

- **Execute**   This method executes, via the CommandText argument, queries in the form of SQL statements, stored procedures, or simply a call to a particular table. It also accepts options, such as the number of records affected, and direction for evaluating the CommandText argument.

- **Close**   This method closes the Connection object, but does not remove it from memory.

- **OpenSchema**   This method enables you to gather schema information from the data provider and accepts arguments such as QueryType, Criteria, and SchemaID BeginTrans—this method is used to begin a new transaction.

- **CommitTrans**   This method saves data changes permanently, in effect, completing the transaction.

- **RollbackTrans**   This method cancels data changes made during the current transaction and ends the transaction.

Using Commands with the Connection object

You probably noticed the Execute method in the previous listing. Like the Command object, you can run commands such as SQL statements, stored procedures, or direct references to database tables with the Connection object—but in a more limited way, just for convenience. You can speed processing of connections that have no requirement to return records by adding the ADO constant adExecuteNoRecords to the Options argument when you Execute your connection.

10

Connection Properties

The properties associated with the Connection object enable you to examine and configure the connection before and during the connection session. For example, the Provider property returns the name of the provider in use, and the Version property returns the version number of ADO running. Here are the properties of the Connection object:

- **Attributes** This property applies to other objects—such as the Parameter object—and has to do with transactions for supporting data providers. For the Connection object, it is read/write.

- **CommandTimeout** This property specifies how long to wait while executing a command until ending processing and producing an error.

- **ConnectionString** This property contains the connection data, such as Provider, Data Source, UserID, Password, and so forth.

- **ConnectionTimeout** Similar to the CommandTimeout, this property specifies how long to wait while trying to make a connection before timing out and producing an error.

- **CursorLocation** This property specifies whether the cursor associated with a connection resides on the client or the server.

- **DefaultDatabase** This property specifies the default database for a connection.

- **IsolationLevel** This property specifies the isolation level of a connection and is useful for keeping your transactions straight.

- **Mode** This property tells you what permissions you have for making modifications to data in a connection, for example, read, write, or exclusive.

- **Provider** This property specifies the name of the data provider for a connection.

- **State**   This property tells you whether the Connection object is open or closed.

- **Version**   This property tells you the ADO version number.

1-Minute Drill

- **What three techniques can be used to specify the information required to open a connection?**

- **What three connection methods actually effect connections, and which one makes records available?**

Many of the properties and methods previously listed have to do with transaction processing or with managing Recordsets you've just made available with the Connection object. These are covered in more detail in Module 11. For now, let's examine the Errors collection, a child of the Connection object within the ADO 2.5 data model.

Advanced Error-Handling Techniques

The Errors collection, as mentioned in Module 9, is contained in the Connection object. This collection consists of an Error object for each error occurring in any given connection to the database via ADO, whether using an explicit Connection object, or making an implicit connection with a Command or Recordset object. If an error occurs when a connection is made, a command is run, or a recordset is retrieved, any existing errors in the Errors collection are removed and the new one(s) inserted. If no error occurs, however, any existing errors *will remain in the collection*. The Errors collection always contains the most recent errors.

10

- A connection string, a .udl file, and a DSN
- The Open, Close, and Execute methods, and the Execute method makes records available.

Handling Errors

Retrieving error values can be done by accessing the Error objects within the Errors collection from the Connection object (MyConn.Errors, for example) or by going through the ActiveConnection property of the Recordset object (myRs.ActiveConnection.Errors, for example). Either way, you find the values you need in each individual Error object. These values include the following properties:

- **Number**   The ADO error number

- **HelpContext**, **HelpFile**   These properties tell you the filename or topic associated with an Error object

- **NativeError**   The error number assigned by the data provider

- **SQLState**   The SQL state code

- **Source**   The object from which the error came

- **Description**   A description of the error

To retrieve these values, you can use code like the following to iterate through all the errors present:

```
For Each erroritem in MyConn.Errors
    Response.Write "The Error number = "  & erroritem.Number & "<BR>"
    Response.Write "The Native Error number is = "  & erroritem.NativeError
& "<BR>"
    Response.Write "The SQL state code is = "  & erroritem.SQLState & "<BR>"
    Response.Write "The Source object of the rror is = "  & erroritem.Source
& "<BR>"
    Response.Write "The Description of the error is = "  &
erroritem.Description & "<BR>"
Next
```

Ask the Expert

Question: What's the difference between the Errors collection and Error objects?

Answer: The Errors collection is simply a child collection of the Connection object, while Error objects represent individual errors that occurred during an ADO operation. They are generated by the data provider and are not cleared out unless a new error occurs.

Question: How are errors generated, and how can they be trapped and worked with?

Answer: When the data provider detects an error, it places an Error object in the Errors collection. Because several errors may occur, several errors may be present in the collection. Examining the Errors collection with the code presented earlier enables you to determine error values and work with them. ADO can also produce errors, and you can trap them just like any other run-time error.

project10-1.zip

Project 10-1: Using The Connection Object

Although the Connection object will be used often when recordsets are discussed in Module 11, let's do a small project now to make and work with connections, with the example Access 2000 database. You can see what Access can do for you as the properties of the connections that can be made are examined.

Step-by-Step

Let's start by making a straightforward connection using a DSN for practice.

Connecting with a DSN

1. The first step in this project is to create the DSN using the method shown earlier in this module. If you've been following along with the book, you should already have a DSN, named "OE1," connected to the Access database file named "OrderEntry1.mdb." If not, make one following the instructions in the earlier section titled "DSNs."

2. Next, build the following code:

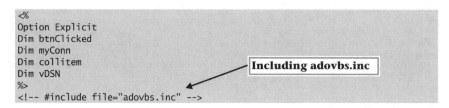

```
<%
Option Explicit
Dim btnClicked
Dim myConn
Dim collitem
Dim vDSN
%>
<!-- #include file="adovbs.inc" -->
```

Including adovbs.inc

```
<html><head><title>Making Database Connections with ADO</title>
<meta http-equiv="Content-Type" content="text/html; charset=iso-8859-1">
</head>
<body bgcolor="#77FF77">
<H2><font size="6">Making ADO Connections</font></H2>
<TABLE border=1><TR><TD>
<H3>Connection Variables and Errors</H3>
</TD></TR><TR><TD bgcolor="white">
<%
btnClicked = Request.Form("btnval")
Select Case btnClicked
      Case "DSN"
             vDSN = Request.Form("DSN")
             Set myConn = Server.CreateObject("ADODB.Connection")
             myConn.Open vDSN
             Response.Write "<B>DSN Connection Values are:</B><P>"
             Response.Write "The value for Attributes is <B>" &
myConn.Attributes & "</B><BR>"
             Response.Write "The value for Command Timeout is <B>" &
myConn.CommandTimeout & "</B><BR>"
             Response.Write "The value for Connection String is <B>" &
myConn.ConnectionString & "</B><BR>"
             Response.Write "The value for Connection Timeout is <B>" &
myConn.ConnectionTimeout & "</B><BR>"
             Response.Write "The value for Cursor Location is <B>" &
myConn.CursorLocation & "</B><BR>"
             Response.Write "The value for Default Database is <B>" &
myConn.DefaultDatabase & "</B><BR>"
             Response.Write "The value for Isolation Level is <B>" &
myConn.IsolationLevel & "</B><BR>"
             Response.Write "The value for Mode is <B>" & myConn.Mode &
"</B><BR>"
             Response.Write "The value for Provider is <B>" & myConn.Provider &
"</B><BR>"
             Response.Write "The value for State is <B>" & myConn.State &
"</B><BR>"
             Response.Write "The value for Version is <B>" & myConn.Version &
"</B><BR>"
             Response.Write "<P><B>Error Values are:</B><P>"
             For each collitem in myConn.Errors
                    Response.Write "Number: " & collitem.Number & "<BR>"
                    Response.Write "NativeError: " & collitem.NativeError &
"<BR>"
                    Response.Write "Source: " & collitem.Source & "<BR>"
                    Response.Write "SQLState: " & collitem.SQLState & "<BR>"

                    Response.Write "Description: " & collitem.Description & "<BR>"
             Next
             myConn.Close
      End Select
%>
</TD></TR></TABLE>
<P>
<TABLE border=1 width="50%">
  <TR>
    <TD bgcolor="#00CC99" COLSPAN=3>
```

Opening the Connection

Iterating through the Errors collection

```
    <H3><font size="6">Connection Values</font></H3>
   </TD>
 </TR>
 <TR>
  <TD colspan="3">
    <form method=POST action="ADOConnections.asp">
     <table width="50%" border="1">
       <tr>
        <td><b>Enter the DSN</b>
          <input type="submit" name="btnval" value="DSN">
        </td>
       </tr>
       <tr>
        <td> <b>DSN: </b>
          <input type="text" name="DSN" size="20">
        </td>
       </tr>
     </table>
    </form>
  </TD>
 </TR>
</TABLE>
</BODY></HTML>
```

3. In the previous code, the first step is to dimension some variables and include the constants file. Then the Select Case structure is used to capture the DSN value returning from the form and open the connection.

4. Next, we write back all the built-in properties of the Connection object that has been opened, followed by the Error properties (iterated through with a For Each structure).

5. The open form initially looks like Figure 10-6, while the displayed connection and error properties are shown in Figure 10-7.

The Command Object

The *Command object* can open connections (implicitly) and has the added advantage of being able to pass parameters to the stored procedures it runs. This gives you the flexibility you need for working with stored procedures, rather than doing all your processing in the scripting code. As previously mentioned, stored procedures usually run much more quickly than scripts.

The Command object can accept several arguments:

- **RecordsAffected**   This is a variable specifying how many records are affected by the command.

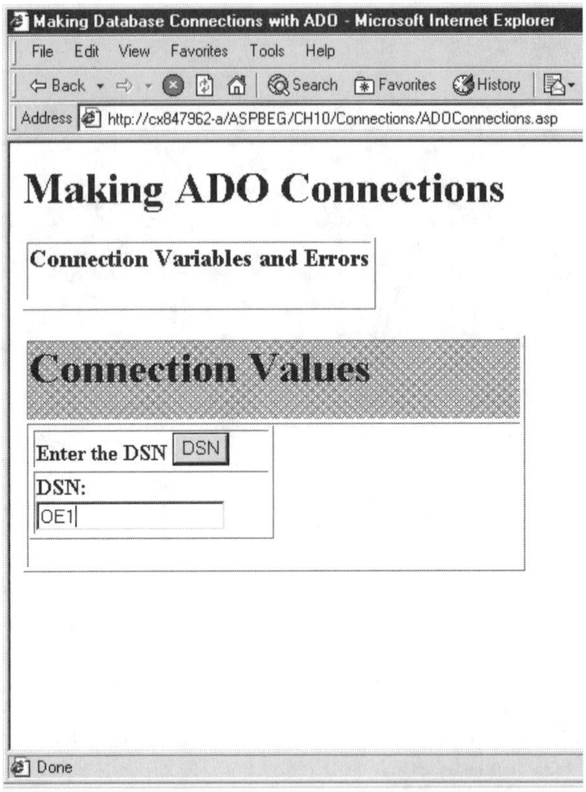

Figure 10-6 The HTML form for opening a connection with a DSN

- **Parameters** This is an array of parameter values. Parameters are discussed in more detail shortly.

- **Options** This value specifies how to process the commands given (as a table, stored procedure, and so forth).

The basic code for opening a connection and running a command is as follows:

```
Set myCmd = Server.CreateObject("ADODB.Command")
myCmd.CommandText = "Products"
Set myRs = myCmd.CommandText
```

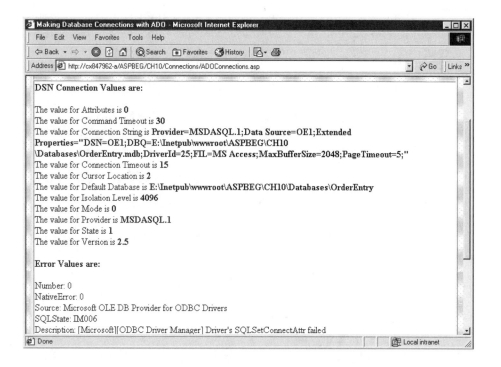

Figure 10-7 The Connection and Error properties displayed

Notice you must set the CommandText property to the name of the table you want to open (or the SQL statement, and so forth) to produce the read-only Recordset that is the default. You can use the CommandType property to set the type of command you are using. This is a good idea when you know the type, because it reduces calls to the provider to determine the CommandType value before completing execution. Insert a line of code like the following (for retrieving a table as a Recordset) after the line setting the CommandText argument:

```
MyCmd.CommandType = adCommandTable
```

Another way to set the arguments for the Command object is simply to put them right in the line of the Execute method, in which the first space represents the RecordsAffected argument, the second space represents the Parameters argument, and the third space represents the Options argument. Your code may look something like the following:

```
Set myCmd = Server.CreateObject("ADODB.Command")
myCmd.CommandText = "Products"
Set myRs = myCmd.Execute(, , adCmdTable)
```

Although Module 11 covers recordsets in greater detail, some discussion about creating recordsets is necessary here because some of the arguments you can use with the Command object directly affect the functionality you get when your recordset is retrieved. The next two sections discuss cursors and locking, and how to use the Command object to set them for a given recordset.

Recordset Cursors

If you open an Access table with records in it, you see a pointer showing which record you are currently on, similar to what is displayed in the following illustration. This pointer defines the current record, and is handled by what is known as a cursor. The purpose of the *cursor* is to manage navigation through a table via the pointer. A cursor is also essential for navigating through a recordset. Without the cursor, you could neither tell what record you are working with nor get to other records.

Cursor Types

When you retrieve a recordset, several types of cursors can be used with it. You must specify the type of cursor you want to use with the recordset or the recordset will be assigned the default cursor. The cursor types are

- **Forward Only**   This is the default cursor type, which enables you only to move forward through the recordset. The ADO Constant for this cursor type is "adOpenForwardOnly."

- **Static**   This cursor type enables movement forward and backward through the recordset, but it does not reflect any changes made by other users. The ADO Constant for this cursor type is "adOpenStatic."

- **Dynamic**   This cursor type enables movement in both directions and reflects changes made by other users. The ADO Constant for this cursor type is "adOpenDynamic."

- **Keyset**   This cursor type enables movement in both directions and reflects changes made by other users, except added records are not visible and deleted records remain in the set. The ADO Constant for this cursor type is "adOpenKeyset."

Coding the Cursor Type   To set the cursor type of a recordset when using a Command object, you need to use the Open method for the recordset. There are several arguments for the Open method of the Recordset object, including the Source (myCmd in the following example) and the Cursor Type (adOpenDynamic in the following example). The code for setting the cursor type could be something similar to this:

```
myRs.Open = myCmd, , adOpenDynamic
```

10

Recordset Locking

Like any data being used by more than one person at a time, some mechanism must exist to prevent records from being overwritten by someone else at the same time. ADO has several constants available that enable the developer to specify a lock type when retrieving a recordset. The lock types you can choose from are

- **Read Only**   This lock type enables you to read records, but not to change them. It is the default type and places the lightest load on the server because no special processing is required. The ADO Constant for this lock type is "adLockReadOnly."

- **Pessimistic**   This lock type locks the record you are changing as soon as you begin to edit it. This is best to ensure data integrity because no other users can work with that record once you start to change it, but this restriction also makes less records available to other users during that time. The ADO Constant for this is "adLockPessimistic."

- **Optimistic**   This lock type doesn't lock the record until the change is committed. Other users can still see the record and make changes to it until it is committed. The ADO Constant for this lock type is "adLockOptimistic."

- **Batch Optimistic**   This lock type enables you to change more than one record in a batch. Lock types are only locked when they are committed.

Coding the Lock Type   To set the lock type of a recordset when using the Command object, the Open method for the recordset is used again. Using the previous example from the Cursor Type section, the code for setting the cursor type could be something similar to

```
myRs.Open = myCmd, , adOpenDynamic, adLockOptimistic
```

1-Minute Drill

● **What default cursor type do you get when you connect to a database?**

● **What cursor type is the most flexible?**

Stored Procedures

As discussed earlier, stored procedures are quite useful for performing interactions with your databases because they are compiled and run from within the database, and they are almost always much faster. In this section, a few stored procedures are built, first ordinary queries, and then using the capability to pass parameters back and forth.

Stored Procedures with Microsoft Access

You can create a stored procedure in Access by building a query that performs an action, such as updating records. Go into the Queries section, click the New button, and go into Design View. In the following illustration, you can see the results of a SELECT query created with the fields of the Products table from the example database named OrderEntry.mdb. Several products are entered—Golf Bags, Golf Clubs, and so forth—as well as prices for each product.

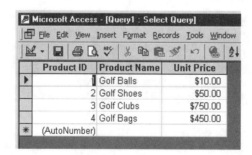

10

● **A Forward-Only cursor**
● **The Dynamic cursor**

To change the query to an UPDATE query, choose Query | Update Query from the menu, and then enter an update value in the Update To: row of the query grid. As you can see in Figure 10-8, the Unit Price times 1.1 is entered. This increases prices by 10 percent.

If you run the query, Access asks if you want to complete the update. If you click OK, the update takes effect. To change the query back to a SELECT query, choose Query | Select Query from the menu and run it again. You see the results shown in the following illustration.

After you look at the updated prices, change this query back to an UPDATE query (the update information should still be in place), name it UpdateProducts, and save it. Now you have a stored procedure you can run from your scripts. The code to call this procedure from your scripts can be something like the following:

```
Set myComm = Server.CreateObject("ADODB.Command")
myComm.ActiveConnection = "OE1"
myComm.CommandText = "UpdateProducts"
myComm.CommandType = adCmdStoredProc
myComm.Execute , , adExecuteNoRecords
Set myComm = Nothing
```

The "OE1" DSN is still being used to create the active connection, but now the command text and command type are being set before executing the command. Also, notice the option "adExecuteNoRecords" is set. This makes the command return no recordset, a good idea considering you don't want records returned, just updated. If you don't set

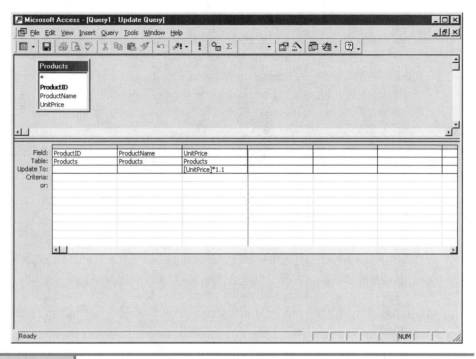

Figure 10-8 The UPDATE query value

this, ADO goes through the process of creating and returning an empty Recordset, useless processing that slows down things.

Stored Procedures with Parameters

By using the capability of Access or other DBMSs to accept and return parameters with their stored procedures, you can dramatically increase the usefulness of stored procedures running from your scripts.

The first step in using parameters with a stored procedure in Access is to build the parameter into the UPDATE query you've already built. To do this, open the query in Design View in Access, and then choose View | SQL View from the menu. Change the SQL code, so it begins with the line "Parameters [UpdatePercentage] Real;". This establishes a parameter named "UpdatePercentage" is to be passed to the query from the script and the data type is "Real" (data types are discussed more in a moment).

Change the SET statement so it reads "SET Products.UnitPrice = [UnitPrice]*[UpdatePercentage];. This inserts the parameter you pass into the query when it runs. Your SQL code should look like that in the following illlustration. Notice Access has replaced the data type "Real" with "IEEESingle" in the SQL code.

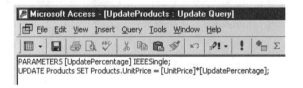

You can find more information about how to create parameter queries in the Help feature in Microsoft Access 2000. A list of acceptable data types is there, as well as some coding examples to assist you in building parameter queries. For your convenience, these are also listed in the table in the next section.

Microsoft Jet SQL Data Types

Thirteen data types are used with the Microsoft Jet database engine, some of which have valid synonyms. Table 10-1 lists them.

Data Type	Size	Description
BINARY	1 byte per character	Any type of binary data.
BIT	1 byte	Yes and No (logical) values.
TINYINT	1 byte	An integer between 0 and 255.
MONEY	8 bytes	A scaled integer between −922,337,203,685,477.5808 and 922,337,203,685,477.5807.
DATETIME	8 bytes	A date/time value between the years 100 and 9,999.

Table 10-1 Data Types for Parameters in Access

Data Type	Size	Description
UNIQUEIDENTIFIER	128 bits	A unique identification number.
REAL	4 bytes	A single-precision floating-point value from −3.402823E38 to −1.401298E-45 for negative values, 1.401298E-45 to 3.402823E38 for positive values, and 0.
FLOAT	8 bytes	A double-precision floating-point value from −1.79769313486232E308 to −4.94065645841247E-324 for negative values, 4.94065645841247E-324 to 1.79769313486232E308 for positive values, and 0.
SMALLINT	2 bytes	A short integer from −32,768 to 32,767.
INTEGER	4 bytes	A long integer from −2,147,483,648 to 2,147,483,647.
DECIMAL	17 bytes	An exact numeric data type. Both precision (1–28) and scale (0—defined precision) can be defined. The default precision and scale are 18 and 0.
TEXT	2 bytes per character	Zero to a maximum of 2.14 gigabytes.
IMAGE	As required	Zero to a maximum of 2.14 gigabytes.
CHARACTER	2 bytes per character	Zero to 255 characters.

Table 10-1 Data Types for Parameters in Access *(continued)*

The Parameters Collection

10

The *Parameters collection* is a collection of the Command object and contains a Parameter object whenever you use the Append method to add one to the collection (one for each parameter you want to pass to the stored procedure). To create Parameter objects, you need to give them a name; a data type; a direction; and, perhaps, a size and a value. While you can create the parameters and their values directly in your scripting code, usually you leave off the value and allow the user to pass the value in by a variable from a form.

Creating Parameter Objects

You can use code like the following to create Parameter objects:

```
Set myParam = myComm.CreateParameter("UpdatePercentage", adSingle,
adParamInput)
myComm.Parameters.Append myParam
```

Make up a variable name, such as myParam, and use the Set command to set it equal to the contents of a CreateParameter method. Inside the CreateParameter method, the first thing you find is the name of the Parameter you're creating.

---Hint---

You can use whatever name you like for the Parameter object, but remembering what you're working with is easier if you use the same name as the parameter you created inside the stored procedure in Access.

The next thing you find is the ADO Constant for the data type. Look in the DataTypeEnum section of your adovbs.inc file to find the allowable data types. In this case, use the Single data type because you want to specify the percentage by which to increase prices of the products.

The last attribute set in the CreateParameter method is the type of Parameter it is, namely, an Input parameter. Parameters can be

- **adParamInput**   They pass values to the stored procedure.

- **adParamOutput**   They accept values being passed from the stored procedure.

- **adParamInputOutput**   They can do either of the previous.

- **adParamReturnValue**   They hold the return status of the stored procedure.

You could also set the size of the parameter, but you needn't do this because the size is fixed by the data type Single at 4. If you were using a text data type, you might want to set the size. And you could set the value but, because you're going to retrieve the value from the user, no need exists to do that either.

Ask the Expert

Question: Stored procedures seem to be the way to go. Instead of writing all my code in ASP to get processing done, I can simply call a query I've made in the database and run that. Besides running faster, what other advantages are there?

Answer: When a database runs a query, it relies on an execution plan to perform the query. *Execution plans* are required because there are often many ways to get the query action accomplished, and some are more efficient than others. The DBMS has a query optimization mechanism in it, and this mechanism attempts to apply the most efficient execution plan to any given query. It then compiles the execution plan ahead of time.

Another advantage is that your SQL code is kept inside the database and may, therefore, be more secure, and certainly keeps your ASP code easier to maintain. If you've ever used a long set of SQL statements to process a query from ASP, you know what I mean.

project10-2.zip

Project 10-2: Using the Command Object

Now that you've worked with the Command object a bit, let's put together a combination form and ASP script to enable running commands with stored procedures and parameters. The format to use is similar to the one used for the Connection object, but some of the coding is specific to the Command object.

Step-by-Step

First, build the form. Next, add the code to run stored procedures, and then run stored procedures with parameters. Use the existing OrderEntry database and the UpdateProducts query you created.

Commands and Stored Procedures

1. The first step in this project is to use the QBE interface to build a query, if you haven't done so already. Make the query described earlier in the section "Stored Procedures," and name it "UpdateProducts."

10

2. Next, make a second query named "UpdateProducts2" and change the SQL code as described in the Parameters section.

3. Next, copy the ADOConnections.asp file to a new file named ADOCommands.asp, and change the code as listed in the following:

```
<%
Option Explicit
Dim btnClicked
Dim myComm
Dim collitem
Dim vParameter
Dim myParam
%>
<!-- #include file="adovbs.inc" -->
<%
%>
<html><head><title>Running Commands against a Database with ADO</title>
<meta http-equiv="Content-Type" content="text/html; charset=iso-8859-1">
</head>
<body bgcolor="#77FF77">
<H2><font size="6">Running ADO Commands</font></H2>
<TABLE border=1>
<TR><TD>
      <H3>Connection Variables and Errors</H3>
      </TD></TR><TR><TD bgcolor="white">
<%
btnClicked = Request.Form("btnval")
Select Case btnClicked
      Case "Update"
            Set myComm = Server.CreateObject("ADODB.Command")
            myComm.ActiveConnection = "OE1"
            myComm.CommandText = "UpdateProducts"
            myComm.CommandType = adCmdStoredProc
            myComm.Execute , , adExecuteNoRecords
            Set myComm = Nothing
      Case "Parameter"
            vParameter = Request.Form("Parameter")
            Set myComm = Server.CreateObject("ADODB.Command")
            myComm.ActiveConnection = "OE1"
            myComm.CommandText = "UpdateProducts2"
            myComm.CommandType = adCmdStoredProc
            Set myParam = myComm.CreateParameter("UpdatePercentage",
adSingle, adParamInput)
            myComm.Parameters.Append myParam
            myComm.Parameters("UpdatePercentage") = vParameter
            myComm.Execute , , adExecuteNoRecords
            Set myComm = Nothing
      End Select
%>
</TD></TR></TABLE>
<P>
<TABLE border=1 width="50%">
  <TR>
    <TD bgcolor="#00CC99" COLSPAN=3>
      <H3><font size="6">Values</font></H3>
```

Set and Append the Parameter.

```
    </TD>
  </TR>
<TR>
    <TD colspan="3">
      <form method=POST action="ADOCommands.asp">
        <table width="50%" border="1">
          <tr>
            <td><b>Update Prices by Ten Percent</b>
              <input type="submit" name="btnval" value="Update">
            </td>
          </tr>
        </table>
      </form>
    </TD>
  </TR>
  <TR>
    <TD colspan="3">
      <form method=POST action="ADOCommands.asp">
        <table width="50%" border="1">
          <tr>
            <td><b>Enter your Parameter for the Price Update</b>
              <input type="submit" name="btnval" value="Parameter">
            </td>
          </tr>
          <tr>
            <td> <b>Price Update Percentage: </b>
              <input type="text" name="Parameter" size="20">
            </td>
          </tr>
        </table>
      </form>
    </TD>
  </TR>
</TABLE>
</BODY></HTML>
```

10

☑ *Mastery Check*

1. What can you do to optimize your database interactions?

A. Limit user searches.

B. Compact your database every time it is accessed.

C. Close connections, use stored procedures, and use only required data.

D. None of the above.

☑ Mastery Check

2. What is the SQL command for specifying a parameter in Access?

    A. PARAMETERS "parametername" data type

    B. INSERT PARAMETER

    C. CREATE VARIABLE

    D. None of the above

3. What does the Direction attribute mean for Parameter objects?

    A. Whether the numeric value is positive or negative

    B. Whether the returned sort order is ascending or descending

    C. Whether data is going to or coming from the stored procedure

    D. None of the above

4. What lock type is the default?

    A. Lock All

    B. Optimistic

    C. Read–Only

    D. Batch Optimistic

Module 11

The ADO Recordset-Related Objects

The Goals of This Module

- Retrieve records with the Recordset object
- Learn about the Record object
- Learn about the Stream object
- Work with the Fields collection
- Navigate records in a recordset
- Learn how to create Bookmarks
- Filter records in a Recordset
- Modify records in a Recordset

Pulling sets of records from a table using the Recordset object and a little SQL is easy. Just think of Recordsets as tables in a kind of spreadsheet view. You can navigate through them; edit; update; add new ones, and delete them; and even filter, sort, and sum them, with the tools available to the Recordset object. And, in ADO 2.5, a few new objects exist: the Record object and the Stream object. These objects provide a great deal of additional functionality, which you learn about in this module.

The Recordset Object

If you've ever built a spreadsheet, you are intimately familiar with the columns and rows format for data. In fact, before computers came along. accountants were busy adding up columns of figures and working out by hand various results based on columns and rows. It's not surprising that a computerized method for doing the same thing was developed long ago. The Recordset object is just another iteration in a long line of information-processing formats people seem to work with easily. Each column represents a field, and each row contains values related to a single instance of the entity type being tracked in the record. The fields in a Recordset are represented by the Fields collection. You can work with the values in a field in a particular record with the following syntax:

```
vMyVariable = MyRecordset.Fields("fieldname")
```

So, to recap, you use the Connection and/or Command objects to make the connection to a data source and, perhaps, set some parameters for retrieving the records with a particular cursor type. You use SQL statements or even calls to entire tables to specify the records retrieved (or commands to run against those data sources when no Recordset is retrieved). Once you create a Recordset, you use the Recordset object and its methods to manipulate the records for your own purposes.

Recordset Methods and Properties

Like other objects encountered, the Recordset object supports a variety of methods and properties. The Recordset methods give you many of the same capabilities you have when a database table is open in front of you, such as enabling you to move around the records, add, edit, and delete them, and so on. Once you get used to these methods, working with records in Recordsets becomes second nature.

Recordset Methods

Here are the supported methods:

- **Open**   This method opens a Recordset and has optional arguments that can set the cursor type, and so forth.

- **Close**   This method closes a Recordset.

- **AddNew**   This method enables you to place a new record in a Recordset and specify the values to be entered in each field.

- **Move**   This method moves the cursor forward or backward a specified number of records through the Recordset.

- **MoveFirst**   This method moves the cursor to the first record in a Recordset.

- **MoveLast**   This method moves the cursor to the last record in a Recordset.

- **MoveNext**   This method moves the cursor to the next record in a Recordset.

- **MovePrevious**   This method moves the cursor to the previous record in a Recordset.

- **Delete**   This method deletes the specified record from the Recordset.

- **Update**   This method saves changes you've made to the current record in a Recordset.

- **UpdateBatch**   This method updates the records affected (specified by an ADO constant for current, filtered, or all records) for changes you've made to these records.

- **NextRecordset**   This method returns the next Recordset when you've placed commands returning more than one Recordset in your command or stored procedure.

11

● **Requery** This method updates the data into your Recordset, based on reexecuting the original query statement.

● **Resync** This method refreshes the data in the Recordset object from the underlying database.

● **Clone** This method creates a duplicate of the current Recordset object.

● **GetRows** This method puts records from a Recordset into an array.

● **Supports** This method returns a value indicating what functions the data provider supports.

● **CancelUpdate** This method cancels changes you've made to records, as long as you use it before the final Update method call.

● **CancelBatch** This method cancels batch updates to records in a Recordset.

Recordset Properties

The properties available with a Recordset tell you quite a bit about where you are in a Recordset, the size and composition of the Recordset, and such things as the source and status of a Recordset. Here are the supported properties:

● **BOF** This property indicates the record pointer for the cursor is located at the beginning of the Recordset, actually before the first record.

● **EOF** This property indicates the record pointer for the cursor is located at the end of the Recordset, after the last record.

● **RecordCount** This property indicates the number of records in the current Recordset.

● **MaxRecords** This property is used to set the number of records to return with a Recordset.

● **PageSize** This property sets or returns the number of records that make up a page of records for the current Recordset.

● **PageCount**   This property indicates the number of pages of records in the current Recordset, based on the PageSize setting.

● **Bookmark**   This property returns or sets a bookmark, which uniquely identifies a specific record in the current Recordset.

● **AbsolutePosition**   This property specifies the ordinal or numeric position of a record within the current Recordset or returns an ADO constant indicating the position is unknown, BOF, or EOF.

● **AbsolutePage**   This property specifies the page for the current record.

● **ActiveConnection**   This property indicates the Connection object to which the Recordset belongs.

● **CacheSize**   This property indicates the number of records in the Recordset that are cached locally in memory.

● **CursorType**   This property tells you what kind of cursor the Recordset has.

● **EditMode**   This property indicates the editing status of the current record, and can be none, in-progress, or AddNew.

● **Filter**   This property enables you to filter records based on criteria, changing the viewable contents of the current Recordset.

● **LockType**   This property reflects the lock type in force when the Recordset was retrieved.

● **MarshallOptions**   This property is only available for client-side Recordsets and is used to optimize performance when sending records back to the server.

● **Source**   This property indicates the source of the records in the Recordset.

● **State**   This property indicates whether the Recordset is open or closed.

● **Status**   This property indicates the status of the current record regarding batch update operations.

11

1-Minute Drill

- **What method of the Recordset object tells you the functions the data provider provides?**

- **If the Recordset BOF property is True, what does this mean?**

Recordset Navigation and Manipulation Operations

In this section, Recordset object methods and properties are used to maneuver around a Recordset and to make some updates and changes. Being familiar with the various connection and command parameters affecting the kind of Recordsets retrieved is important because some of the Recordset methods and properties may be unavailable, unless they're supported by the provider and specified in the commands used.

Creating and Using Recordsets

To start manipulating records programmatically with Recordsets, you need to make a connection, run some commands, and retrieve some records. The first thing to do is to make sure you have plenty of records to play with in the example database. Open the example database you've been using and enter some records for products, customers, employees, and orders. You can use the files provided on the Web site, rather than entering your own data, if you'd like your operations to match what's in the book exactly.

Next, let's write some code that makes the connection and returns a Recordset that can be worked with, meaning a dynamic cursor type. Try this on your server:

```
Set myConn = Server.CreateObject("ADODB.Connection")
myConn.Open "OE1"                                      Creates a
Set myRs = Server.CreateObject("ADODB.Recordset")      Connection.
With myRs
        .Source = "Products"          Builds a Dynamic
        .ActiveConnection = myConn    recordset from the
        .CursorType = adOpenDynamic   Products table.
        .LockType = adLockOptimistic
        .Open
End With
```

- **The Supports method**
- **You have reached a record position before the first record.**

As you can see from the code, the Connection object was used to open a connection via our "OE1" DSN. Then you use the Recordset object and the With command to set the Source, ActiveConnection, CursorType, and LockType for the Recordset.

If you want to view the properties of the Recordset, you can use code like the following:

```
Response.Write "The AbsolutePage Property of the Recordset is <B>"
& myRs.AbsolutePage & "</B><BR>"
```

Navigating Through the Recordset   To navigate the open Recordset, the first thing you want to do is check to see whether any records were returned. Following this check, you can use the Move methods of the Recordset to navigate around. Use code like this to get started:

```
If myRs.EOF Then
                Response.Write "There are no records in this table"
        Else
                myRs.MoveFirst
                Response.Write "The Product Name is " &
myRs.Fields("ProductName") & " and the Unit Price is " &
myRs.Fields("UnitPrice")
                End If
```

The code to go to the next, previous, and last records is essentially the same, substituting in the MoveNext, MovePrevious, and MoveLast methods for the MoveFirst method. Because you might end up outside the Recordset at BOF or EOF, use some additional code (after the rst.MovePrevious, for instance) for the next and previous records that checks for this condition, such as

```
If myRs.BOF OR myRs.EOF Then
                    Response.Write "You are not on a record"
            Else
                    Response.Write "The Product Name is " &
myRs.Fields("ProductName") & " and the Unit Price is " &
myRs.Fields("UnitPrice")
                    End If
```

To move to a specific record in the Recordset, use code like this:

```
MyRs.Move vMoveNumber
```

In this case, vMoveNumber is a number contained in a variable representing the record number to which to move. If you like, you can collect this number from the user via an HTML form. This can become the basis for a system enabling the user to navigate records in a Recordset.

1-Minute Drill

- **What common programming structure checks whether any records have been retrieved?**

- **What common programming structure enables you to travel through records one at a time until you've traversed the entire Recordset?**

Editing Records in a Recordset   Now that you can move through the records and, perhaps, find a specific record, being able to change the contents of a record would be nice. To make this possible, you need to display the contents of the record in such a way that changes are possible. An easy way to do this is to make the field values show up inside HTML form elements. The user can then make changes to the form elements, and the changed values can be used to update the record they came from. It's as simple as the following code:

```
%>
            <Form Method=Post Action="ADORecordsets.asp">
<Table><TR><TD><B>Product ID</B></TD><TD><B>Product Name</B></TD><TD><B>Unit
Price</B></TD><TD><B>Delete?</B></TD></TR>
<%
            Do While not myRs.EOF
            %>
            <TR><TD><INPUT TYPE="text" name="ProductID<%
Response.Write myRs.Fields("ProductID") %>" value="<% Response.Write
myRs.Fields("ProductID") %>"></TD>
<TD><INPUT TYPE="text" name="ProductName<% Response.Write
myRs.Fields("ProductID") %>" value ="<% Response.Write
myRs.Fields("ProductName") %>"></TD>
<TD><INPUT TYPE="text" name="UnitPrice<% Response.Write
myRs.Fields("ProductID") %>" value = "<% Response.Write
myRs.Fields("UnitPrice") %>"></B></TD>
<TD><INPUT TYPE="checkbox" name="chkbx<% Response.Write
myRs.Fields("ProductID") %>"></TD></TR>
```

Starts the form and begins a table showing column headers.

This block (and the Do While loop) return each row with ProductID attached to indicate the record they came from. And don't forget the MoveNext command before the Loop.

- You can use the If recordset.EOF Then structure to check for no records returned.
- You can use the Do While Not recordset.EOF structure to visit all the records.

```
         <%
      myRs.MoveNext
      Loop
      %>
         <TR><TD COLSPAN=3><INPUT TYPE="submit" name="btnval"
value="Change Records"><INPUT TYPE="submit" name="btnval" value="Delete
Records"></TD></TR></Form></Table>
         <%
```

> **This just ends the table and creates the submission buttons.**

Ask the Expert

Question: Recordsets seem to be pretty powerful objects. What are the primary limitations, and how can I cope with them?

Answer: Like most data structures related to a database, Recordsets are just a snapshot of data and must be locked appropriately to update the values your users change accurately. If you are running a multiuser environment, you have the same types of concurrency problems you would with an ordinary application. Fortunately, you can use a variety of lock types, and the Requery method can update the contents of the Recordset as often as necessary.

Question: How do I know what methods a given provider supports? I know the Supports method is available, but examining all the available properties every time I want to connect to a data source seems like a lot of work. Is there some easy way around this?

Answer: Chances are, you'll be using a data provider whose properties are familiar to you, so you'll know what functions the provider supports without having to check every time you connect. If you're connecting to multiple unfamiliar data sources, you can program a tool that immediately checks all functions supported as soon as a connection is made. The programming logic would be a bit complex—similar to using the browser capabilities component to check the functions the user's platform supports—but it's worth it as you attempt to provide your users with the functionality they need to work with your application.

11

project11-1.zip

Project 11-1: Building a Data Management Page

One of the things you run into often is the need for a data management page. Users want you to make their data and records available for additions, updates, deletions, and so forth. You can use the functions coded for the Recordset object to do just that, in a fairly straightforward way.

Supported Features

For Access databases, the provider does not support bookmarks. In the code in this project, you can see the Bookmark property statement is commented out, because bookmarks are not supported. You can determine what the data provider supports using the Supports method. For example, you can code a conditional statement, such as the following, to determine whether a particular data provider supports bookmarks:

```
If myRs.Supports(adBookmark) Then
    Response.Write "The bookmark is " & myRs.Bookmark
End If
```

Step-by-Step

Let's build a single page that enables the user to reveal all the properties of a connection, navigate the records, and make changes to them as desired. We use the typical Select Case structure to capture which button they pressed, combined with an HTML form to let the user give input to the processing. Figure 11-1 shows how the Web page looks before activating any of the Recordset functions.

1. Set up the variables and include the adovbs.inc file, like so:

```
<%
Option Explicit
Dim btnClicked
Dim myConn
Dim myRs
Dim collitem
Dim vParameter
Dim myParam
Dim vMoveNumber
Dim vProductName
Dim vProductNamen
Dim vUnitPricen
```

```
Dim vUnitPrice
Dim intI
Dim vRecordToDelete
%>
<!-- #include file="adovbs.inc" -->
<%
```

2. Lay out the HTML for the top of the resulting page, as follows:

```
%>
<html><head><title>Working with ADO Recordsets</title>
<meta http-equiv="Content-Type" content="text/html;
charset=iso-8859-1">
</head>
<body bgcolor="#77FF77">
<H2><font size="6">Working with ADO Recordsets</font></H2>
<TABLE border=1><TR><TD>
     <H3>Recordset Properties and Data</H3>
   </TD></TR><TR><TD bgcolor="white">
<%
```

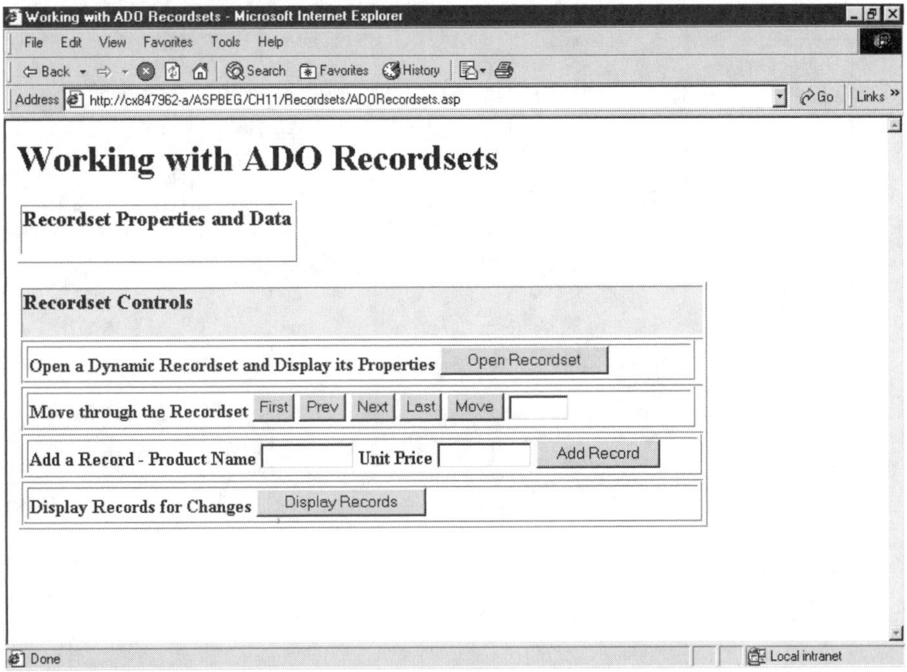

Figure 11-1 The Initial Recordset Web page

3. Set up the capture of the value of the button clicked using the name of the button (they're all named "btnval") and the variable "btnClicked", and then begin the first case for the Select Case structure. This case shows the properties available for this data provider and is shown in Figure 11-2.

```
btnClicked = Request.Form("btnval")
Select Case btnClicked
      Case "Open Recordset"
            Set myConn = Server.CreateObject("ADODB.Connection")
            myConn.Open "OE1"
            Set myRs = Server.CreateObject("ADODB.Recordset")
            With myRs
            .Source = "Products"
            .ActiveConnection = myConn
            .CursorType = adOpenDynamic
            .LockType = adLockOptimistic
            .Open
            End With
            Response.Write "The AbsolutePage Property of the Recordset is
<B>" & myRs.AbsolutePage & "</B><BR>"
            Response.Write "The AbsolutePosition Property of the Recordset
is <B>" & myRs.AbsolutePosition & "</B><BR>"
            Response.Write "The ActiveConnection Property of the Recordset
is <B>" & myRs.ActiveConnection & "</B><BR>"
            Response.Write "The BOF Property of the Recordset is <B>" &
myRs.BOF & "</B><BR>"
            'Response.Write "The Bookmark Property of the Recordset is <B>"
& myRs.Bookmark & "</B><BR>"
            Response.Write "The CacheSize Property of the Recordset is <B>"
& myRs.CacheSize & "</B><BR>"
            Response.Write "The CursorLocation Property of the Recordset is
<B>" & myRs.CursorLocation & "</B><BR>"
            Response.Write "The CursorType Property of the Recordset is <B>"
& myRs.CursorType & "</B><BR>"
            Response.Write "The EditMode Property of the Recordset is <B>" &
myRs.EditMode & "</B><BR>"
            Response.Write "The EOF Property of the Recordset is <B>" &
myRs.EOF & "</B><BR>"
            Response.Write "The Filter Property of the Recordset is <B>" &
myRs.Filter & "</B><BR>"
            Response.Write "The LockType Property of the Recordset is <B>" &
myRs.LockType & "</B><BR>"
            Response.Write "The MarshalOptions Property of the Recordset is
<B>" & myRs.MarshalOptions & "</B><BR>"
            Response.Write "The MaxRecords Property of the Recordset is <B>"
& myRs.MaxRecords & "</B><BR>"
            Response.Write "The PageCount Property of the Recordset is <B>"
```

This property was not supported, and so was commented out.

```
& myRs.PageCount & "</B><BR>"
            Response.Write "The PageSize Property of the Recordset is <B>" &
myRs.PageSize & "</B><BR>"
            Response.Write "The RecordCount Property of the Recordset is
<B>" & myRs.RecordCount & "</B><BR>"
            Response.Write "The Source Property of the Recordset is <B>" &
myRs.Source & "</B><BR>"
            Response.Write "The State Property of the Recordset is <B>" &
myRs.State & "</B><BR>"
            Response.Write "The Status Property of the Recordset is <B>" &
myRs.Status & "</B><BR>"
            Set myRs = Nothing
            Set myConn = Nothing
```

> **Notice both the Recordset and the Connection are set to Nothing.**

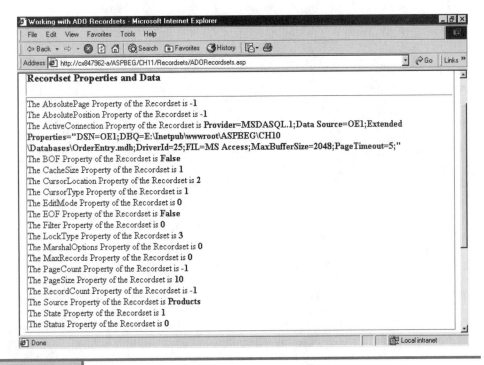

Figure 11-2   **The Properties returned for the Recordset**

11

4. The next five cases all use similar structures to navigate the
Recordset. They open the Recordset, and then use the "If myRs.EOF
Then" structure to check whether any records were actually
returned, and then call the appropriate method to move through
the Recordset. The last case (the Move method) accepts input from
the user to determine to what record to move. Figure 11–3 shows
the results returned for one of the records after navigating to it.

```
Case "First"
        Set myConn = Server.CreateObject("ADODB.Connection")
        myConn.Open "OE1"
        Set myRs = Server.CreateObject("ADODB.Recordset")
        With myRs
        .Source = "Products"
        .ActiveConnection = myConn
        .CursorType = adOpenDynamic
        .LockType = adLockOptimistic
        .Open
        End With
        If myRs.EOF Then
                Response.Write "There are no records in this table"
        Else
                myRs.MoveFirst
                Response.Write "The Product Name is " &
myRs.Fields("ProductName") & " and the Unit Price is " &
myRs.Fields("UnitPrice")
        End If
        Set myRs = Nothing
        Set myConn = Nothing
    Case "Prev"
        Set myConn = Server.CreateObject("ADODB.Connection")
        myConn.Open "OE1"
        Set myRs = Server.CreateObject("ADODB.Recordset")
        With myRs
        .Source = "Products"
        .ActiveConnection = myConn
        .CursorType = adOpenDynamic
        .LockType = adLockOptimistic
        .Open
        End With
        If myRs.EOF Then
                Response.Write "There are no records in this table"
        Else
                myRs.MovePrevious
                If myRs.BOF OR myRs.EOF Then
                        Response.Write "You are not on a record"
                Else
                        Response.Write "The Product Name is " &
myRs.Fields("ProductName") & " and the Unit Price is " &
myRs.Fields("UnitPrice")
                End If
        End If
        Set myRs = Nothing
        Set myConn = Nothing
```

```
    Case "Next"
        Set myConn = Server.CreateObject("ADODB.Connection")
        myConn.Open "OE1"
        Set myRs = Server.CreateObject("ADODB.Recordset")
        With myRs
        .Source = "Products"
        .ActiveConnection = myConn
        .CursorType = adOpenDynamic
        .LockType = adLockOptimistic
        .Open
        End With
        If myRs.EOF Then
            Response.Write "There are no records in this table"
        Else
            myRs.MoveNext
            If myRs.BOF OR myRs.EOF Then
                Response.Write "You are not on a record"
            Else
                Response.Write "The Product Name is " &
myRs.Fields("ProductName") & " and the Unit Price is " &
myRs.Fields("UnitPrice")
            End If
        End If
        Set myRs = Nothing
        Set myConn = Nothing
    Case "Last"
        Set myConn = Server.CreateObject("ADODB.Connection")
        myConn.Open "OE1"
        Set myRs = Server.CreateObject("ADODB.Recordset")
        With myRs
        .Source = "Products"
        .ActiveConnection = myConn
        .CursorType = adOpenDynamic
        .LockType = adLockOptimistic
        .Open
        End With
        If myRs.EOF Then
            Response.Write "There are no records in this table"
        Else
            myRs.MoveLast
            If myRs.BOF OR myRs.EOF Then
                Response.Write "You are not on a record"
            Else
                Response.Write "The Product Name is " &
myRs.Fields("ProductName") & " and the Unit Price is " &
myRs.Fields("UnitPrice")
            End If
        End If
        Set myRs = Nothing
        Set myConn = Nothing
    Case "Move"
        vMoveNumber = request.form("MoveNumber")
        Set myConn = Server.CreateObject("ADODB.Connection")
        myConn.Open "OE1"
        Set myRs = Server.CreateObject("ADODB.Recordset")
        With myRs
        .Source = "Products"
```

11

```
           .ActiveConnection = myConn
           .CursorType = adOpenDynamic
           .LockType = adLockOptimistic
           .Open
           End With
           If myRs.EOF Then
                 Response.Write "There are no records in this table"
           Else
                 myRs.Move vMoveNumber
                 If myRs.BOF OR myRs.EOF Then
                       Response.Write "You are not on a record"
                 Else
                       Response.Write "The Product Name is <B>" &
myRs.Fields("ProductName") & "</B> and the Unit Price is <B>" &
myRs.Fields("UnitPrice") & "</B>"
                 End If
           End If
           Set myRs = Nothing
           Set myConn = Nothing
```

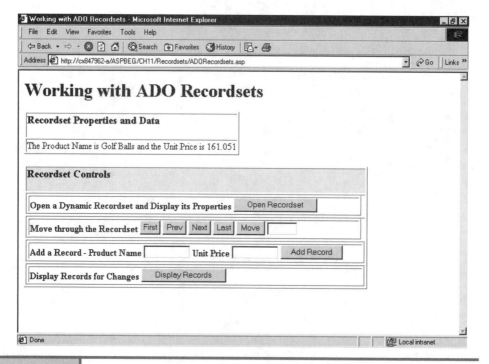

Figure 11-3 Navigating to the first record with the first button

5. The next cases enable the user to Add, Change, and Delete records. This is done using the AddNew method, the Update method, and the Delete method. Of course, you need to collect the additions, changes, and deletions from the user, so you use HTML form elements to capture this data and insert it into the appropriate places. The resulting records are displayed, as shown in Figure 11-4 after adding a record, Figure 11-5 after changing a record, and Figure 11-6 when ready to delete a record.

```
Case "Add Record"
        vProductName = request.form("ProductName")
        vUnitPrice = request.form("UnitPrice")
        Set myConn = Server.CreateObject("ADODB.Connection")
        myConn.Open "OE1"
        Set myRs = Server.CreateObject("ADODB.Recordset")
        With myRs
        .Source = "Products"
        .ActiveConnection = myConn
        .CursorType = adOpenDynamic
        .LockType = adLockOptimistic
        .Open
        End With
        With myRs
        .AddNew
                .Fields("ProductName") = vProductName
                .Fields("UnitPrice") = vUnitPrice
        .Update
        End With
        'With myRs
        '.AddNew Array("ProductName", "UnitPrice"), Array(vProductName,
vUnitPrice)
        'End With
        myRs.Requery
        Response.Write "<TABLE border=1>"
        Do While not myRs.EOF
                Response.Write "ProductID is " &
myRs.Fields("ProductID") & "</B></TD> <TR><TD> ProductName is <B>" &
myRs.Fields("ProductName") & "</B></TD>  <TD> / <B>UnitPrice is <TD> / <B>"
& myRs.Fields("UnitPrice") & "</B></TD></TR>"
                myRs.MoveNext
        Loop
        Response.Write "</table>"
        Set myRs = Nothing
        Set myConn = Nothing
    Case "Display Records"
        Set myConn = Server.CreateObject("ADODB.Connection")
        myConn.Open "OE1"
        Set myRs = Server.CreateObject("ADODB.Recordset")
        With myRs
        .Source = "Products"
        .ActiveConnection = myConn
        .CursorType = adOpenDynamic
        .LockType = adLockOptimistic
        .Open
```

11

```
                End With
                %>
                <Form Method=Post Action="ADORecordsets.asp"><Table>
                <%
                Do While not myRs.EOF
                    %>
                    <TR><TD>ProductID is <B><INPUT TYPE="text"
name="ProductID<% Response.Write myRs.Fields("ProductID") %>" value="<%
Response.Write myRs.Fields("ProductID") %>"></B></TD><TD>ProductName is <B>
<INPUT TYPE="text" name="ProductName<% Response.Write
myRs.Fields("ProductID") %>" value ="<% Response.Write
myRs.Fields("ProductName") %>"></B></TD><TD> UnitPrice is <B><INPUT
TYPE="text" name="UnitPrice<% Response.Write myRs.Fields("ProductID") %>"
value = "<% Response.Write myRs.Fields("UnitPrice") %>"></B></TD></TR>
                    <%
                myRs.MoveNext
                Loop
                %>
                <TR><TD COLSPAN=3><INPUT TYPE="submit" name="btnval"
value="Change Records"></TD></TR></Form></Table>
                <%
                Set myRs = Nothing
                Set myConn = Nothing
```

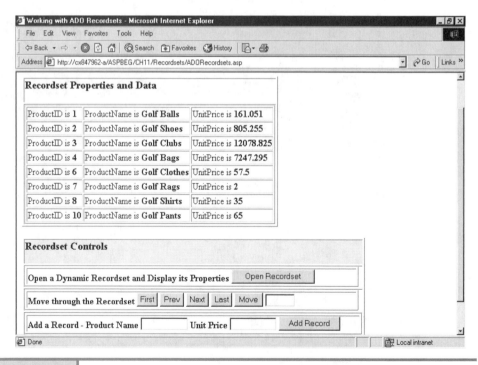

Figure 11-4   The Displayed Records after adding a record

```
Case "Change Records"
        Set myConn = Server.CreateObject("ADODB.Connection")
        myConn.Open "OE1"
        Set myRs = Server.CreateObject("ADODB.Recordset")
        With myRs
        .Source = "Products"
        .ActiveConnection = myConn
        .CursorType = adOpenDynamic
        .LockType = adLockOptimistic
        .Open
        End With
        Do While not myRs.EOF
                vProductNamen = "ProductName" & myRs.Fields("ProductID")
                vProductName = request.form(vProductNamen)
                vUnitPricen = "UnitPrice" & myRs.Fields("ProductID")
                vUnitPrice = request.form(vUnitPricen)
                With myRs
                .Fields("ProductName") = vProductName
                .Fields("UnitPrice") = vUnitPrice
                .Update
                End With
        myRs.MoveNext
        Loop
        myRs.Requery
        %>
        <Form Method=Post Action="ADORecordsets.asp">
<Table><TR><TD><B>Product ID</B></TD><TD><B>Product Name</B></TD><TD><B>Unit
Price</B></TD><TD><B>Delete?</B></TD></TR>
        <%
        Do While not myRs.EOF
                %>
                <TR><TD><INPUT TYPE="text" name="ProductID<%
Response.Write myRs.Fields("ProductID") %>" value="<% Response.Write
myRs.Fields("ProductID") %>"></TD><TD><INPUT TYPE="text" name="ProductName<%
Response.Write myRs.Fields("ProductID") %>" value ="<% Response.Write
myRs.Fields("ProductName") %>"></TD><TD><INPUT TYPE="text" name="UnitPrice<%
Response.Write myRs.Fields("ProductID") %>" value = "<% Response.Write
myRs.Fields("UnitPrice") %>"></B></TD><TD><INPUT TYPE="checkbox"
name="chkbx<% Response.Write myRs.Fields("ProductID") %>"></TD></TR>
                <%
        myRs.MoveNext
        Loop
        %>
        <TR><TD COLSPAN=3><INPUT TYPE="submit" name="btnval"
value="Change Records"><INPUT TYPE="submit" name="btnval" value="Delete
Records"></TD></TR></Form></Table>
        <%
        Set myRs = Nothing
        Set myConn = Nothing
```

11

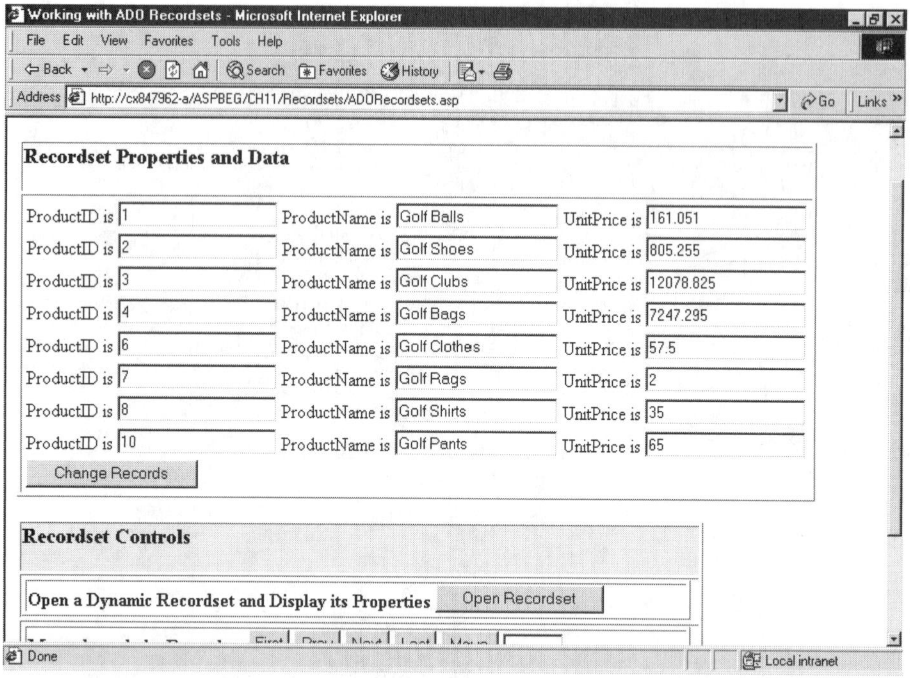

Figure 11-5 The Displayed Records ready for changes

```
Case "Delete Records"
        Set myConn = Server.CreateObject("ADODB.Connection")
        myConn.Open "OE1"
        Set myRs = Server.CreateObject("ADODB.Recordset")
        With myRs
        .Source = "Products"
        .ActiveConnection = myConn
        .CursorType = adOpenDynamic
        .LockType = adLockOptimistic
        .Open
        End With
        For Each collitem in Request.Form
            If Left(collitem, 5) = "chkbx" Then
                vRecordToDelete = Mid(collitem, 6, 10)
                myRs.Find "ProductID = " & vRecordToDelete & ""
```

```
                        If myRs.BOF Then
                                Response.Write "Record " & vRecordToDelete & "
was not found.<BR>"
                        Else
                            If myRs.EOF Then
                                    Response.Write "Record " &
vRecordToDelete & " was not found.<BR>"
                                Else
                                myRs.Delete
                                Response.Write "Record " & vRecordToDelete & "
was deleted.<BR>"
                                End If
                        End If
                    End If
            Next
            myRs.Requery
            %>
            <Form Method=Post Action="ADORecordsets.asp">
<Table><TR><TD><B>Product ID</B></TD><TD><B>Product Name</B></TD><TD><B>Unit
Price</B></TD><TD><B>Delete?</B></TD></TR>
            <%
            Do While not myRs.EOF
                %>
                <TR><TD><INPUT TYPE="text" name="ProductID<%
Response.Write myRs.Fields("ProductID") %>" value="<% Response.Write
myRs.Fields("ProductID") %>"></TD><TD><INPUT TYPE="text" name="ProductName<%
Response.Write myRs.Fields("ProductID") %>" value ="<% Response.Write
myRs.Fields("ProductName") %>"></TD><TD><INPUT TYPE="text" name="UnitPrice<%
Response.Write myRs.Fields("ProductID") %>" value = "<% Response.Write
myRs.Fields("UnitPrice") %>"></B></TD><TD><INPUT TYPE="checkbox"
name="chkbx<% Response.Write myRs.Fields("ProductID") %>"></TD></TR>
                <%
            myRs.MoveNext
            Loop
            %>
            <TR><TD COLSPAN=3><INPUT TYPE="submit" name="btnval"
value="Change Records"><INPUT TYPE="submit" name="btnval" value="Delete
Records"></TD></TR></Form></Table>
            <%
            Set myRs = Nothing
            Set myConn = Nothing
End Select
```

11

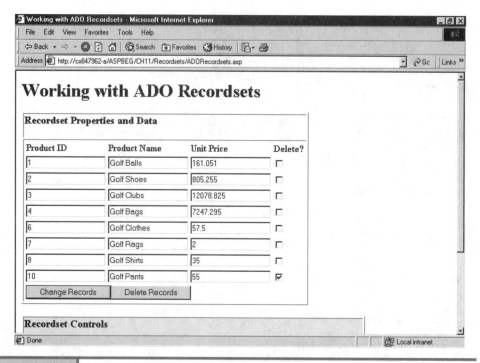

The Displayed records ready to be deleted

6. The last job with this management page is to set up the rest of the part the user sees, essentially a series of tables and form elements—mainly buttons—for controlling the page.

```
%>
</TD></TR></TABLE>
<P>
<TABLE border=1 width="80%"><TR>
    <TD bgcolor="#00CC99" COLSPAN=3>
      <H3>Recordset Controls</H3>
    </TD></TR><TR>
    <TD colspan="3">
      <form method=POST action="ADORecordsets.asp">
        <table width="99%" border="1">
          <tr>
            <td><b>Open a Dynamic Recordset and Display its Properties</b>
              <input type="submit" name="btnval" value="Open Recordset">
            </td></tr></table>
    </TD></TR><TR>
    <TD colspan="3">
```

```
        <table width="99%" border="1"><tr>
            <td><b>Move through the Recordset</b>
              <input type="submit" name="btnval" value="First">
              <input type="submit" name="btnval" value="Prev">
              <input type="submit" name="btnval" value="Next">
              <input type="submit" name="btnval" value="Last">
              <input type="submit" name="btnval" value="Move">
              <input type="text" name="MoveNumber" size="5">
            </td></tr></table>
    </TD></TR><TR>
    <TD colspan="3">
      <table width="100%" border="1">
        <tr>
          <td><B>Add a Record - Product Name</B>
            <input type="text" name="ProductName" size="10">
            <B>Unit Price</B>
            <input type="text" name="UnitPrice" size="10">
            <input type="submit" name="btnval" value="Add Record">
          </td></tr></table>
    </TD></TR><TR>
  <TD colspan="3">
 <table width="100%" border="1">
        <tr><td><B>Display Records for Changes</B>
            <input type="submit" name="btnval" value="Display Records">
          </td></tr>
      </table></TD></TR>
</form>
  </TR></TABLE>
</BODY></HTML>
```

The Stream and Record Objects

The *Stream* and *Record* objects represent important new capabilities for
ADO. Previous versions of ADO allowed access to simple Recordset
and field data, but many data sources are not structured as database tables,
so the need for additional objects to support other data structures became
apparent. The Stream and Record objects provide this capability
(however, we don't define the workings of the Stream object within this
book, as its use is limited at present).

The Record object can be used to work with folders and files in a file
system, e-mail and folders in an e-mail system, and rows in a Recordset.
It has somewhat different methods and properties than a Recordset object
because the Record object has unique properties dependent on the data
source being represented.

11

Record Object Properties and Methods

The Record object, like the Recordset object, enables you to work with fields via the Fields collection and, if a Record object happens to represent a row in a Recordset, you can get back to the Recordset from the Record. In addition, the Record object can also represent hierarchical data structures such as file systems and allows another method for manipulating and navigating around these data structures.

When you open a Record object, a connection is created implicitly and, if you choose, you can also set the connection explicitly. Like other ADO objects, Records have their own methods and properties.

Record Object Methods

The Record object has the following methods:

- **Open and Close**   These methods open or close the Record object.

- **CopyRecord, MoveRecord, and DeleteRecord**   These methods can copy, move, or delete files, folders, and subfolders represented by a Record object.

- **GetChildren**   This method opens a Recordset with rows representing each subfolder or file of the current Record object.

- **Cancel**   This method cancels an asynchronous operation of the Record object.

Record Object Properties

The Record object has the following properties:

- **ActiveConnection**   This property sets or retrieves the connection for the Record object.

- **Mode**   This property tells what permissions are available for the Record object.

- **ParentURL**   This property tells the name of the folder that contains the file or folder represented by the Record object.

- **Source**   This property tells the absolute URL, relative URL, or Recordset associated with the Record object.

- **RecordType**   This property tells whether the Record type is "simple," "collection," or "structured document."

- **State**   This property tells whether the Record object is open or closed.

Stream Object Properties and Methods

The Stream object can be used with the Recordset and Record objects to provide access to the actual contents of files, including binary data. It's useful for working not only with typical text files, but also all kinds of other file types, including images. The Stream object, like other ADO objects, has properties and methods associated with it.

In a hierarchical data structure such as a file system or an e-mail system, the Record object can also deliver a stream of bits representing the file or resource. This stream consists of the contents of the file or resource, and is a Stream object. The Stream object can be used to manipulate fields or records containing binary data. A Stream object can be generated using a variety of methods. For example, you could retrieve a Stream object from a URL, you could open the default Stream object of a Record object, or you could actually instantiate a Stream object using the OBJECT tag.

Stream Object Methods

The Stream object has the following methods:

- **Open**   This method opens a stream from a Record object or a particular URL.

- **Close**   This method closes an open Stream object.

- **Write and WriteText**   These methods write bytes or plain text to a stream, effectively inserting them into the stream.

- **Read and ReadText**   These methods read bytes or text from a stream.

11

- **Flush**   This method sends any data remaining in the buffer to the underlying object associated with the stream.

- **CopyTo**   This method enables you to specify a certain number of characters from one open stream to another stream.

- **SetEOS**   This method sets the position considered as the end of a stream.

- **SkipLine**   This method skips an entire line when reading text from a stream.

- **SaveToFile**   This method saves the contents of a stream to a file, the name of which you can specify.

- **LoadFromFile**   This method loads the contents of a file you can specify into a stream.

- **Cancel**   This method terminates an asynchronous call to the Open method.

Stream Object Properties

The Stream object also has the following properties:

- **LineSeparator**   This property sets or retrieves the character to be used as a line separator in a stream.

- **EOS**   This property tells whether the current position is at the end of the stream.

- **Charset**   This property tells into what character set the stream should be translated.

- **Size**   This property tells the size of the stream in bytes.

- **Position**   This property tells the position, as a Long value, the number of bytes from the beginning of the stream.

- **Type**   This property tells whether the type of data is text or binary.

- **State**   This property tells whether the stream is open or closed.

- **Mode**   This property tells, via an ADO constant, what permissions are available for working with the stream.

Record and Stream Object Overview

Record and Stream objects are relatively new, and not many applications can be covered for them here. However, it should be apparent from the methods and properties associated with the Record and Stream object that they will come to play an important role in your applications.

1-Minute Drill

- **How does the Record object differ primarily from the Recordset object?**
- **What special type of data does the Stream object handle?**

Ask the Expert

Question: For what kinds of applications can I use the Record and Stream objects? Why wouldn't I use the FileSystemObject object and other related objects to perform these kinds of functions?

Answer: Good question. For the time being, you'll end up using the FileSystemObject and its related objects because the Record and Stream objects aren't currently as well supported, but you'll find the Record and Stream objects are useful for XML applications. XML documents are hierarchical in nature, so the Record and Stream objects are a natural fit.

11

- **The Record object has special properties depending on the type of data source it represents.**
- **Binary data**

☑ *Mastery Check*

1. What is the difference between the Requery and Resync methods of the Recordset object?

    A. Requery and Resync both perform the same function, but Requery is faster.

    B. Requery reperforms the original query, while Resync refreshes the existing data in the Recordset.

    C. Requery works for the Recordset object, and Resync doesn't.

    D. None of the above.

2. What property would you set to limit the number of records returned in a Recordset?

    A. PageSize

    B. PageCount

    C. MaxRecords

    D. RecordCount

    E. None of the above

3. What mechanism could you use to gather user data for record updates?

    A. Hard-coded HTML Form elements

    B. HTML Form elements named after unique records

    C. HTML Form elements with cookies attached

    D. All of the above

☑ Mastery Check

4. What property of a Stream object is similar to the Recordset's BOF and EOF properties?

A. Position

B. SetEOS

C. EOS

D. None of the above

5. What information does the State property convey, for many ADO objects?

A. What state the user is in, for tax purposes

B. What state the object is in, receiving or sending

C. Whether the object is open or closed

D. Whether the object is positive or negative

11

Part 3

Client/Server Applications

Module 12

ASP Transactions

The Goals of This Module

- Learn what transaction processing means
- Get and install SQL Server 7.0 demo
- Verify Component Services is installed
- Create a transacted ASP application
- Design a database structure for simple financial records
- Create the database tables using SQL Server
- Design an interface format using HTML
- Delete and Insert records within the transaction

To introduce you to transactions and show how they are important to ASP applications, let's create a little scenario. Suppose you have a user registration form on your Web site. While users are being registered, they can also order a copy of the weekly e-mail newsletter you publish. Your business rules state no unregistered users can receive the newsletter. On the back end, you maintain user registration data in one table, and subscriptions to the newsletter in another.

Transactions and Transaction-Based Data Processing

When users register, their personal or contact data is recorded in the users table and their subscription data is recorded in the subscriptions table. This means two records are created, one in each table. Now suppose the process you are using to create these records fails in one instance, but not in the other. You could potentially have a subscription record in the subscriptions table without an associated user record in the users table.

Now imagine the previous scenario multiplied many thousands of times, using highly complex sets of business rules. It's easy to see some mechanism must exist to ensure that whenever a set of record modifications (adds, edits, deletes, and so forth) must be completed together, they are either all completed or they all fail. And, if they fail, a means of reverting everything back to how it was before any of the modifications started must exist.

Linking separate processing steps together so they succeed or fail as a whole makes them a *transaction*. When formed into a transaction, they are no longer considered separate steps; they are now considered one atomic step, *atomic* meaning you can't break them apart into smaller pieces.

Consistency and the ACID Test

If you have done your database design properly, when you first start using it, the database is said to be in a *consistent* state, which means no exceptions exist to the business rules you have programmed in. No values are out of range, no child records exist without the appropriate parent records, and so on. Each time a modification of records occurs, the end result of the modification still leaves the database in a consistent state.

In this scenario, if the creation of a user record failed, then the creation of a subscription record wouldn't occur, thereby leaving the database still in a consistent state. Typically, in the scenario described, the database itself wouldn't let you add a record to the subscribers table without a corresponding record in the user table, because you would have set referential integrity. Many instances may occur, however, in which the database itself wouldn't automatically enforce your business rules and, in these cases, you would undoubtedly build in a means to capture the error or try the modifications again until they succeed. The point is, you may need to set up transactions for your applications explicitly; and, to make your transactions function properly, you may need to build additional support into your application to cope with potential failure points. Fortunately, there are tools you can use to make it easier to create and properly complete application transactions, and these tools are discussed in just a moment. First, let's talk about the ACID test.

ACID (Atomicity, Consistency, Isolation, and Durability)

When a system meets the ACID test, it is said to embody the ACID properties. The ACID properties are

- **Atomicity**   This property means either all changes are effected or none are. Typically, before any change is committed to permanent storage, they are all written to temporary storage of some kind, and then written as a group to permanent storage.

- **Consistency**   This property means the application remains in a consistent state after the entire set of modifications is made. The assumption here, of course, is that the system was in a consistent state before the transaction started.

- **Isolation**   This property means any data or records taking part in a transaction are isolated from all other uses or transactions, until the entire transaction is either committed or aborted. Locking the data being used by a transaction ensures that other users or transactions won't be able to view inconsistent or partially modified records.

12

- **Durability**   This property means once a transaction is committed, the changes to data are permanent and can be recovered, even if a system crash or hardware failure occurs.

The ACID properties are good guidelines for creating industrial-strength applications, but the actual implementation is somewhat more complicated because many of today's applications function in a distributed fashion. *Distributed* means many components, databases, and other players at many different locations may be involved when a transaction is performed, and all must either complete the transaction or abort the transaction as a group.

Two-Phase Commit and Microsoft-Distributed Transaction Coordinator

To enable distributed transactions to be performed correctly, a protocol called the *two-phase commit* breaks the commit process into two steps. The first step is to notify all players in the transaction to write the transaction to disk, but in a buffer, waiting for the final go-ahead. Once all players have done this and returned a signal that they are ready to commit, the second phase is to write the change to disk permanently, provided the *Distributed Transaction Coordinator (DTC)* receives no failure signals from any player. If a failure signal is received, the transaction is rolled back across all players.

ASP Transactions

Because ASP is a widely used tool for creating online applications, Microsoft has incorporated support for transactions into ASP. If you need to call several components or databases to get a particular job done in its entirety, you can do so from an ASP script. You should do two things to ensure consistent transactions, however:

- Put all your transaction-related actions on one script page. While you may have a single business process that spans several ASP files, you should break the business process into physical transactions that each fit on a single script. In ASP 3.0, the Server.Execute and Server.Transfer methods enable you to write transacted scripts that span several ASP files, but it isn't recommended.

- Manually code roll-back procedures into your scripts. You should do this because, while your script can receive notification of the success or failure of a particular transaction, the transaction coordinator cannot roll back variables and values set within the context of the script itself, such as Application and Session variables, or other nontransactional resources. Upon notification, your script must reset these values on its own.

Component Services

Component Services must be running to make use of the transaction management capabilities built into the Web server. You have probably installed it during the installation of Windows 2000, and if you open it up you will see the transaction-processing parts (as shown in Figure 12–1).

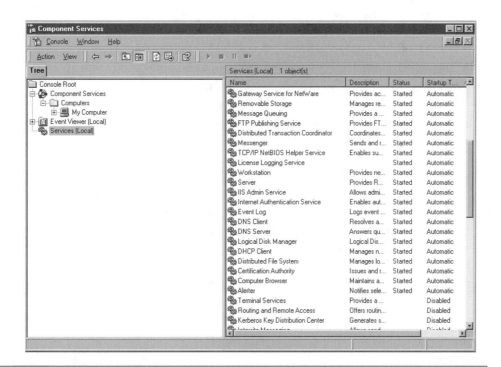

Figure 12-1 | **The Component Services Manager**

To declare your ASP script as a transaction, use the following statement as the **first** statement in the file:

```
<%@ TRANSACTION=Required %>
```

You could also include the LANGUAGE attribute in this statement, if you like. The Required value is one of several settings the TRANSACTION directive can take. These settings give you some degree of control over how your script behaves. The settings are

- **Required**   Starts a new transaction or joins one that already exists

- **Supported**   Joins a transaction that already exists, but does not start a new one

- **Not_Supported**   Neither starts nor joins a transaction

- **Requires_New**   Starts a new transaction every time

Using Components in Transacted ASP Scripts

If your transactions require the use of components, you can use the properties of the components and the ObjectContext object to perform transactions within an ASP script. The TRANSACTION directive must still be the first line of your script, and you simply create the objects in the usual way, using the Set myObj = Server.CreateObject("componentname") statement.

Your script should then evaluate whether the transaction processing for each individual component succeeded or failed and, unless all components return the appropriate value to show they succeeded, should change the ObjectContext of the objects to SetAbort, aborting or rolling back the transaction.

Transaction Events

In the example project, a SQL Server database for processing a transaction is used. SQL Server is one of a number of databases supported for transactions by Component Services. When a change is made to the database within the ASP script (started by the TRANSACTION directive), Component Services processes the transaction. Inside the ASP script, you can tell whether the transaction succeeded or aborted by listening for either of two events: OnTransactionCommit and OnTransactionAbort.

To code the workings of these two objects into your script, you use something like the following:

```
<%@ TRANSACTION=Required %>
Make a change to the database
Sub OnTransactionCommit
Do something if the transaction committed
End Sub
Sub OnTransactionAbort
Do something if the transaction aborted
End Sub
```

1-Minute Drill

● **What makes a transaction different from ordinary database updates?**

● **How can ASP scripts tell whether a change has been made?**

● A transaction usually has more than one change to make, and all changes must be complete, or none of them will be committed to permanent memory.
● The OnTransactionCommit and OnTransactionAbort events tell ASP whether a change has been made.

12

SQL Server Databases

Before you start on your project, you first need a database that supports the transaction environment. For Project 12–1, you use a SQL Server database. To start, you need to make sure SQL Server is properly installed.

Getting and Installing SQL Server 7.0

If you aren't in a position to buy SQL Server, but you know you're going to need it and you'd like to get started immediately, you can download a demo version of SQL Server 7.0 from the Microsoft Web site. The download for Windows NT is broken into 22 individual files, each about 10MB in size. You can download them and install them according to the installation instructions, and then you'll be set to go. Remember, though, the demo version doesn't specifically say it is compatible with Windows 2000 Advanced Server, so you may want to run it on a machine running Windows NT 4.0 or so.

project12-1.zip

Project 12–1: ASP Transactions on SQL Server

To build an ASP transaction, you first need a database that supports the transaction environment. For this exercise, you use a SQL Server database (named "myDATABASE") running on Windows NT 4.0, just to make sure you don't have any odd compatibility problems. Also, your system administrator has kindly configured a system DSN to your database named "myDSN", so your connection can be easily established.

The Design

The objective of Project 12–1 is to demonstrate transactions, so you need to have several things to update at once. This project allows the entry of simple financial data, such as you might keep to balance a checkbook and forecast your next month's expenses. Therefore, you have one table for the beginning checking balance and all existing deposits and withdrawals, and another table for all forecasted deposits and withdrawals. Your HTML pages and forms enable you to view the checking records and the forecasted records, and add, delete, or modify any records in either table. You can also see what the balance is at every record.

The Application's SQL Server Tables

For your application, you need the following two tables:

- **CurTransRec**   Contains all the current transaction records
- **ForTransRec**   Contains all the forecasted transaction records

    Each table requires the following fields:

- **TransactionID**   An autonumbering primary key field for tracking each individual record
- **TType**   The type of the transaction
- **TDate**   The date of the transaction
- **TAmount**   The amount of the transaction
- **AuthorizedBy**   The name of the person authorizing the transaction (and, in this case, physically making the transaction)
- **ForWhat**   A general description of the purpose of the deposit or withdrawal
- **CheckNumber**   If the transaction had a check written for it, the check number
- **MadeOutTo**   The name the check was made out to, if applicable
- **ToAccountNumber**   The account number the payment was made for, if applicable

    The current balance is calculated by the application and displayed next to each record, and the starting balance for forecasted deposits and withdrawals is always the existing balance in the CurTransRec table. At the top of each table, the beginning date, beginning balance, ending date, and ending balance are displayed; and on the last row is a space for entering new records. Each record has a Delete button so it can be deleted, but there is no capability to modify existing records after adding them (they can be deleted and reentered, if necessary).

12

Step-by-Step

Using the design just discussed, you're going to make a set of tables in your SQL Server database to support an online management system that tracks simple financial records for a small company you can call Online Systems Services. Your first step is to make a script to create the tables (although you could do this function with the visual interface SQL Server provides, better practice is to use pure SQL statements in a script). Note, if you do it correctly, you only have to use this script once.

1. The code for the script should look something like this:

```
<%
set Conn = Server.CreateObject("ADODB.Connection")
Set rst = Server.CreateObject("ADODB.RecordSet")
Conn.Open "DSN=myDSN;UID=myUID;PWD=myPWD;DATABASE=myDATABASE"
sql = "CREATE TABLE CurTransRec (TransactionID INTEGER IDENTITY NOT
NULL PRIMARY KEY, "
sql = sql & "TType VARCHAR(20), TDate DATETIME, "
sql = sql & "TAmount MONEY DEFAULT 0, AuthorizedBy VARCHAR(10), "
sql = sql & "ForWhat VARCHAR(50), CheckNumber VARCHAR(6), MadeOutTo
VARCHAR(50), "
sql = sql & "ToAccountNumber VARCHAR(20))"
rst.Open sql, Conn
Response.Write "Table Created"
%>
```

Notice the connection string contains the DSN your administrator set up, the database in SQL Server the administrator has created for your use, and a simple username and password. The rest of the code simply constructs a CREATE TABLE statement in SQL and loads it into the variable "sql". The data type assigned to the first field (INTEGER IDENTITY) is specific to SQL Server, results in an autonumbering, unique value for this field, and is ideal for a primary key field. The rest of the data types are standard SQL data types, such as VARCHAR, MONEY, and DATETIME. To make calculations easier, the value for the Amount field is set to default to zero if an amount has not been entered. The final Response.Write statement tells you the table was created. Then you can substitute in the table name "ForTransRec" and create another table just like the first one, except the second table is for forecasted records.

2. Your next step is to build an ASP script to process data in and out of the database, and an include file to display the results of our processing. First, you build the interface screen. You can use an ordinary HTML editor, such as Dreamweaver, to construct the interface screen and a simple text editor, such as Notepad, to make the script file.

3. The purpose of the interface screen is to show the current financial records as rows in a table, with the balance showing on each row and all the necessary fields also showing. On the same page, you also show the forecasted deposits and withdrawals as a table, with basically the same information displayed. The interface screen could be made up of HTML, such as the following (see Figure 12–2 for an example):

```
<html><head><title>Online Services Systems</title>
<meta http-equiv="Content-Type" content="text/html; charset=iso-8859-1">
</head>
<body bgcolor="#77FF77">
<H2><font size="6">Online Services Systems - Financial
Transactions</font></H2>
<%
set Conn = Server.CreateObject("ADODB.Connection")
Set rst = Server.CreateObject("ADODB.RecordSet")
Conn.Open "DSN=myDSN;UID=myUID;PWD=myPWD;DATABASE=myDATABASE"
sql = "SELECT SUM(TAmount) As SumTAmount FROM CurTransRec"
rst.Open sql, Conn
If Not rst.EOF Then
      vCurBal = rst.Fields("SumTAmount")
Else
      vCurBal = 0
End If
Set rst = Nothing
set Conn = Server.CreateObject("ADODB.Connection")
Set rst = Server.CreateObject("ADODB.RecordSet")
Conn.Open "DSN=myDSN;UID=myUID;PWD=myPWD;DATABASE=myDATABASE"
sql = "SELECT SUM(TAmount) As SumTAmount FROM ForTransRec"
rst.Open sql, Conn
If Not  rst.EOF Then
      vCurBFor = rst.Fields("SumTAmount")
Else
      vCurBFor = 0
End If
Set rst = Nothing
set Conn = Server.CreateObject("ADODB.Connection")
Set rst = Server.CreateObject("ADODB.RecordSet")
Conn.Open "DSN=myDSN;UID=myUID;PWD=myPWD;DATABASE=myDATABASE"
sql = "SELECT TAmount, TDate FROM CurTransRec WHERE TType = 'Start'"
rst.Open sql, Conn
If Not rst.EOF Then
      vStartAmount = rst.Fields("TAmount")
      vStartDate = rst.Fields("TDate")
```

This query pulls the sum of all amounts in the current records table, or sets the vCurBal variable to zero if no records exist yet. A similar query does the same for the forecasted records table just a few lines down.

This query pulls all the records from the current records table for display.

12

This query pulls the beginning amount and date of the first record in the current records table, based on the record type "Start". One requirement for using this system is to have one (but only one) "Start" record, in case the account is started with an existing balance. Notice that if there is no starting record, the variables are set to zero. A similar query does the same for the forecasted records table just a few lines down.

```
Else
        vStartAmount = 0
        vStartDate = 0
End If
Set rst = Nothing
set Conn = Server.CreateObject("ADODB.Connection")
Set rst = Server.CreateObject("ADODB.RecordSet")
Conn.Open "DSN=myDSN;UID=myUID;PWD=myPWD;DATABASE=myDATABASE"
sql = "SELECT TAmount, TDate FROM ForTransRec WHERE TType = 'Start'"
rst.Open sql, Conn
If Not rst.EOF Then
     vStartAFor = rst.Fields("TAmount")
     vStartDFor = rst.Fields("TDate")
Else
     vStartAFor = 0
     vStartDFor = 0
End If
Set rst = Nothing
set Conn = Server.CreateObject("ADODB.Connection")
Set rst = Server.CreateObject("ADODB.RecordSet")
Conn.Open "DSN=myDSN;UID=myUID;PWD=myPWD;DATABASE=myDATABASE"
sql = "SELECT * FROM CurTransRec ORDER BY TDate"
rst.Open sql, Conn
%>
<form method="post" action="FinancialTransactions.asp">
  <table border=1 width="885">
    <tr>
      <td bgcolor="#00CC99" colspan=4>
        <h3>Current Transactions</h3>
      </td></tr><tr>
        <td bgcolor="#00CC99" width="196">
          <div align="left"><b>Beginning Date: <% Response.Write vStartDate
%></b></div>
        </td><td bgcolor="#00CC99" width="216">
          <div align="left"><b>Beginning Balance: <% Response.Write
vStartAmount %></b></div>
        </td><td bgcolor="#00CC99" width="256">
          <div align="left"><b>Ending Balance: <% Response.Write vCurBal
%></b></div>
        </td></tr><tr><td colspan="4">
          <table width="100%" border="1">
            <tr valign="top">
              <td width="4%" height="7">
                <div align="center"><font size="-1"></font></div>
              </td><td width="4%" height="7">
                <div align="center"><font size="-1"><b>ID</b></font></div>
              </td><td width="4%" height="7">
                <div align="center"><font
size="-1"><b>Balance</b></font></div>
              </td><td width="10%" height="7">
                <div align="center"><font size="-1"><b>Type</b></font></div>
              </td><td width="8%" height="7">
                <div align="center"><font size="-1"><b>Date</b></font></div>
              </td><td width="8%" height="7">
                <div align="center">
                  <p><font size="-1"><b>Amount</b></font></p>
                </div></td><td width="8%" height="7">
```

Each table has a form pointing back to the ASP script for initiating Adds and Deletes.

The second row of each table shows the beginning date (of the first, or "Start" reccord), the beginning balance, and the ending balance.

```
                    <div align="center"><font size="-1"><b>Authorized<br>
                 By</b></font></div>
              </td><td width="16%" height="7">
                    <div align="center"><font size="-1"><b>For
What</b></font></div>
              </td><td width="5%" height="7">
                    <div align="center"><font size="-1"><b>Check
#</b></font></div>
              </td><td width="16%" height="7">
                    <div align="center"><font size="-1"><b>Made Out
To</b></font></div>
              </td><td width="17%" height="7">
                    <div align="center"><font size="-1"><b>To Account
#</b></font></div>
              </td></tr>
        <% If Not rst.EOF Then
               vRecordBal = rst.Fields("TAmount")
        Else
               vRecordBal = 0
        End If
        Do While Not rst.EOF
        %>
         <tr><td width="4%">
                 <input type="submit" name="cmdButton" value="DeleteCur<%
Response.Write rst.Fields("TransactionID") %>">
                 </td><td width="4%"><font size="-1"><% Response.Write
rst.Fields("TransactionID") %></font></td>
                 <td width="4%"><font size="-1"><% Response.Write vRecordBal
%></font></td>
                 <td width="10%"><font size="-1"><% Response.Write
rst.Fields("TType") %></font></td>
                 <td width="8%"><font size="-1"><% Response.Write
rst.Fields("TDate") %></font></td>
                 <td width="8%"><font size="-1"><% Response.Write
rst.Fields("TAmount") %></font></td>
                 <td width="8%"><font size="-1"><% Response.Write
rst.Fields("AuthorizedBy") %></font></td>
                 <td width="16%"><font size="-1"><% Response.Write
rst.Fields("ForWhat") %></font></td>
                 <td width="5%"><font size="-1"><% Response.Write
rst.Fields("CheckNumber") %></font></td>
                 <td width="16%"><font size="-1"><% Response.Write
rst.Fields("MadeOutTo") %></font></td>
                 <td width="17%"><font size="-1"><% Response.Write
rst.Fields("ToAccountNumber") %></font></td>
            </tr>
        <%
        If Not rst.Fields("TType") = "Start" Then
               vRecordBal = vRecordBal + rst.Fields("TAmount")
        End If
        rst.MoveNext
        Loop
        Set rst = Nothing
        %>
          <tr><td width="4%">
                 <input type="submit" name="cmdButton" value="AddCur">
                 </td><td width="4%"> </td>
```

> On the records row, each table starts with a delete button keyed to the record number (assigned automatically by SQL Server when the record is first created). This allows easy matching of the delete button to the appropriate record for deletion.

> This code calculates the balance for the current record, so long as the record is not the "Start" record.

12

> This code begins a row that allows records to be inserted, so the contents of each cell are form elements. The first two cells are blank, because they are the ID and balance, which are not required for a record to be inserted.

```html
            <td width="4%">  </td>
            <td width="10%">
              <select name="TType">
                <option value="Start">Start</option>
                <option value="Deposit">Deposit</option>
                <option value="Withdrawal">Withdrawal</option>
              </select>
            </td><td width="8%">
              <input type="text" name="TDate" size="10" maxlength="10">
            </td><td width="8%">
              <input type="text" name="TAmount" size="10" maxlength="10">
            </td><td width="8%">
              <select name="AuthorizedBy">
                <option value="John">John</option>
                <option value="Jimmy">Jimmy</option>
                <option value="Roger">Roger</option>
                <option value="Steve">Steve</option>
              </select>
            </td><td width="16%">
              <input type="text" name="ForWhat">
            </td><td width="5%">
              <input type="text" name="CheckNumber" size="6" maxlength="6">
            </td><td width="16%">
              <input type="text" name="MadeOutTo">
            </td><td width="17%">
              <input type="text" name="ToAccountNumber">
            </td></tr></table>
      </td></tr></table>
  <p></p><p>
  <table border=1 width="885">
    <tr><td bgcolor="#00CC99" colspan=4>
        <h3>Forecasted Transactions</h3>
    </td></tr><tr><td bgcolor="#00CC99" width="196">
        <div align="left"><b>Beginning Date: <% Response.Write vStartDFor
%></b></div>
      </td><td bgcolor="#00CC99" width="216">
        <div align="left"><b>Beginning Balance: <% Response.Write vStartAFor
%></b></div>
      </td><td bgcolor="#00CC99" width="256">
        <div align="left"><b>Ending Balance: <% Response.Write vCurBFor
%></b></div>
      </td></tr><tr><td colspan="4">
        <table width="100%" border="1">
          <tr valign="top">
          <td width="4%" height="7">
            <div align="center"><font size="-1"></font></div>
          </td><td width="4%" height="7">
            <div align="center"><font size="-1"><b>ID</b></font></div>
          </td><td width="4%" height="7">
            <div align="center"><font
size="-1"><b>Balance</b></font></div>
          </td><td width="10%" height="7">
            <div align="center"><font size="-1"><b>Type</b></font></div>
          </td><td width="8%" height="7">
            <div align="center"><font size="-1"><b>Date</b></font></div>
          </td><td width="8%" height="7">
            <div align="center">
```

> The forecasted records table begins here, and many of the same techniques are used to gather and display the data and records.

```
                    <p><font size="-1"><b>Amount</b></font></p>
                </div></td><td width="8%" height="7">
                <div align="center"><font size="-1"><b>Authorized<br>
                By</b></font></div>
            </td><td width="16%" height="7">
                <div align="center"><font size="-1"><b>For
What</b></font></div>
            </td><td width="5%" height="7">
                <div align="center"><font size="-1"><b>Check
#</b></font></div>
            </td><td width="16%" height="7">
                <div align="center"><font size="-1"><b>Made Out
To</b></font></div>
            </td><td width="17%" height="7">
                <div align="center"><font size="-1"><b>To Account
#</b></font></div>
            </td></tr>
        <%
    set Conn = Server.CreateObject("ADODB.Connection")
    Set rst = Server.CreateObject("ADODB.RecordSet")
    Conn.Open "DSN=myDSN;UID=myUID;PWD=myPWD;DATABASE=myDATABASE"
    sql = "SELECT * FROM ForTransRec ORDER BY TDate"
    rst.Open sql, Conn
    If Not rst.EOf Then
        vRecordBal = rst.Fields("TAmount")
    Else
        vRecordBal = 0
    End If
    Do While Not rst.EOF
    %>
     <tr><td width="4%">
            <input type="submit" name="cmdButton" value="DeleteFor<%
Response.Write rst.Fields("TransactionID") %>">
            </td>
            <td width="4%"><font size="-1"><% Response.Write
rst.Fields("TransactionID") %></font></td>
            <td width="4%"><font size="-1"><% Response.Write vRecordBal
%></font></td>
            <td width="10%"><font size="-1"><% Response.Write
rst.Fields("TType") %></font></td>
            <td width="8%"><font size="-1"><% Response.Write
rst.Fields("TDate") %></font></td>
            <td width="8%"><font size="-1"><% Response.Write
rst.Fields("TAmount") %></font></td>
            <td width="8%"><font size="-1"><% Response.Write
rst.Fields("AuthorizedBy") %></font></td>
            <td width="16%"><font size="-1"><% Response.Write
rst.Fields("ForWhat") %></font></td>
            <td width="5%"><font size="-1"><% Response.Write
rst.Fields("CheckNumber") %></font></td>
            <td width="16%"><font size="-1"><% Response.Write
rst.Fields("MadeOutTo") %></font></td>
            <td width="17%"><font size="-1"><% Response.Write
rst.Fields("ToAccountNumber") %></font></td>
        </tr>
<%
    If Not rst.Fields("TType") = "Start" Then
```

12

```
            vRecordBal = vRecordBal + rst.Fields("TAmount")
        End If
        rst.MoveNext
        Loop
        Set rst = Nothing
        %>
            <tr><td width="4%">
                <input type="submit" name="cmdButton" value="AddFor">
            </td>
            <td width="4%"> </td>
            <td width="4%">  </td>
            <td width="10%">
              <select name="TType2">
                <option value="Start">Start</option>
                <option value="Deposit">Deposit</option>
                <option value="Withdrawal">Withdrawal</option>
              </select>
            </td><td width="8%">
              <input type="text" name="TDate2" size="10" maxlength="10">
            </td><td width="8%">
              <input type="text" name="TAmount2" size="10" maxlength="10">
            </td>
            <td width="8%">
              <select name="AuthorizedBy2">
                <option value="John">John</option>
                <option value="Jimmy">Jimmy</option>
                <option value="Roger">Roger</option>
                <option value="Steve">Steve</option>
              </select>
            </td><td width="16%">
              <input type="text" name="ForWhat2">
            </td><td width="5%">
              <input type="text" name="CheckNumber2" size="6" maxlength="6">
            </td><td width="16%">
              <input type="text" name="MadeOutTo2">
            </td><td width="17%">
              <input type="text" name="ToAccountNumber2">
            </td></tr></table>
        </td></tr></table>
</form>
<p> </p>
</BODY></HTML>
```

4. The next step in the construction of your application is the creation of the script to process the transaction; it has only four functions. This step adds a record to either the current or the forecasted records tables, or it deletes a record form either table. There is no

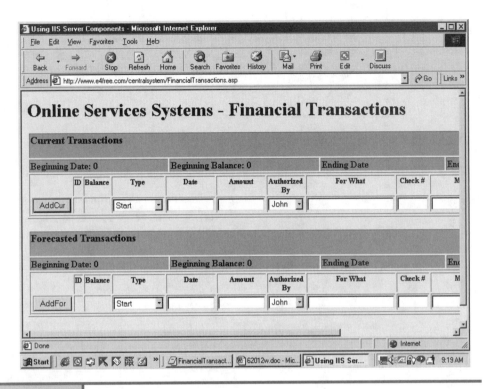

Figure 12-2 The table display interface screen

update or edit, because it's easy enough simply to delete a record and reenter the data. The code looks like this:

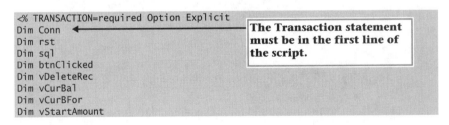

```
<% TRANSACTION=required Option Explicit
Dim Conn
Dim rst
Dim sql
Dim btnClicked
Dim vDeleteRec
Dim vCurBal
Dim vCurBFor
Dim vStartAmount
```

The Transaction statement must be in the first line of the script.

12

```
Dim vStartAFor
Dim vStartDate
Dim vStartDFor
Dim vRecordBal
Dim collitem
If Left(Request.Form("cmdButton"), 9) = "DeleteCur" Then
    btnClicked = "DeleteCur"
End If
If Left(Request.Form("cmdButton"), 9) = "DeleteFor" Then
    btnClicked = "DeleteFor"
End If
If Request.Form("cmdButton") = "AddCur" Then
    btnClicked = "AddCur"
End If
If Request.Form("cmdButton") = "AddFor" Then
    btnClicked = "AddFor"
End If
Select Case btnClicked
    Case "DeleteCur"
        vDeleteRec = Mid(Request.Form("cmdButton"), 10, 10)
        set Conn = Server.CreateObject("ADODB.Connection")
        Set rst = Server.CreateObject("ADODB.RecordSet")
        Conn.Open "DSN=myDSN;UID=myUID;PWD=myPWD;DATABASE=myDATABASE"
        sql = "DELETE FROM CurTransRec WHERE TransactionID = " &
vDeleteRec & ""
        rst.Open sql, Conn
        Sub OnTransactionCommit()
        %>
        <!-- #include file="IncludeDisplayTransactions.txt" -->
        <%
        End Sub
        Sub OnTransactionAbort()
        Response.Write "Unable to delete this record at this time.
Please try again later."
        End Sub
    Case "DeleteFor"
        vDeleteRec = Mid(Request.Form("cmdButton"), 10, 10)
        set Conn = Server.CreateObject("ADODB.Connection")
        Set rst = Server.CreateObject("ADODB.RecordSet")
        Conn.Open "DSN=myDSN;UID=myUID;PWD=myPWD;DATABASE=myDATABASE"
        sql = "DELETE FROM ForTransRec WHERE TransactionID = " &
vDeleteRec & ""
        rst.Open sql, Conn
        Sub OnTransactionCommit()
        %>
        <!-- #include file="IncludeDisplayTransactions.txt" -->
        <%
        End Sub
        Sub OnTransactionAbort()
        Response.Write "Unable to delete this record at this time.
Please try again later."
        End Sub
    Case "AddCur"
        set Conn = Server.CreateObject("ADODB.Connection")
        Set rst = Server.CreateObject("ADODB.RecordSet")
        Conn.Open "DSN=myDSN;UID=myUID;PWD=myPWD;DATABASE=myDATABASE"
        sql = "INSERT INTO CurTransRec (TType, TDate, "
```

> These next If...Then statements determine what case will be used to process the transaction by separating out the first part of the Submit button's (named "cmdButton") value and setting the "btnClicked" variable equal to it.

> The first line in the case pulls out the record number from the value of the Submit button (in this case, the record number is attached to the end of the value "DeleteCur").

> The query deletes the appropriate record and then, if the transaction is successful, displays the include file again. If unsuccessful, an error message is displayed.

> This case is processed in a similar manner as the deletion of current records.

```
              sql = sql & "TAmount, AuthorizedBy, ForWhat, CheckNumber, "
              sql = sql & "MadeOutTo, ToAccountNumber) VALUES "
              sql = sql & "('" & Request.Form("TType") & "', "
              sql = sql & "'" & Request.Form("TDate") & "', " &
Request.Form("TAmount") & ", "
              sql = sql & "'" & Request.Form("AuthorizedBy") & "', '" &
Request.Form("ForWhat") & "', "
              sql = sql & "'" & Request.Form("CheckNumber") & "', '" &
Request.Form("MadeOutTo") & "', "
              sql = sql & "'" & Request.Form("ToAccountNumber") & "')"
              rst.Open sql, Conn
              Sub OnTransactionCommit()
              %>
              <!-- #include file="IncludeDisplayTransactions.txt" -->
              <%
              End Sub
              Sub OnTransactionAbort()
              Response.Write "Unable to add this record at this time. Please
try again later."
              End Sub
      Case "AddFor"
              set Conn = Server.CreateObject("ADODConection")
              Set rst = Server.CreateObject("ADODB.RecordSet")
              Conn.Open "DSN=myDSN;UID=myUID;PWD=myPWD;DATABASE=myDATABASE"
              sql = "INSERT INTO ForTransRec (TType, TDate, "
              sql = sql & "TAmount, AuthorizedBy, ForWhat, CheckNumber, "
              sql = sql & "MadeOutTo, ToAccountNumber) VALUES "
              sql = sql & "('" & Request.Form("TType2") & "', "
              sql = sql & "'" & Request.Form("TDate2") & "', " &
Request.Form("TAmount2") & ", "
              sql = sql & "'" & Request.Form("AuthorizedBy2") & "', '" &
Request.Form("ForWhat2") & "', "
              sql = sql & "'" & Request.Form("CheckNumber2") & "', '" &
Request.Form("MadeOutTo2") & "', "
              sql = sql & "'" & Request.Form("ToAccountNumber2") & "')"
              rst.Open sql, Conn
              Sub OnTransactionCommit()
              %>
              <!-- #include file="IncludeDisplayTransactions.txt" -->
              <%
              End Sub
              Sub OnTransactionAbort()
              Response.Write "Unable to add this record at this time. Please
try again later."
              End Sub
      End Select
      If LEN(Request.Form("cmdButton")) = 0 Then
              %>
              <!-- #include file="IncludeDisplayTransactions.txt" -->
              <%
      End If
%>
```

> The insertion of records is accomplished by using the INSERT statement, and picks up the values passed by the request object. The same Transaction processing mechanism is used, but the error message is modified slightly for additions.

> If the application is being accessed initially, there will be no cmdButton value, so these statements are added to initiate display of the form.

12

☑️*Mastery Check*

1. What four properties are the mark of a valid transaction?

A. Atomicity, Synchronicity, Isolation, and Durability

B. Atomicity, Consistency, Immolation, and Durability

C. Atomicity, Consistency, Information, and Durability

D. Atomicity, Consistency, Isolation, and Durability

2. In the context of a transaction, what does Isolation mean and why is it important?

A. Isolation means each part of an individual transaction is isolated from the other parts, so the failure of one part does not stop the other parts from being completed.

B. Isolation means each transaction is isolated from other transactions, so each transaction operates as if it alone had total control over the resources it is updating.

C. Isolation means, if one update within a transaction fails, the entire transaction will be rolled back.

D. None of the above.

3. If you program a script with ASP as a transaction and the transaction fails, how does Component Services tell your script about this, and what measures must you take to support transactions in your script?

A. Component Services has two events—OnTransactionCommit and OnTransactionAbort—that tell ASP about the success or failure of a transaction, and, upon failure, rolls back all changes made within the transaction.

B. Your ASP script can detect the events triggered in Component Services signaling the success or failure of a transaction, but you must manually roll back all changes made because Component Services cannot perform the rollback when a transaction is performed within an ASP script.

☑ *Mastery Check*

   C. Although your ASP script can detect the success or failure of a transaction, you must manually roll back the parts of the transaction that aren't supported under Component Services, such as Application and Session variables and file system changes.

   D. None of the above.

4. What is the SQL statement to build a table in SQL Server, and how is an autonumbering Primary Key established?

   A. "Build Table *tablename*" is the statement, and Primary Key is the attribute that sets an autonumbering Primary Key in SQL Server when a field or column is being named.

   B. "CREATE TABLE *tablename*" is the statement, and setting a data type of INTEGER IDENTITY creates an autonumbering field in SQL Server.

   C. "CREATE TABLE *tablename*" is the statement, and you can use the AUTO attribute to create an autonumbering field in SQL Server.

   D. None of the above.

5. What should the connection string to a SQL Server database include?

   A. It should include the name of the DSN, the username, the password, and the name of the database.

   B. It should include the DSN only.

   C. It should include the username, password, and name of the database only.

   D. None of the above.

12

Module 13

ASP Collaboration and Security

The Goals of This Module

- Learn about the latest collaborative Web technologies
- Design an ASP e-mail application
- Learn about Internet, network, and workstation security
- Understand weaknesses in typical Web site applications
- Understand weaknesses in operating systems
- Learn how to design test procedures for Web site applications
- Learn how to assess security and recommend improvements
- Design Web site applications with security in mind

437

One of the most common CGI scripts available with traditional Web hosting accounts is one that takes the name–value pairs submitted with a Web page form and turns them into e-mail, and then sends them to the Web site owner. The capability to send e-mail from an application opens up a whole new world of possibilities and, naturally, ways exist to do the same thing with ASP. The enabling technology is called *Collaboration Data Objects (CDO)*.

Collaborative Technologies and CDONTS

CDO works with Microsoft Exchange Server to provide e-mail, calendaring, collaboration, and workflow services that are accessible to your ASP applications. A subset of these capabilities, called *CDO for Windows NT Server* (*CDONTS*), provides only the e-mail service when your Windows 2000 SMTP Service is installed. Using CDONTS for sending e-mail makes it easy to whip up an application quickly with e-mail capability. Unfortunately, at press time, CDONTS doesn't seem to offer direct support for such collaborative capabilities as whiteboarding, remote client control, and videoconferencing. These collaborative capabilities can be generated using Microsoft NetMeeting and its associated server. As yet, however, no direct way exists to manipulate NetMeeting or the server from ASP, although a simple scripting interface has been added in the latest version that enables developers to embed NetMeeting in Web pages.

The CDONTS Object Model

The object model for CDONTS has two primary objects at the top level: the Session object and the NewMail object. First, you learn about how the NewMail object works, and then you learn about the Session object.

The NewMail Object

The *NewMail* object is essentially an e-mail message in programmatic form, and it has properties containing the appropriate values for things such as who the message is from, who it is addressed to, and so on. If you were to imagine the screen of a common e-mail client in which you are sending a new e-mail message, the NewMail object has a property for each text field on the screen. It also has a property for Importance, which is not yet common in e-mail clients, but seems pretty handy from a programming perspective.

The From, To, CC, BCC, and Subject properties are self-explanatory; just make sure the values they take on are equivalent to what you would enter if you were in the new message screen of a typical e-mail client. As you see shortly, you can retrieve these values from an HTML form in a Web page, and then assign them to the appropriate properties of a NewMail object before you send it..

The *Importance property* is a little different. The values it can take on are 2, 1, and 0, representing High, Normal, and Low importance. If you use an HTML form to capture the Importance value a user assigns to her message, make sure to use the numerical values rather than the text equivalents. And, remember, support for importance values is not solid across the Internet, so it may not provide any additional functionality.

The *Body property* contains the contents of the message and, by default, it is formatted as plain text. You can change the BodyFormat property to HTML using the CdoBodyFormatHTML constant; in that case, you could send a message formatted as HTML to a user, and it would be properly rendered (assuming his e-mail client supports HTML). The MailFormat property is, by default, plain text, but you can change that to *Multipurpose Internet Mail Extension* (*MIME*) if you need to send a message in a rich content format. Setting the MailFormat property to equal CdoMailFormatMIME does the trick. The Version property of the NewMail object returns the version of CDONTS being used.

Hint

To use CDO constants, you can set a reference to the CDO type library in the global.asa file, or you can reference the available constants from an include file you build yourself, as long as you know what the constants are.

13

The Send method of the NewMail object actually sends your e-mail message, and the AttachFile method attaches files to the message. The Send method can be used by itself once the appropriate properties are set, or these properties can be used as parameters in a single line sending a message, like so:

```
ObjEmail.Send(From, To, Subject, Body, Importance)
```

The AttachFile method has syntax like the following:

```
ObjEmail.AttachFile(pathandfilename, caption, encodingmethod)
```

The caption can be the filename, so the user knows what the attachment is, and the encoding method can be changed from the default (UUENCODE) to Base64.

1-Minute Drill

- **What does setting the Importance property do for your e-mail?**
- **What happens if you send e-mail without setting the From property?**

The Session Object and Child Objects

The CDONTS object model also contains a Session object, and related to this object are a number of children objects that work with it to provide a great deal more e-mail functionality to your applications than just being able to generate and send e-mail messages. The children are

- **The Folder object** This object allows access to the default folders (Inbox and Outbox) in the Session, and you can view, add, and delete any messages in it, as well as through its Messages collection.

- **The Message object** This object can be accessed through the Messages collection (from the Folder object) and enables you to retrieve the message properties of messages in the collection, as

---

- Possibly nothing, unless all e-mail servers and the receiving client can make use of the value.
- The e-mail will still be sent, but the From area will be blank.

well as send or delete individual messages (the delete method of the Messages collection deletes all messages in the folder).

- **The Attachment object**   This object allows access to an individual attachment on a message (the Attachments collection of the message allows access to all attachments on a message). You can review the attachments properties to see what kind of attachment it is (name, source, type, and so on), and you can also delete, load data to, or save an attachment.

- **The Recipient object**   This object represents a single recipient among a group of recipients (accessible through the Recipients collection of the Message object) and enables you to view the name, address, and type of recipient (To, CC, BCC).

Now that you've reviewed the primary objects in CDONTS, make a simple application for sending e-mail from a Web page.

project13-1.zip

Project 13-1: An E-Mail Sending Web Page

You might never want your users to be able to log in to your Web site and send e-mail directly, but creating a page to do that can illustrate how you can use the NewMail object easily to send e-mail from an ASP application. What you do with it after that is your business, but, please note, just because you can easily send mass quantities of e-mail using a database of e-mail addresses doesn't mean you should. Spam is usually unwelcome, and making the extra effort to verify those on the list actually want to hear from you can pay big dividends down the road.

Step-by-Step

1. Make sure your SMTP server is properly set up to send e-mail. If you installed SMPT service during the installation of Windows 2000 and IIS, there's little to do other than make sure the Default Virtual SMTP Server is pointing to a valid domain, as shown in the following illustration. If you didn't install it, do so using the administrative functions and the setup procedures under IIS.

13

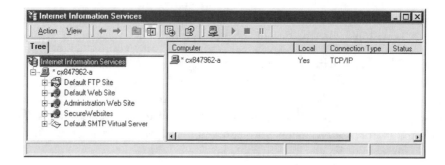

2. To start the application, build the user a nice e-mail sending screen (shown in Figure 13–1), using an HTML form to collect the appropriate value for each property you're going to send, like this:

```
<html><head><title>Project 13-1</title>
<meta http-equiv="Content-Type" content="text/html; charset=iso-8859-1">
</head>
<body bgcolor="#FFFFFF" link="#663333">
<table width="100%" border="1" bordercolordark="#CC9966"
bordercolorlight="#CC9966">
  <tr><td colspan=2>
    <table width="100%" border="0">
      <tr><td width="100%" valign="top" height="247" colspan="2">
        <table width="100%" border="1" bordercolor="#FFCC99"
bordercolorlight="#CC9966" bordercolordark="#CC9966">
          <tr bgcolor="#CC9966">
            <td><b><font face="Arial, Helvetica, sans-serif" size="+1"
color="#FFFFFF">SEND E-MAIL </font></b></td>
          </tr></table><form method="POST" action="SendE-mail.asp" name="">
          <table width="100%" border="0" bordercolordark="#CC9966"
bordercolorlight="#CC9966">
            <tr valign="top" bgcolor="#CC9966"><td> </td>
            </tr><tr valign="top"><td>
              <table border="0" width="100%">
                <tr bordercolor="#CC9966" bgcolor="#FFCC99">
                  <td align="right" colspan="2">
                    <div align="left"><b><font face="Arial, Helvetica,
sans-serif" color="#FFFFFF"><font color="#663333" size="+1">Fill In All Fields,
Please</font></font></b></div>
                  </td></tr>
                <tr bordercolor="#CC9966" bgcolor="#FFCC99">
                  <td align="right" width="12%"><div align="center"></div>
                  </td><td align="right" width="88%">
                    <div align="left"><b><font face="Arial, Helvetica,
sans-serif" size="+1" color="#FFFFFF"><font color="#663333"><font
size="-1"></font></font></font></b></div>
                  </td></tr><tr><td width="12%" align="right">
                    <div align="left"><font face="Arial, Helvetica,
sans-serif" color="#663333" size="-1"><b>From: </b></font></div>
                  </td><td width="88%">
                    <input type="text" name="From" size="40" tabindex="1">
```

```
</td></tr><tr><td width="12%" align="right">
        <div align="left"><font face="Arial, Helvetica,
sans-serif" color="#663333" size="-1"><b>To:
        </b></font></div>
    </td><td width="88%">
        <input type="text" name="To" size="40" tabindex="3">
    </td></tr><tr><td width="12%" align="right">
        <div align="left"><font face="Arial, Helvetica,
sans-serif" color="#663333" size="-1"><b>CC:</b></font></div>
    </td><td width="88%">
        <input type="text" name="CC" size="40">
    </td></tr><tr><td width="12%" align="right">
        <div align="left"><font face="Arial, Helvetica,
sans-serif" color="#663333" size="-1"><b>BCC:</b></font></div>
    </td><td width="88%">
        <input type="text" name="BCC" size="40" tabindex="6">
    </td></tr><tr><td width="12%" align="right">
        <div align="left"><font face="Arial, Helvetica,
sans-serif" color="#663333" size="-1"><b>Importance:</b></font></div>
    </td><td width="88%">
        <select name="Importance">
          <option value=2>High</option>
          <option value=1 selected>Normal</option>
          <option value=0>Low</option>
        </select>
    </td></tr><tr><td width="12%" align="right">
        <div align="left"><b><font size="-1" face="Arial,
Helvetica, sans-serif" color="#663333">Subject:</font></b></div>
    </td><td width="88%"><input type="text" name="Subject" size="40">
    </td></tr><tr><td align="right" bgcolor="#FFCC99" colspan="2">
        <div align="left"><font face="Arial, Helvetica,
sans-serif" color="#663333" size="-1"><b><font face="Arial, Helvetica,
sans-serif" size="+1" color="#FFFFFF"><font color="#663333">BODY</font></font>
        </b></font></div></td></tr><tr>
        <td width="12%" align="right"><font face="Arial,
Helvetica, sans-serif" color="#663333" size="-1"></font></td>
    <td width="88%"><textarea name="Body" cols="100" rows="10"></textarea>
        </td></tr><tr bordercolor="#CC9966" bgcolor="#FFCC99">
        <td width="12%" align="right"><font face="Arial,
Helvetica, sans-serif" color="#663333" size="-1">
        <input type="submit" value="Send E-mail" name="B1">
        </font></td>
        <td width="88%">  </td>
    </tr></table></form></table></td>
</tr></table></td></tr></table></body></html>
```

3. Now that you have a beautiful form, you can set up the backend
processing like this:

```
<% Option Explicit
Dim objEmail
Set objEmail = CreateObject("CDONTS.NewMail")
objEmail.From = request.Form("From")
objEmail.To = request.Form("To")
objEmail.Cc = request.Form("CC")
```

```
objEmail.Bcc = request.Form("BCC")
objEmail.Importance = request.Form("Importance")
objEmail.Subject = request.Form("Subject")
objEmail.Body = request.Form("Body")
objEmail.Send
Set objEmail = Nothing
Response.Write "<HTML><HEAD><TITLE>Project
13-1</TITLE><BODY><CENTER><B>Message Sent</B></CENTER></BODY></HTML>"
```

4. Notice that after you set all the properties for the e-mail, you send it using the Send method, and then respond to the user with a "Message Sent" notice formatted as a Web page, as shown in the following illustration.

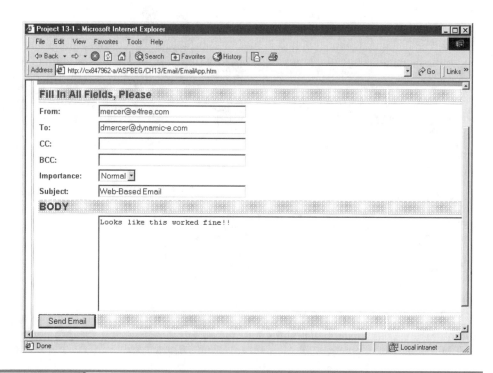

Figure 13-1 The e-mail sending form

Ask the Expert

Question: I understand how it would be useful to send e-mail to myself when someone submits a form, but how else would I really use this capability? Why not just keep the contents in a database?

Answer: One big advantage of using e-mail (and you can use it in addition to putting the contents in a database) is you get instant notification. As soon as you click, the e-mail is sent. If you happen to be online with your e-mail client open and checking for mail on a regular basis, you could almost receive notification in real time.

Also plenty of e-mail–to–fax applications are available, and these work well for businesses that either don't have e-mail (still a significant number, believe it or not) or don't want to go online to check e-mail all the time. Sometimes, the person collecting the information or taking the order is just an employee working behind a counter, and having the fax machine spit out online orders is convenient.

Other uses for e-mail capability run more toward server and application management. For instance, suppose you want the server to notify you when a certain value in the database reaches a threshold, or when a particular customer is shopping, or when a particular error is generated? Triggering e-mail through ASP lets you do these things easily.

Security Overview

High-profile attacks on e-commerce Web sites are becoming more and more common, and fraudulent transactions are also a growing problem. While they get lots of press and attention, security, privacy, and reliability issues have been around practically since data processing began. If you look into the history of commerce and communications in general, you'll find innovative methods employed to verify identity, keep information private, and ensure accurate delivery under adverse conditions since people first started communicating.

The point I'm making is that security, in its broadest terms, goes far beyond simply using SSL on your Web server, or making users provide a username and password. When you think about security, think about all

13

the potential threats to your system, your data, and the services you are attempting to provide users. Start at the highest level and work down to build in security, and you'll have a much more secure and reliable application.

Security Defined

In its broadest terms, building a secure system means protecting the data and services your system works with from all threats that would gain unauthorized access to, misuse, destroy, or render inoperable that data and/or those services. This means any potential threat to the system, regardless of whether it is natural or manmade, malicious or just careless, must be factored into the equation. Let's discuss the subtopics implied by this definition:

- **Reliability** An unreliable system is just as bad as a hacked system, especially if you are running mission-critical applications.

- **Privacy** A privacy policy that enables you to sell user's personal data without notifying them (still perfectly legal at this time, by the way) could be damaging to you and your user base in the long run, almost as bad as having a hacker steal the data.

- **Secure transactions and storage** Employing SSL to collect sensitive data, but leaving your database files hackable, is like closing the barn door after the horses are already gone.

So where do you start building a properly secured system, keeping in mind that no system can be guaranteed completely secure under all circumstances? Good security policy goes hand in hand with good security architecture.

Security Policy

Depending on the circumstance under which you are working, you might assist the systems administrator and other members of the IT department (along with other upper-level managers in the organization) in preparing a comprehensive security policy for the organization, or you might be in the position of developing the entire policy yourself, with a little input from your client. From one end of the spectrum to the other, you still need to have a formal, written security policy in hand, even if it's not elaborate. It's like having a business plan or any other kind of plan; if you don't have one, it's much harder to figure out where you're going, much less actually get there.

A good security policy covers specific computer and Internet-related issues such as SSL, encryption, and so forth; but it also covers password generation, permissions for employees or users, training, and other issues having more to do with the way people work with your system. Start your security policy by defining the objectives of the policy—in measurable terms—so you can measure whether it's working. For example, if the system is mission-critical, perhaps you must have it up and accessible 100 percent of the time. Then, if it ever goes down for any reason, you will be missing your objective (hopefully, not by much). At least it's measurable and gives you a means to quantify the effectiveness of the measures built into your security policy.

Next, define the roles and responsibilities of each player or group expected to have access to the system, and make sure to include a discussion of those folks who are uninvited. By this I mean, include not only what users, managers, and administrators are supposed to do, but also hackers, ex-employees, and Internet users in general. Remember, if enough users try to access your site, even by accidentally entering a wrong URL in their browsers, they can bring down your application. So it's important to define what you expect of authorized users, but it's also important to outline what you think unauthorized users might do and plan for it.

Finally, your security policy should include regular assessments, updates, revision, and effectiveness measurements. Security, like so many other areas of interest on the Internet, changes pretty rapidly, and you need to put in place some system of regular accounting for and coping with rapid change.

Software, Applications, and Networking Security

Assuming you have a reasonable security policy in place that covers noncomputer-related issues well, then it's time to look at security concerns about your software, applications, and how your networks are configured.

This includes your operating systems, programs, and applications, as well as the physical and logical arrangement of your networks.

Operating System Security

Operating system security is a good starting point because you can do many things at the operating system level to make it more difficult for unauthorized users to gain access to restricted areas or services. For example, you can create partitions on your hard drive with a variety of formats. Making a separate partition for the Web server and Web applications is a smart move, especially when you format the partition as NTFS. NTFS enables you to set permissions much more finely than the typical FAT format. And NTFS enables you to set *Access Control Lists (ACLs)*, set disk quotas, and encrypt files.

Another area deserving attention is the removal of capabilities not needed to run the application or manage the server. For example, you can remove the capability of the operating system to generate DOS-style filenames and extensions, to allow anonymous network access, and to allow access to common administrator tools. Your system administrator should be familiar with how to disable these functions, but a good idea is to check with them and see what they've done or plan to do.

The system administrator should also remove access to unneeded network services, such as WINS, NetBIOS, and LMHOSTS lookup, and should set TCP/IP filtering so unnecessary ports are unavailable. The responsibility of the system administrator is also to install and configure the firewall and any proxy servers properly.

Web Server Security

Following a review of operating system security (note, this is as much or more the job of the system administrator) comes a review of the configuration of your Web server software, in your case IIS 5.0. By default, when IIS is installed, some capabilities that aren't required for all Web applications will be installed. For example, FrontPage Server Extensions is only required if the Web pages call them, and this should only happen if you are using the advanced features of FrontPage when you create your pages. If you don't use the advanced features in FrontPage (such as the Search function or the Form Handler), then you don't need FrontPage Server Extensions installed. This can be construed as a general rule, namely, that you shouldn't install or should uninstall any services or features not specifically required by your applications.

If you maintain the Web server, another area deserving close attention is the release of patches for the server. For example, I went to the Microsoft site and searched for IIS 5.0, and found nine different security bulletins about IIS 5.0 vulnerabilities, such as

- **MS00-031**—Patch Available for "Undelimited .HTR Request" and "File Fragment Reading via .HTR" Vulnerabilities.

- **MS00-030**—Patch Available for "Malformed Extension Data in URL" Vulnerability.

- **MS00-023**—Patch Available for "Myriad Escaped Characters" Vulnerability.

Examining the available patches to see if they apply to your IIS configuration or your Web application is crucial to the continuing security of your Web site.

Like most servers, IIS 5.0 can maintain log files; and using the components discussed in previous modules, you can create custom log files to use for whatever you want. For some applications, you may find this capability makes tracking who is doing what within your application easier. This has implications not only for telling what happened after an attack, but also for alerting you during an attack or an attempt to gain unauthorized entry.

Authentication and Certificates

You can set your application to require one of three levels of authentication when users enter your Web site: Anonymous, Basic, and IWA. Anonymous authentication requires no username and password; essentially, by requesting a page, a user gets access to it. Basic authentication means users will be requested to supply a username and password when connecting, and they are then transmitted in clear text format. *Integrated Windows Authentication* (*IWA*) makes use of either the Kerberos Network Authentication Protocol, or the old Windows NT Challenge/Response Protocol, depending on the client being used.

13

The point of authentication is to verify the user is who she says she is. Each of the three methods mentioned has appropriate uses under various circumstances and can work with other security measures to provide secure communications to the appropriate party.

Certificates, which can be bought from a number of sources, provide a layer of encryption to your communications, both personal and server based. The use of certificates is part of the answer to the problem of making sure the person you are dealing with is actually the person you think he is. Without going into too much detail, the overall problem of security and encryption has been fairly well solved from the standpoint of generating hard-to-break encryption codes, but not as well when it comes to verifying identity unambiguously. Certificates from trusted sources help solve that portion of the problem.

You can buy personal certificates and server certificates from companies such as Verisign, and then install them on your browser and your Web server, respectively. These certificates help prove who you are and make it much easier to communicate securely with e-commerce Web sites and with your own customers. Once you have a certificate in place, it's a fairly simple matter to set up SSL on IIS 5.0, and you can even become your own certificate authority (rather than buy from Verisign) if you want.

1-Minute Drill

- **What should you have in place before you start setting up security measures for your Web site?**
- **Who is responsible for Web site application security?**

project13-2.zip

Project 13-2: Building a User Log-In Application

Requiring users to log in to your site is a common miniapplication these days, so let's build a simple registration and log-in mechanism for your security-oriented project here. To make log-in secure, you can run the registration and log-in pages under SSL, but remember to place all your

---

- A well-thought-out security policy
- Everyone developing or using the application

files (including images) in the secure area (accessed by the secure URL) so your users don't get that warning pop-up box that tells them nonsecure items are in the page they are about to view securely.

Building the Databases, Scripts, and Include Files

To store and search for usernames and passwords, use a simple Access database. If you like, you can attach passwords to the database for added security. You can often add the username and password fields to the user records; but, in some cases, you'll want to make a separate table with a one-to-one relationship to the user records.

For the registration page, use an HTML form with fields for username and password (and leave the password in plain view rather than making that form element display only asterisks to the user, so he can see if he made a mistake). On the backend, the registration function checks the existing database to see if anyone else has already used that username. If so, she needs to pick a new one, and if not, she will be registered. If you like, you can use the LEN function in VBScript to make sure her password is of a certain length, and you can do more sophisticated matching if you want to make sure she's chosen a string password.

For the log-in page use a simple search function to verify his username and password exist on his record. If not, he will go to the failed log-in page. If his record is found, a Session variable representing log-in status will be set to "Yes," and another Session variable containing his UserID will also be set. You'll find it useful to maintain his UserID throughout
his session, so you can record his actions (for his benefit, of course). Also useful is to know his logged-in status whenever he attempts to reach pages to which only logged-in users are supposed to have access.

Step-by-Step

1. Create an Access database with a table named Users and, in the Users table, create fields for the standard personal info, plus username and password fields. Make them text fields ten characters in size.

2. Create a Registration page (shown in Figure 13–2) like the following code:

```
<html><head><title>Material Bids.com</title>
<meta http-equiv="Content-Type" content="text/html; charset=iso-8859-1">
</head>
```

13

```html
<body bgcolor="#FFFFFF" link="#663333">
<table width="100%" border="0" bordercolordark="#CC9966"
bordercolorlight="#CC9966">
  <tr>
    <td width="100%" colspan="2">
      <table width="11%" border="5" align="left" bordercolordark="#CC9966"
bordercolorlight="#CC9966">
        <tr bgcolor="#CC9966">
          <td>
            <div align="center"><font color="#FFFFFF"><b><font face="Arial,
Helvetica, sans-serif"><a href="Register.htm"><font
size="-1">Register</font></a></font></b></font></div>
          </td></tr>
        <tr bgcolor="#CC9966">
          <td height="5">
            <div align="center"><font color="#FFFFFF"><b><font face="Arial,
Helvetica, sans-serif"><a href="LogIn.htm"><font
size="-1">Log-In</font></a></font></b></font></div>
          </td></tr>
      </table>
    </td></tr>
</table>
<table width="100%" border="1" bordercolordark="#CC9966"
bordercolorlight="#CC9966">
  <tr><td colspan=2>
      <table width="100%" border="0">
        <tr>
          <td width="100%" valign="top" height="247" colspan="2">
            <table width="100%" border="1" bordercolor="#FFCC99"
bordercolorlight="#CC9966" bordercolordark="#CC9966">
              <tr bgcolor="#CC9966">
                <td><b><font face="Arial, Helvetica, sans-serif" size="+1"
color="#FFFFFF">REGISTER HERE </font></b></td>
              </tr>
            </table><form method="POST" action="register.asp" name="">
            <table width="100%" border="0" bordercolordark="#CC9966"
bordercolorlight="#CC9966">
              <tr valign="top" bgcolor="#CC9966">
                <td><p align="center"><b></b></p>
              </td></tr>
              <tr valign="top">
                <td>
                  <table border="0" width="100%">
                    <tr bordercolor="#CC9966" bgcolor="#FFCC99">
                      <td align="right" colspan="2">
                        <div align="left"><b><font face="Arial, Helvetica,
sans-serif" color="#FFFFFF"><font color="#663333" size="+1">STEP 1 - ALL
REGISTRANTS FILL IN CONTACT DATA</font></font></b></div>
                      </td></tr>
                    <tr bordercolor="#CC9966" bgcolor="#FFCC99">
                      <td align="right" width="20%">
                        <div align="center"></div>
                      </td>
                      <td align="right" width="80%">
                        <div align="left"><b><font face="Arial, Helvetica,
sans-serif" size="+1" color="#FFFFFF"><font color="#663333"><font
size="-1"></font></font></font></b></div>
```

```
                        </td></tr>
                  <tr>
                        <td width="20%" align="right"><font face="Arial,
Helvetica, sans-serif" color="#663333" size="-1"><b>First and Last
Name:</b></font></td>
                        <td width="80%">
                           <input type="text" name="FirstName" size="20"
tabindex="1">
                           <input type="text" name="LastName" size="20"
tabindex="2">
                        </td></tr>

                  <tr>
                        <td width="20%" align="right"><font face="Arial,
Helvetica, sans-serif" color="#663333" size="-1"><b>Address:</b></font></td>
                        <td width="80%">
                           <input type="text" name="Address" size="40"
tabindex="3">
                        </td></tr>

                  <tr><td width="20%" align="right"><font face="Arial,
Helvetica, sans-serif" color="#663333" size="-1"><b>City, State,
Zip:</b></font></td>
                        <td width="80%">
                           <input type="text" name="City" size="20"
maxlength="20">
                           <input type="text" name="State" size="2"
tabindex="4">
                           <input type="text" name="ZipCode" size="10"
tabindex="5">
                        </td></tr>

                  <tr><td width="20%" align="right"><font face="Arial,
Helvetica, sans-serif" color="#663333" size="-1"><b>Phone,
Fax:</b></font></td>
                        <td width="80%">
                           <input type="text" name="Phone" size="20"
tabindex="6">
                           <input type="text" name="Fax" size="20"
tabindex="7">
                        </td></tr>

                  <tr>
                        <td width="20%" align="right"><font face="Arial,
Helvetica, sans-serif" color="#663333" size="-1"><b>Email:</b></font></td>
                        <td width="80%">
                           <input type="text" name="Email" size="40">
                        </td></tr>

                  <tr><td align="right" bgcolor="#FFCC99" colspan="2">

                        <div align="left"><font face="Arial, Helvetica,
sans-serif" color="#663333" size="-1"><b><font face="Arial, Helvetica,
sans-serif" size="+1" color="#FFFFFF"><font color="#663333">STEP 2 - CHOOSE
USER NAME AND PASSWORD </font></font> </b></font></div>
                        </td></tr>
```

13

```
                    <tr><td width="20%" align="right"><font face="Arial,
Helvetica, sans-serif" color="#663333" size="-1"><b>User Name,
Password:</b></font></td>
                        <td width="80%">
                            <input type="text" name="UserName" size="20"
tabindex="15">
                            <input type="text" name="Password" size="20"
tabindex="16">
                        </td></tr>

                    <tr bordercolor="#CC9966" bgcolor="#FFCC99">

                        <td width="20%" align="right"><font face="Arial,
Helvetica, sans-serif" color="#663333" size="-1"></font></td>
                        <td width="80%">
                            <input type="submit" value="Submit" name="B1">
                            <input type="reset" value="Reset" name="B2">
                        </td></tr>
                </table></form>
            </table></td></tr></table></td></tr></table>
</body></html>
```

3. Next, create an ASP script that processes the registration and returns a valid registration, an invalid registration (if the username is already taken), or a page listing any required fields that still need to be completed. On this page, a good idea is to turn values from the HTML form into variables and to replace any unwanted characters, like so:

```
<%
Dim vMissingFields
Dim vFirstName
Dim vLastName
Dim vAddress
Dim vCity
Dim vState
Dim vZipCode
Dim vCountry
Dim vPhone
Dim vFax
Dim vEmail
Dim vUserName
Dim vPassword
For Each collitem in Request.Form
    If Len(request.form(collitem)) < 1 Then
        vMissingFields = vMissingFields & collitem & ", "
    End If
Next
If Len(vMissingFields) < 1 Then
    vFirstName = request.form("FirstName")
    vFirstName = Replace(vFirstName, "<", "")
    vFirstName = Replace(vFirstName, ">", "")
    vFirstName = Replace(vFirstName, "%", "")
    vFirstName = Replace(vFirstName, "'", "''")
```

```
vLastName = request.form("LastName")
vLastName = Replace(vLastName, "<", "")
vLastName = Replace(vLastName, ">", "")
vLastName = Replace(vLastName, "%", "")
vLastName = Replace(vLastName, "'", "''")
vAddress = request.form("Address")
vAddress = Replace(vAddress, "<", "")
vAddress = Replace(vAddress, ">", "")
vAddress = Replace(vAddress, "%", "")
vAddress = Replace(vAddress, "'", "''")
vCity = request.form("City")
vCity = Replace(vCity, "<", "")
vCity = Replace(vCity, ">", "")
vCity = Replace(vCity, "%", "")
vCity = Replace(vCity, "'", "''")
vState = request.form("State")
vState = Replace(vState, "<", "")
vState = Replace(vState, ">", "")
vState = Replace(vState, "%", "")
vState = Replace(vState, "'", "''")
vZipCode = request.form("ZipCode")
vZipCode = Replace(vZipCode, "<", "")
vZipCode = Replace(vZipCode, ">", "")
vZipCode = Replace(vZipCode, "%", "")
vZipCode = Replace(vZipCode, "'", "''")
vCountry = request.form("Country")
vCountry = Replace(vCountry, "<", "")
vCountry = Replace(vCountry, ">", "")
vCountry = Replace(vCountry, "%", "")
vCountry = Replace(vCountry, "'", "''")
vPhone = request.form("Phone")
vPhone = Replace(vPhone, "<", "")
vPhone = Replace(vPhone, ">", "")
vPhone = Replace(vPhone, "%", "")
vPhone = Replace(vPhone, "'", "''")
vFax = request.form("Fax")
vFax = Replace(vFax, "<", "")
vFax = Replace(vFax, ">", "")
vFax = Replace(vFax, "%", "")
vFax = Replace(vFax, "'", "''")
vEmail = request.form("Email")
vEmail = Replace(vEmail, "<", "")
vEmail = Replace(vEmail, ">", "")
vEmail = Replace(vEmail, "%", "")
vEmail = Replace(vEmail, "'", "''")
vUserName = request.form("UserName")
vUserName = Replace(vUserName, "<", "")
vUserName = Replace(vUserName, ">", "")
vUserName = Replace(vUserName, "%", "")
vUserName = Replace(vUserName, "'", "''")
vPassword = request.form("Password")
vPassword = Replace(vPassword, "<", "")
vPassword = Replace(vPassword, ">", "")
vPassword = Replace(vPassword, "%", "")
vPassword = Replace(vPassword, "'", "''")
Set Conn = Server.CreateObject("ADODB.Connection")
Conn.Open "registration"
```

13

```
      sql= "SELECT Username, Password From Users WHERE Username = '" &
request.form("UserName") & "';"
      Set myRs = Conn.Execute(sql)
      If myRs.EOF Then
Set Conn = Server.CreateObject("ADODB.Connection")
Conn.Open "registration"
sql= "INSERT INTO Users "
sql= sql & "(FirstName,"
sql= sql & " LastName,"
sql= sql & " Address,"
sql= sql & " City,"
sql= sql & " State,"
sql= sql & " ZipCode,"
sql= sql & " Country,"
sql= sql & " Phone,"
sql= sql & " Fax,"
sql= sql & " Email,"
sql= sql & " UserName,"
sql= sql & " Password,"
sql= sql & " SignUpDate) VALUES "
sql= sql & "('" & vFirstName & "', "
sql= sql & "'" & vLastName & "', "
sql= sql & "'" & vAddress & "', "
sql= sql & "'" & vCity & "', "
sql= sql & "'" & vState & "', "
sql= sql & "'" & vZipCode & "', "
sql= sql & "'" & vCountry & "', "
sql= sql & "'" & vPhone & "', "
sql= sql & "'" & vFax & "', "
sql= sql & "'" & vEmail & "', "
sql= sql & "'" & vUserName & "', "
sql= sql & "'" & vPassword & "', "
sql= sql & "'" & Date & "')"
Conn.Execute (sql)
Conn.Close
%>
<!-- #include file="IncludeRegister1.txt" -->
<%
Else
%>
<!-- #include file="IncludeRegister2.txt" -->
<%
End If
Else
%>
<!-- #include file="IncludeRegister3.txt" -->
<%
End If
%>
```

4. Notice in the code you just wrote the use of a DSN named
   registration. You want to create this DSN and point it at your
   registration.mdb file, using the appropriate drivers. Your next job is
   to make the four include text files named IncludeRegistration1.txt,

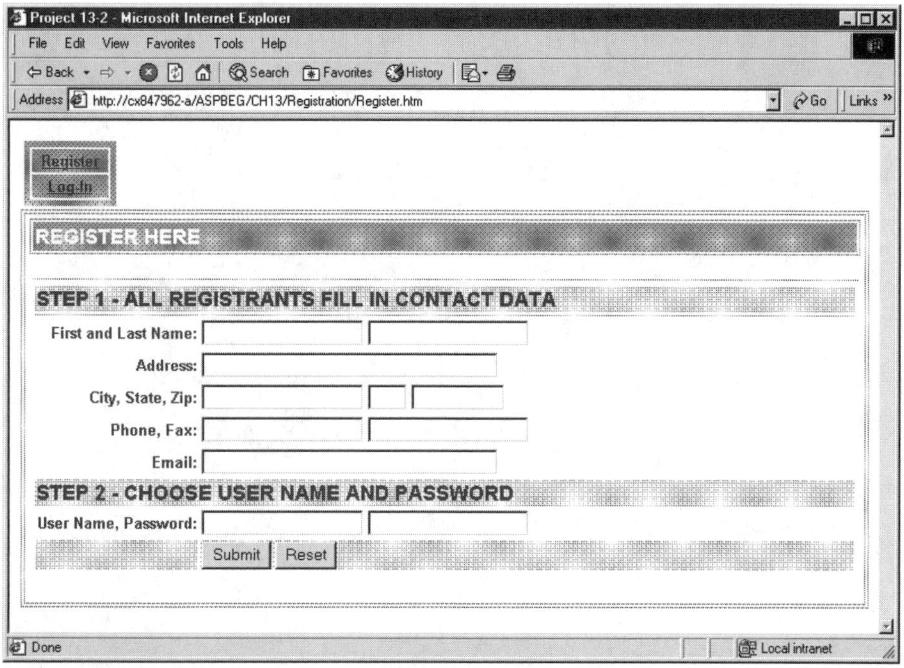

Figure 13-2 The Registration page

IncludeRegistration2.txt, and IncludeRegistration3.txt. The first text file returns the valid registration message, the second text file returns the invalid registration message and asks the user to go back and try again, and the third lists the required fields (taken from the vMissingFields variable).

5. Once you create the Registration function and have that working, you can concentrate on the log-in pages. like the one shown in Figure 13–3. To start, you need an HTML page with a simple form on it, something like this:

```
<html><head><title>Project 13-2</title>
<meta http-equiv="Content-Type" content="text/html; charset=iso-8859-1">
</head>
<body bgcolor="#FFFFFF" link="#663333">
<table width="100%" border="0" bordercolordark="#CC9966"
bordercolorlight="#CC9966">
  <tr>
```

13

```
    <td width="100%" colspan="2">
      <table width="13%" border="5" align="left" bordercolordark="#CC9966"
bordercolorlight="#CC9966">
        <tr bgcolor="#CC9966">
          <td>
            <div align="center"><font color="#FFFFFF"><b><font face="Arial,
Helvetica, sans-serif"><a href="Register.htm"><font
size="-1">Register</font></a></font></b></font></div>
          </td></tr>
        <tr bgcolor="#CC9966">
          <td height="5">
            <div align="center"><font color="#FFFFFF"><b><font face="Arial,
Helvetica, sans-serif"><a href="LogIn.htm"><font
size="-1">Log-In</font></a></font></b></font></div>
          </td></tr>
      </table>
    </td></tr>
</table>
<table width="100%" border="1" bordercolordark="#CC9966"
bordercolorlight="#CC9966">
  <tr>
    <td colspan=2>
      <table width="100%" border="0">
        <tr>
          <td width="100%" valign="top" height="247" colspan="2">
            <table width="100%" border="1" bordercolor="#FFCC99"
bordercolorlight="#CC9966" bordercolordark="#CC9966">
              <tr bgcolor="#CC9966">
                <td><b><font face="Arial, Helvetica, sans-serif" size="+1"
color="#FFFFFF">LOG-IN HERE </font></b></td>
              </tr>
            </table>
            <table width="100%" border="0" bordercolordark="#CC9966"
bordercolorlight="#CC9966">
              <tr valign="top" bgcolor="#CC9966">
                <td>
                  <p><b></b></p>
                </td>
              </tr>
              <tr valign="top">
                <td height="98"> <font size="3"><font color="#663333"><font
face="Arial, Helvetica, sans-serif"><b>
                  </b></font></font></font>
                  <form method="post" action="login.asp" name="">
                    <table width="65%" border="0" align="left">
                      <tr>
                        <td><font size="3"><font color="#663333"><font
face="Arial, Helvetica, sans-serif"><b>Username:
</b></font></font></font></td>
                        <td><font size="3"><font color="#663333"><font
face="Arial, Helvetica, sans-serif"><b>
                          <input type="text" name="Username">
                          </b></font></font></font></td>
                      </tr><tr>
                        <td><b><font face="Arial, Helvetica, sans-serif"
size="3" color="#663333">Password:
                          </font></b></td>
```

```
                    <td><b><font face="Arial, Helvetica, sans-serif"
size="3" color="#663333">
                        <input type="password" name="Password">
                        </font></b></td>
                    </tr><tr>
                    <td><b><font face="Arial, Helvetica, sans-serif"
size="3" color="#663333">
                        <input type="submit" name="Submit" value="Log-in">
                        <input type="reset" name="Submit2" value="Clear">
                        </font></b></td>
                    <td> </td>
                    </tr></table>
                <p> </p>
                <p><font size="3"><font color="#663333"><font
face="Arial, Helvetica, sans-serif"><b><br>
                    </b></font></font></font><b><font face="Arial,
Helvetica, sans-serif" size="3" color="#663333"><br>
                    </font></b> </p>
                </form>
                <p align="left"> </p>
            </td></tr></table>
        </td></tr></table>
    </td></tr></table>
</body></html>
```

6. The Log-in form references an ASP script named "login.asp," naturally. This script searches the database entries to see if the

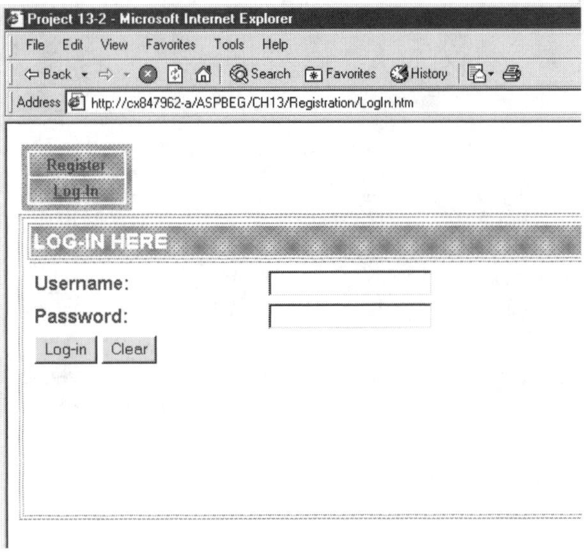

Figure 13-3 | The Log-in form

13

username and password combination are present. If so, it sets the Session variable for log-in status to "Yes" and the Session variable for UserID to the value of the UserID found in the record containing the username and password. It then returns a page telling the user she is logged in. If it doesn't find her username and password in the database, it returns a page suggesting she either register (if she hasn't done so already) or try to log in again (on the assumption that she might have made a mistake logging in). The code for login.asp looks like this:

```
<%
Dim vUserName
Dim vPassword
vUserName = request.form("UserName")
vUserName = Replace(vUserName, "<", "")
vUserName = Replace(vUserName, ">", "")
vUserName = Replace(vUserName, "%", "")
vUserName = Replace(vUserName, "'", "''")
vPassword = request.form("Password")
vPassword = Replace(vPassword, "<", "")
vPassword = Replace(vPassword, ">", "")
vPassword = Replace(vPassword, "%", "")
vPassword = Replace(vPassword, "'", "''")
Set Conn = Server.CreateObject("ADODB.Connection")
Conn.Open "registration"
sql= "SELECT UserID, Username, Password From Users WHERE Username = '" &
vUserName & "' AND Password = '" & vPassword & "';"
Set myRs = Conn.Execute(sql)
If myRs.EOF Then
%>
<!-- #include file="failedloginNew.txt" -->
<%
Else
     Session("LoginStatus") = "Yes"
     Session("UserID") = myRs.Fields("UserID")
%>
<!-- #include file="approvedlogin.txt" -->
<%
End If
%>
```

7. Other than making the Include files for approved and failed registration (which are basically only HTML pages with a message),

you want to build some mechanism that prevents users from seeing pages they shouldn't if they aren't logged in. The following code, when attached at the beginning of your Web pages (turning them into ASP scripts, by the way), does just that:

```
<%
If Session("LoginStatus") = "No" Then
%>
<!-- #include file="failedlogin.txt" -->
<%
Else
%>
<html><head><title>Project 13-2</title>
<meta http-equiv="Content-Type" content="text/html; charset=iso-8859-1">
</head>
<body bgcolor="#FFFFFF" link="#663333">
Whatever page you want protected can go here
</body></html>
<%
End If
%>
```

8. And of course, don't forget your global.asa file, in which you keep your Session variables. It might look like this:

```
<SCRIPT Language="VBScript" RUNAT="server">
Sub Application_onStart()
End Sub
Sub Application_onEnd()
End Sub
Sub Session_onStart()
Dim vLoggedIn
vUID = 0
vLoggedIn = "No"
Session("LoginStatus") = vLoggedIn
Session("UserID") = vUID
End Sub
Sub Session_onEnd()
vUID = 0
vLoggedIn = "No"
Session("LoginStatus") = vLoggedIn
Session("UserID") = vUID
End Sub
</SCRIPT>
```

13

Mastery Check

1. What is the difference between CDO and CDONTS?

    A. CDO means Comma Delimited Object, while CDONTS means Collaboration Data Objects for Windows NT Server.

    B. CDO contains the capability to perform collaborative functions for all platforms, while CDONTS can perform collaboration functions only on Windows NT Server.

    C. CDO has more collaborative functions than CDONTS.

    D. None of the above.

2. What property would you set to send an e-mail to someone without others knowing the e-mail was sent to that person?

    A. To

    B. From

    C. CC

    D. BCC

    E. None of the above

3. What encryption method is unbreakable above a certain bit size?

    A. PGP

    B. RSA

    C. Dual-key

    D. None of the above

☑ Mastery Check

4. What kind of security does authentication provide?

   A. Authentication tells you the person or system you are communicating with is actually the person or system they have told you they are.

   B. Authentication verifies the message you are reading hasn't been tampered with.

   C. Authentication hides the contents of a message from unauthorized viewers.

   D. None of the above.

5. What VBScript method could you use to determine whether a password was long enough to be a valid password?

   A. CStr, which counts the length of a string

   B. Fix, which fixes the length of a string

   C. Len, which measures the length of a string

   D. Lbound, which rejects any strings below the lower bound in size

13

Part 4

Appendixes

Appendix A

Answers to
Mastery Checks

Module 1: Active Server Pages—Getting Set Up

1. On what platform does ASP run, and how much does it cost?

B. Windows NT, and it's free

2. What is the primary functionality ASP brings to a Web site, and why is it so important?

Answer: ASP brings interactivity and programmability to Web sites, making your Web site come alive.

3. What is a partition, and why does it matter how it is formatted when installing IIS?

Answer: A partition is a separate area on a hard drive, and the format is important because IIS can only set permissions allowed by the partition format.

4. What process is advisable to use when designing a Web site?

C. Use reverse engineering and usability testing to determine how to arrive at the desired functionality, and then conform to the client's wishes as closely as possible.

5. What is bandwidth and why is it an important consideration in the design of a modern Web site?

Answer: Bandwidth is the amount of data that can be transmitted within a given time, and it is important because it constrains Web site performance (speed of access).

Module 2: ASP and the Web—Programming Basics

1. What languages are commonly used to construct Web pages and online applications?

E. All of the above

2. Hypertext Transport Protocol defines communications between Web server and Web browser. What kinds of messages are included in these communications?

F. All of the above

3. Delimiters are characters used to define commands in programming languages. The delimiters for HTML are **<** and **>**. The delimiters for ASP code within HTML are **<%** and **%>**.

4. Describe three common coding practices that make your code more readable, more debuggable, and less error prone.

Answer: Commenting your code, using standard naming conventions, and using the Option Explicit statement.

5. Who decides what the layout, look, and feel of a Web site should be? Who should have input?

E. All of the above

Module 3: The Request and Response Objects

1. When you write "Request.Form("fieldname")" what does the word "Form" represent?

C. A collection of the Request object

2. What code could be used to send the message "Thank You!" back to the user, within the context of an HTML page?

D. All of the above

3. What object collection could we retrieve to get a cookie from the user?

C. Both of the above

4. When is it a good idea to buffer the results generated by your scripts?

E. All of the above

A

5. To send the user results processed immediately, you would use the **Flush** method of the Response object. To stop processing, you would use the **End** method of the Response object. To send their browser to another location, you would use the **Redirect** method of the Response object.

Module 4: The Server Object

1. Server-side includes are a legacy technology. Besides the "include" directive, what other directives are there?

   A. Config, flastmod, fsize, echo, exec

2. What is the proper extension for an included file that contains ASP code?

   B. .txt

3. What is the default timeout for ASP scripts, and what is the syntax for resetting the timeout property to 100 seconds?

   A. 1.5 minutes, and <% ScriptTimeout = 100 %>

4. Why is it sometimes necessary to encode HTML characters?

   C. HTML characters are sometimes part of a string, and will be misinterpreted by the browser if unencoded.

5. How can you, as the developer, change error messages the server generates?

   C. Modify the existing error pages

Module 5: The Application and Session Objects

1. What does scope mean, in the context of ASP?

   C. Defines which variables can be seen by which scripts

2. What is the difference between Application and Session scope?

C. Application scope maintains variables that can be seen by any script running within the application, while Session scope maintains variables that can be seen only by scripts running within the session of that individual user.

3. By what mechanism does the global.asa file permit you to run code when your applications and sessions start or finish?

D. Events

4. How does your application identify an individual user and establish a session?

C. Using a Session Cookie

5. The code to add a variable to the Application is **Application ("variable") = value**. The code to abandon a Session is **Session.Abandon**. The code to remove all variables from a Session is **Session.Contents.RemoveAll()**.

Module 6: The Scripting Object Model and SOM Objects

1. What is an object model?

C. A description or illustration of the relationships of objects to each other

2. What does the Dictionary object contain, and how can it be changed?

B. Name/value pairs, and they can be changed by using Dictionary object properties.

3. In the File object, what attributes can be set when using the CreateTextFile method?

A. filepath, overwrite, unicode

4. Which Scripting Library objects can be used to create text files?

D. Only the FileSystemObject object, Folder object, File object, and TextStream object

A

5. Working with files sometimes requires navigating within them to find and edit particular sections of text. To move from one line to the next within a file, you would use the **SkipLine()** method of the **TextStream** object. To write a blank line into a file, you would use the **WriteBlankLines(numberoflines)** method of the **TextStream** object. To determine what column you are in within a text file, you would use the **Column** property of the **TextStream** object.

Module 7: Major Active Server Components

1. What capabilities does the Ad Rotator component offer?

C. It provides a means of accessing banner ads for random rotation according to a set percentage for display.

2. Why is the Browser Capabilities component so important, and where is the content it uses kept?

A. It detects browser types, providing a means to display customized Web content based on browser type and version. The content it uses to accomplish this is kept in a text file named browscap.ini.

3. How does the Content Linking component perform its job?

B. It refers to a content-linking text file for information about path, title, and description of the files in your Web site, and uses methods and properties to assist the user in navigating the site.

4. What is one of the primary advantages of using the Content Rotator component?

B. You can rotate text and hyperlinks across your pages according to the percentage paid for by advertisers.

Module 8: More Active Server Components

1. What is the difference between the Counter component and the Page Counter component?

C. The Counters component can create as many counters as you want.

2. What are some of the steps you must take to use the Permission Checker component?

B. Set permissions on the resource, ensure the partition type is NTFS, and disallow anonymous access.

3. Using the OpenLogFile method of the Logging Utility, I can specify the log file to open with the **filename** attribute, set the reading or writing attribute with **io_mode**, and set the format for the output with the optional **output_format** attribute.

4. What does the ProcessForm method of the Tools component use to build new customized files?

C. Templates, insertion points, and the output path and filename

5. What is the correct syntax for including the DLL file when using the Logging Utility ForReading and ForWriting attrbitues?

D. You must use the path and filename that are appropriate for your system.

Module 9: ActiveX Data Objects and SQL Overview

1. What is the process of determining the end result and working backward to determine requirements called?

C. Reverse engineering

2. What is the SQL command for specifying criteria in a SELECT statement?

B. WHERE

3. What are the SQL text field delimiters?

A Single-quote marks

4. What takes the place of traditional DBMS navigational forms on a Web site?

E. Both C and D will suffice.

Module 10: The ADO Connection-Related Objects

1. What can you do to optimize your database interactions?

C. Close connections, use stored procedures, and use only required data.

2. What is the SQL command for specifying a parameter in Access?

A. PARAMETERS ["parametername"] data type

3. What does the Direction attribute mean for Parameter objects?

C. Whether data is going to or coming from the stored procedure

4. What lock type is the default?

C. Read-only

Module 11: The ADO Recordset-Related Objects

1. What is the difference between the Requery and Resync methods of the Recordset object?

    B. Requery reperforms the original query, while Resync only refreshes the existing data in the recordset.

2. What property would you set to limit the number of records returned in a recordset?

    C. MaxRecords

3. What mechanism could you use to gather user data for record updates?

    D. All of the above

4. What property of a Stream object is similar to the Recordset's BOF and EOF properties?

    C. EOS

5. What information does the State property convey, for many ADO objects?

    C. Whether the object is open or closed

Module 12: ASP Transactions

1. What four properties are the mark of a valid transaction?

    D. Atomicity, Consistency, Isolation, and Durability

2. In the context of a transaction, what does Isolation mean and why is it important?

    B. Isolation means each transaction is isolated from other transactions, so each transaction operates as if it alone had total control over the resources it is updating.

3. If you program a script with ASP as a transaction, and the transaction fails, how does Component Services tell your script about this, and what measures must you take to support transactions in your script?

C. Although your ASP script can detect the success or failure of a transaction, you must manually roll back the parts of the transaction that are not supported under Component Services, such as Application and Session variables and file system changes.

4. What is the SQL statement to build a table in SQL Server, and how is an auto-numbering Primary Key established?

B. "CREATE TABLE tablename" is the statement, and setting a data type of INTEGER IDENTITY creates an autonumbering field in SQL Server.

5. What should the connection string to a SQL Server database include?

A. It should include the name of the DSN, the username, the password, and the name of the database.

Module 13: ASP Collaboration and Security

1. What is the difference between CDO and CDONTS?

C. CDO has more collaborative functions than CDONTS.

2. What property would you set to send e-mail to someone without others knowing the e-mail was sent to that person?

D. None of the above

3. What encryption method is unbreakable above a certain bit size?

D. None of the above

4. What kind of security does authentication provide?

A. Authentication tells you the person or system you are communicating with is actually the person or system they have said they are.

5. What VBScript method could you use to determine whether a password was long enough to be a valid password?

C. Len, which measures the length of a string

Appendix B

HTML 4.01

Within this appendix are a list of commonly used HTML tags and attributes, in alphabetical order. It is useful for rapidly identifying the function of a particular tag or attribute. If you are unsure of correct syntax, please refer to **http://www.w3.org** at the HTML 4.01 recommendation pages.

A	The anchor tag. Used for creating hyperlinks. Most commonly used with the HREF attribute to open another Web page.
ABBR	Indicates a sequence of characters that compose an acronym.
ACRONYM	Indicates a sequence of characters that compose an acronym.
ADDRESS	Indicates a portion of text that constitutes contact information, like an address, phone number, or URL.
APPLET	Executes Java or other executable code.
AREA	Used for inline image mapping. Defines a "clickable space" in the client-side image map.
B	The Bold tag. Encapsulated text will be bold. DO NOT OVERUSE THIS TAG.
BASE	Specifies the URL from which all relative links are referenced.
BASEFONT	The default font for the Web page.
BDO	Turns off the bidirectional rendering algorithm for selected fragments of text.
BIG	Makes text larger.
BLOCKQUOTE	Denotes a long quotation. Separates the quote from the body text.
BODY	Begins and ends the main section of the Web page. Defines many key properties of the Web page, such as bgcolor (background color) and background (background image).
BR	Line Break
BUTTON	Renders an HTML button. The enclosed text is used as the button's name.
CAPTION	Specifies a caption to be placed next to a table.
CENTER	Centers the enclosed information. Frequently, one tag encloses LOTS of stuff.
CITE	Renders text in italics.
CODE	Renders text as a code sample in fixed-width font.
COL	Used to specify column-based defaults for a table.
COLGROUP	Used as a container for a group of columns.
DD	Definition of an item in a definition list. Usually indented from other text.
DEL	Indicates a section of the document that has been deleted since a previous version.
DFN	The defining instance of a term.

DIR	Renders text so it appears like a directory-style file listing.
DIV	Defines a container section within the page and can hold other elements.
DL	Definition list.
DT	Definition term.
ME	Renders text as emphasized, usually in italics.
FIELDSET	Draws a box around contained elements to indicate related items.
FONT	Specifies font attributes for contained text such as size and typeface.
FORM	Contains form elements and describes what is to be done with the gathered data.
FRAME	Used to create a frame within a frameset. Can include several attributes to control borders, spacing, and so forth.
FRAMESET	Defines a group of frames and their collective properties, such as the number of columns and rows.
H1–H6	Heading tags: H1 is the largest and H6 is the smallest.
HEAD	Denotes the header portion of the document.
HR	A horizontal rule. Used for separating sections of a Web page.
HTML	Contains the entire Web page.
I	Italicizes enclosed text. DO NOT OVERUSE.
IFRAME	Creates a floating frame within the page.
IMG	Embeds an image. The attribute "src" defines the location of the desired image.
INPUT	An input field to be used with a form.
INS	Indicates a portion of text that has been inserted since the previous version.
ISINDEX	Part of a searchable index.
KBD	Renders text in a fixed-width format.
LABEL	Creates a label that may be linked to directly, even if it's in the middle of the page.
LEGEND	Defines the title text to be used by the "box" created by the fieldset tag.
LI	List item. Used with UL or OL.
LINK	Defines a hyperlink. Used most commonly with the HREF attribute.
MAP	Defines an inline image map.
MENU	Renders the following block of text as individual items.
META	Provides instructions and information to the browser. This information isn't seen in the rendered view of the page.
NOFRAMES	Encloses text to be seen only on a browser that doesn't support frames.

NOSCRIPT	Encloses text to be seen only on a browser that doesn't support scripting.
OBJECT	Inserts an object, or other non-HTML item or control, into the Web page.
OL	An Ordered List. Used with LI.
OPTGROUP	Creates a collapsible and hierarchical list of options. Not widely supported.
OPTION	An item in a selection field.
P	Starts a new paragraph. End tag optional.
PARAM	Used in an OBJECT or APPLET tag to get the object's parameters.
PRE	Renders text in fixed-width type.
Q	A short quotation, such as the URL of the source document or a message.
S	Renders text in strikethrough type.
SAMP	Renders text in code sample listing, usually in a smaller font.
SCRIPT	Specifies a script for the page.
SELECT	Creates a list box or drop-down list.
SMALL	Renders text with a smaller font than the current font.
SPAN	Used to define nonstandard attributes for text on the page. Used only with style sheets.
STRIKE	Renders text in strikethrough type.
STRONG	Renders text in boldface type.
STYLE	Specifies the style properties used from a style sheet.
SUB	Renders text in subscript.
SUP	Renders text in superscript.
TABLE	Creates a table. Used with TR, and TD, and contains control attributes for borders, cell spacing, and so forth.
TBODY	Denotes the body of the table. Not required.
TD	Contains the data for one cell in the table.
TEXTAREA	A large text-entry field used with forms.
TFOOT	A set of rows to be used as the table footer.
TH	Defines a header row in the table.
THEAD	Denotes a set of rows to be used as the header for the table.
TITLE	Defines the title for the Web page.
TR	Defines a table row. Includes one or more TD tags.
TT	Renders text in fixed-width type.
U	Renders text with an underline.
UL	Unordered list. Used with the LI tag.
VAR	Renders text as a small fixed-width font.

Appendix C

JScript

Within this appendix is a list of all JScript functions, operators, reserved words, Methods, and Properties, in alphabetical order. For further explanation of syntax and usage please see **http://www.microsoft.com**, at the JScript documentation pages.

JScript Command	Explanation
! Operator	Logical negation.
!= Operator	Expression inequality.
!== Operator	Expression inequality or value or value inequality.
0. . .n Properties	Returns value of argument from argument object.
$1. . .$9 Properties	The nine previous regular expression matches found.
% Operator	Modulo division.
%= Operator	Modulo division assignment.
& Operator	Bitwise AND.
&= Operator	Bitwise AND assignment.
&& Operator	Logical AND.
* Operator	Multiply.
*= Operator	Multiply assignment.
+ Operator	Adds two expressions or concatenates two strings.
++ Operator	Increment.
+= Operator	Addition assignment.
, Operator	Sequential execution.
– Operator	Subtracts two expressions or negates a numerical expression.
-- Operator	Decrements.
-= Operator	Subtraction assignment.
/ Operator	Division.
/*. .*/ (Multiline Comment Statement)	Multiline comment.
// (Single-line Comment Statement)	Single-line comment.
/= Operator	Division assignment.
< Operator	Less than.
<< Operator	Left shift.
<<= Operator	Left-shift assignment.
<= Operator	Less than or equal to.

C

JScript Command	Explanation
= Operator	Assignment.
== Operator	Equality.
=== Operator	Equality and type equality.
> Operator	Greater than.
>= Operator	Greater than or equal to.
>> Operator	Right shift.
>>= Operator	Right-shift assignment.
>>> Operator	Right shift without maintaining sign.
>>>= Operator	Right shift without maintaining sign assignment.
?: Operator	Conditional execution.
~ Operator	Bitwise NOT.
| Operator	Bitwise OR.
|= Operator	Bitwise OR assignment.
|| Operator	Logical OR.
^ Operator	Bitwise exclusive OR.
^= Operator	Bitwise exclusive OR assignment.
@cc_on Statement	Activates conditional compilation support.
@if Statement	Conditional execution.
@set Statement	Creates variables used with conditional compilation statements.
abs Method	Absolute value.
acos Method	Arccosine.
ActiveXObject Object	Enables and returns a reference to an Automation object.
Addition Operator (+)	Adds two expressions or concatenates two strings.
anchor Method	Places an HTML anchor with a NAME attribute around specified text in the object.
apply Method	Applies a method of an object, substituting another object for the current object.
arguments Property	Arguments passed to function.
Array Object	Create an array of any data type.
asin Method	Arcsine.
Assignment Operator (=)	Assignment.

JScript Command	Explanation
atan Method	Arctangent.
atan2 Method	Returns the angle in radians from the X axis to a point (*y,x*).
atEnd Method	Indicates if enumerator is at the end.
big Method	Places HTML <BIG> tags around text in a String object.
Bitwise AND Operator (&)	Bitwise AND.
Bitwise Left Shift Operator (<<)	Left shift.
Bitwise NOT Operator (~)	Bitwise NOT.
Bitwise OR Operator (|)	Bitwise OR.
Bitwise Right Shift Operator (>>)	Right shift.
Bitwise XOR Operator (^)	Bitwise exclusive OR.
blink Method	Places HTML <BLINK> tags around text in a String object.
bold Method	Places HTML <B> tags around text in a String object.
Boolean Object	New Boolean object.
break Statement	Terminates current loop to resume execution at next statement.
call Method	Calls a method of an object, substituting another object for the current object.
callee Property	Returns function being executed.
caller Property	References function that called current function.
catch Statement	statements executed upon error in "try" block.
ceil Method	Smallest integer greater than or equal to a given number.
charAt Method	Returns the character at the specified index.
charCodeAt Method	Returns the Unicode encoding of the specified character.
Comma Operator (,)	Sequential execution.
Comment Statement— Multiline (/*. .*/)	Multiline comment.
Comment Statement—Single-Line (//)	Single-line comment.
compile Method	Compiles a regular expression into an internal format.
concat Method (Array)	Concatenates two arrays.

JScript Command	Explanation
concat Method (String)	Concatenates two strings.
Conditional (ternary) Operator (?:)	Conditional execution.
constructor Property	Function that creates an object.
continue Statement	Terminates current loop iteration and starts next iteration.
cos Method	Cosine.
Date Object	Enables date manipulation.
decodeURI Method	Decodes URI.
decodeURIComponent Method	Decodes URI component.
Decrement Operator (--)	Decrements.
delete Operator	Deletes an object property or an array element.
description Property	Returns or sets the numeric value associated with a specific error.
Dictionary Object	Stores key/value pairs.
dimensions Method	Returns number of dimensions in a VBArray.
Division Operator (/)	Division.
do. . .while Statement	Loops while a condition is true; always executes the first iteration.
E Property	Returns Euler's constant.
encodeURI Method	Encodes URI.
encodeURIComponent Method	Encodes URI component.
Enumerator Object	Enables enumeration of items in a collection.
Equality Operator (==)	Equality.
Error Object	Information about run-time errors.
escape Method	Encodes strings for reading on different computers.
eval Method	Evaluates JScript.
exec Method	Starts a search for a pattern.
exp Method	*e* raised to a power.
FileSystemObject Object	File system access.
fixed Method	Places HTML <TT> tags around text in a String object.
floor Method	Returns highest integer less than or equal to a number.

JScript Command	Explanation
fontcolor Method	Places an HTML <FONT> tag with the COLOR attribute around the text in a String object.
fontsize Method	Places an HTML <FONT> tag with the SIZE attribute around the text in a String object.
for Statement	Executes a statement for as long as the condition is true.
for. . .in Statement	Executes a statement for each element in an array.
fromCharCode Method	Returns a string from a Unicode value.
Function Object	Creates new function.
function Statement	Declares new function.
getDate Method	Returns day of the month.
getDay Method	Returns day of the week.
getFullYear Method	Returns the year.
getHours Method	Returns the hours.
getItem Method	Returns item at a location.
getMilliseconds Method	Returns milliseconds.
getMinutes Method	Returns minutes.
getMonth Method	Returns month.
GetObject Function	Returns a reference to an Automation object from a file.
getSeconds Method	Returns seconds.
getTime Method	Returns time.
getTimezoneOffset Method	Difference in minutes between UTC and host computer.
getUTCDate Method	Date in UTC.
getUTCDay Method	Day of the week in UTC.
getUTCFullYear Method	Year in UTC.
getUTCHours Method	Hours in UTC.
getUTCMilliseconds Method	Milliseconds in UTC.
getUTCMinutes Method	Minutes in UTC.
getUTCMonth Method	Month in UTC.
getUTCSeconds Method	Seconds in UTC.
getVarDate Method	Returns the VT_DATE value in a Date object.
getYear Method	Year.

C

JScript Command	Explanation
Global Object	An intrinsic object whose purpose is to collect global methods into one object.
Global Property	State of global flag (g).
Greater than Operator (>)	Greater than.
Greater than or equal to Operator (>=)	Greater than or equal to.
hasOwnProperty Method	Indicates whether the object has a property with the given name.
Identity Operator (===)	Equal and same type.
if...else Statement	Conditional execution.
ignoreCase Property	State of ignoreCase flag (i).
Increment Operator (++)	Increment.
index Property	Character position of first successful match.
indexOf Method	Character position of first substring match.
Inequality Operator (!=)	Inequality.
Infinity Property	Returns an initial value of Number POSITIVE_INFINITY.
input Property	Returns string that was searched.
instanceof Operator	Indicates whether the object is an instance of a specific class.
isFinite Method	Indicates whether object is finite.
isNaN Method	Indicates whether the object is not a number.
isPrototypeOf Method	Returns a Boolean value indicating whether an object exists in another object's prototype chain.
italics Method	Places HTML <I> tags around text in a String object.
item Method	Returns the current item in the collection.
join Method	Concatenates an array to a string.
Labeled Statement	Identifies a statement.
lastIndex Property	Character position of last match.
lastIndexOf Method	Last occurrence of substring within a String object.
lastMatch Property ($)	Last matched characters of a regular expression search.

JScript Command	Explanation
lastParen Property ($+)	The last parenthesized submatch from any regular expression search.
lbound Method	Lowest index value in a VBArray dimension.
leftContext Property ($`)	Number of arguments passed to a function.
length Property (Arguments)	Returns the actual number of arguments passed to a function by the caller.
length Property (Array)	Length of array.
length Property (Function)	Number of arguments for a function.
length Property (String)	Length of string object.
Less than Operator (<)	Less than.
Less than or equal to Operator (<=)	Less than or equal to.
link Method	Places an HTML anchor with an HREF attribute around the text in a String object.
LN2 Property	Natural logarithm of 2.
LN10 Property	Natural logarithm of 10.
localeCompare Method	Indicates whether two strings are equivalent in the current locale.
log Method	Natural logarithm.
LOG2E Property	Base-2 logarithm of *e*, Euler's constant.
LOG10E Property	Base-10 logarithm of *e*, Euler's constant.
Logical AND Operator (&&)	Logical conjunction.
Logical NOT Operator (!)	Logical negation.
Logical OR Operator (‖)	Logical disjunction.
match Method	Returns the results of a regular expression search.
Math Object	Provides basic mathematics functions and constants.
max Method	Returns the greater of two numbers.
MAX_VALUE Property	Returns the greatest numerical value that can be represented in JScript.
message Property	Returns an error message string.
min Method	Returns the lesser of two numbers.
MIN_VALUE Property	Returns the number closest to zero that can be represented in JScript.
Modulus Operator (%)	Modulo division.

JScript Command	**Explanation**
moveFirst Method	Sets current item in collection to the first item.
moveNext Method	Sets current item in collection to next item.
multiline Property	State of multiline flag (m).
Multiplication Operator (*)	Multiplication.
name Property	Name of an error.
NaN Property (Global)	Not a number.
NaN Property (Number)	Not a number.
NEGATIVE_INFINITY Property	A value more negative than the largest negative number that can be represented by JScript.
new Operator	Creates a new object.
Nonidentity Operator (!==)	Not equal or not the same data type.
Number Object	Object representation of the number type or a placeholder for a number constant.
number Property	Returns or sets the numeric value associated with a specific error.
Object Object	Functionality common to all JScript objects.
Operator Precedence	Information about the precedence of operators.
parse Method	Returns milliseconds since the date represented by a string and Midnight, Jan. 1, 1970.
parseFloat Method	Converts a string to a floating-point number.
parseInt Method	Converts a string to an integer.
PI Property	Returns mathematical constant PI.
pop Method	Removes last element of an array and returns it.
POSITIVE_INFINITY Property	Returns a value larger than the largest value that can be represented by JScript.
pow Method	Raises an expression to a power.
propertyIsEnumerable Property	Indicates whether the specified property is enumerable.
prototype Property	Returns reference to prototype of a class of objects.

JScript Command	Explanation
push Method	Appends elements to the end of an array and returns the new length.
random Method	Pseudorandom number between 0 and 1.
RegExp Object	Information about Regular Expression pattern searches.
Regular Expression Object	Contains a regular expression pattern.
Regular Expression Syntax	List of special characters used with regular expressions.
replace Method	Returns result of regular expression replacement.
return Statement	Exits current function and returns a value.
reverse Method	Returns array with elements reversed.
rightContext Property ($')	Returns characters after last match to the end of the searched string.
round Method	Rounds numeric expression to the nearest integer and returns result.
Run-time Errors	List of JScript run-time errors.
ScriptEngine Function	Indicates scripting language in use.
ScriptEngineBuildVersion Function	Build version of scripting engine.
ScriptEngineMajorVersion Function	Major version of scripting engine.
ScriptEngineMinorVersion Function	Minor version of scripting engine.
search Method	Returns position of first match in a regular expression search.
setDate Method	Sets the numeric date of the Date object using local time.
setFullYear Method	Sets the year value in the Date object using local time.
setHours Method	Sets the hour value in the Date object using local time.
setMilliseconds Method	Sets the milliseconds value in the Date object using local time.
setMinutes Method	Sets the minutes value in the Date object using local time.
setMonth Method	Sets the month value in the Date object using local time.
setSeconds Method	Sets the seconds value in the Date object using local time.
setTime Method	Sets the date and time value in the Date object.

JScript Command	**Explanation**
setUTCDate Method	Sets the numeric date in the Date object using Universal Coordinated Time (UTC).
setUTCFullYear Method	Sets the year value in the Date object using Universal Coordinated Time (UTC).
setUTCHours Method	Sets the hours value in the Date object using Universal Coordinated Time (UTC).
setUTCMilliseconds Method	Sets the milliseconds value in the Date object using Universal Coordinated Time (UTC).
setUTCMinutes Method	Sets the minutes value in the Date object using Universal Coordinated Time (UTC).
setUTCMonth Method	Sets the month value in the Date object using Universal Coordinated Time (UTC).
setUTCSeconds Method	Sets the seconds value in the Date object using Universal Coordinated Time (UTC).
setYear Method	Sets the year value in the Date object.
shift Method	Removes the first element from an array and returns it.
sin Method	Sine.
slice Method (Array)	Returns a portion of an array.
slice Method (String)	Returns a portion of a string.
small Method	Places HTML <SMALL> tags around text in a String object.
sort Method	Returns sorted array.
source Property	Returns a copy of the text of the regular expression pattern.
splice Method	Removes or replaces elements in an array and returns result.
split Method	Returns the array of strings that results when a string is separated into substrings.
sqrt Method	Square root.
SQRT1_2 Property	Returns the square root of one half.
SQRT2 Property	Returns the square root of 2.
strike Method	Places HTML <STRIKE> tags around text in a String object.
String Object	Allows manipulation of character strings including location of substrings.

JScript Command	Explanation
sub Method	Places HTML <SUB> tags around text in a String object.
substr Method	Returns a substring beginning at a specified location and having a specified length.
substring Method	Returns the substring at a specified location within a String object.
Subtraction Operator (–)	Subtraction.
sup Method	Places HTML <SUP> tags around text in a String object.
switch Statement	Executes statements based on several sets of conditions.
Syntax Errors	List of JScript syntax errors.
tan Method	Tangent.
test Method	Indicates the presence of a substring within a String object.
this Statement	Reference to current object.
throw Statement	Activates an error to be handled by a catch statement.
toArray Method	Convert JScript array to VBArray.
toDateString Method	Returns data as string.
toExponential Method	Returns a string representing a number in exponential notation.
toFixed Method	Returns a string containing a number in fixed-point notation.
toGMTString Method	Returns a date converted to a string using Greenwich Mean Time.
toLocaleDateString Method	Returns date as string for host's locale.
toLocaleLowercase Method	Converts string to lowercase, acknowledging host's locale.
toLocaleString Method	Converts date to string using current locale.
toLocaleTimeString Method	Returns time as string for host's locale.
toLocaleUppercase Method	Converts string to uppercase, acknowledging current locale.
toLowerCase Method	Converts string to lowercase.
toString Method	Returns object as a string representation.
toPrecision Method	String representing number with specified number of digits.

JScript Command	Explanation
toTimeString Method	Time as a string.
toUpperCase Method	Converts to uppercase.
toUTCString Method	Date to string using UTC.
try Statement	Error handling.
typeof Operator	Returns data type.
ubound Method	Highest index value of VBArray.
Unary Negation Operator (−)	Unary negation.
undefined Property	Returns an undefined value.
unescape Method	Decodes strings encoded with 'escape.'
unshift Method	Inserts elements at the beginning of an array.
Unsigned Right Shift Operator (>>>)	Right shift without maintaining sign.
UTC Method	Returns number of milliseconds after the epoch in UTC.
valueOf Method	Returns value of object.
var Statement	Declares variable.
VBArray Object	Access to Visual Basic safe arrays.
void Operator	Prevents statement from returning.
while Statement	Loops while a condition is true.
with Statement	Assigns the default object for a statement.

Appendix D

VBScript

Within this appendix is a list of the commands, operators, constants, methods, and properties of VBScript. For more explanation and description of the syntax, as well as examples, please visit **http://www.microsoft.com**, at the VBScript documentation.

ARRAY HANDLING

Dim	Declares array type. Can be static or dynamic array size.
ReDim	Changes size of dynamic array.
Preserve	Keyword used for retaining the values in an array when resizing. Only used when resizing the rightmost index.
LBound	Returns the lowest subscript for the array dimension, which is always zero.
UBound	Returns the highest subscript for the array dimension, which is the size of the array.

ASSIGNMENTS

Let	Sets a variable to a value.
Set	Assigns an object reference to a variable.

CONSTANTS

	VALUE
Empty	Variable created, but not assigned a value.
Nothing	Used to remove an object reference.
Null	Not valid.
True	Value is true, numerical value of –1.
False	Value is false, numerical value of 0.

Error

vbObjectErrror	&h80040000

System Colors

vbBlack	&h00
vbRed	&hFF
vbGreen	&hFF00
vbYellow	&hFFFF
vbBlue	&hFF0000
vbMagenta	&hFF00FF
vbCyan	&hFFFF00
vbWhite	&hFFFFFF

Comparison

vbBinaryCompare	0
vbTextCompare	1
vbDatabaseCompare	2

Date & Time

vbSunday	1
vbMonday	2
vbTuesday	3
vbWednesday	4
vbThursday	5
vbFriday	6
vbSaturday	7
vbFirstJan1	1
vbFirstFourDays	2
vbFirstFullWeek	3
vbUseSystem	0
vbUseSystemDayOfWeek	0

Date Format

vbGeneralDate	0
vbLongDate	1
vbShortDate	2
vbLongTime	3
vbShortTime	4

File I/O

ForReading	1
ForWriting	2
ForAppending	8

String

vbCr	Chr(13)
vbCrLf	Chr(13)&Chr(10)
vbLf	Chr(10)
vbNewLine	-
vbNullChar	Chr(0)
vbNullString	-
vbTab	Chr(9)

Tristate

TristateTrue	−1
TristateFalse	0
TristateUseDefault	−2

VarType

vbEmpty	0
vbNull	1
vbInteger	2
vbLong	3
vbSingle	4
vbDouble	5
vbCurrency	6
vbDate	7
vbString	8
vbObjectError	9
vbError	10
vbBoolean	11
vbVariant	12
vbDataObject	13
vbDecimal	14
vbByte	17
vbArray	8192

CONTROL FLOW

For...Next	Repeats a block of code a specified number of times.
For Each...Next Statement	Repeats a block of code for each element in an array.
Do...Loop	Executes a block of code while a condition is true.
If...Then...Else	Conditional execution of a statement.
Select Case	Used to replace If...Then...Else when many conditions need to be tested.
While...When	Loop through a block of code while a condition is true.

FUNCTIONS

Conversion Functions

Asc	Returns ASCII code of first character in string.
AscB	As previous, but for use with byte data contained in a string.

D

AscW	As previous, but for use with Unicode characters; returns the wide character code.
Chr	Coverts an ASCII code to a single character in a string.
ChrB	As previous, but for use with byte data contained in a string.
ChrW	As previous, but for use with Unicode characters; takes a wide character code.
CBool	Converts to a Variant of subtype Boolean.
CByte	Converts to a Variant of subtype Byte.
CDate	Converts to a Variant of subtype Date.
CDbl	Converts to a Variant of subtype Double.
CInt	Converts to a Variant of subtype Integer.
CLng	Converts to a Variant of subtype Long.
CSng	Converts to a Variant of subtype Single.
CStr	Converts to a Variant of subtype String.
Fix	Returns the Integer part of a number.
Hex	Returns a string representing the hexadecimal value of a number.
Int	Returns the Integer part of a number.
Oct	Returns a string representing the octal value of a number.
Round	Rounds a number to the specified number of decimal places.
Sgn	Returns an integer representing the sign on a number.

Date & Time

Date	Returns Date.
DateAdd	Returns a date to which a time interval has been added.
DateDiff	Returns time between two dates.
DatePart	Returns a portion of a date.
DateSerial	Returns a Variant of subtype Date for a specified date.
DateValue	Returns a Variant of subtype Date.
Day	Returns the day(1…31).
Hour	Returns the hour(0…23).

Minute	Returns the minute(0...59).
Month	Returns the month(1...12).
MonthName	Returns the name of a month.
Now	Returns the current date and time.
Second	Returns the second(0...59).
Time	Returns a Variant of subtype Date indicating the current time.
TimeSerial	Returns a Variant of subtype Date for a given hour, minute, and second.
TimeValue	Returns a Variant of subtype Date containing the time.
Weekday	Returns the day of the week.
WeekdayName	Returns the name of the day of the week.
Year	Returns the year.

Math Functions

Atn	Arctangent.
Cos	Cosine.
Exp	*e* raised to a power.
Log	natural logarithm.
Randomize	Initializes the random number generator.
Rnd	Returns a random number.
Sin	Sin.
Sqr	Square root.
Tan	Tangent.

Object Management

CreateObject	Creates and returns a reference to an ActiveX or OLE Automation Object.
GetObject	Returns a reference to an ActiveX or OLE Automation Object.
LoadPicture	Returns a Picture object.

Script Engine Identification

ScriptEngine	Major, minor, and build versions of the script engine.
ScriptEngineMajorVersion	Major version of script engine.
ScriptEngineMinorVersion	Minor version of script engine.
ScriptEngineBuildVersion	Build version of script engine.

D

String Functions

Filter	Returns an array from a string array based on filter criteria.
FormatCurrency	Formats as currency.
FormatDateTime	Formats as Date or Time.
FormatNumber	Formats as a Number.
FormatPercent	Formats as percent.
InStr	Returns the position of one string within another.
InStrB	Same as previous, but for use with byte data in a string.
InstrRev	Same as InStr, but starts from the end of the string.
Join	Creates a large string from multiple smaller strings in an array.
LCase	Converts to lowercase.
Left	Returns a number of characters from the left of a string.
LeftB	Same as previous, but for use with byte data in a string.
Len	Returns number of bytes used by a variable.
LenB	Same as previous, but for use with byte data in a string.
LTrim	Trims spaces from the left.
Mid	Returns a certain number of characters from a string.
MidB	Same as previous, but for use with byte data in a string.
Replace	Replaces a given substring with another.
Right	Returns a specified number of characters from the right of a string.
RightB	Same as previous, but for use with byte data in a string.
RTrim	Trims spaces from the right.
Space	Makes a string of spaces.
Split	Creates an array of smaller strings from a large string.
StrComp	Compares the values of two strings.

String	Creates a string made of a given character repeated.
StrReverse	Reverses the order of the characters.
Trim	Trims spaces from both sides of a string.
UCase	Converts to uppercase.

Variable Testing

IsArray	Is the variable and array?
IsDate	Is the variable a date?
IsEmpty	Is the variable empty?
IsNull	Is the variable null?
IsNumeric	Is the variable numeric?
IsObject	Is the variable an object?
VarType	Returns the subtype of a variable.

ERROR HANDLING

On Error Resume Next	If error is encountered, continue to next statement.
Err	Provides information about run-time errors.

I/O

InputBox	Pop-up box to enter text.
MsgBox	Pop-up box for output.

MsgBox Constants	**Value**
vbOKOnly	0
vbOKCancel	1
vbAbortRetryIgnore	2
vbYesNoCancel	3
vbYesNo	4
vbRetryCancel	5
vbDefaultButton1	0
vbDefaultButton2	256
vbDefaultButton3	512
vbDefaultButton4	768
vbCritical	16
vbQuestion	32
vbExclamation	48
vbInformation	64

vbApplicationModel	0
vbSystemModel	4096
vbOK	1
vbCancel	2
vbAbort	3
vbRetry	4
vbIgnore	5
vbYes	6
vbNo	7

D

PROCEDURES

Call	Calls a subroutine.
Function	Defines a function.
Sub	Defines a subroutine.

OTHER KEYWORDS

Rem	Comment.
Option Explicit	Forces variable declaration.

Glossary

ADO (Active Data Objects)	Constructs ASP can use to work with conforming databases.
Application	Any set of pages, programming logic, and data stores that together create an interactive application. Not necessarily just ASP applications, or Web/Internet based, application also refers to traditional programs such as word processors or spreadsheets.
ASP	Active Server Pages, a set of objects and functions that can be called by a number of scripting languages to work easily with Web sites and Web pages.
Attribute	A variable within an HTML command that affects the properties of the command as displayed or used in a Web page.
Authentication	The process of verifying the identity of a party with whom you are communicating.
Bandwidth	The amount of data that can be transmitted over a given medium within a given time frame. For example, 28.8 modems can transmit 28,800 bits per second across a standard phone line.
Browser	The software used to view Web pages, such as Internet Explorer. Also called the platform on which Web pages are viewed.
Certificate	A unique number supporting secure communications, such as a public key.
Client-server	A methodology employed to effect communications between a central server and a variety of distributed client programs.
Collection	A set of values attached to an object, such as the form field values attached to the Request object when a form is filled out and submitted.
Common Gateway Interface (CGI)	The technology used on UNIX-based operating systems and Web servers to provide interactivity.
Component	A small program with an interface to its methods, properties, and events, typically accessible to ASP scripts. For example, the Content Rotator component is accessible to ASP scripts.

Concatenation	Making two or more strings into a single string by connecting values together.
Connection String	A text string containing connection information.
Contention	In this context, refers to programs vying for a single resource concurrently.
Cookie	A small amount of unique text information stored on the user's browser to facilitate the creation of "state" across the Internet/Web.
Data Type	The name of the type of data stored in a variable, such as Text, Number, Logical (Yes/No), and so forth.
DBMS	Also RDBMS, meaning Relational Database Management System.
Debugging	The process of finding and eliminating causes of unwanted or incorrect behavior in your programs and applications.
Delimiter	The symbol used to denote the beginning or end of a command in a programming language, such as the less-than and greater-than symbols used to enclose HTML commands (for example, <B> for Bold).
Deprecated	Used to refer to HTML tags that won't be supported in future versions of the HTML.
Development Environment	The tools and conditions present on your system when you are developing applications.
Domain Name	An alias given to an IP address to make it easy to remember, such as www.e4free.com, which refers to the IP address 216.188.38.204.
Dynamic Web Page	A Web page that presents a variety of information dependent on the context and user defined.
Element	An HTML command that creates an object in an HTML document, such as the <TABLE> tag.
Encoding	In this context, refers to modifying characters in input or output streams to legal characters. For example, spaces in a URL could be changed to their legal numerical values.

Event	Some condition that, when it occurs, can trigger actions for objects. For example, the OnApplicationStart event can trigger processing when your ASP application starts.
FAT (File Allocation Table)	A hard drive partition format, typically 16 or 32 bit (meaning the number of files that can be addressed).
Firewall	Programming logic embedded in hardware, software, or both, that filters incoming and outgoing data packets on a network, looking for traffic not conforming to the filtering rules with which it has been configured.
Global.asa File	Used to set and control global variables and processing for your ASP applications, at both the application and session levels.
Hosting	Providing space on a server computer for a Web site or application, typically with high-speed, dedicated Internet access.
HTML (Hypertext Markup Language)	The language used to direct browsers to display information content.
Instantiate	To create an instance of an object.
Interactivity	The capability of an application to communicate, in real time, with users, presenting information, receiving feedback, processing the feedback in the context of the information presented, and returning additional information.
Internet Information Server (IIS)	Microsoft's industrial-strength Web server software.
Interpreter	A program that interprets scripting language commands in real time, performing essentially the same function as a compiler, but in real time, as the commands are being processed.
IP Address	The set of numbers that make a unique address on the Internet for your Web site or your connection.

Locking	When several users want to make changes to the same file, database record, or other data resource, locks are used to make sure the changes are made one at a time.
Method	An action that can be performed by an object, such as the Write method (which writes data back to the user) of the Response object.
Multitier	An application in which three or more "tiers" of operation exist, including the front-end interface, the back-end data sources, and one or more levels of programming logic and data in between.
Namespace	The range of names that may be assigned. For instance, domain names can (at press time) consist of up to 67 characters from the standard alphabet. All those possible names constitute the namespace available for domain names.
NNTP (Network News Transport Protocol)	The name for a standard newsgroup protocol.
NTFS (NT File System)	A hard drive partition format designed for Windows NT, offering a higher degree of security.
Null	A nonvalue for a field in which no value resides. Rather than a zero for a numerical value or a zero-length string for a string value, a null value means a value has not yet been set.
Object	A programming term referring to a structure that holds both instructions and data, often a "thing" (such as a counter or form element) within a program or displayed in an application.
Object Model	Defines the relationship of programming structures to one another. For example, the Request object is related to the Form collection in that the Form collection consists of all Form name/value pairs received during a request from a browser when a form is submitted.

ODBC (Open Database Connectivity)	The standard by which most databases can be accessed.
Operating System	The software that sets the operating environment for the application and server software, and manages the hardware. Typical operating systems include UNIX and Windows NT.
Parameter	A value to be inserted into a query, often selected or entered in real time by a user.
Partition	A separate area on your hard drive that may be formatted one of several ways, depending on what you intend to do with it and with the operating system.
Permissions	Various levels of capabilities that can be granted or denied by a System Administrator or designated authority on an operating system or within an application. For example, users may be allowed to read the contents of a file, but not to execute a file.
Platform	In this context, refers to the operating system or browser in use.
Production Server	A server being actively used for production work, such as serving Web pages to the public, rather than being used for development or testing.
Programmatic Structure	Structures created by developers in programs that control the flow of the program, such as Do...While, If...Then, and on on.
Property	A value associated with an object, such as the Timeout property of the Session object.
Proprietary	In this context, refers to software, protocols, or systems that are not open standards.
Protocol	Any defined format for communication on networks, the Internet, and so on.
Proxy Server	A server that acts as an intermediary between a client and server, making requests for the client and passing results back to the client.

Query String	A text string containing SQL commands.
Reserved Word	If a word is reserved, you shouldn't use it as a variable name. For example, the word "Date" is reserved in VBScript to imply the value of the current date. Attempting to create a variable named Date would generate an error.
RFC (Request For Comments)	The method used to solicit comments concerning proposed changes to Internet protocols.
Scope	The range of visibility of values and states within an application. For example, global scope means all parts of an application can "see" a value.
Scripting Language	A programming language in which the commands don't need to be compiled to run.
Server Directive	A command that activates specific server capabilities, such as the capability to include text files within ASP scripting files.
Server Extensions	Additional programs placed on a server that provide greater functionality than just the server alone. For example, Microsoft's FrontPage requires FrontPage Server extensions for some of its features to operate correctly.
Session	A unique set of interactions within a running application, such as a user session with an ASP script.
SMTP (Simple Mail Transport Protocol)	The name for a standard mail transport protocol.
Source Code	The original programming instructions entered by the developer to create a program, as opposed to compiled machine language instructions that constitute a traditional finished program.
SQL (Structured Query Language or Standard Query Language)	A standard language by which most databases can be queried.
State	The current condition of an object within an application, such as open or closed.

Static Web Page	A Web page that presents the same information, regardless of circumstances or context.
Streaming Media	A technology for breaking up large media files and sending them across the Internet to be received and played back while being sent, rather than after the entire file has been sent.
Style Sheet	A separate file that contains information defining styles for a Web page.
TCP/IP (Transmission Control Protocol and Internet Protocol)	The two protocols by which Internet communications can flow across all platforms.
Thread	The basic unit of processing that can be done individually by a Central Processing Unit (CPU).
Transaction	A set of data source changes that must be completed as a unit, as in transferring money from one bank account to another.
Troubleshooting	The process of identifying causes of misbehavior in your software or hardware.
URL (Universal Resource Locator)	The computer name (domain name), folder, and filename of the resource (such as a file or Web page) you are seeking.
Variable	A data storage unit within a program.
XML (Extensible Markup Language)	The specification for creating markup languages of your own.

Index

C